Birnbaum's Country Inns and Back Roads, North America

A BIRNBAUM TRAVEL GUIDE

Alexandra Mayes Birnbaum
EDITORIAL CONSULTANT

Lois Spritzer
Editorial Director

Laura L. Brengelman
Managing Editor

Mary Callahan
Beth Schlau
Senior Editors

Patricia Canole
Gene Gold
Susan McClung
Associate Editors

Jonathan Goodnough
Map Coordinator

Susan Cutter Snyder
Editorial Assistant

HarperPerennial
A Division of HarperCollinsPublishers

BIRNBAUM'S COUNTRY INNS AND BACK ROADS, NORTH AMERICA. Copyright © 1997 by HarperCollins Publishers. All rights reserved. Printed in the United States of America. No part of this book may be used or reproduced in any manner whatsoever without written permission except in the case of brief quotations embodied in critical articles and reviews. For information address HarperCollins*Publishers*, 10 East 53rd Street, New York, NY 10022.

ISSN 0749-2561 (Birnbaum Travel Guides)
ISSN 70-615664 (Country Inns and Back Roads, North America)
ISBN 0-06-278253-3 (pbk.)

97 98 99 00 ❖/RRD 5 4 3 2 1

Cover design © Drenttel Doyle Partners
Cover photograph © Hilary Wilkes/International Stock

BIRNBAUM TRAVEL GUIDES

Bahamas, and Turks & Caicos
Bermuda
Canada
Cancun, Cozumel & Isla Mujeres
Caribbean
Country Inns and Back Roads
Disneyland
Hawaii
Mexico
Miami & Ft. Lauderdale
United States
Walt Disney World
Walt Disney World for Kids, By Kids

Writer/Editor

Suzi Forbes Chase

Contributing Editors

Diana Brubaker
Kathryn Clark
Martin Hintz
Arline Inge
Rob Musial
Donna Peck
June Naylor Rodriguez

Maps

Mark Stein Studios

Contents

Vermont

Southern New England

Mid-Atlantic and Ontario

Upper South

Deep South

Midwest

Southwest, Plains, and Rocky Mountains

Pacific Northwest, Alaska, and British Columbia

Alaska

Oregon

Washington

British Columbia, Canada

Index ... *419*

Foreword

A HarperCollins book since the early 1980s and now a member of the *Birnbaum Travel Guides* series, *Country Inns & Back Roads* is, we believe, a natural outgrowth and expansion of some of the information already found in *Birnbaum's United States* and *Canada* guidebooks—with a delightful difference. A geographic listing of our favorite getaways in the US and Canada, *Country Inns* is written especially for those who prefer small towns to big cities, cedar furnishings to chrome, and sylvan settings to spectacular skylines (although we list some special urban oases as well).

Obviously, our larger country books could not possibly cover the broad range of wonderful inns that dot the landscape across both countries. But here, in a book dedicated solely to chintz curtains, down comforters, grandfather clocks, and home-baked muffins, the breadth of our coverage has expanded greatly. All you need to do is select a destination, turn to the table of contents, and we'll do the rest.

We have organized this guide by region. Within each regional section, inns are listed alphabetically by state or province, then area, city, island, or town. Maps indicate major cities and have legends that point out, by number, towns in which our favorite inns are located. For example, if you'd like to visit Cape Cod, Massachusetts, you can see at a glance which places we recommend. An index listing the properties alphabetically by name is another easy-to-use resource.

As with the rest of the books in the *Birnbaum Travel Guides* series, no part of this text is carved in stone. In our annual revisions we will continue to refine, expand, and further hone our material to serve your travel needs better. Not surprisingly, we are inundated with mail from innkeepers from all parts of the country, whose properties are not included in this guide. Over the next year we will make every effort to visit these various properties with an eye toward their possible inclusion in a future edition of *Country Inns & Back Roads.* Likewise, we will continue to visit inns that are already included in this book, to ensure that our readers will find things much the same as (or better than) last year.

In addition to our own research, nothing is of greater value to us than your personal reaction to what we have written and your own experiences while staying in American and Canadian inns. Please write to us at 10 East 53rd Street, New York, NY 10022.

Northern New England and Quebec

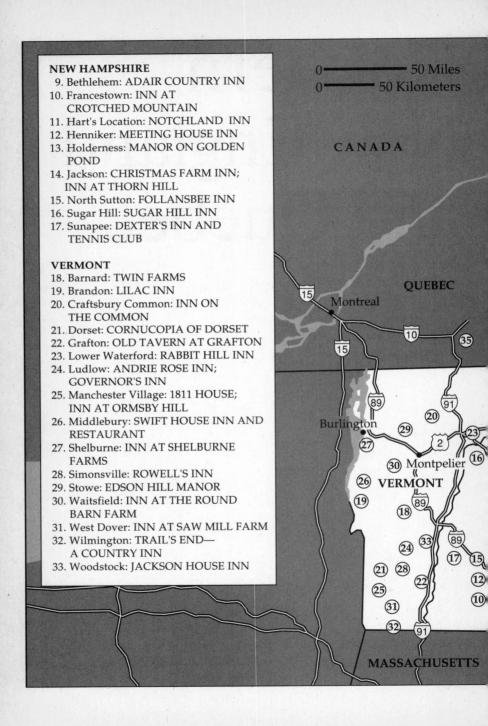

0 ———— 50 Miles
0 ——— 50 Kilometers

CANADA

QUEBEC

Montreal

Burlington

Montpelier

VERMONT

MASSACHUSETTS

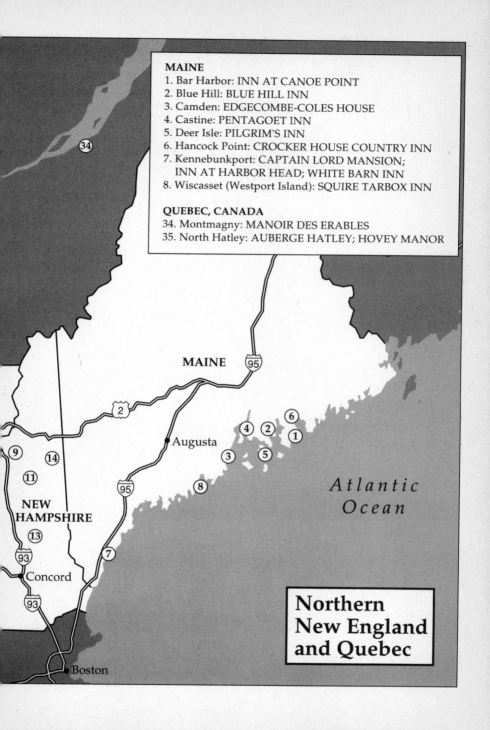

MAINE
1. Bar Harbor: INN AT CANOE POINT
2. Blue Hill: BLUE HILL INN
3. Camden: EDGECOMBE-COLES HOUSE
4. Castine: PENTAGOET INN
5. Deer Isle: PILGRIM'S INN
6. Hancock Point: CROCKER HOUSE COUNTRY INN
7. Kennebunkport: CAPTAIN LORD MANSION;
   INN AT HARBOR HEAD; WHITE BARN INN
8. Wiscasset (Westport Island): SQUIRE TARBOX INN

QUEBEC, CANADA
34. Montmagny: MANOIR DES ERABLES
35. North Hatley: AUBERGE HATLEY; HOVEY MANOR

MAINE 95

2

Augusta

9

14

11

NEW HAMPSHIRE

13

93

Concord

93

7

4 2 6

3 5 1

8

95

Atlantic Ocean

Boston

Northern New England and Quebec

Northern New England and Quebec

Maine

INN AT CANOE POINT

BAR HARBOR, MAINE

As you drive down this property's curving, tree-lined driveway, with glimpses of water beyond, you know you're in for a treat. Then the *Inn at Canoe Point* appears—an oasis of tranquillity on two secluded acres at the edge of Frenchman's Bay.

This English Tudor–style inn was built as a family summer cottage in 1889 and remained a private residence until 1986, when it was purchased by Don Johnson and Esther Cavagnaro and fully renovated to welcome guests. The peace and quiet of this retreat is in marked contrast to the bustle of Bar Harbor, just 2 miles away.

Though its mood is relaxed, the inn also has an elegant air; the decor is a harmonious mixture of antiques and traditional furniture. The main entry hall/living room features a fireplace and a baby grand piano. A granite fireplace dominates one side of the *Ocean Room;* on the other is a panoramic view of Frenchman's Bay. Enjoy a full breakfast either in the *Ocean Room* or on the outside deck. Specialties include cranberry-walnut pancakes, blueberry French toast, and spinach quiche.

The five guestrooms echo the inn's warm, casual style. Overlooking either the water or the rocky shoreline, all have modern bathrooms; some have private balconies. In the master suite, amenities include both a fireplace and a deck, while the *Garret Suite,* the inn's largest, takes up the entire third floor and includes a bedroom with French windows as well as a sitting room with a balcony.

The inn is a quarter mile from *Acadia National Park* and 2 miles from Bar Harbor. Local activities include bicycling, hiking, whale watching and naturalist cruises, antiquing, and visiting art galleries.

INN AT CANOE POINT Box 216K, Bar Harbor, ME 04609 (phone: 207-288-9511; fax: 207-288-8028). This cottage has five guestrooms with private baths and queen- or king-size beds. Open year-round. Rate for a double room (including full breakfast) *Memorial Day* through October: $135 to $250; rest of the year $90 to $165. No credit cards accepted. Not appropriate for children under 12. No pets. Nikki, a German shepherd, in residence. No smoking. Don Johnson and Esther Cavagnaro, innkeepers.

DIRECTIONS: Traveling north on I-95, take Exit 30 in Augusta to Route 3. Follow Route 3 (which becomes Route 1 and 3 shortly after Belfast) north. At Ellsworth continue on Route 3 another 15 miles south toward Bar Harbor. Drive a quarter mile past the entrance to *Acadia National Park,* and turn into the inn's driveway on the left.

BLUE HILL INN

BLUE HILL, MAINE

Blue Hill, a village of impressive houses on streets lined with majestic elm trees, is located on lovely Blue Hill Bay, on the east coast of the Penobscot peninsula. The *Blue Hill Inn,* commanding a prominent location in the center of this quaint village, has been a part of local history since 1840.

When Don and Mary Hartley purchased the inn in 1987, they focused on maintaining its historic authenticity as they renovated it. The original pumpkin-colored pine floors have been polished and accented with Oriental carpets, and the two parlors feature antiques, including an 1850 melodeon and an 18th-century English chest inlaid with rosewood and walnut. Easy chairs and comfortable sofas are grouped around the fireplace.

The guestrooms, furnished with antiques and reproductions, are equally attractive. Five of the rooms have wood-burning fireplaces, and some of the bathrooms feature old-fashioned claw-foot tubs.

One of this hostelry's most popular attractions is its acclaimed restaurant. Dinner is a particularly wonderful affair, beginning with the "innkeeper's reception," held in the parlor on chilly days or in the garden on warm evenings. Afterward comes an elaborate five-course meal (open to nonguests by reservation only) served in the formal dining room, which glows by the 20 candles of a 19th-century brass chandelier. The set menu changes daily but always begins with soup or an appetizer, followed by a sorbet, an entrée (perhaps salmon with ginger and lime, or guinea hen with champagne grapes and wild mushrooms), and a salad. Dessert might be a mint soufflé with bitter chocolate sauce or pears poached in red wine and cassis. An extensive wine list and a selection of fine ports round out the experience. A full breakfast is offered to guests each morning.

The inn's gardens abound with flowers and comfortable spots for relaxing, including a hammock. Don arranges sailing excursions on the 54-foot pinky schooner *Summertime* (a replica of an 1830s fishing boat) or on a 30-foot Catalina sailboat. A canoe also is available. Guests enjoy exploring nearby *Acadia National Park* and the numerous craft shops and art galleries in the area.

BLUE HILL INN Union St., Rte. 177, PO Box 403, Blue Hill, ME 04614 (phone: 207-374-2844; 800-826-7415; fax: 207-374-2829). This historic inn has 11 guestrooms with private baths and twin, double, queen-, or king-size beds. Partially wheelchair accessible. Closed January through mid-May. Rate for a double room (including full breakfast and dinner): $155 to $185. Two-night minimum stay on weekends. MasterCard and Visa accepted. Not appropriate for children under 13. No pets. No smoking. Donald and Mary Hartley, innkeepers.

DIRECTIONS: Traveling north on I-95, take the Augusta exit to Route 3 east. Follow Route 3 east through Belfast to Bucksport. Four miles beyond Bucksport, turn onto Route 15 south toward Blue Hill. Follow Route 15 south for 8 miles to the inn sign (it's 4⁷/₁₀ miles from here). Leave Route 15 south at the sign (there's no road name), and the road soon merges with Route 177, which leads east to the inn. From Bangor take Route 15 south to Bucksport and follow signs to Route 177 east to the inn.

EDGECOMBE-COLES HOUSE
CAMDEN, MAINE

High on a hillside overlooking Penobscot Bay, this historic inn gracefully bridges the 19th and 20th centuries. The original section, dating back to 1800, was incorporated as a side wing when the main building was constructed in 1891. Restored in the 1980s, by innkeepers Terry and Louise Price, the entire house showcases a fine collection of 19th-century antique furnishings, Oriental rugs, and original oil paintings.

With sensational ocean views and a carved-wood fireplace, the living room is a popular place for guests to relax. The den, which also features a carved fireplace and a view of Penobscot Bay, contains the inn's extensive library; embroidered samplers hang on the walls.

The six guestrooms overlook the ocean, the forest behind the inn, or the well-landscaped gardens. Like the public areas, the bedrooms are furnished with 19th-century antiques and original art; four of them also have fireplaces.

Breakfast is a special ritual—and an ideal opportunity for guests to get to know one another. In the dining room, Louise sets the pub-style cherry table with her antique blue-and-white china (including Blue Willow and Phoenix patterns–there's even a set of child-size dishes). The menu changes daily, but entrées may include blueberry pancakes, "Dutch babies" (a cross between popovers and pancakes, served with butter and syrup), and pastries, as well as fresh fruit and juices. In winter, there's sure to be a fire blazing in the fireplace; summertime guests may choose to eat on the porch.

After breakfast you can take a leisurely bicycle ride through the charming village of Camden (bikes are provided by the inn) or go sailing, fishing, or hiking. Other nearby attractions include chamber music concerts and theatrical productions in summer.

EDGECOMBE-COLES HOUSE 64 High St., HCR 60, Box 3010, Camden, ME 04843 (phone: 207-236-2336; fax: 207-236-6227). This country mansion has six guestrooms with private baths, queen- or king-size beds, and telephones. Open year-round. Rate for a double room (including full breakfast): $85 to $185. Two-night minimum stay mid-July through August. Major credit cards accepted. Not appropriate for children under eight. No pets. Several dogs, including Marley, Amy, and Stella, in residence. No smoking. Terry and Louise Price, innkeepers.

DIRECTIONS: Take I-95 north to Exit 22 (Brunswick/Bath), then follow Highway 1 north approximately 60 miles to Camden. Continue north on Highway 1 (High Street) for just over ½ mile; the inn is on the left.

PENTAGOET INN

CASTINE, MAINE

A quintessential New England village with tree-lined streets, a village green, and numerous restored Georgian and Federal houses, Castine is tucked away off the beaten track. The town was settled after the Revolutionary War by British Loyalists, who retained their allegiance to the crown rather than to the newly formed United States. Now very much a bit of Americana, Castine boasts one of Maine's best inns—the Victorian *Pentagoet*.

Originally built in 1894 to house summer tourists, the inn was purchased by Lindsey and Virginia Miller in 1985. The adjacent annex dates back even earlier than the main house—it was erected in the late 1700s—and the *Pentagoet*'s decor reflects these two periods with a pleasant mix of 19th-century antiques, including wicker and walnut furniture in the main house and colonial and period pieces in the annex. The main house has 11 guestrooms decorated in Victorian style with lace curtains and floral wallpaper; the five bedrooms in the annex feature patchwork quilts, Windsor chairs, hooked rugs, and colonial sideboards. One of the suites in the annex has a fireplace.

The broad porch that nearly encircles the house is a favorite gathering place. With its wicker furniture, rocking chairs, and swings, it re-creates the mood of a Victorian summer by the seashore; snacks and iced tea are served here on summer afternoons. Another favorite spot is the library, which houses the Millers' extensive collection of books and a Bosendorfer piano.

A pot of coffee (brewed from freshly ground beans) arrives at guests' doors each morning, and breakfast is served in the dining room shortly thereafter. Good entrée choices include scrambled eggs with cream cheese and chives and bread pudding with warm berry sauce. Homemade breads, bacon, juice, and coffee also are offered.

A wide range of activities is available, including visiting *Acadia National Park,* golf, tennis, swimming, shopping, and attending cultural events.

PENTAGOET INN Main St., PO Box 4, Castine, ME 04221 (phone: 207-326-8616; 800-845-1701 outside Maine; fax: 207-326-9382). This Victorian inn has 16 guestrooms with private baths and twin, double, queen-, or king-size beds. Closed from November through April. Rate for a double room (including full breakfast): $95 to $125. MasterCard and Visa accepted. Not appropriate for children under 13. No pets. One German shepherd, Tara, in residence. No smoking. Lindsey and Virginia Miller, innkeepers.

DIRECTIONS: From I-95 north take Exit 30 in Augusta onto Route 3 and continue north to Belfast. In Belfast take Route 1 north. Three miles past Bucksport turn onto Route 175 south and follow it about 4 miles to Route 166. Continuing south on Route 166 toward Castine, watch for the *Maine Maritime Academy*'s sign and turn left there onto Main Street. The inn is on the right, on the corner of Perkins Street.

PILGRIM'S INN

DEER ISLE, MAINE

This inn has an ideal location on secluded Deer Isle, which juts into Penobscot Bay from the Blue Hill peninsula. Built in 1793 by a local entrepreneur, the Greek Revival–style building is listed on the National Register of Historic Places. The four-story, barn-red structure features a gambrel roof and several mullioned windows. The front of the house overlooks Northwest Harbor, and there is a millpond in back.

Stepping through the front door is like passing into another era. The common rooms, which include a library, gameroom, taproom, and living room, have a colonial feel to them, with eight-foot fireplaces, wood stoves, beehive ovens, brick walls, and pumpkin-colored pine floors. The warm, friendly atmosphere reflects the personalities of Jean and Dud Hendrick, who have owned the inn since 1982.

The 13 large guestrooms are decorated with fine colonial antiques and Laura Ashley fabrics. A separate two-story cottage near the harbor, complete with a kitchen, a living room with a fireplace, a dining room, and a bedroom, is also available for rent. Decorated in the same romantic style as the guestrooms, it's a perfect honeymoon hideaway—its rear deck affords splendid views, especially at sunset.

An attached barn houses the noteworthy dining room (open to non-guests), where jute mats cover the original wood floors. After a convivial cocktail hour with hors d'oeuvres, dinner is served. The menu changes nightly but always features local ingredients, including seafood, free-range chicken, fruit, and shiitake mushrooms from Deer Isle, as well as herbs, vegetables, and edible flowers from the hotel's own gardens. A full buffet breakfast is served to guests daily.

A small building behind the inn houses the *Rugosa Rose,* a shop featuring fine gifts made in Maine. The inn offers sailboat rental and instruction, as well as bicycles for exploring the country roads. You also can arrange a trip to the serene Isle au Haut or a sea excursion to watch seals and dolphins at play in the ocean (the inn will pack a picnic lunch for you). *Acadia National Park* and the famed *Haystack School of Crafts* are both nearby.

PILGRIM'S INN Main St., Deer Isle, ME 04627 (phone: 207-348-6615). **This colonial inn has one cottage and 13 guestrooms (10 with private baths) with twin, double, or queen-size beds. Limited wheelchair accessibility. Closed mid-October through mid-May. Rate for a double room (including full breakfast and dinner): $140 to $200. MasterCard and Visa accepted. Guestrooms in the inn are not appropriate for children under 10, but younger children are welcome in the cottage. No pets. One English springer spaniel, Mr. Beau Dandy, in residence. No smoking. Jean and Dud Hendrick, innkeepers.**

DIRECTIONS: From I-95 north take Exit 30 in Augusta to Route 3, then head north to Belfast. From Belfast, follow Route 1 north beyond Bucksport to the intersection with Route 15 south. Follow Route 15 south to Deer Isle Village and turn right onto Main Street. The inn is one block up the street on the left.

CROCKER HOUSE COUNTRY INN

HANCOCK POINT, MAINE

Hidden away on Hancock Point, three minutes' walk from Frenchman's Bay, this establishment is the sole remnant of a 19th-century village that served as the terminus of the Washington, DC–Bar Harbor railway line. Cobblestones quarried near here were used to pave the streets of Boston, New York, and Philadelphia.

The living room, with its wicker furniture, handmade needlepoint rug, abundant plants, and bright floral watercolors, offers a cheerful, comfortable atmosphere. The guestrooms are decorated in warm apricot and peach and accented by stenciled walls, locally made quilts, and needlepoint rugs. One room is equipped with a king-size, pencil-post pine bed with matching dresser. An adjacent carriage house offers two additional guestrooms, a spa, and a common room, where the inn's only TV set is located.

The popular, highly acclaimed dining room (open to non-guests) serves excellent continental dishes prepared by owner Rick Malaby, who was a chef in Washington, DC, before opening the inn in 1979. Sample entrées include fresh local scallops sautéed with mushrooms, scallions, garlic, and tomatoes and rack of lamb marinated in garlic and mustard with an herbed crust. A jazz pianist plays on Friday and Saturday evenings. A full breakfast is offered daily.

On the grounds guests can play croquet and go bicycling. Boat moorings are available, and boat rentals are possible in nearby Bar Harbor. Tennis courts, Mount Desert Island, and *Acadia National Park* are close as well.

CROCKER HOUSE COUNTRY INN Hancock Point Road, HC 77, Box 171, Hancock Point, ME 04640 (phone: 207-422-6806; fax: 207-422-3105). This rustic inn has 11 guestrooms with private baths and double, queen-, or king-size beds. Wheelchair accessible. Closed January through April; open weekends only November and December. Rate for a double room (including full breakfast): $95 to $125. Major credit cards accepted. Children welcome. Pets allowed by prior arrangement only. Smoking permitted in one common room and in one dining room. Richard and Elizabeth Malaby, innkeepers.

DIRECTIONS: Traveling north on I-95, take Exit 30 in Augusta to Route 3. Follow Route 3 north to Belfast, then take Route 1 approximately 8 miles past Ellsworth. Turn right at the sign for Hancock Point and continue approximately 5 miles to the inn, which is on the right.

CAPTAIN LORD MANSION

KENNEBUNKPORT, MAINE

During the War of 1812, the British naval blockade made shipbuilding impossible for Captain Nathaniel Lord. Rather than allow his sailors to remain idle, he employed them to build a magnificent house. Using wood intended for Lord's ships, they constructed a three-story, Federal-style mansion with elaborate arched doorways, plenty of fireplaces, soaring ceilings, wide-plank pine floors, and a suspended elliptical staircase. At the very top of the house is an octagonal cupola, a lookout point from which Captain Lord could view the daily activity on the Kennebunk River. Today, guests of the *Captain Lord Mansion,* now an upscale country inn, can do the same.

Beautifully restored by innkeepers Bev Davis and Rick Litchfield, this house has become one of Maine's showpieces. Painted Jamestown yellow with white trim and surrounded by elegant gardens, the inn is listed on the National Register of Historic Places.

The uniqueness of the architecture is evident in the grand entrance hall with the unusual staircase; the inn also boasts the kitchen's original fireplace. Today, the main gathering area is the living room, where tea, coffee, and homemade scones are offered every afternoon.

The 22 bedrooms are distributed between the mansion, an adjacent cottage called the *Captain's Hideaway,* and *Phebe's Fantasy,* an 1807 Federal home. Each is elegantly furnished with high-quality antiques and a canopied four-poster; 20 of the rooms also have fireplaces, and 10 have mini-refrigerators stocked with cold drinks. The most romantic accommodation is the *Captain's Room,* which has a double Jacuzzi in the opulent bathroom. (In keeping with the mansion's old-fashioned atmosphere, just two of the guestrooms have TV sets, though a third is available to all in a common room.)

Breakfast is served family-style, each day, at the two harvest tables in the large colonial kitchen. Abundant offerings include fresh fruit, homemade muffins, and a hot entrée—waffles, pancakes, or cheese strata (a soufflé-like dish made with cheese, eggs, milk, and herbs). A gift shop sells small antiques, local crafts, and souvenirs of the mansion.

Golf, tennis, bicycling, and the *Rachel Carson Wildlife Refuge* are all nearby, and whale watching trips can be arranged.

CAPTAIN LORD MANSION Green St., PO Box 800, Kennebunkport, ME 04046 (phone: 207-967-3141; fax: 207-967-3172). This historic inn has 22 guestrooms with private baths, double, queen-, or king-size beds, and telephones. Open year-round. Rate for a double room (including full breakfast and afternoon tea) January through April: $85 to $175; May through December: $149 to $249. Two-night minimum stay on weekends. Discover, MasterCard, and Visa accepted. Not appropriate for children under six. No pets. No smoking. Bev Davis and Rick Litchfield, innkeepers; Rebecca Steens, assistant innkeeper.

DIRECTIONS: Traveling north on I-95, take Exit 3 (Kennebunk). Take Route 35/9A and follow the signs through Kennebunk to Kennebunkport. Go over the drawbridge and take the first right onto Ocean Avenue. After 5 blocks turn left onto Green Street; the mansion is 2 blocks up on the left.

INN AT HARBOR HEAD

KENNEBUNKPORT, MAINE

For pure romance, it's hard to beat this lovely bed and breakfast establishment. Set in a rambling, gray-shingled country house with a spectacular view of Cape Porpoise Harbor, the inn has the breezy, casual feeling of a seaside cottage. The public areas and guestrooms, however, are sophisticated, displaying the artistic talent of innkeeper Joan Sutter. The sitting room, for example, is appointed with Oriental rugs, a Chinese screen, and a sparkling crystal chandelier. Here, though, "elegant" doesn't mean "stuffy": Guests feel right at home snuggling into a wing chair by the fire or lying in the hammock watching boats in the harbor.

All of the guestrooms (which have luxurious private baths) are furnished with antiques, down comforters and pillows, and stereos. The decor of each has been individually created by Joan, and her expressive murals grace many of the walls. For example, in the *Summer Suite* (which has a fireplace and its own balcony) hand-painted clouds drift across the ceiling over the king-size wicker bed; its elevated, cathedral-ceilinged bath has a Jacuzzi and commands a splendid ocean view. The *Harbor Suite* features a fireplace, a queen-size bed with a lacy canopy, as well as more of Joan's artwork—a trompe l'oeil mural in the sitting room, which also has a balcony with a spectacular view, and a serene island mural in the bedroom.

Breakfast is served in the formal dining room on a mahogany table laid with gilt-edged Lenox china, lacy placemats, and linen napkins in sterling silver rings. Choices might include poached pears with Grand Marnier custard sauce or French toast stuffed with ricotta and cream cheese, covered with fresh fruit. Low-fat breakfasts also are available. Afternoon refreshments— wine, sherry, cheese, tea, cappuccino, and cookies—are served as well.

Activities in the area include basking on the beautiful beach (the inn provides passes and towels), golf, fishing, tennis, whale watching excursions, visits to historical museums, and shopping.

INN AT HARBOR HEAD 41 Pier Rd., Cape Porpoise, Kennebunkport, ME 04046-6916 (phone: 207-967-5564 or 207-967-4873; fax: 207-967-1294). The inn has five guestrooms with private baths and queen- or king-size beds. Open year-round. Rate for a double room (including full breakfast and afternoon refreshments): $110 to $275. Two-night minimum stay on weekends and holidays. MasterCard and Visa accepted. Not appropriate for children under 13. No pets. No smoking indoors. Joan and David Sutter, innkeepers.

DIRECTIONS: From I-95 north, take Exit 3 and follow Route 35/9A to Kennebunkport. Make a left at the intersection of Routes 9 and 35. Cross the bridge and follow Route 9 east through Dock Square, then follow the signs to Cape Porpoise. Past the *Wayfarer* restaurant at the head of the cove, the inn is the eighth house on the right.

WHITE BARN INN

KENNEBUNKPORT, MAINE

With its picture-postcard scenery, Kennebunkport is the quintessential Maine village. This peaceful town—best known as former President George Bush's New England vacation spot—is the perfect setting for the *White Barn Inn.* The upscale retreat occupies several historic buildings—the oldest of them, the farmhouse and barn, dating to 1820—on six acres. Until 1988 the property was used as a boardinghouse, but since that time it's taken a quantum leap forward. Distributed among the various buildings, today, are 24 luxurious guestrooms, many outfitted with marble baths (several with whirlpools) and decorated with antiques or top-quality reproductions, fresh flowers, and English-style fabrics, including chintz. Many rooms have working fireplaces and TV sets hidden away in armoires, and several boast four-poster, canopy, or sleigh beds. The 13 guestrooms in the main building feature period furnishings whimsically hand-painted by a local artist. Nightly turndown service includes treats left on the nightstand—anything from strawberries dipped in chocolate to petits fours.

The restaurant (open to non-guests), in two high-ceilinged barns furnished with antiques, is one of the most highly acclaimed in New England. Candlelight plays across the polished floors and reflects in the china, crystal, and silver. The menu changes nightly but always features fresh local seafood and herbs and vegetables grown in the inn's gardens. The offerings (described with a touch of whimsy) might include a "roasted salmon impersonating a filet mignon" or roasted rack of lamb and medallions of Kennebunk venison on a flaky pastry of sweet potato with Granny Smith apple puree, followed by a white-chocolate orange-flavored mousse swan with clementine sauce and orange segments. A hearty continental breakfast and afternoon tea with port and brandy (both included in the room rate) are offered daily.

The inn's genteel surroundings include flower gardens, patios, and a swimming pool. Boating, bicycling (the inn provides bicycles), golf, fishing, tennis, cross-country skiing, and browsing through Kennebunkport's antiques shops are all possible diversions nearby.

WHITE BARN INN Beach St., PO Box 560C, Kennebunkport, ME 04046 (phone: 207-967-2321; fax: 207-967-1100). This historic inn has 24 guestrooms with private baths and double, queen-, or king-size beds, telephones, TV sets, and air conditioning. Open year-round; restaurant closed January 3 through early February. Rate for a double room (including continental breakfast and afternoon tea): $150 to $375. Two-night minimum stay on weekends; three nights on holiday weekends. Major credit cards accepted. Not appropriate for children under 12. No pets. Smoking permitted in bar only. Laurence Bongiorno and Laurie Cameron, innkeepers.

DIRECTIONS: From I-95 north take Exit 2 (Ogunquit/Wells). Follow Route 9 west to Route 35. Turn right onto Beach Street; the inn is a quarter mile up the street on the right.

SQUIRE TARBOX INN

WISCASSET (WESTPORT ISLAND), MAINE

The *Squire Tarbox Inn* is not only a quaint New England inn, but also a fine restaurant, a goat farm, and a thriving local producer of *chèvre* (goat cheese). Its charming setting near Squam Creek provides a scenic feast of buttercups and lupines, country lanes, and birds—the perfect antidote to the hassles of city living.

Prior to opening the *Squire Tarbox Inn,* Karen and Bill Mitman worked at Boston's *Copley Plaza* hotel, and that experience stands them in good stead. They know how to create a friendly, welcoming atmosphere, and they are eager to show visitors around the farm.

The original building dates to 1763, but a clapboard, Federal-style main house was added by Squire Samuel Tarbox in 1825, to form one large, rambling, colonial farmhouse. Listed on the National Register of Historic Places, the inn still has its original pumpkin-colored pine floors, carved moldings, hand-hewn beams, and a large hearth with an oven. A three-story barn with exposed beams contains three sitting rooms (two with fireplaces and one with a wood-burning stove). A screened deck off the main dining room is a pleasant place to sit in warm weather (binoculars are provided for bird watching).

The 11 guestrooms are decorated in country style—mahogany antiques, intricate handmade quilts, and braided rugs—and several have fireplaces or private balconies.

The food alone is well worth the trip to Maine. Dinner begins with a sampling of the inn's cheeses (which are sold locally and by mail order), accompanied by wine. A five-course meal is served nightly in the dining room, which is open to non-guests. The fare often features dairy products made on the premises, as well as whey buns (made from a recipe devised by Karen). Other dishes that might appear include *chèvre* ravioli, beef tenderloin with burgundy-mushroom sauce, swordfish with lemon-caper sauce, and dark chocolate mousse with Grand Marnier and whipped cream. A full breakfast of juice, fresh fruit, granola, homemade bread, oatmeal, and quiche is offered daily.

The inn is located on 12 acres that include wooded trails, pastures, and a cove with a rowboat. Activities off the inn's grounds include swimming at nearby beaches, sailing, bicycling, antiquing, and feasting on lobsters. The nearby *Maine Maritime Museum* holds many fascinations.

SQUIRE TARBOX INN Westport Island, RD 2, Box 620, Wiscasset, ME 04578 (phone: 207-882-7693). This inn and goat farm near Boothbay Harbor has 11 guestrooms with private baths and double, queen-, or king-size beds. Closed November through April. Rate for a double room (including full breakfast and dinner): $110 to $225; bed and breakfast: $90 to $194. Two-night minimum stay required on weekends from mid-July through October. Major credit cards accepted. Not appropriate for children under 12. No pets. Various farm animals on the property. Smoking on weather-protected deck only. Karen and Bill Mitman, innkeepers.

DIRECTIONS: Take I-95 north to Exit 22 (Brunswick). Follow Route 1 north past the Bath bridge for 7 miles to Route 144. Turning south onto Route 144, continue for 8½ miles to Westport Island and the inn.

New Hampshire

ADAIR COUNTRY INN

BETHLEHEM, NEW HAMPSHIRE

When prominent Washington, DC lawyer Frank Hogan built *Adair* as a wedding present for his daughter Dorothy in 1927, he spared no expense. He built a stately three-story Georgian Colonial Revival clapboard home with maple floors, wide box moldings, and a majestic stairway with a maple balustrade. Finally, he commissioned the Olmsted brothers (creators of New York's Central Park and Boston's Common) to landscape the 200-acre grounds. The grand estate was Dorothy's home until she died in 1991.

Purchased in 1992 by Hardy and Patricia Banfield, the mansion has been lovingly restored to its original elegance. Commanding an impressive site on a knoll with dramatic views of the White Mountains, the white house sits at the end of a driveway lined with birch trees, and abundant flower gardens accent the front lawns.

The wide central hallway is flanked by a dining room on one side and a living room on the other. The latter has Oriental rugs, a painted fireplace mantel, lovely flowered wallpaper, and overstuffed sofas and chairs. Downstairs is a taproom constructed of granite slabs (even the beamed ceiling is granite) with a fireplace; here guests watch movies on the VCR and play pool on the antique table. There's a collection of games, a video library, a piano, and an honor-system bar as well.

Upstairs are nine luxurious guestrooms—three rooms and two suites on the second floor and four rooms on the third—each with a private bath. The period reproduction furniture includes four-poster beds and upholstered headboards. *Waterford* boasts a massive mahogany Empire bed; *Lincoln* a Scottish four-poster with turned posts. Muted pastel colors prevail.

At the breakfast room window a bird feeder outfitted with a one-way mirror attracts an early-morning flock of doves and thrush. A full breakfast is offered every morning. Among the specialties are baked egg blossoms (eggs baked in phyllo) or Murphy's Irish toast (raisin toast dipped in milk spiked with Irish Cream). Don't miss the lighter-than-air popovers.

The dining room is leased to Tim and Biruta Carr, who moved their popular local restaurant *Tim-Bir Alley* (open to non-guests) to the inn when it opened. A typical dinner might feature grilled eggplant with warm goat cheese on roasted red-pepper *coulis,* followed by duck breast with fig-almond chutney on a pear purée, and, for a finale, white-chocolate raspberry tart with sweet brandy sauce. A small but well-chosen wine list is offered.

On the grounds are an all-weather tennis court, a mile-long walking trail, gardens with a pond, and terraces on which guests can spend a leisurely afternoon. Across the street, *Rocks Estate* comprises 1,300 acres and 4 miles of hiking and cross-country ski trails. Franconia Notch is just south of the inn, and the *White Mountain National Forest* has 760,000 acres that include numerous hiking trails. Two excellent golf courses are located nearby, as are the *Cannon, Bretton Woods,* and *Loon* ski areas. Nearby attractions include the *Weathervane Theater* and the *Robert Frost Museum.*

ADAIR COUNTRY INN Old Littleton Rd., Bethlehem, NH 03574 (phone: 603-444-2600; 800-441-2606; 888-444-2600; fax: 603-444-4823). This grand manor house has nine guestrooms and suites with private baths and queen- or king-size beds. Open year-round; dining room open Wednesdays through Sundays from May through October and from December through March. Rate for a double room (including full breakfast and afternoon tea): $125 to $175; rate for a double room (including full breakfast, afternoon tea, and dinner): $190 to $210. Two-night minimum stay on holiday weekends and during fall foliage season. Major credit cards accepted. Not appropriate for children under 13. No pets. Two dogs, Jackson, a standard poodle, and Duke, at inn. No smoking. Patricia and Hardy Banfield, innkeepers; Nancy Banfield, Manager.

DIRECTIONS: From I-93 take exit 40 onto Route 302 east toward Bethlehem. You will see the inn's sign after about a quarter mile.

INN AT CROTCHED MOUNTAIN
FRANCESTOWN, NEW HAMPSHIRE

Built in 1822 as a farmhouse, this historic inn once served as a stop on the Underground Railroad, which helped slaves escape to Canada; a secret tunnel led from the cellar to the road. During the late 1920s it became a renowned farm, with prize-winning livestock, including sheep, cattle, horses,

and Angora goats. Although part of the house was destroyed by fire and rebuilt in 1935, much of the original brick building still remains. John and Rose Perry purchased the inn in 1976 and have been improving it ever since.

On a 65-acre parcel of land, the inn offers a tranquil setting and a breathtaking view across the Piscataquog Valley. The decor is elegantly rustic—rich wood tones are accented with vivid, jewel-like colors and striking paintings, and flowers grace the public and private rooms. Its 13 cozy guestrooms are furnished with lovely antiques befitting a country estate. The house also has nine working fireplaces (five in the common rooms, four in guestrooms).

The two dining rooms (also open to non-guests) are warmed by the original fireplaces, and the main one contains the built-in bookcases and books (including a history of the inn) from the old house. This room also has restful views across the manicured lawns and gardens.

In addition to her role of gracious hostess, Rose stars as the chef. Her artistry combines an eye for enticing presentation with creative use of well-matched fresh ingredients—many of the vegetables, herbs, and edible flowers she uses are grown on the grounds. The result is delectable continental fare fused with culinary elements from her native Singapore. Dinner, which is served Friday and Saturday nights, may include cranberry port pot roast, shrimp scampi served with pasta, and lamb chops with mint-apple jelly. For desert, house specialties are a sinfully dense, dark chocolate mousse and a flavorful, not-too-sweet raspberry sherbet—order both. After dinner, guests usually congregate in the library/tavern for a nightcap in front of still another fireplace. A full breakfast is served every morning.

A mountainside swimming pool, a wading pool, ice skating, and two clay tennis courts are on the grounds, an 18-hole golf course is nearby, and hiking paths (which double as groomed cross-country ski trails in winter) thread through the woods. The less athletically inclined can find entertainment at several of the area's cultural attractions, including the *Sharon Art Center, Peterborough Players, Monadnock Music Festival,* and *American Stage Festival.*

INN AT CROTCHED MOUNTAIN Mountain Rd., Francestown, NH 03043 (phone: 603-588-6840). This historic inn in southern New Hampshire has 13 guestrooms (eight with private baths) with twin, double, or queen-size beds. Wheelchair accessible. Closed April and November; dinner served Friday and Saturday nights only; breakfast available daily. Rate for a double room (including full breakfast and dinner): $120 to $140; bed and breakfast: $60 to $70 on weekdays; $100 to $120 on weekends. No credit cards accepted. Children welcome. Pets allowed ($5 additional charge per day). Three English cocker spaniels, Winslow, Lucy, and Frances, in residence. Smoking allowed in tavern and sitting room. Rose and John Perry, innkeepers.

DIRECTIONS: From Boston follow Route 3 north through Nashua to 101A to Milford. In Milford take Route 13 to New Boston, then Route 136 to Francestown. From Francestown follow Route 47 for 2½ miles and turn left onto Mountain Road. The inn is a mile up the road on the right.

NOTCHLAND INN

HART'S LOCATION, NEW HAMPSHIRE

A unique feature of New Hampshire's granite-based terrain is the presence of rugged notches left from the last glacial age, from which the *Notchland Inn* gets its name. Just 10 miles from Mount Washington, the highest peak in New England, the inn sits on a picturesque knoll in *White Mountains National Forest,* commanding a view of the Saco River and its valley. The grounds—400 acres laced with hiking and cross-country ski trails—touch the base of four mountains. The Davis Path, which leads to Mount Crawford and, eventually, to the summit of Mount Washington, starts just across the street. The property also boasts two swimming holes, a pond, and for warmer soaks, a hot tub located in a gazebo overlooking the pond.

Off a major highway, the inn has served travelers for more than 70 years. Dr. Samuel Bemis, a dentist and inventor, completed the English-style manor house in 1862, using native granite blocks and timber. The former *Mount Crawford House,* an inn that was also on this property and dates to 1790, is now the dining room, while an 1852 schoolhouse contains two suites.

After being abandoned for many years, the inn has been painstakingly restored, its huge brick chimneys, embossed-tin ceilings, tiled fireplaces, and Gothic-style hardwood paneling carefully refurbished. One of the most unusual rooms is the *Stickley Room,* which was designed in the 1890s by architect and designer Gustav Stickley. It has six-foot-high wainscoting stained gray-green and a Tudor-style hearth with a high, arched canopy of wrought iron. In the music room, guests are encouraged to perform impromptu selections on the piano.

The seven guestrooms and four suites have their own fireplaces; tile floors and vanities in the bathrooms are recent additions. Bright and cheerful, the rooms are furnished with antiques from England and colonial America, accented by contemporary designer wall coverings and fabrics. The antique beds (two are four-posters) are strategically placed to showcase the incredible mountain views seen from most of the rooms.

Another entrancing aspect of this inn is its menagerie. Coco, a friendly Bernese mountain dog, acts as official greeter; Dolly, the Belgian draft horse, takes guests on sleigh and carriage rides; and Mork and Mindy, miniature horses, like to frolic with D. C. and Cid, the llamas.

Dinners at the *Notchland* (open to non-guests) have achieved legendary status in local circles. The menu varies seasonally but always includes a choice of two soups, two appetizers, three entrées, and three desserts. Popular dishes include lightly curried butternut squash–and–sweet potato soup, chicken champagne, chocolate walnut tart, and a very lemon pie. A full breakfast featuring juice, fresh fruit, and an entrée (perhaps cinnamon almond French toast, an egg dish, or pancakes) is available to inn guests.

Mount Washington's craggy granite cliffs, snow-fed streams, forests of pine, spruce, and fir, and crystalline air offer some of the most invigorating wilderness in the country—ideal for hiking, fishing, cross-country skiing, and other outdoor activities. For railroad buffs, the *Crawford Notch Line,* a scenic railroad that began operation in 1878, once again is winding its way along the trestles that connect the precipices to Crawford Notch, a spectacularly panoramic trip that passes right by the *Notchland Inn.* Nearby towns provide antiquing, and theatrical productions are staged in summer.

NOTCHLAND INN Hart's Location, NH 03812 (phone: 603-374-6131; 800-866-6131; fax: 603-374-6168). This historic inn near Crawford Notch has 11 guestrooms with private baths, queen- or king-size beds, and fireplaces. Open year-round. Rate for a double room (including full breakfast and dinner): $170 to $250; bed and breakfast: $130 to $210. Two-night minimum stay on weekends; three nights on holidays and during fall foliage season. Major credit cards accepted. Not appropriate for children under 13. No pets. One Bernese mountain dog, Coco; a Belgian draft horse, Dolly; miniature horses, Mork and Mindy; llamas, Cid and D.C., on the property. No smoking. Les Schoof and Ed Butler, innkeepers.

DIRECTIONS: Traveling north on I-93, take Exit 35 onto Route 3 to Twin Mountain. Turn right in Twin Mountain onto Route 302 east and travel 20 miles through Crawford Notch to the inn.

MEETING HOUSE INN

HENNIKER, NEW HAMPSHIRE

Located on five acres in the lovely Contoocook Valley and nestled at the base of *Pat's Peak* ski area, this property is a quiet retreat in a small rural village. The inn takes its name from a log meetinghouse, built in the 1760s, that sat at the base of Craney Hill, about a quarter mile away.

The inn's special personality is a reflection of its owners, June and Bill Davis, their daughter Cheryl, and her husband, Peter Bakke. They have decorated it in an eclectic style, with antiques that have been in both families for generations (such as the 1780 grandfather clock), hand-stitched needlework, and unique artwork.

Another unusual element of the decor is "The Sands of Time," a display of small, sand-filled plastic bags that hang from the walls of the restaurant, which is housed in a meticulously restored barn. The bags, contributed by hotel guests, contain sand from exotic spots around the world, including Mount Everest and the floor of the Atlantic Ocean.

The six guestrooms have wide-plank pine floors and antique colonial-era furnishings (including canopy and brass beds). The elegant decor is accented by floral chintz fabrics. Room amenities include a decanter of sherry and a basket of crackers.

A full breakfast is delivered in a picnic basket to guests' rooms, where it may be enjoyed in a leisurely fashion. The hot breakfast entrée is always a surprise, but some of the most popular are Meeting House Sunrise, a baked dish of ham, potatoes, fresh local vegetables, and cheese topped with an egg, or a baked French toast sandwich with fresh fruit and one of June's special syrups. A full dinner featuring hearty New England fare is served in the restaurant (which is open to the public). The evening might start with one of Bill's 14-ingredient bloody marys, then continue with such entrées as seared tuna with raspberry sauce or roast duck with apples and cashews. An interesting wine list is available.

For pampering, there's a hot tub and sauna. Guests enjoy walking through the inn's extensive herb and flower gardens, where they are delighted by the love poems Cheryl hand-painted on slates and placed among the flowers, and by the quaint birdhouses that Peter made by hand. Tennis, golf, downhill and cross-country skiing, antiquing, craft shops, water sports, and theaters are all nearby.

MEETING HOUSE INN 35 Flanders Rd., Henniker, NH 03242 (phone: 603-428-3228; fax: 603-428-6334). In south-central New Hampshire, this country inn has six guestrooms with private baths, double or queen-size beds, and air conditioning. Wheelchair accessible. Open year round, except for two weeks in March; restaurant closed Monday and Tuesday dinner. Rate for a double room (including full breakfast): $65 to $105. Two-night minimum stay on weekends in October and February and on holidays. Major credit cards accepted. Children welcome with advance notice. No pets. One cat, Grensil, in residence. No smoking. June and Bill Davis, Cheryl Davis Bakke, and Peter Bakke, innkeepers.

DIRECTIONS: Take I-89 west to Exit 5, then travel west on Route 9/202 to Route 114 south, continuing about 2 miles to the *Pat's Peak* sign. Turn right onto Flanders Road; the inn is a half mile up the hill on the right.

MANOR ON GOLDEN POND

HOLDERNESS, NEW HAMPSHIRE

If Squam Lake had not been showcased in the movie *On Golden Pond,* starring Katharine Hepburn and Henry Fonda, it might have remained in relative obscurity. Since the world found out about it, however, the lake has had no shortage of visitors—particularly in summer and fall.

There are many reasons to come to this delightful area. In summer, Squam Lake is ideal for swimming, fishing, and boating; in winter, ice fishing is popular; and, in fall, mirror images of the autumn foliage reflect in the water. An Englishman named Isaac Van Horn first discovered the pleasures of the area in 1903 and built an English-style manor house on a 14-

acre parcel of land overlooking the water. In 1992, David and Bambi Arnold purchased the house and its outbuildings, a collection of rustic cottages, and ambitiously began renovating the property.

They have turned it into a first class hotel. The manor house is furnished throughout with period antiques, with a quintessentially British ambience. The upstairs library offers an extensive collection of books and jigsaw puzzles, as well as leather chairs with hassocks for relaxed reading. Downstairs are a second library (strikingly decorated with a table made from a bellows and several Beatrix Potter lamps) and a living room with hand-carved mahogany woodwork and a marble fireplace. On occasion, a pianist plays in the cozy *Three Cocks Pub,* which has a copper bar, copper-topped tables, and an old English pub sign.

All of the guestrooms are supremely comfortable, their private baths featuring the original pedestal sinks. Most rooms have wood-burning fireplaces; three have two-person whirlpool tubs. Done up in blue and white, the *Churchill Suite* has a light blue carpet and leaded windows, a canopy bed, a fireplace, an antique wardrobe closet, and a writing desk placed to capture views of the lake. The *Buckingham Suite* offers a canopied four-poster bed, a marble fireplace, a tapestry wall hanging, and a porch overlooking the water. The four two-bedroom cottages and the carriage house have a more rustic flavor and are ideal for families. All have kitchens and grassy yards; three have fireplaces.

The three dining rooms (open to the public) boast additional marble fireplaces. The formal evening meal consists of five courses with such entrées as pan-seared filet mignon with crawfish and hollandaise and rack of veal with berry-and-port sauce. A heavenly dessert of warm timbale of flourless chocolate torte, served on *crème anglaise* and berry sauces, is accompanied by white and dark chocolate "fettuccine" (chocolate strings). A full breakfast is served to inn guests.

On the grounds are a pool, tennis courts, a croquet lawn, volleyball, horseshoes, and a sandy beach; the inn has a number of canoes and boats for guests' use. Activities in the area include downhill and cross-country skiing, hiking, golf, horseback riding, visiting *White Mountains National Forest,* and exploring the *Squam Lake Science Center.*

MANOR ON GOLDEN POND Box T, Rte. 3, Holderness, NH 03245 (phone: 603-968-3348; 800-545-2141; fax: 603-968-2116). Set in a manor house and several cottages, this inn offers 26 guestrooms and suites with private baths, twin, double, queen-, or king-size beds, air conditioning, and TV sets. Main house open year-round; cottages and carriage house open May through October. Rate for a double room in the manor house (including full breakfast and dinner): $180 to $325. Two-night minimum stay on major holidays and in autumn. Major credit cards accepted. Children welcome in cottages; manor house not appropriate for children under 12. No pets. No smoking. David and Bambi Arnold, innkeepers.

DIRECTIONS: From I-93 north, take Exit 24 in Ashland, then travel Highway 3 for 4 miles to Holderness. In Holderness cross the bridge and look for the sign to the inn, 2 blocks farther on the right.

CHRISTMAS FARM INN

JACKSON, NEW HAMPSHIRE

The inn's white clapboard farmhouse, built in 1777 on 14 acres of rolling land, is located on a country road at the base of the White Mountains. At first the green-shuttered house can be seen only in brief glimpses through a filter of large maple trees. Then it reveals itself—its long front porch decorated with hanging flower baskets and a row of green rocking chairs.

Sydna and Bill Zeliff purchased the inn in 1976. It had been called *Christmas Farm Inn* since 1946, and they were quick to seize the Yuletide theme. Several of the 37 guestrooms are named for Santa's reindeer and elves, meals are served in the *Mistletoe Pub* and the *Sugar Plum Dining Room,* and the overall color scheme is red and green. In addition, the Zeliffs hold a *Christmas* celebration in July.

There are guestrooms in the main house, in a 1778 saltbox, and in a barn. In addition, several two-bedroom cottages set in the woods are available for rent—each with its own fireplace, yard, and porch. The guestrooms and cottages are furnished with high-quality reproductions and decorated in Laura Ashley fabrics; several have four-poster or canopy beds and Jacuzzis.

The dining room, which affords a splendid view of the extensive flower gardens, serves well-prepared continental fare. Breads and rolls are baked on the premises. Typical entrées include baked duck breast stuffed with apples and walnuts and served with an apple-and-butter sauce, and roast pork tenderloin with a cranberry-apple compote. Be sure to leave room for the amaretto-soaked sponge cake served in a pool of raspberry sauce and topped with chocolate shavings. A full breakfast is also offered, and meals are open to non-guests.

Plenty of recreational activities are available. The inn's grounds boast a swimming pool, a putting green, horseshoes, shuffleboard, volleyball, table tennis, a children's play area, and a sauna. Golf, tennis, fishing, hiking, and cultural activities are also nearby.

CHRISTMAS FARM INN PO Box CC, Rte. 16B, Jackson, NH 03846 (phone: 603-383-4313; 800-HI-ELVES; fax: 603-383-6495). Located in the Mount Washington Valley, this inn has 37 guestrooms with private baths, twin, double, queen-, or king-size beds, and telephones. Open year-round. Rate for a double room (including full breakfast and dinner): $136 to $190; children ages 12 to 18 (in their parents' room): $50; children ages two to 12: $25; children under two: free. Two-night minimum stay during school vacations, fall foliage season, and winter weekends. Major credit cards accepted. No pets. Smoking permitted in the pub and in some guestrooms. Sydna and Bill Zeliff, innkeepers.

DIRECTIONS: From I-95 north, take Exit 4 (Spaulding Turnpike), which becomes Route 16. Take Route 16 for approximately 70 miles. Turn off onto Route 16A to Jackson. Continue across the covered bridge for a half mile. At the schoolhouse on the right, turn left onto Route 16B and travel a half mile. The inn is on the right.

INN AT THORN HILL

JACKSON, NEW HAMPSHIRE

Architecture and nature buffs alike will find much to occupy them at this grand country estate located on nine acres in northern New Hampshire.

Designed by famed architect Stanford White, the estate's main house retains several features that are characteristic of his work, including leaded-glass sliding doors and a gambrel roof. The manmade beauty is matched by that of the nature show that unfolds before the broad front porch—whether you're watching nearby Mount Washington become shrouded by dusk or enjoying the vivid colors of sunrise.

If Stanford White could see the *Inn at Thorn Hill* today, he'd undoubtedly feel right at home, as it has been faithfully restored by Jim and Ibby Cooper, who bought the place in 1992. White built the 14-room mansion in 1895 for Katherine Prescott Wormeley, a distinguished translator of the works of Balzac. Judging from the enormous rooms, she must have enjoyed lavish entertaining: The dining room seats 42, and the living room is so massive that it's now divided into three separate areas, where guests congregate to socialize or play board games. The smaller parlor contains the only television set, and the spacious drawing room has a Steinway baby grand piano and a soapstone wood stove.

The main inn's 10 guestrooms feature views of the mountains. Accommodations also are available in the adjacent *Carriage House,* whose 40-foot-long *Great Room* is highlighted by a fireplace, and in three cottages, each outfitted with a gas fireplace, Jacuzzi, and a deck or porch. These rooms, too, are tastefully decorated with Victorian antiques.

The dining room (which is open to non-guests for dinner) is justifiably noted for its haute cuisine. Choices include an appetizer of grilled scallops with sautéed plums, spinach, and prosciutto with a basil-and-citrus sauce, and such entrées as grilled quail with sautéed parmesan and orange semolina gnocchi. Full breakfast and afternoon tea are offered as well.

The property has an Olympic-size pool, and volleyball, badminton, and croquet courts. In addition, the Coopers often host special activities such

as wine-tasting dinners. Guests can go hiking, skiing (downhill and cross-country), golfing, canoeing, horseback riding, and mountain biking nearby. They can also attend outdoor concerts and summer theater.

INN AT THORN HILL Thorn Hill Rd., Box A, Jackson, NH 03846 (phone: 603-383-4242; 800-289-8990; fax: 603-383-8062). This luxurious country inn has 19 guestrooms with private baths and twin, double, queen-, or king-size beds. Limited wheelchair access. Rate for a double room (including full breakfast, afternoon tea, and dinner): $150 to $275. Major credit cards accepted. Not appropriate for children under 10. No pets. One cat, Gizmo, on premises. No smoking. Jim and Ibby Cooper, innkeepers.

DIRECTIONS: From I-95 north, take Exit 4 (Spaulding Turnpike), which becomes Route 16. Follow Route 16 for approximately 70 miles to Jackson. Once in the village, take Route 16A through the covered bridge to Thorn Hill Road and turn right. The inn is up the hill.

FOLLANSBEE INN

NORTH SUTTON, NEW HAMPSHIRE

Set in a distinctive, rambling farmhouse built in the 1840s, this inn is surrounded by three acres of land adjoining Kezar Lake. Four miles from New London, the *Follansbee* and the placid village of North Sutton have hosted visitors for more than a century. Some of this history is recorded in an album available to guests, which includes intriguing old photographs and postcards, and written reminiscences.

Owned by Dick and Sandy Reilein since 1985, the crisp white clapboard house has green trim and a broad front porch, accented with bright flowers in summer. Guests can sit on the porch and gaze at the peaceful lake, or watch the sunset from a bench built into the dock.

The warm hospitality extended here makes you feel as if you're staying with old friends. The sitting room, paneled with weathered barn siding and furnished with overstuffed chairs, presents an inviting setting for socializing. The room is particularly pleasant in winter, when the wood-burning stove offers a respite from the chill. A second parlor contains another fireplace, comfortable seating, and a small service bar, which has an impressive selection of wines and local beers.

The public areas are decorated with numerous folksy touches. Named after the Follansbees and other local forebears, the 23 comfortable guestrooms feature low ceilings and country antiques. Only 11 of the rooms have private baths, but the shared baths are large. Several have claw-foot tubs.

In the morning, guests congregate in the spacious dining room overlooking the lake to enjoy homemade granola, yogurt, juice, and coffee, and then are invited to the kitchen to select from a hot buffet, which may consist of an egg soufflé, pancakes, or French toast. Dinner is served to guests

with advance notice. A typical menu might include tortellini vegetable soup; spinach salad with feta cheese, *tamari* dressing, and marinated vegetables; savory dill bread; Cornish game hens; and chocolate cheesecake.

The inn has two sailboards, a rowboat, a canoe, and a paddleboat; for a memorable afternoon, take a self-powered excursion to the island in the middle of the lake. Guests also can stroll the scenic 3-mile path around the lake or take a bicycle ride on secluded roads. Anglers can drop a line in the state-stocked waters for bass, perch, and pickerel. In winter, there is cross-country skiing on the miles of groomed trails in the adjacent 500 acres. Mount Sunapee, a downhill skiing area, is nearby.

Musterfield Farm, a collection of early homestead buildings; the *Hay Estate*, former mansion and gardens of US statesman John Hay; the *Indian Museum* at Mount Kearsarge; and historic homes in the area make interesting excursions.

FOLLANSBEE INN PO Box 92, North Sutton, NH 03260 (phone: 603-927-4221; 800-626-4221). On Lake Kezar near New London, this inn offers 23 guestrooms (11 with private baths) with twin, double, queen-, or king-size beds. Closed briefly in April and November. Rate for a double room (including full breakfast): $75 to $105. Two-night minimum stay on some peak weekends. MasterCard and Visa accepted. Not appropriate for children under 11. No pets. One English springer spaniel, Samantha, in residence. No smoking. Dick and Sandy Reilein, innkeepers.

DIRECTIONS: Located 90 miles from Boston. From I-89 north, take Exit 10. Turn left at the end of the ramp and follow signs to North Sutton, turning right onto Route 114 north. The inn is behind the white church, across Keyser Road from the lake.

SUGAR HILL INN

SUGAR HILL, NEW HAMPSHIRE

Built in 1789, the *Sugar Hill Inn* was originally the home of one of the many hardy families who came to the White Mountains to farm. Traditional post-and-beam construction was employed for the house; massive rock fireplaces provided heat; and wide pine planks were used for walls and floors. A working farm until the 1920s, the property became an inn in 1929, and over the years three cottages were added. Jim and Barbara Quinn purchased the inn in 1986 and decorated it in colonial style. Their daughter Kelly Ritarossi and her husband, Stephen, joined them as innkeepers in 1995.

The two charming common rooms have original fireplaces, and guests congregate around a player piano in the living room for evening sing-alongs. In the small pub is another fireplace, a pine bar, and a piano that has been computerized to play CDs. The house's wide verandahs are filled with pots of flowers and white wicker furniture.

The 10 guestrooms in the main inn and six cottage suites feature antique beds, hand-braided rag rugs, and handmade quilts. Barbara stenciled the walls according to original patterns found during the renovations. The suites have private decks and wood-burning fireplaces.

In the morning, guests awaken to the aroma of freshly baked muffins and brewing coffee. A full breakfast, which might feature walnut pancakes with fresh fruit, is served in the dining room. Every afternoon the parlor is set for tea, served from a silver service on a cart laden with scones, sweet rolls, and breads. In the evening, the dining room (also open to non-guests by reservation) glows with candlelight, and a flutist and pianist play background music. Jim and Stephen are the chefs. The baked stuffed shrimp and the chicken breast with crabmeat topped with hollandaise sauce, are especially popular. A selection of wines is available. Desserts include bread pudding with warm whiskey sauce.

Downhill and cross-country skiing, tennis, concerts, the *Robert Frost Historic Home,* summer theater, golf, biking, and craft shows are nearby. Guests can use the powerful telescope on the verandah for stargazing.

SUGAR HILL INN Rte. 117 (mailing address: Franconia, NH 03580), Sugar Hill, NH (phone: 603-823-5621; 800-548-4748; fax: 603-823-5639). This inn has 16 guestrooms with private baths and twin, double, queen-, or king-size beds. Open year-round except *Christmas* week; dining room closed Tuesdays and Wednesdays. Rate for a double room (including full breakfast, afternoon tea, and dinner) during fall foliage season: $199 to $249; rate for double room (including full breakfast and afternoon tea) November through August: $109 to $145. Two-night minimum stay during fall foliage season. Major credit cards accepted. Children welcome in summer; not appropriate for children under 10 at other times of the year. No pets. One chocolate Labrador, Mr. Chuck, on premises. No smoking. Jim and Barbara Quinn and Kelly and Stephen Ritarossi, innkeepers.

DIRECTIONS: Traveling north on I-93 from Boston, take Exit 38 and follow Route 18 north through Franconia. In Franconia turn left onto Route 117. The inn is half a mile up the hill on the right.

DEXTER'S INN AND TENNIS CLUB

SUNAPEE, NEW HAMPSHIRE

New Hampshire in the summer is a kaleidoscope of blue skies, green trees, and sunshine, while in fall the colors change to red and orange. On 20 acres overlooking Lake Sunapee, *Dexter's* is itself a palette of bright yellow clapboard, green shutters, white trim, and colorful flower beds.

Built in 1803, the Colonial Revival main house was part of a private estate until 1948. It has since been thoroughly restored and furnished with period reproductions. Frank and Shirley Simpson purchased the inn in 1969, and their daughter Holly and her husband, Michael Durfor, are now the innkeepers.

Popular gathering places for guests include the screened porch, with white wicker furniture and a ceiling painted to look like a tent, and the large family room, which doubles as a small bar at night. In the evening, guests enjoy cheese and crackers in the cozy library/living room, which has a fireplace and a piano and is furnished with comfortable love seats.

Each of the 19 guestrooms is carpeted and individually decorated with antiques or 1940s oak furniture; three have four-poster or canopy beds, and five are air conditioned. Most are reached by little hallways that zigzag through the wings of the main house, although several are located in the annex barn across the street. Next to the main house is the *Holly House Cottage,* which accommodates up to six guests in two bedrooms, and includes a living room with a fireplace and a fully-equipped kitchen.

The full breakfast might include eggs Benedict or an omelette, and hearty country fare is served at dinner. Both meals also are open to non-guests. Dinner selections might include poached salmon, lamb chops, or chicken *piccata* and, for dessert, butterscotch-pecan pie or a chocolate-walnut torte. The cocktail lounge is a convivial place for after-dinner drinks.

One of the primary attractions at *Dexter's* is the variety of outdoor activities. There are three Plexipave tennis courts with a resident pro, a pool, and various lawn games, such as horseshoes, shuffleboard, and volleyball. Guests can golf, hike, or swim in a lake nearby. Local attractions include a visit to a maple syrup sap house, live entertainment at *Sunapee Harbor Marine*, summer stock at the *New London Barn Playhouse*, and historic tours at the *Saint-Gaudens National Historic Site*.

DEXTER'S INN AND TENNIS CLUB Stagecoach Rd., Box 703, Sunapee, NH 03782 (phone: 603-763-5571; 800-232-5571). Near Lake Sunapee, this country inn and tennis club has 19 guestrooms with private baths and twin, double, queen-, or king-size beds. Wheelchair accessible. Closed November through April (the cottage may be available in the winter); dinner served every day except Tuesday from *Memorial Day* through *Columbus Day*. Rate for a double room (including full breakfast and dinner): $135 to $190; rate for a double room (including full breakfast only when dining room is closed): $110 to 165; children under 12 (in parents' room): $35 to $45. Two-night minimum stay on weekends. Discover, MasterCard, and Visa accepted. Pets allowed in the annex and *Holly House Cottage* ($10 additional per night). No smoking except in lounge and on the porch. Michael Durfor and Holly Simpson-Durfor, innkeepers.

DIRECTIONS: Located 50 miles from Manchester, New Hampshire, and 100 miles from Boston. From I-89 north take Exit 12 to Route 11 west. Travel 5½ miles, turn left onto Winn Hill Road (which becomes Stagecoach Road), and continue another 2 miles. The main inn is on the right.

Vermont

TWIN FARMS

BARNARD, VERMONT

When Nobel Prize–winning novelist Sinclair Lewis and his wife, writer Dorothy Thompson, purchased a property with two farmhouses in this bucolic valley, they treasured the peaceful setting. Today, guests can experience that same sense of serenity on their former farm.

Twin Farms is no ordinary inn. Painstaking attention to detail has created an exclusive retreat that spoils guests for future experiences. The staff members are so helpful and friendly, yet so professional, that they seem to anticipate every need.

The architecture of the inn is stunning; the ambience highly personal. There is no lobby, cashier, or reception area, but a multitude of common rooms. The *Barn Room,* highlighted by the massive picture window Lewis installed so that he could see Mount Ascutney, has raftered ceilings and an enormous fireplace, making it snug in winter and bright and airy in summer. The walls of the foyer are decorated with charming hand-painted murals depicting Barnard and other Vermont scenes. An eclectic array of original paintings and art objects from the private collection of the owners, the Twigg-Smith family, lends a whimsical air. A garden terrace, a covered bridge to the pub and gameroom, a fully equipped fitness center, and a forest building containing a *furo* (a Japanese-style soaking tub) are just a few of the features. The pub contains a pool table and a complimentary bar.

Each of the guestrooms is unique and spacious, with amenity-laden baths, featherbeds, interesting fabrics, fine woodwork, and abundant fireplaces. There are four guest accommodations in the main house; among them are *Red's Room* (a nickname Lewis earned for his red hair) and the *Guest Room*, which has an oak sleigh bed facing a green marble fireplace, a dressing room, and bath with a claw-foot tub and a separate shower. Its walls and windows are hung with green French toile. Next to the main house is a former artist's studio that has been made over into two more guest-rooms. Seven new stone-and-timber cottages have been built in wooded settings near the main house, though they look as if they've been there for a hundred years. The *Orchard Cottage,* for example, is set amid apple trees in the old orchard, where it surveys, through its wall of windows, the ter-raced beaver ponds and ski slopes beyond. It has two carved granite fire-places and a split-ash herringbone ceiling, and is decorated in neutral tones accented by cranberry and teal. The *Treehouse* has a lofty ceiling and an ebony four-poster bed. Its screened porch looks across the fields at tree-top level.

Before dinner, guests (unless they have chosen to eat privately in their room) gather for drinks and hors d'oeuvres; the exact location, announced on an easel, might be the pub, the *Barn Room,* or the wine cellar. Dinner is served in the dining room, which has a soaring ceiling and a fireplace at each end. Tables are set with antique English china, fine crystal, and sil-ver. Guests may dine at a private table or share a larger table with other guests, heightening the sense of visiting with friends at their country estate. A fine wine selection complements the superb cuisine of Neil Wigglesworth, who is justifiably proud of the kitchen garden, where he grows herbs, edi-ble flowers, and vegetables. An evening's four-course meal may include a shrimp timbale with three-grain *blini,* char-grilled black sea bass with a compote of fiddleheads and fennel, and a dessert of apple chrysalis—a blown-sugar apple filled with Granny Smith mousse, accompanied by a warm caramel sauce.

The full breakfast might include berry-filled crêpes or blueberry pan-cakes with homemade sausage. A variety of fresh-baked croissants and other breads arrives in a basket. A full lunch also is served and, in the after-noon, delicate sandwiches, cakes, cookies, and tea tempt even folks who have spent the morning in the fitness center.

Bicycle and walking trails lace the 255-acre property. Tennis courts, a private ski slope and tow, croquet lawns, canoeing, swimming, and fishing in the seven-acre trout-stocked lake all are available. The inn will pack a picnic of lobster and champagne for an excursion on a mountain bike. Nearby is Woodstock, with its quaint shops and museums (including *Billings Farm Museum*), as well as facilities for golf and additional downhill and cross-country skiing.

TWIN FARMS (mailing address: PO Box 115) Barnard, VT 05031 (phone: 802-234-9999; 800-TWIN-FARMS; fax: 802-234-9990). This country retreat in a very rural, wooded setting in central Vermont has six suites and seven cottages

with private baths, queen- or king-size beds, telephones, TV/VCR sets, and air conditioning. Wheelchair accessible. Closed April. Rate for a double room (including breakfast, lunch, afternoon tea, dinner, all alcoholic beverages, all activities, and use of sports equipment): $700 to $1,500, plus a 15% gratuity. Two-night minimum stay on weekends; three nights on holidays. Major credit cards accepted. Not appropriate for children. No pets. One dog, Maple, in residence. No smoking. Shaun and Beverley Matthews, managing directors.

DIRECTIONS: Take I-91 north to the White River Junction/Lebanon exit. Get on I-89 north and turn off at Exit 1. Turn left onto Route 4 and head to Woodstock. In Woodstock take Route 12 north to Barnard. Turn right at the general store and drive for 1½ miles, bearing left at the fork. Two stone pillars mark the entrance to *Twin Farms* on the right; push button by gate for admittance.

LILAC INN

BRANDON, VERMONT

Painted the same pale yellow as the rare lilacs that bloom in the courtyard in spring, the *Lilac Inn* exudes a charm and gentility that's as special as its namesake blossoms. A mix of Greek Revival and Southern Plantation architectural styles, this nine-room hostelry is the pride and joy of innkeepers Michael and Melanie Shane, who have put their own unique stamp on its decor and gracious ambience.

Prior to opening in 1993, the inn underwent a two-year restoration overseen by Melanie, an architect, and Michael, a contractor. Today, it boasts polished oak floors, a curving staircase, and an elegant ballroom and cozy library, both adorned with carved fireplace mantels and fine antiques. The owners' museum-quality collections give the inn a distinctive character; there are enameled Russian box lids in the library, and Melanie's beautifully outfitted dolls are displayed in every guestroom.

Each spacious guestroom has a private tiled bath, many with a pedestal sink or claw-foot tub. In some cases, sinks have been placed in antique dressers or tables in the bedroom to allow more room in the baths. All the rooms are special, but two of our favorites are *Room No. 5* and the *Bridal Suite.* The former, with pink walls and yellow trim, features an antique bed with Ralph Lauren floral linen, and a deep green marble-topped dresser that contains the sink. The *Bridal Suite,* decorated in shades of pink and plum, has a massive iron canopy bed, a large oak table with twisted legs and claw feet, a wood-burning fireplace, a built-in vanity, and a bath with a two-person Jacuzzi. Impressive bride and groom dolls, accompanied by their bridal party, sit atop the armoire.

A full breakfast (included in the room rate) is served to overnight guests; the pastries are a house specialty. On Sundays the inn offers a huge brunch that's also open to non-guests; be sure to try the cream-filled caramelized French toast.

The inviting restaurant, which features a tavern and a more formal dining room, draws food lovers from far and wide. Lunch and dinner are served to overnight guests and others on Wednesdays through Saturdays. The dining room, romantically lit at night by candlelight, offers views of the garden, where the trees are adorned with hundreds of tiny white lights. Entrées may include rosemary lamb tenderloin or Brandon haddock, a local fish prepared with seasoned bread crumbs. The chocolate coffee *crème brûlée,* a house specialty, is a masterpiece. Lighter fare is offered in the tavern, which features a cozy seating area in front of a carved oak fireplace.

Another pleasant common area is the broad marble-tiled verandah, a secluded oasis lined with antique wicker chairs and sofas. The gazebo in the garden has become a favorite backdrop for weddings, while the putting green is a pleasant place to fritter away an afternoon.

Special inn events—from lawn concerts to wine tastings—take place throughout the year. Brandon lies in the Otter Valley between the Adirondack and the Green Mountains; the Battenkill River meanders through town. Hiking on the Long Trail, downhill and cross-country skiing, golf, fishing, and boating are all nearby, as is *Middlebury College Performing Arts Center* and *Fort Ticonderoga* in New York state.

LILAC INN 53 Park Street, Brandon, VT 05733 (phone: 802-247-5463; 800-221-0720; fax: 802-247-5499). A nine-guestroom Victorian mansion with private baths, twin, queen-, or king-size beds, telephones, and TV sets. Open year-round; dining room closed January, and for dinner Sundays through Tuesdays. Rate for a double room (including full breakfast): $100 to $250. Two-night minimum during fall foliage times and holiday weekends. Major credit cards accepted. Children welcome. No pets. Three cats and two pugs, Bella Noir and Dr. Watson, on premises. No smoking. Michael and Melanie Shane, innkeepers.

DIRECTIONS: From I-87, take Exit 20 in Glens Falls, New York, and follow NY 149 east to US 4 in Fort Ann, New York. Follow US 4 north and east to Rutland, Vermont. In Rutland, take US 7 north to Brandon. At the monument on the village green, follow signs for Route 73 north. The inn is in the first block on the right.

INN ON THE COMMON

Craftsbury Common, Vermont

Tucked away on a rural hilltop in Vermont's Northeast Kingdom, in a village that's hardly changed a street sign or a clapboard in its more than 200-year history, the *Inn on the Common* is a decidedly uncommon inn.

But, in truth, the name is something of a misnomer. The inn, which comprises three historic white clapboard houses, is only partially located on Craftsbury Common's village green. The two main houses are on its broad Main Street, about a quarter mile distant. Not that it matters. Romantic and serene, the 15-acre property includes lush perennial and rose gardens and walking trails that lead past quaint birdhouses to a garden with Leutens benches, a formal English croquet lawn, a red-clay tennis court, and a belvedere where Adirondack chairs provide front-row seats for watching the sun set behind Mount Mansfield. In winter, when the fields are covered with snow, cross-country ski trails lace the grounds. There's also a free-form swimming pool.

Penny and Michael Schmitt, owners of the inn since 1973, have anticipated every guest need. The common rooms, decorated with fine English antiques, are gracious and warm. Oriental rugs cover wide-plank pine floors, and wood-burning fireplaces glow in winter. An honor bar is discreetly placed within a cabinet in the library of the *Main Inn,* where guests can read old cookbooks, chat, and nibble hors d'oeuvres before dinner. In the *South Annex,* there's a guest pantry which offers snacks, coffee, tea, sodas, and freshly baked cookies, as well as a large collection of classic movies and a large-screen TV/VCR set.

The 16 guestrooms reflect the same careful attention to detail as the rest of the inn. The antique furnishings include four-poster and canopy beds and elegant dressers; some rooms have fireplaces or wood-burning stoves. Distinctive decorative touches include a huge butter churn in one room, a pine bed with fishnet canopy in another, and English furnishings in a third.

A full breakfast and dinner (also open to non-guests) are served either in the formal dining room decorated with elegant oil portraits and antiques, or on the outside deck in warm weather. Fine sterling silver, elegant china and crystal, tall tapered candles, and an extensive wine list create the backdrop for romantic and intimate dinners. The menu changes nightly, but game and fish are often featured; there might be venison cutlets with brandied peaches and plums, or sea bass accompanied by pineapple and jalapeño salsa. A delicate chocolate-raspberry torte is a tasty dessert selection. Coffee, chocolates, and cordials are available in the library following dinner.

The *Craftsbury Nordic Ski Center* is nearby, as are opportunities for golf, mountain biking, canoeing, and horseback riding.

INN ON THE COMMON Main Street, Craftsbury Common, VT 05827 (phone: 802-586-9619; 800-521-2233; fax: 802-586-2249). A genteel, sophisticated country inn in Vermont's remote Northeast Kingdom with 16 guestrooms with private baths, and twin, double, queen-, or king-size beds. Open year-round. Rate for a double room (including full breakfast, afternoon hors d'oeuvres, and dinner): $200 to $270. Two-night minimum stay during fall foliage season and *Christmastime.* MasterCard and Visa accepted. Children welcome. Pets welcome with prior permission (additional charge of $15 per pet). Bernese mountain dog, Samantha, in residence. Smoking permitted in some guestrooms. Michael and Penny Schmitt, innkeepers.

DIRECTIONS From I-91 take Exit 21 in St. Johnsbury and follow US 2 west to Danville. In Danville take Route 15 west to Hardwick and from there follow Route 14 north for 8 miles. Take a sharp right at the sign for Craftsbury Common and follow this road for 3 miles. The inn office will be on the right before the village green.

CORNUCOPIA OF DORSET

DORSET, VERMONT

Dorset is an appealing little mountain community with an unusual all-marble church, marble sidewalks, a spate of white clapboard houses and inns with green shutters, and an old-fashioned country store. If you haven't already guessed, one of the first commercial marble quarries was located nearby. Amidst all this marble, along the main street and under a canopy of trees, *Cornucopia of Dorset* is a special find.

Bill and Linda Ley, both with backgrounds in the travel business, have owned the white clapboard, 1880s inn since 1986 and they bring to it a friendliness and a commitment to guest comfort that are exceptional. If desired, coffee or tea is delivered to guests' rooms in the morning, along with a vase of fresh flowers, and a selection of fine wines may be enjoyed in front of either the living room or the library fireplace in the evening. Throughout the day, refreshments such as cookies, cake, or fresh fruit are laid out.

The living room is furnished with priceless antiques and family heirlooms. An abundance of books is available in the library, where a friendly game of backgammon may be in progress. A large sunroom contains videos for viewing on the VCR and, in the warmer months, guests enjoy relaxing on the patio, the side porch, and in the gardens.

The inn has four rooms and a cottage suite, each one awash with color. Four-poster or canopy beds are covered with colorful hand-knotted Vermont quilts in the summer and European down comforters in cooler weather. Four of the rooms have either wood-burning fireplaces or free-standing gas stoves, and each has a private bath stocked with Crabtree and Evelyn toiletries, hair dryers, and fluffy terry robes. The charming cottage suite in back has a full kitchen, a loft bedroom with skylights, and a living room with a cathedral ceiling and a fireplace. French doors lead to a private deck.

Breakfasts are served in the formal dining room. The table is set with one of Linda's many antique china services—maybe the Wedgwood or the Lenox "Monroe" pattern. Sterling silver is used, and linen napkins are folded into stemmed glasses. A typical breakfast might include a melon boat filled with fresh local berries topped with *crème fraîche,* followed by cinnamon puff pancakes with Vermont maple syrup or cheese blintzes with warm cranberry and raspberry toppings.

The inn is within walking distance of fine restaurants and the famed *Dorset Playhouse.* Art galleries, skiing, tennis, swimming, golf, and horseback riding are nearby.

CORNUCOPIA OF DORSET PO Box 307, Rte. 30, Dorset, VT 05251 (phone: 802-867-5751; fax: 802-867-5753). This country inn has four guestrooms and one cottage suite with private baths, twin, queen-, or king-size beds, and air conditioning; four have fireplaces or gas stoves. Open year-round. Rate for a double room (including full breakfast): $105 to $140; rate for cottage suite: $185 to $205. Major credit cards accepted. Not appropriate for children under 12. No pets. A dog, Kitt, in residence; Rutland, a rabbit, makes his summer home outside in a hutch. No smoking. Bill and Linda Ley, innkeepers.

DIRECTIONS: From Manchester Center take Route 30 north approximately 6 miles to Dorset. The inn is on the right, just south of the Dorset village green.

OLD TAVERN AT GRAFTON

GRAFTON, VERMONT

Little has changed in the sleepy village of Grafton since the 1800s, or at least it seems that way. A horse-drawn wagon still deposits travelers at the doorstep of the *Old Tavern at Grafton,* just as the Boston-to-Montreal stagecoach once did.

The illusion that the 19th century lives on here is by design. The Windham Foundation, a not-for-profit organization established in 1963, has restored and operates many of the local businesses, including the inn and the Grafton Village Cheese Company, which began production in 1890.

A fine white brick and clapboard structure, the *Old Tavern at Grafton* was built in 1801. Daniel Webster, Oliver Wendell Holmes, Ulysses S. Grant, Nathaniel Hawthorne, Ralph Waldo Emerson, Rudyard Kipling, and Henry David Thoreau are but a few of the American notables who have rocked gently on the wraparound porch. It remains a popular spot for an afternoon libation to this day.

Thanks to meticulous restoration, the exterior and interior of this historic inn fairly gleam. Colonial-era antiques furnish the common rooms as well as the guestrooms. Fireplaces grace the *Kipling Library,* with its floor-to-ceiling bookcases, and the lobby.

The inn offers 66 guestrooms, 14 of them in the main inn, 22 in *Homestead* and *Windham Cottages* across the street, 29 in six guesthouses located in the village, and one in a honeymoon cottage. All the rooms are charming, with colonial-style fabrics and antique furnishings; all but four have private baths. Nearly half the rooms have four-poster or canopy beds so high that step stools are set by them, and ten have private porches. The room rate includes a breakfast buffet of fresh fruit, muffins, bagels, cold and hot cereal, and yogurt.

The dining room is noted for its fine fare. Among the traditions are Grafton garlic-cheddar-and-ale soup and New England lobster pie, but the chef also has added lighter entrées to the menu such as grilled sesame chicken and halibut filet. For smaller meals—or a sampling of more than a dozen Vermont ales—there's also the *Phelps Barn Pub,* the restored original barn. Sofas are positioned near the pub's downstairs fireplace, and a loft contains a game and TV lounge with another fireplace. Entertainment— perhaps jazz, country music, or Old English ballads—takes place here nightly.

Guests may enjoy such local pleasures as a stroll of museum-like Grafton, with its stately old homes; blacksmith shop; exhibits of old tools, carriages, and photos at the *Windham Foundation Center;* the *Grafton Historical Society Museum;* the *Grafton Museum of Natural History;* and numerous craft, art, and antique shops. Visitors may watch cheese being made (and purchase it, too) at the *Grafton Village Cheese Company.* Other activities include swimming in the inn's pond, cross-country skiing, tennis, fly-fishing, and downhill skiing nearby.

OLD TAVERN AT GRAFTON Grafton, VT 05146 (phone: 802-843-2231; 800-843-1801; fax: 802-843-2245). This Georgian-era inn has 66 guestrooms (62 with private baths) with twin or queen-size beds. Wheelchair accessible. Closed April and *Christmas Day.* Rate for a double room (including continental buffet breakfast) weekends: $79 to $220; midweek: $95. Rate for entire guesthouses (with four to seven rooms each): $460 to $510. Two-night minimum stay on holiday weekends. MasterCard and Visa accepted. Children welcome. No pets. Smoking permitted in the *Phelps Barn Pub* only. Tom List II, innkeeper.

DIRECTIONS: From I-91 north, take Exit 52 in Bellows Falls. Bear right off the exit ramp; at the end of the access road turn left onto Route 5. Travel 5 miles to a traffic light. Turn left onto Route 121 west and continue 12 miles to Grafton. The inn is in the center of town.

RABBIT HILL INN
LOWER WATERFORD, VERMONT

Just above the meandering Connecticut River in the hamlet of Lower Waterford, with the White Mountains as its backdrop, the *Rabbit Hill Inn* sits on a village green that has changed little in 150 years. With its steepled Congregational church, tiny post office, honor-system library, and cluster of restored homes, the village is so perfectly preserved it feels as if time has stood still.

The inn is composed of two restored buildings—the Jonathan Cummings home, dating from 1825, and Samuel Hodby's 1795 tavern. Polished wide-plank pine floors and fireplaces are found in the common rooms. Outside are spacious porches and decks furnished with antique wicker. Across the manicured lawns and past the flower and herb garden is a charming gazebo and a swimming pond.

It's obvious that innkeepers John and Maureen Magee love the history of their inn and the surrounding countryside. The 21 guestrooms are named for people who had a connection with the place, and they're furnished accordingly. For example, a Victorian dressing-room suite on the top floor of the old tavern is furnished with hatboxes, bonnets, and letters of the period, and Victorian clothing hangs in the wardrobe. The guestrooms' priceless antiques, canopy and four-poster beds, fireplaces, and balconies are enhanced by such modern creature comforts as radios with cassette tape players, in-room coffee makers, and terry robes. The "Fantasy Suites" are outfitted with Jacuzzis, glassed-in showers, fireplaces, separate dressing areas, and numerous extras.

To complete guests' immersion in the Federal era, candles light the common and dining rooms at night. The Federal-period parlor in the main inn is decorated with period antiques and original oil paintings, as is the sitting room, where guests also will find a collection of hand-cut mahogany puzzles and unusual gameboards. A bountiful afternoon tea is set out here. The video den, with the inn's only television, contains an extensive videocassette library (bowls of freshly popped popcorn are available on request). The *Snooty Fox Pub* is a convivial spot to enjoy an aperitif.

A stay at the *Rabbit Hill Inn* includes a four-course breakfast, afternoon tea, and dinner (also open to non-guests), and the food is certainly one of the highlights. Dinner, by the expert hand of chef Russell Stannard, may include an appetizer of smoked chicken and sweet potato pie with pecans and dried apples; an entrée of beef tenderloin with blue goat cheese, oregano sauce, and rosemary-garlic noodles; and the inn's specialty dessert, chocolate bourbon pecan pie. Heart-healthy menu items are provided as well. Live chamber music accompanies the meal, frequently with Maureen, a music teacher, performer, and arranger, playing the flute.

The inn is located on 15 acres of grounds. In summer, guests enjoy croquet, horseshoes, shuffleboard, a pond for swimming, fishing and canoeing on the river, and hiking trails that lead over bridges spanning a stream and past meadows of grazing cows. There are snowshoes and toboggans for winter entertainment. Nearby are golf courses, *Franconia Notch State Park, Fairbanks Museum and Planetarium,* and downhill and cross-country skiing.

RABBIT HILL INN Rte. 18 and Pucker St., Lower Waterford, VT 05848 (phone: 802-748-5168; 800-76-BUNNY; fax: 802-748-8342). This luxurious country inn has 21 guestrooms with private baths and twin, queen-, or king-size beds; 17 of the rooms have air conditioning; 12 have fireplaces. Wheelchair accessible. Closed April and the first two weeks in November. Rate for a double room (including full breakfast, afternoon tea, and dinner): $179 to $269; bed and breakfast: $139 to $229. Two-night minimum stay if Saturday is included. Major credit cards accepted. Not appropriate for children under 13. No pets. One cat, Zeke, in residence. No smoking. John and Maureen Magee, innkeepers.

DIRECTIONS: Traveling north on I-89, take Exit 44 to Route 18. Follow Route 18 north for 2 miles. The inn is on the left. From I-91 north take Exit 19 to I-93 south. Then take Exit 1 to Route 18 south and follow this for 7 miles. The inn is on the right.

ANDRIE ROSE INN

LUDLOW, VERMONT

The *Andrie Rose Inn* is one of those places you love so much you don't even want to tell your best friend about it. What makes it so special? The main inn, a former farmhouse dating to 1829, the 1840s Greek Revival *Solitude Building,* and the 1833 Federal-style *Guesthouse* certainly have interesting features. There's a wraparound porch for afternoon relaxation, as well as patios, decks, and a rose garden. The main building has a fireplace in the living room and an inviting dining room with an alcove where breakfast is served. But it's the guestrooms that make this inn so appealing.

Although the main inn has been welcoming guests since Andrie Rose opened her home to skiers in the 1950s, it wasn't until Jack and Ellen Fisher purchased the property in 1991 that it began to take on its current sophisticated style. Today, the majority of accommodations are romantic suites, boasting spectacular baths, 16 of them with spacious whirlpool tubs. In the *Solitude Building,* the whirlpool tubs, romantically placed in front of fireplaces, are encased in creamy-white faux onyx. The furniture is country pine, accented by Laura Ashley fabrics and wallcoverings. The luxury suites in the *Guesthouse* are even more sumptuous, complete with canopy beds, fireplaces, whirlpool tubs, telephones, hair dryers, refrigerators, instant hot water, and TV sets.

Jack and Ellen offer numerous little "perks" throughout the inn: Cookie jars, candy dishes, and fruit bowls are always filled with treats, and turndown service includes a Vermont chocolate. In the afternoon, hot teas and chocolate (or iced tea and lemonade in the summer) are set out. There's a tiny bar where drinks are served and a tray of locally made cheeses, fruits, breads, and crackers is offered in the evening. A variety of games and books is available.

Breakfast is served by candlelight and may include cinnamon walnut French toast or blueberry pancakes topped with Ben & Jerry's Vermont ice cream, as well as juice, fruit, cereal, and homemade breads. A six-course dinner (exclusively for inn guests) is served every Saturday night. A typical menu will include an appetizer, soup, salad, intermezzo, and a choice of entrée. Beef Wellington, roasted double breast of pheasant with roasted garlic hollandaise sauce, or fresh Atlantic salmon served with orange-basil butter, are possible entrées. Perhaps the dessert will be the luscious *crème brûlée.*

Ludlow is a sleepy village at the base of *Okemo* ski area in the Green Mountains and also close to the *Killington* ski areas. The *Weston Playhouse* is nearby, as is the village of Woodstock.

ANDRIE ROSE INN 13 Pleasant St., Ludlow, VT 05149 (phone: 802-228-4846; 800-223-4846; fax: 802-228-7910). This village bed and breakfast has 20 guestrooms with private baths, and twin, double, queen-, or king-size beds; most with telephones, TV sets, fireplaces, and Jacuzzis. Open year-round. Rate for a double room (including full breakfast): $70 to $205; luxury suites (not including breakfast): $250. Two-night minimum on weekends July through October and mid-December through March. Major credit cards accepted. Children welcome. No pets. One dachshund, Schultz, at inn. No smoking. Jack and Ellen Fisher, innkeepers.

DIRECTIONS: From I-91 take Exit 6 and travel north on Route 103 to Ludlow. In the village, turn south at the only traffic light onto Depot Street. At the next intersection, turn right onto Pleasant Street. The inn will be on the left.

GOVERNOR'S INN

LUDLOW, VERMONT

Built as a summer home by Vermont governor William Wallace Stickney in the 1890s, the Victorian mansion known as the *Governor's Inn* retains much of its former elegance. Exquisite examples of stained glass grace the tea alcove, the parlor, and the second- and third-floor stair landings. Unusual marbleized slate fireplaces warm the parlor and the front hall.

Charlie and Deedy Marble, who have owned the inn since 1982, have decorated the rooms with family heirlooms and original art. All of the eight guestrooms have antique beds—burled walnut in one, a brass four-poster in another. Private baths with a variety of amenities reflect the innkeepers' thoughtful attention to guest comfort. There's even one luxury suite with a whirlpool tub. There's also a "welcome to the inn" gift, a cordial and chocolates at turndown time, and a box of maple-sugar candy at departure. A stay, here, is not just a night in the country. It's an unforgettable and romantic experience.

As lovely as the common rooms and guestrooms are, the inn also is renowned for its food. Both Charlie and Deedy are accomplished cooks: Charlie is the breakfast chef, and Deedy prepares dinner. She's won too many awards to list, but it would be wise to fast for several days prior to a visit in order to savor all the culinary pleasures here.

Plan to arrive no later than 3 PM for afternoon tea, an array of perfect little sandwiches and delectable pastries served on silver trays and antique china.

Dinner guests gather in the den for hors d'oeuvres and cocktails at 6 PM. At 7 they are escorted to their tables by waitresses clad in Victorian dresses. The candlelit tables are set with antique bone china and silver, perhaps gilded and hand-painted porcelain oyster plates and some of the 110 different knife rests. Deedy describes the menu as soon as the guests are seated, then fully describes each dish again as each of the six courses is presented. An appetizer might be artichoke hearts in a puff pocket with Vermont cheese custard scented with tarragon; this will be followed by a homemade sorbet, eaten with little sterling silver spoons. The entrée might be pan-seared Vermont veal with raspberry sauce, accompanied by a beet-and-apple puree, and two of the inn's most requested dishes: the potato soufflé and the corn pudding. Desserts are equally innovative. Following the evening meal, coffee is poured from one of the lovely Limoges chocolate pots. Dinner is also open to non-guests.

The next morning Charlie's five-course breakfast may include apple pie, just as our colonial ancestors ate, or a three-cheese soufflé served in puff pastry. If you've saved room—or run 20 miles after breakfast—order one of Deedy's picnic baskets to take on a hike through the forest. Even if you don't picnic, you'll get one of the unique baskets when you leave. It's thoughtfully made to fit under an airline seat.

Throughout the year the Marbles sponsor "Culinary Magic Cooking Seminars," during which Deedy shares her secrets. A box of recipe cards is for sale at all times. Other special events include an antiques extravaganza, a weekend in September when guests are taken to a farm to select their *Christmas* tree (it will later be cut and shipped to them), and an apple-picking weekend. Downhill and cross-country skiing, hiking, summer theater, and antiquing are all available in the area.

GOVERNOR'S INN 86 Main St., Ludlow, VT 05149 (phone: 802-228-8830; 800-GOVERNOR). This inn has eight guestrooms with private baths, twin, double, or queen-size beds, and air conditioning. Open year-round. Rate for a double room (including full breakfast, afternoon tea, and dinner): $170 to $299; with full breakfast and afternoon tea only: $95 to $259. Two-night minimum stay on weekends during fall foliage season and at *Christmas*. MasterCard and Visa accepted. Not appropriate for children under nine. No pets. No smoking. Charlie and Deedy Marble, innkeepers.

DIRECTIONS: Traveling north on I-91, take Exit 6 to Route 103 north. Ludlow is located at the junction of Route 103 and Route 100. The inn is just off the village green on Route 103.

1811 HOUSE

MANCHESTER VILLAGE, VERMONT

Except for the brief period when Mary Lincoln Isham, President Lincoln's granddaughter, used it as a residence, this house has been a wayside inn since it was built in the 1770s. Purchased by Marnie and Bruce Duff in 1990, it has been meticulously restored to its Federal-period style: twelve-over-twelve windows and clapboard siding characterize the structure. Located in a charming historic village with broad, tree-lined streets, marble sidewalks, and magnificent vintage houses, the *1811 House,* listed on the National Register of Historic Places, sits on seven and one-half acres with views of the surrounding mountains. Its landscaped gardens—including a pond, colorful flower beds, and a rose garden—are all carefully tended by Bruce.

The inn's rooms are filled with authentic English and American antiques and Oriental rugs, giving guests the opportunity to stay in a living museum, yet one that encourages relaxation and comfort. Chinese porcelain lamps and sterling and china objets d'art grace polished mahogany tables. Original oils and drawings line the walls.

A roaring fire in the library/gameroom attracts guests for a game of chess, but the hub of the inn is the dark-beamed pub. The windows are draped with the MacDuff family tartan, and a pewter collection, gleaming

brass horns, pub tables, and a regulation dartboard add to the thoroughly British atmosphere. You know this is the real thing when you see the choice of 49 single-malt whiskies and the Scottish ale on tap. A downstairs recreation room houses pool and Ping-Pong tables.

There are 14 guestrooms, six with fireplaces, each with a private bath. Lace-canopied four-poster beds, exquisite Persian rugs, stenciling, and fine fabrics decorate the rooms.

Marnie used to be a cooking teacher, and not surprisingly, breakfast is one of the highlights of a stay here. Vermont products such as Harrington ham and Cabot cheddar cheese are featured, as are herbs and edible flowers from the Duffs' own gardens. The meal is served on fine china with Georgian sterling silver and fine old linen. A typical breakfast might include fresh-squeezed juice, fruit, home-baked breads, and an entrée such as French toast or a casserole served with homemade chicken-sausage patties.

Several excellent golf courses are in the area, as are tennis, fly fishing, and skiing. Also nearby are a tony factory-outlet village and a number of historic attractions, including *Hildene,* the former home of Robert Todd Lincoln.

1811 HOUSE Rte. 7A, PO Box 39, Manchester Village, VT 05254 (phone: 802-362-1811; 800-432-1811; fax: 802-362-2443). This historic inn has 14 guestrooms with private baths, double, queen-, or king-size beds, and air conditioning. Closed one week prior to *Christmas.* Rate for a double room (including full breakfast): $110 to $210. Two-night minimum stay on weekends; three nights on holidays and during fall foliage season. Major credit cards accepted. Not appropriate for children under 17. No pets. Heath and Heather, two cats "who love guests," in residence. No smoking. Bruce and Marnie Duff, innkeepers.

DIRECTIONS: Traveling north on Route 7 in Vermont, exit at Manchester Center. Turn left at the bottom of the ramp and travel through town to Route 7A. Turn left onto 7A south. The inn is just over a mile farther, at the monument in Manchester Village.

INN AT ORMSBY HILL

MANCHESTER VILLAGE, VERMONT

During the early 1900s, Manchester Village was the hub of a glittering social scene. Here, Robert Todd Lincoln, President Lincoln's only child to survive to adulthood, built his glorious estate, *Hildene,* overlooking the Battenkill River. One of Lincoln's law partners, Edward Swift Isham, adapted a 1790s farmhouse into his own grand estate in 1890, creating the manor house now known as the *Inn at Ormsby Hill.* It is believed that Isham was the first to call the house "Ormsby Hill," after Captain Gideon Ormsby of the Green Mountain Boys. The inn supposedly offered refuge to Ethan Allen when he was fleeing the British. A "secret" room is still here, so be sure to ask to see it. Sometime during Isham's stewardship, President Taft was a visitor.

Since 1991 the inn has taken on a new look: New siding, new paint, new porches, a sunny conservatory overlooking newly landscaped gardens, polished floors, beautiful antiques, fireplaces, and whirlpool tubs. Yet the core of this magnificent home is still the original 1790 keeping room with its huge kitchen fireplace. Today, this room and two others are comfortable sitting rooms.

Since purchasing the inn in 1995, Ted and Chris Sprague have almost doubled its size and they've redecorated the common and guestrooms as well. The 10 guestrooms are enormous. Nine have working fireplaces, whirlpool tubs, and antique queen- or king-size (they've been enlarged)

four-poster or canopy beds with step stools to reach them. The rooms are decorated with tasteful chintz bed drapes, down comforters, bouquets of fresh flowers, upholstered chairs or love seats, and antique desks; all have views of the surrounding mountains. Isham's former library (now one of the guestrooms) retains the clubby look of a man's den: painted a rich ever-green with creamy white wood trim, it has a fireplace and bookcases lining three walls. The *Taft Room* has a fireplace, a canopy bed, and a private breakfast room. Its bath contains a whirlpool, a bidet, and an ample stall shower. All the bathrooms have heat lamps, hair dryers, and terry robes.

Dinner, for house guests only, is served Friday and Saturday nights. On Friday night, it's a casual affair—a pot of soup (perhaps a meaty chicken noodle) simmering on the stove and a basket of sourdough bread on the table; guests arrive anytime between 6:30 and 9:30 PM and congregate in the spacious kitchen to meet and eat. For dessert, Chris might prepare her three-layer carrot cake with cream-cheese frosting. The price is a mere $20 for two. On Saturday night, the mood is more formal. Guests who have chosen to eat in (price: $60 for two) will have hors d'oeuvres and drinks at 6:30 PM. At 7 the four-course sit-down dinner begins. Perhaps rack of lamb with a Cabernet-and-shiitake-mushroom sauce as an entrée. The spectac-ular dessert of double-chocolate truffle torte with white chocolate sauce receives raves.

Breakfast is another four-star, four-course event, served in the conser-vatory, which has bow-shaped windows at the end of the room, wainscoted ceilings, and a spectacular carved walnut fireplace. A buffet of fruit, juice, breads, and cereals is set out between 8 and 10 AM and a hot entrée (maybe individual high-rise baked pancakes with lemon and powdered sugar) is served at 9. This is followed by a typical New England–style breakfast dessert such as hot apple crisp or warm gingerbread with vanilla ice cream.

The inn's two and one-half acres include flower gardens with paths for strolling. Guests who enjoy golf, fishing, or skiing will find outstanding facil-ities nearby (the Orvis Flyfishing School is located here). Others may pre-fer a visit to *Hildene* (Robert Todd Lincoln's home is now a historic house museum), the *Dorset Playhouse,* or some of the area's many art galleries and discount outlets (Christian Dior and Ralph Lauren, Brooks Brothers, Giorgio Armani, among others).

INN AT ORMSBY HILL Historic Rte. 7A, RR2, PO Box 3264, Manchester Village, VT 05255 (phone: 802-362-1163; 800-670-2841; fax: 802-362-5176). This Federal-style inn just outside historic Manchester Village has 10 guestrooms with private baths, queen- or king-size beds, and air conditioning; nine have fireplaces and two-person whirlpool tubs. Wheelchair accessible. Open year-round. Rate for a double room (including full breakfast): $110 to $210. Two-night minimum stay on weekends and during fall foliage season. Major credit cards accepted. Not appropriate for children under 11. No pets. Truffles, a yellow Lab, in residence. Smoking permitted outside only. Ted and Chris Sprague, innkeepers.

DIRECTIONS: Traveling north on Route 7 in Vermont, take Exit 3 (Arlington/Manchester Village) onto Route 7A toward Manchester. Follow Route 7A north. The inn is on the right, about 2 miles north of the Basket Barn store and before Manchester Village.

Swift House Inn

SWIFT HOUSE INN AND RESTAURANT

MIDDLEBURY, VERMONT

When Andrea and John Nelson purchased this inn in 1985, they embarked on an extensive renovation project—not the first that this sophisticated spot has seen in its lifetime. The main house was built by Samuel Swift in 1815 and later became the home of Vermont governor John W. Stewart, who moved to the house when his daughter Jessica was five years old. Jessica became a Swift when she married the builder's grandson, and she lived in the house until she died at the age of 110 in 1981. Over the years a carriage house and a Victorian gatehouse were added to the three-and-a-half-acre property. Today each of these buildings, set amid formal gardens that contain more than 200 rosebushes and are terraced by low stone walls, contains guestrooms or suites.

The main house has five common rooms, including a formal dining room with cherry paneling and a marble fireplace. The elegant parlors, in shades of peach and buttercup, are furnished with Queen Anne antiques and reproductions, architectural renderings and paintings of the house, and English chintz. Oriental rugs cover the oak and maple floors.

The 21 guestrooms are equally elegant, especially in the main house, where the lavishly draped rooms have antique four-poster or canopy beds, fine armoires, exquisite antique desks and chests, fireplaces, and private balconies. The *Swift Room,* for example, has a cherry canopy bed with an eyelet spread, a fireplace, and a private terrace; the *Governor's Room* also has a fireplace, an antique armoire, and is decorated in a handsome marine blue. The *Addison Room* contains a quilt handed down through Andrea's family. Some baths in the main house maintain their old-fashioned quality with claw-foot tubs and pedestal sinks, although most have been updated. The *Carriage House,* which was renovated in 1990, offers six spacious rooms with new baths and Jacuzzis, as well as a communal sauna and steamroom—especially popular after a day on the ski slopes. The *Gatehouse,* a splendid turreted Victorian that overlooks busy Route 7, has a porch furnished with antique wicker, Tennessee rockers, and an old buckboard seat. The Victorian atmosphere carries inside with fretwork and period chandeliers and furniture. Here, the guestrooms are more whimsically decorated: *No. 32* is pretty in shades of pink, for example, and *No. 35* has purple walls.

Candlelit dinners (also open to the public) are served nightly in the dining rooms and on a pretty side porch. The menu features Vermont products. Appetizers might include smoked Maine salmon with an endive-and-radicchio salad dressed with watercress aiole and croustades; the entrée might be pan-seared pork tenderloins with a sauce of Vermont cheddar and ale, served with fruit compote. For dessert, try Andy's famous coffee toffee pecan torte. A continental breakfast is included in the room rate, but a full breakfast is available for an additional charge.

Guests enjoy visiting Middlebury, a delightful college town with exceptional craft and art galleries. Don't miss the *Frog Hollow Vermont State Craft Center,* where Vermont's finest artisans sell their wares. Skiing, hiking, and golf also are nearby, as are the *Morgan Horse Farm* and the *Sheldon Museum.*

SWIFT HOUSE INN AND RESTAURANT 25 Stewart La., Middlebury, VT 05753 (phone: 802-388-9925; fax: 802-388-9927). In historic Middlebury, this inn has 21 guestrooms with private baths, twin, double, queen-, or king-size beds, telephones, and air conditioning; 19 with TV sets; 12 with whirlpool tubs. Wheelchair accessible. Open year-round; dining room closed Tuesdays and Wednesdays. Rate for a double room (including continental breakfast): $100 to $175. Children welcome. No pets. Smoking permitted in some guestrooms. Andrea and John Nelson, innkeepers.

DIRECTIONS: On Route 7, Middlebury is 30 miles north of Rutland and 35 miles south of Burlington. The inn is 2 blocks north of the village green, on the corner of Stewart Lane and Route 7.

INN AT SHELBURNE FARMS

SHELBURNE, VERMONT

This inn, set on 1,400 hilltop acres overlooking Lake Champlain, was for many years a Vanderbilt family retreat. The imposing brick turn-of-the-century Queen Anne mansion was built in 1888 by railroad baron Dr. William Seward Webb and his wife, Lila Vanderbilt Webb. It sits high on

the hill amid lawns and gardens designed by Frederick Law Olmsted, who was assisted in the selection of trees by Gifford Pinchot, founder of the *US Forest Service.*

The manor house shares the property with *Shelburne Farms,* a nonprofit educational and working farm where Brown Swiss cows produce the milk from which the farm makes its renowned creamy Vermont cheddar. Even the livestock was beautifully housed in the Vanderbilts' day: The massive *Farm Barn,* where 40 teams of horses once were quartered, resembles a French château, with an interior courtyard and turreted brick walls.

Past the barn, some 2 miles farther up the driveway, is the inn itself. The mansion counts among its treasures elaborate oak paneling, arched doorways, common rooms with massive fireplaces, and family portraits. Lila Vanderbilt's gardening books are still in the library. The Vanderbilt era lives on in such details as the original chandeliers, sconces, and bathroom fixtures, even as the inn is updated with modern creature comforts.

The 24 guestrooms (most with private baths) retain exquisite Vanderbilt and Webb antiques—including canopy beds, armoires, and elaborate dressers—in their original settings. *Frederica's Room* (the Webbs' daughter's bedroom) still holds her bookcases filled with books, her carved canopy bed with its horsehair mattress, a pink satin striped chaise, and an ornate bureau; a wall of windows overlooks the terraced gardens with Lake Champlain and the mountains beyond. The bath includes its original claw-foot tub and double pedestal sink. The *Brown Room* contains a stunning 10-piece suite of marquetry furniture. Even the rooms on the third floor, once the children's quarters, are large and very special (some share baths). The light and pretty *White Room* has a coffered ceiling, a half-canopied bed with a pink satin bedskirt, wicker furniture, and a long hallway to an enormous private bath with a claw-foot tub.

Guests enjoy afternoon tea in the sunny parlor in the north wing, just as the Webbs did. Breakfast and dinner (open to the public) are served in the dining room, which retains its marble floor, spectacular carved ceiling, and a massive white marble, claw-footed serving buffet. The 13 tables are laid with heirloom silver, pretty china, and crystal—a fitting setting for the impressive meals. Appetizers might include puff pastry with a sauté of wild mushrooms, marjoram, and lemon or a salad of Miskell tomatoes grown at the farm. Entrées include roasted rack of Vermont lamb with fennel purée and grilled filet of beef tenderloin with a Tennessee bourbon and rosemary sauce. An extensive selection of wines is available. Picnic lunches are prepared for guests by request. No meals are included in the room rate.

Guests may enjoy a 90-minute tour around the farm in an open wagon. The journey includes the *Farm Barn,* where children can collect eggs, pet farm animals, and watch cheese being made; the *Dairy Barn;* the *Coach Barn;* and the inn's spectacular gardens. Just beyond the front gates is a gift shop purveying cheeses, jams, and maple syrup.

A tennis court, a beach, rowboat, kayak, and canoes also are on site, and summer concerts frequently are held on the grounds. Among the nearby attractions is the *Shelburne Museum,* one of the country's finest collections of Americana. Located in 37 buildings on 45 acres adjacent to Shelburne Farms—and including everything from hats and quilts to a grand private railroad car—it was assembled by Electra Havemeyer Webb, who married the eldest Webb son, James Watson Webb. Also in the area are the *Morgan Horse Farm* and *Ben and Jerry's Ice Cream Factory* (where tours and samples are offered).

INN AT SHELBURNE FARMS 102 Harbor Road, Shelburne, VT 05482 (phone: 802-985-8498; fax: 802-985-8123). This manor house and farm on Lake Champlain has 24 guestrooms (17 with private baths) with twin, double, or queen-size beds, and telephones. Closed mid-October to mid-May. Rate for a double room: $85 to $285. Two-night minimum stay on weekends. Major credit cards accepted. Children welcome. No pets. Farm animals on property. No smoking. Kevin G. O'Donnell, director.

DIRECTIONS: From I-89, take Exit 13 in Burlington and drive south on Route 7 for approximately 5 miles. Turn right at the stoplight in the center of Shelburne. Drive 1⅔ miles to the entrance of *Shelburne Farms.* Turn left through the stone gate beside the *Visitors' Center* and follow signs for 2 miles up the driveway to the inn.

ROWELL'S INN

SIMONSVILLE, VERMONT

Established in 1820 as a stagecoach stop, this venerable inn presides over a bend in Route 11 between Londonderry and Chester beside Lyman Brook. Restored by innkeepers Lee and Beth Davis, its five guestrooms and five

common rooms are brimming with antiques and oddities that always offer small surprises, even for its many repeat visitors.

The inn, on the National Register of Historic Places, boasts broad brick walls and expansive porches lined with rockers. The lobby/parlor, which formerly served as Simonsville's stagecoach stop, general store, and post office, contains photographs of the inn and of visitors who stayed here in the 1920s.

Overlooking the Green Mountains, the library features a fireplace, built-in bookcases, wing chairs, and custom-woven English carpets. The inviting *Tavern Room,* in a 1790s farmhouse, offers a selection of English ales, porters, and stouts, as well as an old-fashioned soda fountain; a toasty wood stove and a moose head complete the picture. In the afternoon an array of cheeses, hors d'oeuvres, cookies, and teas is served in the sunroom. Guests often spill out onto the slate patio with its Adirondack chairs to watch the goings-on at the bird feeder.

Guestrooms (some with fireplaces) feature brass beds and Oriental rugs. Pedestal basins, claw-foot tubs, and heated towel bars enhance the baths. Two suites have been carved out of the top-floor ballroom. *Room No. 1,* on the second floor, has a wood-burning fireplace and a bath with a deep tub.

Dinners at *Rowell's Inn* (open to the public by reservation) are five-course meals featuring Yankee fare. Selections include roast chicken, a New England boiled dinner, and such traditional desserts as chocolate cake, bread pudding, and apple pie. A full breakfast is served to guests.

The inn has two acres of grounds; hiking, biking, downhill and cross-country skiing, golf, tennis, fishing, and theaters are all nearby.

ROWELL'S INN RR1, Box 267-D, Simonsville, VT 05143 (phone: 802-875-3658; 800-728-0842; fax: 802-875-3680). In the mountains of central Vermont, this inn has five guestrooms with private baths and twin, double, queen-, or king-size beds; most have air conditioning. Closed April through mid-May and the first two weeks of November. Rate for a double room (including full breakfast, afternoon tea, and dinner): $160 to $175; bed and breakfast (available Sundays through Thursdays mid-November through March): $110 to $125. Two-night minimum stay on weekends. MasterCard and Visa accepted. Not appropriate for children under 13. No pets. Outside cat, Oscar. Smoking in tavern only. Beth and Lee Davis, innkeepers.

DIRECTIONS: From I-91 take Exit 6 at Bellows Falls and drive north on Route 103 to Chester. Turn west onto Route 11 and travel 7 miles to Simonsville. The inn is on your right.

EDSON HILL MANOR

STOWE, VERMONT

Serenely situated on a hilltop surrounded by 225 acres of forest laced with hiking, horseback-riding, and groomed cross-country ski trails, *Edson Hill Manor* is truly an inn for all seasons.

As guests wind up the driveway past the inn's private riding stables and pond, views of the spacious lawns, abundant flower beds, and secluded pool come into view. The handsome wood-and-brick manor house sits on the hillside, surveying its domain.

Inside, the gracious pine-paneled living room has tapestry-covered chairs and sofas, pine floors covered with Persian rugs, a massive fireplace, elegant oil paintings (including one of the owner's ancestor Sophie Bronfman), and a multitude of books and games. The beams here were originally hewn for Ira and Ethan Allen's barn, a structure that once stood in North Burlington.

The manor house contains nine antiques-filled guestrooms, most with canopy beds and fireplaces. Dormer windows, fabric wall coverings, fireplaces with imported Dutch tile, and goose-down comforters in pretty duvets are typical embellishments. Yet the bathrooms are what leave the most lasting impression. Each has been hand-painted by artist Gail Kiesler with exuberant scenes of flower gardens and playful birds, cats, dogs, and fish. Four carriage houses just up the hill from the manor house contain 16 additional pine-paneled guestrooms, each with a fireplace and hand-crafted Shaker-style furniture.

More whimsical murals adorn the dining room. Painted stone arches frame sponge-painted walls, and the ceiling is painted with beams and ivy to create the illusion of a secluded arbor in Provence. Elegant French provincial furniture and leaded casement windows add to the ambience. A large covered flagstone terrace serves as an additional dining room in summer. Another mural, a pastel garden scene, greets guests in the dining room foyer, and the bar downstairs, which has its own patio, is painted with hunt scenes and stenciled designs. Even more lovely than the painted panoramas are the real views, down to a lake and beyond, that can be glimpsed from this hilltop aerie.

A full breakfast and dinner (both open to non-guests) are served on marvelous oversized china hand-painted especially for the inn. The bill of fare at dinner might include fresh salmon wrapped in bacon or a spectacular Cornish game hen.

In addition to horseback riding and cross-country skiing, the inn offers hayrides and carriage rides in summer, and sleigh rides in winter. Nearby, guests will find downhill skiing, mountain biking, golf, and tennis. Stowe's 6-mile recreation path is one of the finest in the nation, offering walkers, joggers, bicyclists, and in-line skaters a broad, paved, dedicated roadway that meanders across covered bridges, alongside rushing streams, and through wooded forests.

EDSON HILL MANOR 1500 Edson Hill Road, Stowe, VT 05672 (phone: 802-253-7371; 800-621-0284; fax: 802-253-4036). A refined 25-guestroom country inn on 225 acres near Vermont's finest ski resorts with private baths, twin, double, queen-, or king-size beds, and telephones; 22 rooms have fireplaces; 18 have TV sets. Open year-round. Rate for a double room (including full breakfast and dinner): $140 to $200; with breakfast only: $100 to $160. Two-night minimum stay during fall foliage season; five nights at *Christmastime*. Major credit cards accepted. Children welcome. No pets. Two dogs, Sophie and Amber, on premises. Smoking in some guestrooms. Eric and Jane Lande, proprietors; William O'Neil, manager.

DIRECTIONS From I-89 take Exit 10 in Waterbury. Travel north on Route 100 for 10 miles to Stowe. In Stowe, take Route 108 north for 3 miles to Edson Hill Road. Follow Edson Hill Road north for 1½ miles to the entrance to the inn, which will be on the left.

INN AT THE ROUND BARN FARM

WAITSFIELD, VERMONT

The Shakers were masters at finding ingenious solutions to everyday problems, and round barns were one of their most clever inventions. Hay was stored on the top level and pitchforked down into a center manger every day. Cows were then brought into the middle level of the barn, where they were placed in a circle to feed while they were milked. The waste was shoveled through holes down to the lowest level, where waiting carts would carry it out to fertilize the fields.

This particular round barn, built in 1910, is actually a 12-sided structure. Now listed on the National Register of Historic Places, it is one of only eight round barns still standing in Vermont. Staying at the *Inn at the Round Barn Farm* presents a rare opportunity to appreciate Shaker craftsmanship up close.

We can thank the Simko family, the innkeepers, for the pleasure. When they purchased the 85-acre property in 1986, the barn, as well as the rest of the farm, was almost beyond repair. Now, after their meticulous research and restoration, the 1810 farmhouse contains beautifully decorated guestrooms; the barn is a special setting for weddings, concerts, and meetings, and also serves, on occasion, as an art gallery. In the fall Vermont's premier juried show, "Art in the Round Barn," is held here.

The common rooms are in the farmhouse. To preserve the polished pine floors, guests are asked to remove their shoes upon entering; in winter they are provided with slippers. Guests congregate in the living room/library for coffee in the morning and hors d'oeuvres and sherry in the evening. The gameroom lures guests with a billiards table, board games, and television. Throughout the inn an abundance of fresh flowers suggests the innkeepers' former occupation: florists.

Guestrooms feature wide-plank pine floors, hand-carved moldings, antique chairs and desks, Oriental rugs, fireplaces, and bookcases. The baths are thoroughly modern, with steam showers (several with Jacuzzis), thick towels, terry robes, special soaps and lotions, and lighted makeup mirrors. Turndown service includes warm chocolate-chip cookies.

A full breakfast, prepared by daughter AnneMarie, is served in the solarium overlooking the meadows. It might be Belgian waffles with maple cream or cottage-cheese pancakes with raspberry sauce. Fresh fruit is served in antique cut-glass goblets.

A stone terrace lined with hibiscus and a formal garden make relaxing summer havens. For the energetic, a 60-foot lap pool is located in the lower level of the barn, and the nearby pond is warm enough for summer swimming; it freezes over in winter for ice skating. There are 19 miles of groomed cross-country ski trails on the property, as well as a ski-touring center. Guests can rent skis here, but ski at no additional charge. The *Round Barn* is the site of the *Green Mountain Cultural Center,* where a lively schedule of performing arts, art workshops, and cultural events take place year-round. There's also plenty of hiking, bicycling, canoeing, golf, tennis, horseback riding, and antiquing in the area.

INN AT THE ROUND BARN FARM E. Warren Rd., RR1 Box 247, Waitsfield, VT 05673 (phone: 802-496-2276; fax: 802-496-8832). In the Mad River Valley of central Vermont, this inn has 11 guestrooms with private baths and twin, double, queen-, or king-size beds, some with air conditioning, and telephone and TV jacks. Closed two weeks in April. Rate for a double room (including full breakfast and evening sherry): $115 to $225. Major credit cards accepted. Not appropriate for children under 14. No pets. A calico cat and a dog, J.B., in residence. No smoking. Jack and Doreen Simko, innkeepers; AnneMarie DeFreest, manager.

DIRECTIONS: From I-89 north take Exit 9 (Moretown/Middlesex) to Route 100 south to Waitsfield. In Waitsfield drive east on Bridge Street, passing through the covered bridge, and travel 1½ miles up East Warren Road to the inn, which is on the left.

INN AT SAW MILL FARM
WEST DOVER, VERMONT

Rod and Ione Williams have owned the *Inn at Sawmill Farm* since 1968. From the beginning, Rod's background in architecture, Ione's decorating wizardry, and their combined love of fine food and wine have made the place a model for other innkeepers. Ione has even traveled to other inns to act as an interior design consultant and Rod has designed numerous renovations for other innkeepers.

Their casual yet sophisticated inn consists of a collection of restored buildings: a massive barn (now the main inn), a millhouse, a woodshed, a farmhouse, and a cider house. The rooms in the main inn are connected by quaint little hallways and staircases. The public rooms all have beamed ceilings. The bar, which is filled with copper tables and upholstered wing chairs, has walls finished with barn siding. It's the living room, however, that is frequently seen in magazines, as it radiates the essence of country-inn warmth. Beamed ceilings and barnwood walls are brightened by a plaid carpet, vibrant red floral chintz upholstery on sofas and wing chairs, and a fireplace that is large enough for an adult to stand in.

The 20 large guestrooms and suites contain four-poster and canopy beds, and antique desks, chests, and chairs; 11 of the rooms have private balconies or patios and 10 have fireplaces. The decor includes quilted spreads, English chintz adorning the windows and chairs, numerous plants, and bookcases filled with books. All have private baths and several have Jacuzzis.

Dinner at the *Inn at Saw Mill Farm* (also open to non-guests) is a very special experience; a jacket is required. Brill Williams, who was a teenager when his parents purchased the inn, is now chef and part owner. Try his appetizer of shrimp in beer batter with pungent fruit sauce or his entrée of baby frogs' legs in a Riesling sauce with sliced truffles. The outstanding *crème brûlée* has a thick bittersweet crust and a creamy, rich center. The 36,000-bottle, award-winning wine cellar will satisfy the most sophisticated oenophile.

The 21-acre property includes gardens with a gazebo, a patio, porches, a swimming pool, tennis courts, trout ponds, and groomed cross-country ski trails. It is near the *Mount Snow, Stratton, Bromley,* and *Magic Mountain* ski areas. There's golf, fishing, and boating in the area. Another popular attraction is the *Marlboro Music Festival,* held in July or August in the town of Marlboro (about an hour's drive from the inn).

INN AT SAW MILL FARM Crosstown Rd., Box 367, West Dover, VT 05356 (phone: 802-464-8131; fax: 802-464-1130). This delightful country inn has 20 guestrooms with private baths, double, queen-, or king-size beds, and air conditioning. Closed April. Rate for a double room (including full breakfast, afternoon tea, and dinner): $340 to $400. Major credit cards accepted. Not appropriate for children under 11. No pets. Smoking permitted. Rodney, Ione, Brill, and Bobbie Dee Williams, innkeepers.

DIRECTIONS: From I-91 north, take Exit 2 in Brattleboro and go west on Route 9 to Route 100 in Wilmington. Travel 6 miles north on Route 100 to West Dover. Take the first left past the church; the inn is on the left.

TRAIL'S END—A COUNTRY INN

WILMINGTON, VERMONT

As its brochure states, *Trail's End* is not an old sea captain's house, an authentic Victorian, or a Federal-style mansion; it is a much newer property, decidedly different from other inns. Built in 1956 as a lodge for the nearby *Mount Snow* ski area, the building was purchased in 1985 by Bill and Mary Kilburn, who transformed it into a 10-acre country haven.

The common rooms are comfortably furnished with antiques. In the living room, a fieldstone fireplace rises s 22 feet to the cathedral ceiling. Hot cider, cookies, pastries, and fruit are served here in winter; in summer there's lemonade. The soaring picture windows overlook the landscaped grounds and meadows; the view from the loft is even more spectacular.

Four of the 15 guestrooms feature fireplaces, and all have brass, wicker, iron, four-poster, or canopy beds, country antiques, and fluffy comforters. Two romantic suites have stone fireplaces, canopy beds, kitchens, skylights, decks, and whirlpools. All the rooms have private baths, and several have Jacuzzis.

Breakfast is served in the dining room and includes home-baked muffins, eggs, pancakes or waffles with Vermont maple syrup, bacon or sausage, and coffee. In the afternoon, Mary bakes a cake or cookies to tide her guests over until dinner. During the *Marlboro Music Festival,* held in July or August, she has another batch of goodies waiting for returning guests.

A heated pool, a clay tennis court, and a trout pond are all on the property. Skiing, golf, and hiking are nearby.

TRAIL'S END—A COUNTRY INN 5 Trail's End Lane, Wilmington, VT 05363 (phone: 802-464-2727; 800-859-2585). This inn has 15 guestrooms with private baths and twin, double, or queen-size beds. Closed *Easter Monday* to mid-May. Rate for a double room (including full breakfast and afternoon refreshments): $90 to $170. Two-night minimum stay on weekends; three nights on holidays. Children welcome. No pets. Madison, a black Labrador, in residence. Smoking permitted. Bill and Mary Kilburn, innkeepers.

DIRECTIONS: From I-91 north, take Exit 2 in Brattleboro to Route 9 west. Wilmington is 17 miles from Brattleboro. At the traffic light in Wilmington, take Route 100 north for 4 miles, then turn right and follow the signs to the inn.

JACKSON HOUSE INN

WOODSTOCK, VERMONT

If the charming town of Woodstock is a reflection of the Rockefellers' commitment to historic preservation, then this inn is certainly a reflection of the similar sensibilities of its owners, Bruce McIlveen and Jack Foster. Listed on the National Register of Historic Places, *Jackson House Inn* is a jewel. A gingerbread Victorian painted yellow with white trim, it's surrounded by exquisite flower gardens and furnished with equally exquisite antiques.

Built in 1890 by Wales Johnson, a local sawmill operator, the house exhibits examples of the finest woods milled in Woodstock: polished floors of the high-quality cherry and maple generally reserved for fine furniture, wainscoting of alternating cherry and maple, decorative exterior woodwork hand-crafted for the house. In 1940, the Jackson family purchased the house and began taking in guests. In 1983, it was purchased by Bruce and Jack, who embarked on a massive renovation project.

The 12 guestrooms are decorated with imagination and wit—each in a different style, with the finest antiques, furnishings, and Scalamandre silks. *Francesca,* for example, is an opulent suite in muted champagne and mauve with a queen-size cherry sleigh bed, burgundy sofa, Italian marble bath, and French doors opening to a deck that overlooks the landscaped grounds. *Miss Gloria Swanson,* named after the star who stayed here in 1948, is done in peach and green and has a floor of curly and bird's-eye maple.

Stroll the three acres of formal gardens, sit on the bench by the pond, or take a cup of tea to the wicker-furnished front porch. Downstairs in the main house is a spa that contains exercise equipment and a steamroom. There's also a film library and a large-screen TV. A wine and champagne bar and a buffet of hors d'oeuvres are offered in the parlor each evening, and turndown service includes a Godiva chocolate on each pillow.

Bountiful breakfasts are served at an antique Queen Anne mahogany table. Jack is the chef, and he's likely to start the meal with buttermilk scones, banana bread, and apple–wheat germ muffins as well as fruit—perhaps bananas and cream with toasted almonds. A main course of chicken au champagne with buttered fettuccine and poached egg may follow, accompanied by mimosas. The round table facilitates convivial conversation.

Just outside Woodstock, the inn is near downhill and cross-country skiing, antiquing, horseback riding, and the *Billings Farm Museum.*

JACKSON HOUSE INN 37 Rte. 4 W., Woodstock, VT 05091 (phone: 802-457-2065). This Victorian inn has 12 guestrooms with private baths and twin, double, or queen-size beds and air conditioning. Open year-round. Rate for a double room (including full breakfast and evening wine and hors d'oeuvres): $135 to $250. Two-night minimum stay on weekends and holidays. No credit cards accepted. Not appropriate for children under 15. No pets. One cat and ducks on the property. No smoking. Bruce McIlveen and Jack Foster, innkeepers.

DIRECTIONS: From I-91 north, take Exit 9 to Route 12 north. When Route 12 crosses Route 4, travel west on Route 4 through Woodstock. The inn is located 1½ miles west of the village on the right.

Quebec

MANOIR DES ERABLES

MONTMAGNY, QUEBEC

Serenely situated on four acres, the *Manoir des Erables* stands back from the road. Accommodations are in a variety of buildings, all of which surround a central courtyard with a flower garden and a pool. *Le Manoir* itself, a stately mansion dating from 1812, contains guestrooms with polished hardwood floors and antique furnishings. The common room and dining room are located here, as are three conference rooms. The rooms in *Le Pavillon Collin* also are furnished with antiques, and *Le Motel* is a collection of nine rooms, some with whirlpools or saunas. A massive suite has a fireplace and a Jacuzzi.

Owned since 1993 by Jean Cyr, the inn is acclaimed for its fine French fare. Cyr's father, a chef, purchased the inn in 1975 and dedicated himself to promoting Quebecois cuisine. Dinner (also open to non-guests) is a relaxing repast that begins with soup, progresses through salad, entrée, and cheese courses, and ends with dessert and coffee. Entrées might include pork medallions with apples or lamb in a port sauce. Following the meal, guests may enjoy a glass of port in the cozy pub. Breakfasts are all-American feasts of bacon, eggs, and toast.

Montmagny is located on the St. Lawrence Seaway, and only a short walk from the inn is an excursion ferry that threads its way through the estuary's 21 islands. Also nearby is the interesting *Centre Educatif des Migrations* (Center of Migration Education), which documents the arrival of millions of Irish immigrants to Quebec in the 19th century. The center also features exhibits on the annual migration of thousands of snow geese to the bird sanctuary on nearby Grosse-Ile. Golf, boating, and downhill skiing also are nearby.

MANOIR DES ERABLES 220 Bd. Taché E. (Rte. 132), Montmagny, QUE G5V 1G5, Canada (phone: 418-248-0100; 800-563-0200; fax: 418-248-9507). On the St. Lawrence Seaway, this inn has 23 guestrooms with private baths, double, queen-, or king-size beds, telephones, and TV sets. Open year-round. Rate for a double room (including full breakfast, dinner, and all gratuities): CN $158 to $283 (US $115 to $207at press time). Major credit cards accepted. Children welcome. Pets allowed by prior arrangement only. Smoking permitted. Jean Cyr, innkeeper.

DIRECTIONS: From Quebec City, cross the seaway and follow Highway 20 east for 36 miles (58 km). Take Exit 376 (Des Poiriers and Montmagny). Follow Route 132 for 1⅓ miles (2 km). The inn is on the right.

AUBERGE HATLEY
NORTH HATLEY, QUEBEC

A retreat in the Quebec countryside may seem as remote to many Americans as a château on the Loire River in France, but North Hatley is only 24 miles from the Vermont border.

Owned by Robert and Liliane Gagnon since 1980, *Auberge Hatley* is a sprawling, gray-shingled, three-story, 30-plus-room house on the shores of Lake Massawippi. Built in 1903 by the Holt family, Canadians with their roots in Scotland, it was then, and is now, an impressive haven. The country French theme of the decor includes antique pine furniture, braided rugs on polished hardwood floors, and bright floral wallpaper. Many of the rooms have Jacuzzis, saunas, fireplaces, and French doors leading to balconies overlooking the lake. Several have four-poster or canopy beds.

Liliane, who once owned an art gallery, has created an octagonal pavilion with a 32-foot ceiling, where the works of Quebec artists are displayed. The living room contains English antiques and leather sofas and chairs, a comfortable spot for reading before the massive brick fireplace or just enjoying the ambience.

As lovely as the rooms are, it's the food that attracts people from miles around. Exotic lettuces, herbs, and edible flowers are grown hydroponically in a spectacular 8,500-square-foot greenhouse. Because of the short local growing season, extensive research went into the construction and maintenance of the greenhouse, which now yields crops in such abundance that the produce itself inspires new recipes.

In a candlelit dining room overlooking Lake Massawippi, dinner (also open to non-guests) is presented with exceptional flair. A meal might start with a *mille-feuille* of salmon and scallops with lime dressing and seaweed, followed by a sliver of Barbary duck leg with fresh foie gras. The extensive

wine list, featuring current and collector vintages, will satisfy the most serious oenophile. Desserts are equally impressive. In the morning, a full buffet breakfast is served.

Auberge Hatley is an inn for all seasons. In the spring, there is horseback riding, fishing, and bird watching on the 10-acre grounds. Summer means swimming in the heated pool or a concert on the lawn. The fall foliage season is ideal for hiking and photography, while ice fishing and skiing occupy guests during the winter months.

AUBERGE HATLEY 325 Chemin Virgin, PO Box 330, North Hatley, QUE J0B 2C0, Canada (phone: 819-842-2451; fax: 819-842-2907). On the shores of Lake Massawippi, this inn has 25 guestrooms with private baths, double, queen-, or king-size beds, telephones, and air conditioning. Wheelchair accessible. Closed two weeks in November; lunch served in summer only. Rate for a double room (including full breakfast and dinner): CN $180 to $350 (US $131 to $255 at press time). Major credit cards accepted. Not appropriate for children under 12. No pets. Smoking permitted. Robert and Liliane Gagnon, innkeepers.

DIRECTIONS: Take I-91 from Vermont north to the Canadian border, then continue on Route 55 north for 18 miles (29 km) to Exit 29 (North Hatley). Follow Route 108 east for 6 miles (10 km) to North Hatley, then follow the signs to the inn, which is 1 mile (1.6 km) from the center of the village.

HOVEY MANOR

NORTH HATLEY, QUEBEC

The village of North Hatley was settled by Loyalists who fled America after the Revolutionary War. *Hovey Manor* was named for one of them, Colonel Ebenezer Hovey, who was granted a plot of land by the crown in 1785. After the Civil War, the village became a popular summer retreat for American Southerners, who had formerly summered in New England. Many of the spectacular homes here are remnants of that era. Today, the area is a haven for artists, writers, theater lovers, and sportsmen.

Inspired by *Mount Vernon,* Henry Atkinson of Atlanta built *Hovey Manor* in 1899. It's a large house with broad verandahs and white columns overlooking Lake Massawippi. Atkinson needed a sizable house: He would arrive for his summer stay with an entourage of 18 servants, 10 horses, and a full housekeeping staff, all packed into two private railway cars and several carriages.

Today *Hovey Manor* is a year-round retreat owned since 1979 by Stephen and Kathy Stafford. The resort is decorated with priceless antiques, many from Atkinson's original collection; spectacular bouquets of fresh flowers abound. Most of the guestrooms have fireplaces, Jacuzzis, antique canopy beds, and balconies with views of the lake, and all have coffee makers. In addition to the 32 guestrooms in the mansion, 10 other rooms are tucked away in the caretaker's residence, the pump house, the icehouse, and the electric house (a former electric plant that has been renovated).

A complimentary full breakfast is served every morning to guests, and an English cream tea is served every afternoon (at additional charge). Dinner (also open to non-guests) is an event, with a menu of contemporary French cuisine (such as duckling with rhubarb galette and caramelized ginger, or lobster and fish with champagne and green papaya salsa). The food is enhanced by herbs and edible flowers from the inn's gardens. Tasting dinners with five or six courses of regional fare (including game in season) also are offered. Classical music often is played on the grand piano for the enjoyment of dinner patrons.

Combining a historic ambience with the facilities often found in a year-round resort, the inn offers guests much to occupy them. In summer, they can roam the resort's 25 acres, where they'll find English gardens, lighted tennis courts, a heated pool, a lake with two beaches, and a private dock with canoes, paddleboats, windsurfers, and sailboats, or they might take a jaunt on one of the inn's touring bikes. Inside, there's an exercise and a massage room. Cruises to North Hatley and water skiing also are possible (for an additional charge). Also nearby is *The Piggery,* a summer stock theater that mounts productions in English. Wintertime attractions are a skating rink, an ice fishing cabin, and 31 miles of groomed cross-country ski trails. Board games, Ping-Pong, and billiards are available in the *Tap Room,* which occupies the old stables and has a fireplace so large that it took 10,000 bricks to build it. Golf and downhill skiing are nearby.

HOVEY MANOR 575 Hovey Rd. (Rte. 108 E.), Box 60, North Hatley, QUE J0B 2C0, Canada (phone: 819-842-2421; 800-661-2421; fax: 819-842-2248). This country house inn has 42 guestrooms with private baths, twin, double, queen-, or king-size beds, and telephones. Wheelchair accessible. Open year-round. Rate for a double room (including full breakfast, dinner, all recreational facilities, and service charges): CN $200 to $410 (US $146 to $299 at press time). Major credit cards accepted. Not appropriate for children. No pets. Smoking permitted, but some guestrooms are designated nonsmoking. Stephen and Kathryn Stafford, innkeepers; Steven G. Beyrouty, manager.

DIRECTIONS: Take I-91 from Vermont north to the Canadian border, then continue on Route 55 north for 18 miles (29 km) to Exit 29 (North Hatley). Follow Route 108 east for 6 miles (10 km) to North Hatley, then follow *Manoir Hovey* signs to the private driveway, which is on the left.

Southern
New England

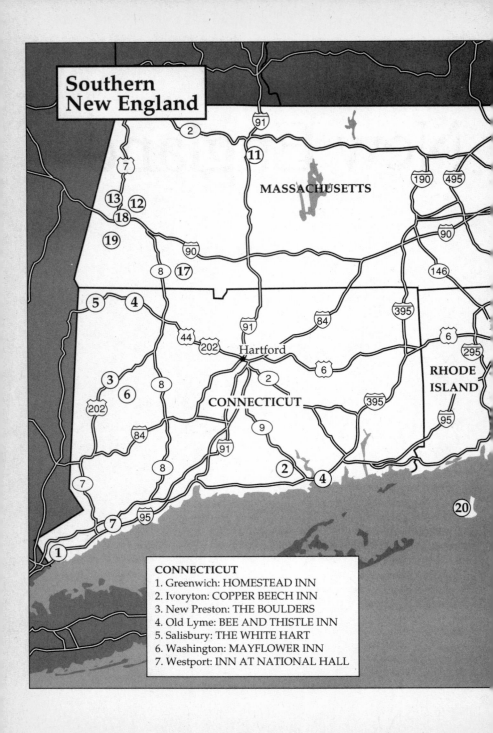

Southern
New England

MASSACHUSETTS

RHODE ISLAND

Hartford

CONNECTICUT

CONNECTICUT
1. Greenwich: HOMESTEAD INN
2. Ivoryton: COPPER BEECH INN
3. New Preston: THE BOULDERS
4. Old Lyme: BEE AND THISTLE INN
5. Salisbury: THE WHITE HART
6. Washington: MAYFLOWER INN
7. Westport: INN AT NATIONAL HALL

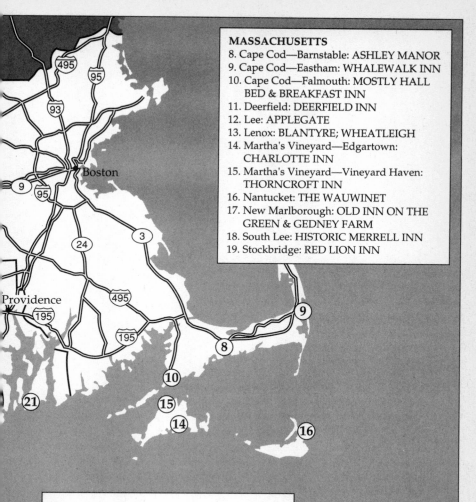

MASSACHUSETTS

8. Cape Cod—Barnstable: ASHLEY MANOR
9. Cape Cod—Eastham: WHALEWALK INN
10. Cape Cod—Falmouth: MOSTLY HALL BED & BREAKFAST INN
11. Deerfield: DEERFIELD INN
12. Lee: APPLEGATE
13. Lenox: BLANTYRE; WHEATLEIGH
14. Martha's Vineyard—Edgartown: CHARLOTTE INN
15. Martha's Vineyard—Vineyard Haven: THORNCROFT INN
16. Nantucket: THE WAUWINET
17. New Marlborough: OLD INN ON THE GREEN & GEDNEY FARM
18. South Lee: HISTORIC MERRELL INN
19. Stockbridge: RED LION INN

RHODE ISLAND

20. Block Island: 1661 INN, HOTEL MANISSES, & NICHOLAS BALL COTTAGE
21. Newport: ELM TREE COTTAGE; FRANCIS MALBONE HOUSE INN; IVY LODGE

Atlantic Ocean

0 ——— 10 Miles
0 ——— 10 Kilometers

Southern New England

Connecticut

HOMESTEAD INN
GREENWICH, CONNECTICUT

Located in a residential neighborhood of elegant estates in one of
Connecticut's most exclusive communities, the *Homestead Inn* was built in
1799. It began welcoming guests in 1859, but not until Nancy Smith and
Lessie Davison purchased it in 1978, did it acquire an upscale reputation.

It's hard to believe that portions of the Victorian Gothic structure are
nearly 200 years old, but if you look closely, remnants of the original square
Federal farmhouse are still visible in front. Today, the High Victorian gingerbread is admired most. The large wraparound porch, with its pretty
antique furniture, is the kind that invites guests to "sit a spell," and the
patio has a murmuring fountain.

Set on a knoll on three acres, surveying orchards, sloping lawns, and
gardens, the inn is superbly furnished with period antiques. The seven-
drawer Philadelphia cherry chest and 1816 tallboy clock in the front hall
are prized treasures.

Guestrooms in the main house retain their historic ambience, right down
to the polished pine floors. Those in the outbuildings, such as the cottage
and barn, have private porches. Each room is individually decorated with
Schumacher and Waverly fabrics, as well as antiques, and includes a queen-
size bed or two twins and a thoroughly modern bathroom.

The dining room, known as *La Grange,* is renowned in the area for its French menu and romantic decor, complete with candlelight and flowers. Dinner entrées include duck with black currant sauce and roast Florida red snapper with an asparagus-and-mushroom ragout. For dessert, the triple chocolate cake puts all diets on hold. A continental breakfast of juice, muffins, and coffee is served in the morning.

There is plenty for guests to do in this suburban Connecticut town and the surrounding region—from playing golf or tennis to exploring local beaches and nature preserves, or visiting the many shops and museums.

HOMESTEAD INN 420 Field Point Rd., Greenwich, CT 06830 (phone/fax: 203-869-7500). This sophisticated suburban inn, 45 minutes from New York City, has 23 guestrooms with private baths, twin or queen-size beds, telephones, TV sets, and air conditioning. The dining room is wheelchair accessible. Open year-round. Rate for a double room (including continental breakfast): $137 to $185. Major credit cards accepted. Older children welcome. No pets. Smoking permitted. Lessie Davison and Nancy Smith, innkeepers; Donna Oldford, manager.

DIRECTIONS: From I-95, take Exit 3 in Greenwich. At the traffic light just before the railroad overpass, turn left onto Horseneck Lane. At the next traffic light turn left onto Field Point Road and continue for a quarter mile. The inn is on the right.

COPPER BEECH INN

IVORYTON, CONNECTICUT

Ivoryton put itself on the map in the 19th century by importing elephant tusks from Africa and transforming them into piano keys and combs. Long before the prohibition of the ivory trade, the town's number one industry was wiped out with the Depression in the 1930s. Since then, the sleepy hamlet, off the traveled tourist routes, has been best known for its topnotch summer theater, the *Ivoryton Playhouse.*

The *Copper Beech Inn* was built as a private home in the 1880s by the foremost ivory importer, A. W. Comstock. It sits beneath the giant spreading arms of a 200-year-old copper beech tree that shelters it from the sun and rain and inspired the inn's name. The seven acres surrounding the inn include both formal and informal gardens, and nearly half the acreage has been carefully retained as natural woodland. There's a sunken side garden, a profusion of plants at the entrance, and a broad variety of evergreen and ornamental trees.

The main floor of the inn houses its acclaimed restaurant as well as a delightful conservatory with a tile floor, cast-iron Victorian furniture, and an extensive collection of 19th-century botanical and Audubon prints—a lovely spot to sip after-dinner coffee and admire the gardens, which are illuminated at night. The main floor also boasts a notable display of the

fine antique Chinese porcelain collected by the innkeepers, Eldon and Sally Senner; some pieces are offered for sale.

Upstairs are four spacious antiques-furnished guestrooms, authentically restored to turn-of-the-century charm, with canopy or brass beds and old-fashioned baths with pedestal sinks. In the serenely private carriage house out back, nine more rooms are beautifully furnished with high-quality reproductions, including some four-poster and canopy beds. These rooms have decks overlooking the woodlands, TV sets, and Jacuzzis. Those on the top floor have raftered cathedral ceilings.

Each of the four elegant dining rooms has its own ambience: The *Comstock Room,* originally the billiard room, has dark oak paneling and an Oriental rug on the floor; the *Ivoryton Room* is distinguished by peachy-toned floral wallpaper; the *Copper Beech Room,* overlooking the gardens, is the most informal room; and the intimate garden porch has dramatic red-sponged walls and a profusion of plants. Each table is set with tall tapered candles and a bud vase containing a single rose. The French-inspired cuisine is equally refined. Dinner entrées may include such French classics as bouillabaisse and sautéed boned breast of pheasant, sliced and served with Madeira-flavored glaze, black truffles, and fresh duck foie gras. Desserts include a fine selection of cheese and fresh fruit, and *gâteau aux framboises* (layers of crisp meringue, sponge cake, and raspberry mousse served with a vanilla custard sauce).

Nearby activities include tennis, hiking, boating, swimming, and antiquing. For music and theater, there's the picturesque *Goodspeed Opera House* (where *Man of La Mancha, Annie,* and *Shenandoah* premiered) in nearby East Haddam, as well as the summer productions at the *Ivoryton Playhouse.*

Guests also may visit *Gillette Castle,* a crenelated extravaganza built by an eccentric actor, high above the river in Hadlyme. The property offers numerous hiking trails and picnic spots.

COPPER BEECH INN 46 Main St., Ivoryton, CT 06442 (phone: 860-767-0330; fax: 860-767-7840). This inn has 13 guestrooms with private baths, twin, double, queen-, or king-size beds, telephones, and air conditioning. Wheelchair accessible. Closed *Christmas Eve, Christmas Day,* and the first week of January; dining room closed Mondays year-round and Tuesdays also from January through March. Rate for a double room (including continental breakfast): $110 to $175. Major credit cards accepted. Not appropriate for children under eight. No pets. No smoking. Eldon and Sally Senner, innkeepers.

DIRECTIONS: From I-95, take Exit 69 in Old Saybrook to Route 9 north. Follow it to Exit 3 west. The inn is 1¾ miles farther on the left.

THE BOULDERS

New Preston, Connecticut

Snugly situated at the base of the Pinnacle Mountains overlooking quiet Lake Waramaug, *The Boulders* offers a warm and inviting atmosphere. Built of massive granite boulders in 1895, it boldly surveys its 27-acre domain. Manicured lawns lead to perennial beds filled with daylilies, phlox, peonies, irises, dahlias, and delphiniums, which, along with a nearby rose garden, supply the inn with cut flowers.

Ulla and Kees Adema, who have owned *The Boulders* since 1988, have infused it with their own special charm. Ulla is a talented artist who made all of the "cut-and-pierced" lamp shades—there are more than 80—that grace the inn. In this unusual form of American folk art, paper is cut in intricate designs that allow light to filter through.

The inn's welcoming living room is furnished with overstuffed sofas and wing chairs, arranged to capture the view across the lake—and to receive the warmth of the fireplace. A gameroom downstairs is equipped with a pool table, darts, an antique pinball machine, and a piano.

The guestrooms are distributed among the main house, a carriage house, and several cottages. Rooms in the main house are furnished with elegant antiques, including canopy and brass beds, and embellished with pretty fabrics. Rooms in the carriage house have a Shaker-style simplicity with pine furnishings and pencil-post beds. The cottages, high on a hill with unobstructed views of the lake, are the most spectacular. These spacious accommodations contain hand-crafted four-poster or canopy beds, quilts, refrigerators, fireplaces, and spacious decks. Spacious bathrooms include whirlpool tubs.

Excellent food is part of the appeal here. Meals are served in three dining rooms or on the terrace in summer. A full breakfast starts with a buffet table of fresh fruits, breads, and cereals and concludes with a hot dish such as "Dutch babies" (a cross between popovers and pancakes, served with butter and syrup) or an omelette. Dinner (which is open to the public) garners rave reviews for its sophisticated American fare. The menu might include pan-seared salmon with cucumber salad and a chili pepper rice cake or crisp-skinned duck breast with gingered black bean salad, brickdough (a Moroccan dough similar to phyllo, but sturdier) vegetable strudel, and a sauce made with star anise and infused orange reduction. There's an excellent wine list (the wine cellar contains 7,000 bottles comprised of 400 selections), and at least 25 wines are available by the glass.

There's something for everyone here. The tennis court is in frequent use in summer, as is the private dock with sailboats, canoes, and paddleboats. Winter brings ice skating on the lake. The surrounding area offers golf, hiking, summer theater, antiquing, and winery visits.

THE BOULDERS E. Shore Rd. (Rte. 45), New Preston, CT 06777 (phone: 860-868-0541; 800-55-BOULDERS; fax: 860-868-1925). This granite inn on the shore of Lake Waramaug has 17 guestrooms with private baths, double, queen-, or king-size beds, telephones, and air conditioning. Wheelchair accessible. Open year-round; restaurant closed Mondays through Wednesdays January through April. Rate for a double room (including full breakfast and dinner): $200 to $350; bed and breakfast: $150 to $300. Two-night minimum stay on weekends. Major credit cards accepted. Not appropriate for children under 12 (younger children by special arrangement). No pets. One cat, Mouse, in residence. Smoking permitted in the cottages, the living room, and the library. Kees and Ulla Adema, innkeepers; Stacey McBreairty, manager.

DIRECTIONS: From I-684 north take I-84 east to Exit 7. Turn onto Route 7 north to New Milford. In New Milford take Route 202 north to New Preston. In New Preston turn onto Route 45 (East Shore Road) and follow the signs to Lake Waramaug. The inn is on the right.

BEE AND THISTLE INN

OLD LYME, CONNECTICUT

In the late 19th century, the historic hamlet of Old Lyme attracted a distinguished array of American Impressionist painters. They lived in the home of art patron Florence Griswold and painted in the nearby fields. Today, their work hangs in the galleries of Old Lyme's *Florence Griswold Museum*.

Next door to the museum is the *Bee and Thistle Inn,* a fine home that long predates the arrival of the Impressionists. Built in 1756 on five and a half acres bordering the Lieutenant River, this gracious, yellow clapboard house recalls its colonial ancestry in its stone garden walls, paneled parlors, grand center hall staircase, and multitude of fireplaces.

The house was transformed into an inn in the 1930s at the suggestion of actress Elsie Ferguson, who was starring in a play at the nearby *Goodspeed Opera House* at the time. It was Ferguson's idea that her friend, who owned the house, should take in boarders, and it is from her Scottish clan emblem of a bee and thistle that the inn's name derives. Today, the inn is run with experienced care and friendliness by Bob and Penny Nelson, their son Jeff (who is the sous chef), and their daughter Lori (who is the manager).

On the main floor, two parlors are filled with antique tables, comfortable sofas, and wing chairs placed before the fireplaces. It's a convivial setting for the weekend entertainment, which ranges from a harpist to a duo singing hits from the 1950s and 1960s.

The eleven guestrooms in the main house are furnished with handsome antiques, including four-poster and canopy beds, elegant nightstands and chests, and baths with the original pedestal sinks and porcelain faucet handles. A cottage in back is more contemporary in style. It has one bedroom, two living areas (one with a fireplace), a deck, and a kitchen.

Meals are served in four dining rooms, two with fireplaces and two on glassed-in porches with views of the gardens. The decor might suggest old-fashioned country fare, but the kitchen turns out sophisticated, contemporary American cuisine. Breakfast (which is not included in the room rate) offers such choices as popovers filled with eggs, bacon, and cheese; homemade sausages; crêpes; and waffles. Dinner begins with melt-in-your-mouth scones that accompany soup or salad. Entrées include salmon served with green-onion sauce, and roasted rack of lamb coated with Dijon mustard, honey, and rosemary breadcrumbs. For dessert, there might be a light bread pudding or an apple-strawberry-rhubarb crisp. Afternoon tea is served Mondays, Wednesdays, and Thursdays from November through April (at an additional charge). Lunch, tea, and dinner are open to non-guests.

Adirondack chairs are placed near the riverbank to capture views of the sunset. In addition to the local museums and the *Goodspeed Opera House,* area attractions include *Mystic Seaport, Gillette Castle,* the *Essex Steam Train,* and *Rocky Neck State Park.* Bicycling is a popular pastime.

BEE AND THISTLE INN 100 Lyme St., Old Lyme, CT 06371 (phone: 860-434-1667; 800-622-4946; fax: 860-434-3402). This colonial mansion and cottage has 11 rooms (nine with private bath), plus a cottage with twin, double, queen-, or king-size beds, air conditioning, and telephones. Closed *Christmas Eve, Christmas Day,* and two weeks in January. Rate for a double room: $69 to $195. Major credit cards accepted. Not appropriate for children under 12. No pets. Two outside dogs, Beau and Jack. Smoking permitted in parlors only. Bob, Penny, Lori, and Jeff Nelson, innkeepers.

DIRECTIONS: From I-95, take Exit 70 in Old Lyme. At the end of the ramp, turn left. Make the first right onto Halls Road (Route 1 north). Go to the end and turn left. The inn is the third house on the left.

THE WHITE HART

SALISBURY, CONNECTICUT

The White Hart was built as a tavern in 1810 at the junction of two stage-coach routes—one heading north into Massachusetts and the other continuing east through Connecticut. Its *Tap Room,* which looks today much as it did originally, with dark walls and a cheery fireplace, has always been the heart of the inn. Additional floors and rooms were added in front and in back as the inn's popularity increased.

The inn has had its good days and its bad. At one time, it was owned and restored by Edsel Ford, who stayed here when visiting his son at one of the prep schools nearby. When Terry and Juliet Moore purchased the

stately dowager at auction in 1989, however, it was definitely in a down mode. Today, after a massive renovation, the inn's glory has been restored.

The broad front lawn serves as the village green, and the front porch, which has painted ivy twining up the pillars and clusters of white wicker chairs and sofas, is the ideal viewing venue for local activities. The town lights a massive evergreen tree on the green every *Christmas,* and in summer antiques and craft shows, as well as musical events, take place here.

Juliet has decorated the guestrooms, many of which have such charming idiosyncracies as slanted ceilings and angled doorways, with spritely floral chintzes, antiques, and high-quality period reproductions. The *Ford Room,* for example, has a canopy bed; *Room No. 15* has a four-poster bed and lace curtains; *No. 18* has a bath with an enormous cast-iron tub and a pedestal sink; *No. 21* is a stunning rooftop suite with slanted ceilings and a boudoir chair and makeup table in the bathroom.

The inn offers three distinctly different dining rooms (which are open to non-guests). The *Tap Room,* with its wide-plank floors, low ceilings, and brick fireplace, is flanked by the inn's bar. The mood here is decidedly British (a reflection of Terry's roots), and much of the food is hearty pub-style fare. The bright and sunny *Garden Room,* with its cathedral ceiling, floor-to-ceiling windows, abundant plants, and flagstone floor, is a delightful place for breakfast and lunch. *Julie's New American Sea Grill* is one of the prettiest formal dining rooms in Connecticut. Mirrors and gilt-framed paintings hang on the salmon-pink walls, and the menu emphasizes fresh fish. Salmon is roasted with an almond crust and served with chive butter, while red snapper comes with a nectarine, rosemary, and Vidalia onion *confit.*

Nearby are downhill and cross-country skiing (the *Salisbury Ski Jump* takes place every February), numerous hiking trails (including the Appalachian Trail, which meanders merely 500 yards beyond *The White Hart's* boundaries), *Lime Rock Raceway,* and summer theaters.

THE WHITE HART 15 Undermountain Road (Junction Routes 41 and 44), Salisbury, CT 06068 (phone: 860-435-0030; 800-832-0041; fax: 860-435-0040). In northwestern Connecticut, this historic inn has 26 guestrooms and suites with private baths, double or queen-size beds, telephones, TV sets, and air conditioning. Wheelchair accessible. Open year-round. Rate for a double room: $75 to $190. Two-night minimum stay on weekends May through October; three nights on holiday weekends. Major credit cards accepted. Children welcome. Pets allowed in designated rooms for a $10 fee per day. Smoking permitted except in two dining rooms. Terry and Juliet Moore, innkeepers; Debra Erickson, manager.

DIRECTIONS: From New York City, take the Henry Hudson Parkway north to the Saw Mill River Parkway to I-684. Follow I-684 north until it becomes Route 22 in Brewster. Continue on Route 22 north to Millerton, New York. In Millerton take Route 44 east for 6 miles to Salisbury. The inn is in the center of town at the junction of Route 44 and Route 41.

MAYFLOWER INN

WASHINGTON, CONNECTICUT

Built in 1894, the *Mayflower Inn* was originally the main building of the *Ridge School.* It was converted to an inn in 1920, but subsequently fell into a sad state of disrepair. Today, the inn is reminiscent of a fine English manor house, thanks to Adriana and Robert Mnuchin, who bought it in 1992 and spared no expense on renovation. The entire place glows with the patina of polished antiques, crystal chandeliers, and friendly spirits.

Common rooms include an elegant English parlor, which has velvet sofas and chairs; a mahogany-paneled library with leather sofas, a window seat below leaded casement windows, a fireplace, and bookcases filled with leather-bound books (including more than 200 first-edition mysteries); and a clubby, intimate bar with forest green walls, a mahogany bar, and a fireplace. Outside, the verandah with its elegant wicker furniture is a pleasant place from which to survey the gardens: 28 acres of stately maples, stone walls, a gazebo, boxwood hedges, ancient rhododendrons, formal perennial and rose gardens, and even a Shakespearean garden complete with a bust of the poet and plaques containing some of his quotations. For the more active, there's a heated pool, a tennis court, and a fitness center, where a battery of exercise machines complements the sauna, steamrooms, and yoga classes. Massages—Swedish, aromatherapy, shiatsu, and reflexology—are available. A separate building, the *Teahouse,* styled like an Adirondack

hunting lodge, is dedicated to corporate meetings. It has sophisticated audiovisual and communications systems.

Guestrooms are furnished with exquisite antiques, and many have balconies and gas fireplaces. The baths are done in marble with mahogany wainscoting; there are silver Limoges fittings on the sinks and handwoven Belgian tapestry rugs on the floors. Decanters of sherry and stemmed crystal glasses stand on sideboards in the suites, and an orchid plant blooms in every room.

Breakfast is available each morning, although it's not included in the room rate. The house specialty is salmon—smoked and cured on the premises—with bagels and cream cheese.

Dinner at the *Mayflower Inn* (also open to non-guests) is as impressive as its decor. Entrées such as Muscovy duck breast with a mushroom-thyme sauce and *gaufrette* potatoes (similar to au gratin) are complemented by an excellent wine selection. Spa-inspired fare is offered to those watching their diets. The outstanding gift shop features local and imported items made especially for the inn, including rugs like those found in the bathrooms.

Located in the Litchfield Hills, the inn is near golf courses, *Steep Rock Nature Preserve,* which has hiking trails, *Red Jacket Farm* for horseback riding, fishing (the inn can provide an angling guide), concerts, theater, and a multitude of antiques shops.

MAYFLOWER INN 118 Woodbury Rd., Rte. 47 (mailing address: Box 1288), Washington, CT 06793 (phone: 860-868-9466; fax: 860-868-1497). This inn has 25 guestrooms with private baths, twin, queen-, or king-size beds, telephones, TV sets, and air conditioning. Wheelchair accessible. Open year-round. Rate for a double room: $250 to $395; for suites: $410 to $560. Two-night minimum stay on weekends; three nights on holiday weekends. Major credit cards accepted. Not appropriate for children under 12. No pets. Smoking permitted in the bar and on guestroom balconies. Robert and Adriana Mnuchin, innkeepers; John Trevenen, manager.

DIRECTIONS: Take I-684 north to Exit 9E (Danbury) onto I-84 east. Travel on I-84 to Exit 7 (Brookfield-New Milford). Take Route 7 north for 4½ miles to the stoplight, then turn left onto Route 202 west. Stay on this for ¹/₁₀ of a mile and turn left onto Silvermine Road (a very small road). Go for 1¹/₁₀ miles to a traffic light. Go straight through the traffic light onto Route 133. Continue on this road for 7 miles to Route 67. Turn right onto Route 67 south and continue for 4 miles. Then turn left onto Route 199 to Washington in 4 miles. Turn right onto Route 47 and you will see the *Mayflower Inn* sign immediately on the left.

INN AT NATIONAL HALL

WESTPORT, CONNECTICUT

A historic 1873 brick Italianate building overlooks the Saugatuck River (and the heart of Westport's National Hall Historic District). Built as a bank, it subsequently served as a newspaper office, as Westport's first high school, and as headquarters for the Connecticut State Police. The capacious first floor was the quintessential town meeting hall and also hosted village concerts, dances, graduations, election-night revelries, and basketball games. Through painstaking care, the building has been restored by owner Arthur Tauck, and today is one of the finest inns in America.

Reminiscent of a fine English manor house, the inn exudes elegance—but spiced with wit. An elevator, whimsically painted to resemble a library, brings guests to the third-floor reception area. The drawing room features a carved wood mantel, English antiques, and a mural that pays homage to all the artisans who worked on the restoration. In the vestibule is a full bar, and there's a boardroom with a spectacular crystal chandelier and a complete audiovisual system for small meetings.

The seven suites and eight guestrooms are equally extravagant, decorated by San Francisco interior designer Joszi Meskan with canopy beds, armoires, and fanciful wall stencils. Some of the ceilings reach to 20 feet. Every room includes a TV/VCR and refrigerator with complimentary soft drinks, as well as such charming touches as a book of bedtime stories placed on the nightstand. The *Turkistan Suite* (No. 304) has pink-and-seafoam-green striped taffeta drapes covering the massive windows, a floor-to-ceiling library, and puffy love seats with needlepoint pillows; the loft bedroom has a bowed balcony (with river views) and a king-size canopy bed. The *Willow Suite* (No. 305), which is decorated in shades of pink and yellow, features a canopy bed; the walls of the bedroom are painted with willow branches, and gardenias are splashed across the walls of the bath. The *Sheriff Room* (No. 207), in peach and black, has stars painted on the ceiling, and

bookcases line three walls of the bath. The baths are so luxurious they are like private spas, with marble showers, floors, and walls, scales, and robes.

On the main floor, *Restaurant Zanghi* is chef-managed and earns high praise for its French/Italian cuisine. An entrée of pan-roasted veal loin chop with wild mushrooms on whipped polenta is one possibility, as is a dessert of burnt-brown-sugar banana *brûlée*. The restaurant will provide room service. A full breakfast is offered to guests.

The inn provides guest passes to the fitness facilities at the nearby *YMCA*, and the village of Westport boasts numerous exclusive boutiques, antiques shops, and gourmet food emporiums. Local recreation options include bicycling, sailing, boating, and golf.

INN AT NATIONAL HALL 2 Post Rd. W., Westport, CT 06889 (phone: 203-221-1351; 800-NAT-HALL; fax: 203-221-0276). This inn on Connecticut's south shore has 15 guestrooms and suites with private baths, twin, queen-, or king-size beds, telephones, TV/VCR sets, and air conditioning. Closed *Christmas*. Rate for a double room (including full breakfast): $195 to $450. Two-night minimum stay on weekends June through November. Major credit cards accepted. Children welcome. No pets. No smoking. Arthur Tauck, owner; Nick Carter, general manager.

DIRECTIONS: From I-95 take Exit 17 (Westport/Saugatuck). At the bottom of the ramp turn left onto Route 33. Proceed for approximately 1½ miles to the traffic light at the intersection with US 1. Continue across US 1 and turn immediately right into the *Inn at National Hall*'s parking area.

Massachusetts

ASHLEY MANOR

BARNSTABLE, CAPE COD, MASSACHUSETTS

A graceful gabled inn whose cedar shingles have weathered to a soft dove gray, *Ashley Manor* is located at the end of a curving driveway, hidden behind privet hedges on two lush acres of manicured lawns.

Steeped in history and exhibiting a variety of architectural styles, the house was built by the Delap family, Tories who fled to Nova Scotia following the American Revolution. The original part of the building was built in 1699; the massive front gable was added in 1750 (the fireplace with its beehive oven in the keeping room also dates from this era). Throughout the inn are reminders of the estate's long history: hand-blown six-over-six windows, open-hearth fireplaces, and hand-glazed wainscoting. Enhancing the sense of history and romance is a "secret" passageway connecting the upstairs and downstairs suites, thought to have been a hiding place for Tories during the Revolution.

Donald and Fay Bain, owners of the inn since 1987, have infused the house with their own warmth and style. Oriental rugs, a baby grand piano, original oil paintings, antiques, plush sofas, and fireplaces characterize the sitting room and the keeping room. A porch and a terrace provide additional places to relax. The suites have canopy beds, most guestrooms have working fireplaces, and all have luxurious bathrooms. Fresh flowers, bedside chocolates, and fragrant soaps and lotions are special touches. Outside, among the flower gardens, are a secluded gazebo, fountain garden, brick terrace, and tennis court.

In the exquisitely appointed dining room, corner cupboards are filled with a fine collection of antique Oriental porcelain, providing an elegant backdrop for the inn's bountiful breakfasts. Guests gather around the pine dining table, where four courses are served by candlelight on Meissen, Lowestoft, and Spode china; when the weather is cool, a fire blazes in the fireplace. In summer, breakfast is served on the brick terrace. In addition to being "chief putterer," Donald is the chef. Expect to start with fresh-squeezed orange juice, followed by a fruit course of stuffed baked apple or strawberries and cream, Donald's renowned granola, homemade muffins and breads, and perhaps a main course of stuffed crêpe with strawberry sauce or French toast. Guests are pampered at *Ashley Manor.* In the afternoons, wine, sherry, and port are set out in decanters in the sitting room, as are freshly baked cookies, chocolates, coffee, and tea.

The inn is near beaches, bicycle trails, bird sanctuaries, antiquing, golf, whale watching, boating, and summer theaters. Bicycles are available for guests' use, and there just might be a lively game of croquet being played on the lawn.

ASHLEY MANOR 3660 Old Kings Hwy. (Rte. 6A), (mailing address: PO Box 856), Barnstable, MA 02630 (phone: 508-362-8044). This country estate on the north shore of Cape Cod has six suites and guestrooms with private baths, double, queen-, or king-size beds, and air conditioning. Open year-round. Rate for a double room (including full breakfast): $115 to $175. Two-night minimum stay on summer weekends; three nights on some holiday weekends. Major credit cards accepted. Not appropriate for children under 15. No pets. Smoking permitted in guestrooms only. Donald and Fay Bain, innkeepers.

DIRECTIONS: From I-495, I-195, or Route 3, take Route 6 across the Sagamore Bridge onto Cape Cod. Continue on Route 6 to Exit 6. At Exit 6 turn left onto Route 132 north. Take this road for a half mile to its end and turn right onto Route 6A east. Travel 3 miles through the village of Barnstable. Continue beyond the light for ⁶/₁₀ of a mile. The inn is on the left.

WHALEWALK INN

EASTHAM, CAPE COD, MASSACHUSETTS

Innkeepers Dick and Carolyn Smith love what they do, and it shows in their gracious hospitality. Their inn is an 1830s whaling master's home with shingles mellowed to a driftwood gray, now artfully restored. Salt-tinged sea breezes, a seashell knocker on the door, three acres of manicured lawns and gardens, and lots of tastefully arranged flowers inside are just a few of the details adding to the *Whalewalk's* appeal.

Guestrooms have a warm, comfortable feeling, thanks to the massive bouquets in wicker baskets, and brass beds piled high with pillows, quilts, and comforters. Other touches: an English pine wardrobe complemented by an artistically painted chest, a pink-and-green wool blanket draped over a white rattan chair, watercolor seascapes on the walls. Small kitchens, wood-burning fireplaces, and private patios complete the facilities found in the suites.

Guests begin their day with fresh fruit, juice, and hot-from-the-oven bread, muffins, or apple–sour cream coffee cake. For an entrée, Dick may prepare cranberry-blueberry pancakes, cheese pie with herbed potatoes, or Grand Marnier French toast. In winter, the meal takes place on the bright sun porch, while in summer tables are set up on the patio. In the afternoon, iced tea or hot cider accompanied by freshly baked cookies provide refreshment. Every evening, hors d'oeuvres (guests may bring their own wine) are served in the living room, where the fireplace glows in cool weather. It's a chance for guests to become acquainted and discuss local activities with the owners. In summer, the get-together takes place on the patio.

The inn is near the *Cape Cod National Seashore,* the Cape Cod Rail Trail Bike Path, regional theatrical productions, whale watching, sailing, and fishing.

WHALEWALK INN 220 Bridge Rd., Eastham, MA 02642 (phone: 508-255-0617; fax: 508-240-0017). This whaling master's home has 12 guestrooms with private baths and twin, double, queen-, or king-size beds and air conditioning. Closed December through March. Rate for a double room (including full breakfast and evening hors d'oeuvres): $110 to $190. Two-night minimum stay June through September and on weekends throughout the year; three nights on holiday weekends. MasterCard and Visa accepted. Not appropriate for children under 13. No pets. No smoking. Carolyn and Dick Smith, innkeepers.

DIRECTIONS: Cross the Sagamore Bridge to Cape Cod. Traveling east on Route 6, go to the Orleans traffic circle. Three-fourths of the way around, exit onto Rock Harbor Road. Take the first right onto Bridge Road. The inn is on the right.

MOSTLY HALL BED & BREAKFAST INN

Falmouth, Cape Cod, Massachusetts

Although *Mostly Hall* was built in 1849 by a Yankee ship captain, it is distinctly Southern in style: A wide verandah encircles the main floor, and there are 13-foot ceilings, a front-to-back central hallway, and massive windows on the upper floors. Like a typical plantation house, it is set back from the road amid rolling lawns and landscaped gardens, yet its location on the historic village green of Falmouth is strictly New England. This seeming contradiction is easily explained: Captain Albert Nye built the house as a wedding present for his New Orleans bride. It received its odd name about a hundred years ago when a child walked through the front doors and exclaimed, "Why, Mama, it's mostly hall!"

Caroline and Jim Lloyd purchased the house in 1986; they have created a refined village inn furnished with Victorian antiques, including Lincoln rockers and a variety of chiming clocks. Among them is a navy clock that strikes bells, a Viennese regulator, a banjo clock, and a French marble mantel clock. The warm peach walls in the living room are accented by Oriental rugs, while the interior wooden shutters are charming reminders of an earlier era.

Each of the spacious corner guestrooms, which overlook clipped lawns and flower beds, has a private bath, a queen-size canopy bed, and Oriental rugs. Converted to a sitting room, the enclosed widow's walk cupola with multiple windows is a favorite hideaway. The gazebo in the garden entices guests outside on balmy days, as does the verandah, where tea and sherry are enjoyed on summer afternoons.

Breakfast is a delight whatever the season. In winter, a fire burns in the gas fireplace in the dining room and guests sit at the spacious table; in summer, tables are set up on the verandah. The meal has become such a tradition that the inn has published a collection of its most popular recipes—treats such as stuffed French toast with apricot sauce, eggs Benedict soufflé, and cheese-blintz muffins with warm blueberry sauce. The entrées are accompanied by fresh fruit and a variety of fresh-baked breads. In the afternoon, tea, coffee, hot chocolate, cider, and iced tea (in summer) are set out in the living room.

Bicycles are available for guests' use; the Shining Sea Bikeway to Woods Hole is a short pedal from the inn. Also nearby are beaches, boating, golf, tennis, and cultural events.

MOSTLY HALL BED & BREAKFAST INN 27 Main St., Falmouth, MA 02540 (phone: 508-548-3786; 800-682-0565). This plantation-style inn on the south shore of Cape Cod has six guestrooms with private baths, queen-size beds, and air conditioning. Closed January through mid-February. Rate for a double room (including full breakfast): $90 to $130. Two-night minimum stay May through October and all weekends. Major credit cards accepted. Not appropriate for children under 16. No pets. No smoking. Caroline and Jim Lloyd, innkeepers.

DIRECTIONS: Traveling north, take I-95 to I-195 and the Cape Cod and Islands exit onto Route 25. Follow Route 25 (a one-way road) 4 miles to Route 28 south. Take Route 28 across the Bourne Bridge into Falmouth. The inn is located on the village green behind a wrought-iron fence and massive rhododendrons.

DEERFIELD INN
DEERFIELD, MASSACHUSETTS

Historic Deerfield Village is the Williamsburg of New England—a perfectly preserved town steeped in authentic colonial history and listed as a National Historic Landmark. Thirteen of the 18th- and 19th-century houses on the mile-long, tree-lined way known as The Street are museums that tell the story of Indian attacks, of the valor of 300 people who were captured by Indians after the Deerfield Massacre in 1704 and forced to march to Canada, and of the town's rebirth and the rural life of its residents. The museum houses sit side by side with privately owned homes of the same vintage, as well as *Deerfield Academy,* one of the oldest boarding schools in the country.

In the midst of all this history is the *Deerfield Inn,* built in 1884 (and substantially rebuilt after a devastating fire in 1981) to replace a 1730s inn that had been on the busy Hartford–New York stage route. When Mr. and Mrs. Henry Flynt bought it in 1936, their collection of antiques that now graces

the inn found a home. The Flynts also were responsible for purchasing the fine old homes that comprise the museums of Historic Deerfield Village (a visitors' center with museum information is across the street from the inn). Today, the inn is owned by Historic Deerfield, Inc.; it has been managed by Karl and Jane Sabo since 1987.

In both the public areas and the guestrooms, the overall look is Early American. The spacious bedrooms are furnished with a combination of antiques and high-quality reproductions and decorated with Greeff and Waverly fabrics; most have four-posters. Old prints of Deerfield Village line the walls. The rooms are named for historic local luminaries, and some guests claim to have seen amiable spirits wandering the hallways.

A full country-style breakfast of fruit, juice, cereal, bacon, eggs, and pancakes is served in the formal dining room, a gracious room with brass chandeliers, a bay window, and candles flickering within hurricane lamps on the tables. Dinner is served here as well. Highly acclaimed entrées include venison, as well as beef tenderloin wrapped in bacon and served with sautéed mushrooms; for dessert, there is chocolate cake or Indian pudding. Afternoon tea, cookies, and other pastries are offered in the parlor. All meals are open to non-guests.

In addition to visits to the historic houses, the area offers several other activities, including hiking and shopping.

DEERFIELD INN The Street, Deerfield, MA 01342 (phone: 413-774-5587; fax: 413-773-8712). This historic inn has 23 guestrooms with private baths, twin or queen-size beds, telephones, TV sets, and air conditioning. Wheelchair accessible. Closed three days at *Christmas.* Rate for a double room (including full breakfast and afternoon tea): $122 to $185. Two-night minimum stay on holiday weekends. Major credit cards accepted. Children welcome. No pets. No smoking. Karl and Jane Sabo, managers.

DIRECTIONS: From I-91 north take Exit 24 at Deerfield to Route 5 north. Travel 6 miles on Route 5, and turn left onto The Street at the "Historic Deerfield" sign. The inn is in the center of town.

APPLEGATE

LEE, MASSACHUSETTS

Driving through the iron gates and up the road to the porte cochère, you'll find a little piece of tranquillity tucked away on six acres in the Berkshires called *Applegate.*

Rick and Nancy Cannata, who were married nearby, have always loved the Berkshires, and they never gave up their desire to live here full-time. Although both were airline employees (Rick is still a pilot, and Nancy was a flight attendant until 1996) they took the plunge in 1990, buying and restoring this stately columned colonial, built in the 1920s .

It's hard to imagine a detail that hasn't been attended to by these thoughtful innkeepers. On arrival, guests find a crystal decanter of brandy with two snifters in their rooms; in the evening, Godiva chocolates are left on the nightstand. The six spacious guestrooms are done in a variety of styles: *No. 1* has a king-size four-poster bed, a fireplace, and a shower built for two (with two shower heads); *No. 2* is furnished with a pine four-poster bed and an antique carved pine dressing table; *No. 5* has a tiger-maple four-poster canopy bed and is painted in pale lavenders and green; *No. 6* has an antique Victorian bed with matching marble-topped dresser.

With a baby grand piano, plush love seats, a fireplace, and a lovely Oriental rug, the formal living room is as refined as the main room in a stately manor house should be, yet it has whimsical touches as well. In the afternoon, wine and cheese are set out here. Martha, Heather, and Claudia, three of Nancy's favorite dolls, observe the daily activity from their antique chairs. Testimony to the Cannatas' love for their adopted business are the framed photographs of inn guests placed on the mantel, in the bookcases, and on tables. Adjacent to the living room is a sun porch with a TV/VCR, a collection of video classics, and games. On the covered verandah, cushioned wicker chairs provide vantage points for viewing the gardens. Just beyond is an inviting swimming pool. Throughout the formal gardens (Rick's passion) and the orchard are pretty benches, perfect for relaxing and watching butterflies flit among the dahlias, delphiniums, and phlox.

Breakfast is served on Nancy's antique bone china in the formal dining room, where the mantelpiece displays a collection of faux apples, many contributed by former guests. It's an elegant setting, with flickering candles in silver candelabra. A selection of fruit and juices, yogurt, granola, and fresh-baked muffins and breads are offered.

There's skiing, golf, tennis, hiking, and biking in the area, and guests can visit *Tanglewood,* the *Norman Rockwell Museum, Jacob's Pillow Dance Festival,* and the *Berkshire Theatre Festival* nearby.

APPLEGATE 279 W. Park St., RR1 Box 576, Lee, MA 01238 (phone: 413-243-4451; 800-691-9012; fax: 413-243-4451). This stately inn has six guestrooms with private baths, double, queen-, or king-size beds, and air conditioning. Open year-round. Rate for a double room (including continental breakfast): $85 to $225. Two-night minimum stay on weekends in June, September, October, and holidays; three nights on weekends in July and August. MasterCard and Visa accepted. Not appropriate for children under 13. No pets. Four cats and two cockatiels on the property. No smoking. Nancy and Rick Cannata, innkeepers.

DIRECTIONS: From Albany or Boston on the Massachusetts Turnpike, take Exit 2 at Lee. At the bottom of the ramp turn right onto Route 20 and follow it through town to the first stop sign. Route 20 turns right here, but you should continue straight ahead. Cross the railroad tracks and ascend the hill. You are now on West Park Street; *Applegate* is approximately one-quarter mile farther on the left.

BLANTYRE

LENOX, MASSACHUSETTS

As imposing as this massive stone manor may appear, the warm greeting guests receive from managing director Roderick Anderson dispels all apprehensions. At *Blantyre,* the tone is unpretentious and friendly.

A 23-room summer "cottage" on 85 acres in the heart of the Berkshires, *Blantyre* was built by a wealthy New Yorker in 1902. To please his wife, he built the house in a style prevalent in her native Scotland. The exterior is embellished with gargoyles, carved friezes, turrets, and balconies. A glass-enclosed conservatory (where continental breakfast is served) and several terraces, surrounded by flower beds, overlook clipped lawns and two tournament-size croquet lawns.

After entering through the ornately carved oak doors of the *Great Hall,* guests find themselves in a room resplendent with stained glass, Oriental rugs, exquisite Victorian antiques, and a castle-size stone fireplace. The music room, the largest of the common rooms, contains a grand piano and a jeweled Tiffany floor lamp, and leads to a covered side terrace. The dignified wood-paneled dining room, with oil paintings and a tapestry on the walls, contains another fireplace, which is lighted on chilly evenings.

The eight guestrooms in the *Manor House* are graciously decorated and furnished with museum-quality chests, dressers, armoires, and beds (some are four-posters). Each has interesting features; one, for example, has a "fainting" couch, another a gilded French chandelier. Twelve more rooms are located in the *Carriage House,* about a quarter-mile away. Although the decor here is more contemporary. Several rooms feature loft bedrooms; others have downstairs sitting rooms with frescoed walls; all have handsome baths with limestone or marble floors and separate dressing areas. Three whimsically decorated cottages complete the picture: *Cottage by the Path,* with a fireplace and a kitchen; *Winter Palace,* with a kitchen; and *Cottage Queen.*

Dining at *Blantyre* (also open to non-guests) is a memorable experience. Guests gather in the *Great Hall,* now bathed in the soft glow of candlelight. As they relax on the plush sofas, listening to a harpist and sipping an aperitif from the honor bar, they make their appetizer and entrée selections.

They are escorted to the dining room when the table has been laid with the appetizers. Chef Michael Roller, who trained in some of America's finest kitchens, prepares such inventive dishes as seared Muscovy duck with mustard, junipers, and wild mushrooms, and pepper-charred yellowfin tuna on grilled onions with a leek-and-blood-orange salad. Dessert might be a bittersweet chocolate *daquoise* or a raspberry *genoise* tart.

Tennis courts, a pool, two regulation croquet lawns, and a spa with a Jacuzzi and sauna are right on the property. Nearby attractions include hiking, bicycling, golf (there's a course adjacent to the inn), horseback riding, *Tanglewood,* the *Norman Rockwell Museum,* the *Berkshire Theatre Festival,* and Edith Wharton's home *The Mount,* where plays are presented by *Shakespeare and Company.*

BLANTYRE 16 Blantyre Rd., PO Box 995, Lenox, MA 01240 (phone: 413-637-3556, May through October; 413-298-1661, November through April; fax: 413-637-4282). This elegant country estate has 23 guestrooms with private baths, double, queen-, or king-size beds, telephones, TV sets, and air conditioning. Wheelchair accessible. Closed November through mid-May; restaurant closed for dinner Mondays throughout the year and open for lunch in July and August only. Rate for a double room (including continental breakfast): $250 to $625. Two-night minimum stay on weekends; three nights on holidays. Major credit cards accepted. Not appropriate for children under 14. No pets. Smoking permitted. Jack and Jane Fitzpatrick, owners; Roderick Anderson, managing director.

DIRECTIONS: From the Massachusetts Turnpike, take Exit 2 at Lee. Follow signs for Route 20 toward Pittsfield. Traveling north on Route 20, pass through the town of Lee and continue for 2 miles. Look for the sign to the inn. Blantyre Road is on the right.

WHEATLEIGH

LENOX, MASSACHUSETTS

When Henry H. Cook, a New York banker, railroad director, and real estate tycoon, learned that his daughter, Georgie, was marrying Spanish count Carlos de Heredia, he commissioned a grand estate for their summer use. It was designed in 1893 in the style of a 16th-century Florentine palazzo; more than 150 artisans were imported from Italy to execute the intricate carvings found both inside and outside. Frederick Law Olmsted was responsible for the 380-acre "Wheatleigh Park," 23 acres of which remain in landscaped gardens with spectacular vistas.

Wheatleigh has been an inn since the 1960s, and many of its exquisite original features remain intact: an unusual wrought-iron and glass canopy over the double entry doors, Tiffany lanterns at the gates, a massive and ornate mantelpiece in the *Great Hall,* 20-foot ceilings, fluted columns that flank grand archways, a spectacular Tiffany window over the stairway. A

olive Metcalf

loggia with a carved oak ceiling runs the length of one side, and a broad terrace extends across the back.

Following a complete refurbishment in 1993, *Wheatleigh*'s furnishings now match the quality of the building itself. The *Great Hall* has Oriental rugs on the parquet floors, and its Queen Anne–style furniture is upholstered in damasks and velvets. There's a grand piano in a parlor, and an antique marquetry table.

Guestrooms range in size from tiny to baronial, but all are decorated with subdued elegance. Those on the second floor, which include the *Count's Room* and the *Countess's Room,* are the grandest, and they have views of the Stockbridge Bowl with the Berkshire Mountains beyond. *Room No. 21,* one of largest, features a tailored half-canopy bed, an antique lady's writing desk of inlaid woods, ornate ceiling moldings, and a private loggia. Leonard Bernstein often stayed in a two-level suite in the former aviary.

The dining room is considered to be one of the finest in the Berkshires. Chef Peter Platt creates original and bold fare. Every evening there are three prix fixe menus (a low-fat, vegetarian, and regular meal), each comprising four courses. Guests may mix and match courses from the three menus, perhaps beginning with a vegetarian appetizer like the wild-mushroom gâteau, then choosing between low-fat roast loin of wild antelope with roasted vegetable couscous and wild black huckleberries, or an entrée from the regular menu, such as seared breast of Muscovy duck with red-cabbage *confit* and Seville orange sauce. An irresistible finish is the sinful warm liquid-center chocolate cake with three ice creams (a fitting reward for those who otherwise adhered to the low-fat menu). Breakfast is also available daily, but is not included in the room rate.

Guests enjoy a heated pool and tennis courts; the inn also has an exercise room with treadmills, a Stairmaster, a Lifecycle, and free weights.

Tanglewood is so close that guests can walk to concerts; so is a small red house that replicates one used by Nathaniel Hawthorne when he lived and wrote in the Berkshires. Other nearby attractions include skiing, hiking, the *Norman Rockwell Museum,* and numerous historic museum houses, including Edith Wharton's *The Mount.*

WHEATLEIGH Hawthorne Rd., Lenox, MA 01240 (phone: 413-637-0610; fax: 413-637-4507). This mansion has 17 guestrooms with private baths and queen- or king-size beds, telephones, TV/VCRs, and air conditioning. Wheelchair accessible. Open year-round. Rate for a double room: $155 to $535. Two-night minimum stay on weekends; three nights on weekends in July and August. Major credit cards accepted. Not appropriate for children under 13. No pets. Smoking permitted except in dining room. Linfield and Susan Simon, owners; François Thomas, general manager.

DIRECTIONS: From the Massachusetts Turnpike take Exit 2 in Lee. At the bottom of the ramp turn right onto Route 20, traveling through the town of Lee. Follow signs to Lenox by turning left onto Route 7 at its junction with Route 20. At the monument in Lenox, take Route 183 south past the entrance to *Tanglewood.* At the next intersection, turn left onto Hawthorne Road. The entrance to *Wheatleigh* is 1 mile farther on the left.

CHARLOTTE INN

EDGARTOWN, MARTHA'S VINEYARD, MASSACHUSETTS

The village of Edgartown on Martha's Vineyard, with its narrow streets and shingled cottages, was settled in the 1670s. Ever since, its inhabitants have made their livelihood from the sea, and Samuel Osborne, owner of a whaling company and the builder of the 19th-century *Charlotte Inn,* was no exception. The main house is a grand, three-story, white Italianate structure with an impressive widow's walk on top, where Osborne's wife watched for the return of his ships.

Gery Conover and his wife, Paula, have been the innkeepers here for 25 years. Their goal has been to offer a quiet and romantic retreat on this very special island—and they do so in grand style. Moreover, their interest in art led them to create a gallery on the main floor of the inn, where fine oils and watercolors, by both 19th-century European and contemporary American painters, are for sale.

Accommodations are scattered among the main house and four adjacent buildings: the *Carriage House,* the *Garden House,* the *Summer House,* and the *Coach House.* The separate buildings are unified into a private compound, with brick walkways, sculpted English boxwood hedges, and an old water pump and gardener's toolshed. All the guestrooms are furnished with fine antiques: four-poster, brass, or pineapple-post beds, polished English chests, and gilt-framed 19th-century English oil paintings, often of

sporting scenes. A number of the rooms have fireplaces; floral or paisley wallpapers and an abundance of fresh flowers add romance.

Despite similarities, each room has its own personality. The huge *Coach House* suite, for example, is entered through a garage that houses a collection of restored antique vehicles, including a surrey with a fringe on top, a 1939 Ford Woody, and a 1933 Ford sedan. The upstairs room has a Palladian window and is outfitted with antique sports equipment—a croquet mallet, a golf club, and tennis racquets. A four-poster bed with a lace spread and an 1860s mahogany dressing table complete the decor.

With large windows and hanging plants, the inn's restaurant, *L'Etoile*, is similar to an English conservatory. It is known for its fine fare. A prix fixe dinner (also open to non-guests) featuring local seafood is served nightly and might include such specialties as an *étouffée* of native lobster, seared bay scallops, and artichoke risotto or roasted red snapper filet with a horseradish-pistachio-scallion crust. Roasted duck breast and grilled filet mignon are also offered. A continental breakfast of juice, fruit, muffins, cereal, coffee, and tea is served here as well. On summer afternoons tea, lemonade, sandwiches, and cookies are offered on the porch.

The ferry ride to Martha's Vineyard is half the fun of getting to the *Charlotte Inn*. The other half is driving along the winding road past blufftop vistas and rose-covered cottages. Guests can enjoy all the island has to offer—from beaches and boating to bicycling and shopping.

CHARLOTTE INN 27 South Summer St., Edgartown, MA 02539 (phone: 508-627-4751 or 508-627-4151; fax: 508-627-4652). This jewel of an inn has 25 guestrooms and suites with private baths, double or queen-size beds, and air conditioning; most have telephones and TV sets. Limited wheelchair accessibility.

Open year-round. Rate for a double room (including continental breakfast and afternoon tea) June through mid-October: $250 to $650; mid-October through May: $125 to $550. Two-night minimum stay on weekends; three nights on holidays. Major credit cards accepted. Not appropriate for children under 15. No pets. A dog, Andrew, and a cat, Oscar, in residence. Smoking permitted. Gery and Paula Conover, innkeepers; Carol Read, manager.

DIRECTIONS: The Woods Hole/Vineyard Haven ferry runs year-round; automobiles may be taken aboard or left in the parking lot at Woods Hole. Taxis are available in Vineyard Haven for the 8-mile trip to Edgartown. Those driving should exit the ferry and follow the signs to Edgartown. In Edgartown proceed down Main Street to the large whaling church on the left. South Summer Street is the second on the right after the church. The inn is the third building on the left.

THORNCROFT INN

VINEYARD HAVEN, MARTHA'S VINEYARD, MASSACHUSETTS

In 1918, when it was the guesthouse on the estate of John Herbert Ware, a Chicago grain merchant who summered on Martha's Vineyard, the *Thorncroft Inn* was filled with visitors enjoying their host's hospitality. It's hard to imagine that they would have been more pampered or had lovelier surroundings than do today's guests. Innkeepers Lynn and Karl Buder, who have owned *Thorncroft* since 1981, make a visit here seem like staying with friends at their country estate. Every need has been anticipated—perhaps that's one reason they have received several prestigious hospitality awards.

A romantic retreat for couples, the inn has accommodations in both the main house and a new *Carriage House*. The spacious rooms and suites have wood-burning fireplaces, private balconies, and palatial baths with claw-foot tubs, two-person Jacuzzis, or hot tubs. All are furnished with antique four-posters with hand-tied fishnet canopies or turn-of-the-century carved mahogany beds. Some house a Victorian doll or two.

For quiet relaxation there is a living room with fireplace. Be sure to note the Seth Thomas mantel clock that fits neatly into a niche, painted by Ware's mother more than a century ago. Outdoors, the three and a half acres of gardens are perfect for strolling or simply sitting.

A stay at the *Thorncroft Inn* includes a full breakfast—perhaps almond French toast or cheese strata (a casserole of bread, eggs, and cheese) and sausage. Generally, the meal will be served either in the formal dining room with its fireplace or a smaller breakfast room, although breakfast in bed is also extremely popular. There's afternoon tea with pastries as well..

Guests may enjoy all the recreational advantages of Martha's Vineyard, including beaches, sailing, and summer theater.

THORNCROFT INN 278 Main St., PO Box 1022, Vineyard Haven, MA 02568 (phone: 508-693-3333; 800-332-1236; fax: 508-693-5419). This exclusive inn on Martha's Vineyard has 13 guestrooms with private baths, double or queen-size beds, telephones, TV sets, and air conditioning. Open year-round. Rate for a double room (including full breakfast and afternoon tea): $169 to $349. Three-night minimum stay on summer weekends and holidays. Major credit cards accepted. Not appropriate for children under 12. No pets. No smoking. Karl and Lynn Buder, innkeepers.

DIRECTIONS: From the Vineyard Haven ferry dock (see *Charlotte Inn,* above), turn right at the first stop sign, then right again onto Main Street. The inn is located 1 mile up Main Street on the left. There's taxi service from the ferry.

THE WAUWINET

NANTUCKET, MASSACHUSETTS

The old *Wauwinet* is no more, but a new one with the same wild, windswept-seacoast ambience has taken its place in a spectacular spot on a remote neck of land between the Atlantic Ocean and Nantucket Bay.

Stephen and Jill Karp, who had summered on Nantucket for a number of years, watched with dismay as the old *Wauwinet* resort, which had operated continuously since 1876, sank into disrepair. In 1986, they purchased the derelict inn and embarked on a $3-million renovation project that restored the weathered exterior but created an entirely new interior.

Rooms were enlarged, and opulent tile bathrooms with wainscoted walls and brass fixtures were installed in each room and suite. The decor—casual beach resort with luxurious overtones—features light colors, antique pine armoires, iron and brass headboards, light wool Berber carpeting, and lovely chintz fabrics. The common areas are decorated in similar fashion, with lots of wicker furniture, rag rugs, flowers, and fireplaces.

The inn's fine restaurant, *Toppers*, specializes in new American cuisine (and also is open to non-guests). Breakfasts are hearty affairs, with muffins, eggs, French toast, cereal, wild turkey hash, and the inn's version of eggs Benedict (made with turkey instead of ham). Dinner entrées are equally interesting, including grilled arctic crab with matchstick potatoes and lemon beurre blanc sauce, and veal chops served with polenta and crisp leeks.

An hourly shuttle bus takes guests the 8 miles from the inn to the cobblestone streets of Nantucket village and back again; a 28-passenger launch makes the journey by water. Other outings include naturalist-led tours to 'Sconset, a quaint old fishing village; visits to the natural cranberry bogs; or bird watching jaunts along the beach. The inn will pack a picnic lunch for a perfect afternoon of sun, sand, water, and wine on a hideaway sand spit. There also are two beaches (one on the Atlantic, the other on Nantucket Bay), 26 miles of Nature Conservancy trails, sailboats, kayaks, rowboats, bicycles, two Har-tru tennis courts, a croquet court, and a whimsical outdoor chess set with waist-high pawns. Golf, sailing, antiquing, shopping, and museums and other cultural attractions are nearby.

THE WAUWINET 120 Wauwinet Rd., PO Box 2580, Nantucket, MA 02584 (phone: 508-228-0145; 800-426-8718; fax: 508-228-6712). This seafront inn has 25 guestrooms and suites in the main inn and five cottages, all with private baths, twin, queen-, or king-size beds, telephones, TV sets, and air conditioning. Wheelchair accessible. Closed November through mid-May. Rate for a double room (including full breakfast): $190 to $790. Rate for a two- to four-bedroom cottage: $390 to $1,400. Four-night minimum stay mid-June through mid-September and major holidays; two- or three-night minimum other times. Major credit cards accepted. Children welcome in cottages. No pets. No smoking. Stephen and Jill Karp, innkeepers; Russ Cleveland, manager.

DIRECTIONS: The inn provides complimentary pick-up and drop-off service at the ferry landing. If you decide to drive, take Orange Street from the ferry to the traffic circle in Nantucket village, then take Milestone Road. Bear left onto Polpis Road, follow it to Wauwinet Road, and take a left. The inn is at the end of Wauwinet Road.

OLD INN ON THE GREEN & GEDNEY FARM

NEW MARLBOROUGH, MASSACHUSETTS

Time seems to stand still in New Marlborough, a village that has remained unchanged for more than 200 years. Sitting back from the road on the pretty village green, the *Old Inn on the Green* shows the same resistance to change. The first building on the property was built in 1760 as a frontier trading post and store. In the late 18th century, the current structure was built to serve as a post office, general store, and inn for travelers on the passing stagecoach route. The two-level porch that spans the front of the building dates to that time, as do the guestrooms upstairs.

Bradford Wagstaff and Leslie Miller have owned the inn since 1973. Respecting its colonial roots, they have made few changes, except for the addition of private bathrooms. The wide-plank red pine floors in the five bedrooms still slant and tilt, showing their years, and the furnishings are as close as possible to those that graced the original.

Gedney Farm, a short distance down the lane from the inn, is another matter. The six suites (some with two levels) and four deluxe guestrooms fill a massive old barn that once housed prize-winning Percheron horses. The architecture is stunning: In the lobby, for example, the ceiling soars 28 feet and there's a cozy fireplace. The four-poster beds are authentic colonial gems with crocheted canopies. Many of the rooms and suites feature fireplaces and boldly tiled Jacuzzis for two (the master suite also has an eating area and a sitting room).

A continental breakfast—juice, fruit, granola, and fresh-baked breads— is served to guests either in the *Tap Room* of the old inn or in the barn of *Gedney Farm.* The *Gallery at Gedney Farm,* where fine and decorative art is displayed, also is the setting for summer weekend lunches.

Dining is one of the joys of a stay at the *Old Inn on the Green.* The intimate dining rooms are lighted only by candles. Four of the six dining rooms have impressive fireplaces, and on the wall in the *Gallery* dining room is a hand-painted mural depicting colonial New Marlborough. In summer and fall, dinner also is served on a canopied garden terrace overlooking a colonial flower and herb garden.

The food matches the setting for drama and excellence. Dinner (which is open to non-guests) is served on a prix fixe basis Saturday nights and à la carte the rest of the week. Frequent wine tastings and special culinary events are held as well. In springtime, one of Chef Christopher Capstick's typical Saturday menus might include an appetizer of lobster-and-scallop boudin with spicy corn relish and main courses such as charred Chilean sea bass with ragout of spaghetti squash and wild mushrooms, and black-trumpet-mushroom–encrusted loin of lamb with grilled vegetable tian. Leslie makes the desserts, and choosing between orange *crème brûlée* or frangipane peach tart with rosewater syrup isn't easy.

The inn is on 170 acres that include gardens, meadows, and fields. Located in a hamlet in the Berkshires, it is near the Appalachian Trail, skiing, art galleries, and music festivals. *Tanglewood* is a 30-minute drive away.

OLD INN ON THE GREEN & GEDNEY FARM Route 57 (mailing address: Star Rte. 70), New Marlborough, MA 01230 (phone: 413-229-3131; 800-286-3139; fax: 413-229-3131). This rural inn has 18 guestrooms with private baths, double or queen-size beds, and telephones. Limited wheelchair accessibility. Open year-round; restaurant closed Mondays through Wednesdays from November through June. Rate for a double room (including continental breakfast): $110 to $275. Two-night minimum stay on weekends from June through October and on holidays. Major credit cards accepted. Children welcome. No pets. Smoking permitted in *Tap Room* and in designated guestrooms. Bradford Wagstaff and Leslie Miller, innkeepers; Michael Smith, manager.

DIRECTIONS: Take the Taconic State Parkway north to the Hillsdale exit and follow Route 23 to Great Barrington, Massachusetts. Continue on Route 23 (it will be joined by Route 7 through town). When Route 23 veers right at the traffic light, follow it about 3½ miles east to Route 57. Bear right onto Route 57 and continue for 5¾ miles. The inn is on the left, on the village green.

HISTORIC MERRELL INN

SOUTH LEE, MASSACHUSETTS

When Charles and Faith Reynolds purchased the *Historic Merrell Inn* on two and a half acres bordering the Housatonic River in 1981, it was already almost 200 years old, but it had been vacant and neglected for the last hundred. The new innkeepers' task was monumental. With the help of the *Society for the Preservation of New England Antiquities,* former owners of the property, they installed electricity, heating, and plumbing—always careful to remain faithful to the building's original Federal style. Charles is a retired history teacher, and he wouldn't have it any other way.

Because of this dedication to historic preservation (the building is on the National Register of Historic Places), guests walk into the inn and into 1794 (when the place was a stop on the Boston–Albany stagecoach run). The redbrick exterior with its first- and second-floor porches was unchanged over the years, and inside, numerous remarkable features remain. There are eight original 18th-century Count Rumford fireplaces (three of them in guestrooms), and the *Tavern Room*'s original circular colonial "birdcage" bar, complete with till drawer, is thought to be the only one remaining in America. The original keeping room still has its grand cooking fireplace.

The guestrooms are furnished with equal attention to historical detail, except that all have thoroughly modern baths. Four rooms were carved from the third-floor ballroom, which was added in 1837. There are antique canopy beds, antique chests, lace curtains, fluffy pillows, and colonial-motif wallcoverings and spreads.

An artist as well as a historian, Charles's most recent contribution to the inn is a mural, in the style of the Hudson River School, that wraps around the entry wall and parades up the staircase. Faith is a gardener (as well as a weaver) and is carefully restoring the gardens, which are bordered by neat stone walls. Down by the river is a pretty gazebo.

Breakfast is served in the *Tavern Room,* where a fire may glow in the fireplace. Candles illuminate the paneled walls, polished wide-plank pine floors, original oil paintings, and period tables and chairs. The meal includes juice, fruit, and perhaps an omelette or blueberry-walnut buttermilk pancakes with sausage and pure maple syrup, all served on Bennington pottery, which is made in nearby Bennington, Vermont.

The inn is in the heart of the Berkshires, near *Tanglewood,* the *Norman Rockwell Museum,* summer theater, skiing, and hiking.

HISTORIC MERRELL INN 1565 Pleasant St. (Route 102), South Lee, MA 01260 (phone: 413-243-1794; 800-243-1794; fax: 413-243-2669). This historic inn has nine guestrooms with private baths, double or queen-size beds, telephones, and air conditioning. Open year-round. Rate for a double room (including full breakfast): $55 to $135. Three-night minimum stay on weekends in July and August. MasterCard and Visa accepted. Not appropriate for children under 10. No pets. No smoking. Charles and Faith Reynolds, innkeepers; Pamela Hurst, manager.

DIRECTIONS: From the Massachusetts Turnpike, take Exit 2 at Lee. Follow signs for Route 102 to Stockbridge. Travel 3 miles east on Route 102; the inn is on the left.

RED LION INN

STOCKBRIDGE, MASSACHUSETTS

From its strategic position at the crossroads in Stockbridge (once on the Albany–Boston Post Road), the *Red Lion Inn* has witnessed more than 200 years of history, and its walls literally tell the story. Photographs, historical documents, old paintings, and prints line the walls from floor to ceiling, and innumerable antiques, many rescued from a disastrous inn fire in 1895, fill the lobby and other public rooms. This inn's lobby, with a fireplace that often glows even in summer, and its broad porch, filled with antique wicker furniture and rockers, are the heart of the village.

Today, the inn is considerably larger than it was in 1773. The main building contains 86 rooms, while an additional 22 are in a variety of historic buildings behind the inn and across the street. Jack and Jane Fitzpatrick have been owners since 1968; their daughters, Nancy and Ann, are co-owners.

"Mrs. Fitz," as Jane is known, furnished all the rooms in colonial style. There are antique four-poster beds with crocheted canopies, mahogany chests, pine mirrors, and colonial-style fabrics. The hallways are lined with original Norman Rockwell drawings and prints. The famed illustrator spent the last 25 years of his life in Stockbridge, and his 1968 painting *Stockbridge Main Street at Christmas* features the *Red Lion Inn.* Every room at the inn contains at least one Rockwell print. The newest room, the *Firehouse Suite,* occupying two floors of the village's former fire station, has a cavernous downstairs living room, an upstairs bedroom with a king-size canopy bed, a private deck, and a spacious tile bath with Jacuzzi tub and separate shower.

The inn's formal dining room, a popular place for family dinners and special occasions, features traditional New England fare (and is open to non-guests). Clam chowder, roast turkey, and salmon cakes are on the menu. For dessert, there's Indian pudding, apple crisp, or sinfully delicious chocolate-chip pie. Meals also can be taken in the *Widow Bingham's Tavern,* in the *Lion's Den* (which has live jazz or folk music in the evenings), or in the courtyard under the trees in summer.

The inn has an extensive gift shop called the *Pink Kitty* and also a swimming pool and an exercise room. Guests can take advantage of the inn's proximity to *Tanglewood,* the *Norman Rockwell Museum,* and summer theaters; it is also near golf, tennis, bicycling, hiking, and skiing.

RED LION INN Main St., Stockbridge, MA 01262 (phone: 413-298-5545; fax: 413-298-5130). This historic inn has 108 guestrooms (92 with private baths) with twin, double, queen-, or king-size beds, telephones, and air conditioning; most have TV sets. Wheelchair accessible. Open year-round. Rate for a double room: $72 to $350; continental breakfast included in rate for rooms without private bath. Two-night minimum stay on weekends in July and August. Major credit cards accepted. Children welcome. No pets. No smoking except in designated guestrooms and in the *Lion's Den.* The Fitzpatrick family, owners; Nancy Fitzpatrick, president; Brooks Bradbury, general manager.

DIRECTIONS: From the Massachusetts Turnpike, take Exit 2 at Lee. Follow signs for Route 102 to Stockbridge. Go 5 miles east on Route 102; the inn is on the left in the center of Stockbridge.

Rhode Island

1661 INN, HOTEL MANISSES, AND NICHOLAS BALL COTTAGE

BLOCK ISLAND, RHODE ISLAND

Block Island is a little oasis—a sheltered retreat with salt marshes, sea-cleft bluffs, and sunny beaches, where herons feed and ospreys build their nests. The island was first charted by Italian explorer Giovanni da Verrazano in 1524, then sighted by Dutch adventurer Adrian Block in 1614. In the early 1960s, the Abrams family—Justin, Joan, and their three children, Rita, Mark, and Rick—made a discovery of their own.

Sailing the waters of Block Island Sound, the Abrams family became enchanted with the island and found themselves returning again and again. Eventually, in 1969, they purchased their first property, a little inn in need of a major overhaul. They all pitched in, and soon the *1661 Inn* was pretty and proud. (It originally had 18 rooms with shared baths but now has nine rooms with private baths, some even boasting Jacuzzis.) The inn is decorated with Early American art and antiques, and its decks afford spectacular views of the ocean.

For the energetic Abrams family, the odyssey had just begun. In 1972, they bought the *Hotel Manisses,* an 1870 relic across the street from the inn that had been boarded up for years and was scheduled for demolition. Despite its run-down condition, the hotel, with its mansard roof and square turret, was a picturesque reminder of the late 1800s, when Block Island was a fashionable seaside resort. Today, its 17 rooms, all named for local shipwrecks and all with private baths (some with Jacuzzis), are decorated in lively fabrics and Victorian furniture; instead of suffering the wrecker's ball, the hotel now is listed on the National Register of Historic Places.

The Abrams historic preservation team still wasn't finished. In succession they tackled the *Nicholas Ball Cottage* (it has three luxurious rooms with fireplaces, Jacuzzis, and lovely antiques), and the nine-room *Guest House* (five rooms have private baths and four share). Today, daughter Rita and her husband, Steven Draper, manage the properties.

A bountiful New England buffet breakfast is served to all guests at the *1661 Inn*. The extravaganza includes such specialties as baked bluefish, hash, and baked beans, as well as eggs, pancakes, muffins, fruit, and juices. In the afternoon a complimentary wine and "nibbles" hour offers guests a chance to mingle with their hosts and other visitors. Dinner, which is served at the *Hotel Manisses* (and is open to non-guests), is a food lover's fantasy, featuring seafood and the provender of the Abrams's gardens. Oysters, mussels, bluefish, and tuna are matched with spinach, peppers, tomatoes, zucchini, string beans, kale, rhubarb, and herbs for a distinctive Block Island taste.

During the nibbles hour, guests can sign up for a free excursion around the island—perhaps a sunset tour, a picnic and walk along the Clayhead Nature Trail, or a tour of the owners' farm, where they raise llamas, pygmy and fainting goats, Scottish Highland steers, and black swans. On their own guests can enjoy nearby ocean beaches and nature walks, whale watching, bicycling, sailing, shopping, and fishing.

1661 INN, HOTEL MANISSES, AND NICHOLAS BALL COTTAGE

1 Spring St., Block Island, RI 02807 (phone: 401-466-2421, 401-466-2063, or 800-MANISSES, inn and hotel; 401-466-2836, restaurant; fax: 401-466-2858). The hotel, inn, and cottages on pastoral Block Island have 38 guestrooms (34 with private baths) with twin, double, queen-, or king-size beds; 34 with telephones. Open year-round; restaurant closed weekdays mid-December through mid-April. Rate for a double room (including full breakfast, afternoon wine, and gratuity): $50 to $350. Three-night minimum stay on weekends in July and August; two nights the rest of year. Major credit cards accepted. *Hotel Manisses* not appropriate for children under 10; all children welcome in the other guestrooms. No pets. Smoking permitted in designated rooms. Justin and Joan Abrams, innkeepers; Steve and Rita Draper, managers.

DIRECTIONS: Block Island is located 13 miles off the Rhode Island coast; car-service ferries make daily runs from Point Judith, Rhode Island. Seasonal service and non-car ferries also go to Block Island from Newport, Rhode Island; New London, Connecticut; and Montauk, New York. From the Point Judith ferry turn left up Main Street, then turn right onto Spring Street (just past the theater) and drive one block; *Hotel Manisses* is on the right and the *1661 Inn* is just up the hill on the left.

ELM TREE COTTAGE

NEWPORT, RHODE ISLAND

Innkeepers Priscilla and Thomas Malone—and their three daughters, Keely, Briana, and Erin—purchased this lovely 1882 house, with its views of Easton's Pond and First Beach, in 1990. They have breathed new life into a home that once had a questionable future. Today, the inn and its landscaped gardens look much as they did when Mrs. Crawford-Hill, the first owner, used to entertain her friend Wallis Simpson at tea.

The gracious entryway with its Oriental rug opens onto a formal parlor overlooking the bay. In the parlor are overstuffed sofas upholstered in white jacquard and a magnificent mirror with garlands of carved roses, purchased at auction. Priscilla, who is a fine artist, painstakingly re-created missing pieces of the mirror's frame and then painted it its original pale blue and ivory.

Such restorations are the Malones' business. In addition to innkeeping, Tom and Priscilla restore stained-glass windows and religious interiors for churches, museums, and corporate and residential clients. Not surprisingly, you'll see some exceptional examples of stained glass here, and you'll understand why the Malones have won numerous awards for their inn.

Adjacent to the parlor is the sun-drenched, wicker-filled morning room. It overlooks the perennial gardens, where an abundance of tulips and daffodils heralds the coming of spring, followed by a procession of peonies, roses, and lilies. A tiny, clubby bar, where guests can mix drinks with their own liquor (the inn does not have a liquor license), has an unusual reverse-painted mirror, featuring the Pekinese dogs Mrs. Crawford-Hill loved so much, and a bar embedded with 1921 silver dollars.

Each guestroom seems more impressive than the last, so it would be hard to select a favorite, but each reflects the Malones' background in interior design, woodworking, and fine arts. Each is decorated with polished French and English antiques, complemented by designer linen and lace. The *Library* has floor-to-ceiling bookshelves, a wood-burning fireplace, and a spectacular carved walnut bed and matching armoire. The *Harriman Room,* also with a wood-burning fireplace and carved walnut bed, was once a gentleman's dressing room. All baths in the house are elegant, but the one in the *Harriman Room* contains a porcelain sink with Austrian crystal legs, a huge porcelain soaking tub, and the original shower stall.

Breakfast is served in the sunny formal dining room, which is accented by arrangements of flowers and potted plants. A buffet is set out every morning on the antique Hepplewhite-style sideboard, where guests can help themselves to an appetizer (perhaps a berry cobbler), fruit, and yogurt. That's followed by an entrée such as puffed pear pancakes. Individual tables are set with floral chintz cloths, and Priscilla selects the daily china to complement the day's entrée.

Newport offers a wealth of extravagant mansions, a cliff walk, sailing, boating, tennis, golf, concerts, antiquing, and shopping.

ELM TREE COTTAGE 336 Gibbs Ave., Newport, RI 02840 (phone: 401-849-1610; 800-882-3ELM; fax: 401-849-2084). This elegant inn has six guestrooms with private baths, queen- or king-size beds, and air conditioning. Closed January and December 24 through 26. Rate for a double room (including full breakfast): $145 to $350. Two-night minimum stay on weekends; three nights on weekends June through *Columbus Day,* holiday weekends, and during special events. Major credit cards accepted. Not appropriate for children under 14. No pets. Rabbit in hutch in back. No smoking. Priscilla and Thomas Malone, innkeepers.

DIRECTIONS: From New York take I-95 north to Exit 3 in Rhode Island. Follow Route 138 east for approximately 30 miles, always following the blue signs to the Newport Bridge. After crossing the bridge, exit at "Scenic Newport" and turn right off the exit ramp. At the second traffic light turn right onto America's Cup Avenue. Follow this road to the seventh traffic light, stay to the left, and proceed up the hill onto Memorial Boulevard toward First Beach. Cross Bellevue Avenue and make a left onto Gibbs Avenue (if you pass *Cliff Walk Manor,* you've gone too far). Proceed to the first stop sign. *Elm Tree Cottage* is the third house after the stop sign on the right. From Boston follow Route 128 south to Route 24 south via the Sakonner River Bridge to Route 138 south (exit at the *Ramada Inn* and bear left). Continue on Route 138 south until you reach the Fleet National Bank on the right. Take a left onto Route 138A south toward Newport Beaches. At the second traffic light bear left and continue past the beaches and up the hill. Make a right onto Gibbs Avenue, then follow directions above.

FRANCIS MALBONE HOUSE INN

NEWPORT, RHODE ISLAND

When guests walk from busy Thames Street through the front doors of the *Francis Malbone House Inn,* they step back to 1760, when ship merchant Francis Malbone built the stately brick home on Newport's waterfront, a perfect vantage point from which to survey his private fleet. The architect he hired was Peter Harrison, who had designed other Newport gems, including the *Touro Synagogue* and *Redwood Library.* Although he seldom admitted it, Malbone traded principally in slaves and rum, and a secret tunnel ran under the street from his house directly to the docks.

In this century, the house was used for many years as a nursing home, but in 1989 it was purchased by a group of Newporters, restored, and converted into an inn. Today, with its graceful colonial woodwork and doors, its 10 fireplaces, 15-foot ceilings, and elegant proportions, it looks much as it did in Malbone's day. Three formal parlors contain lovely Federal-era antiques, and fires glow in the fireplaces on chilly nights. In 1996, nine additional guestrooms and a new 40-seat dining room were added in a wing to the rear, in a style faithful to the original house, including the hardwood floors and ornate moldings. The king-size rooms feature wood-burning fireplaces and French doors leading to private patios.

Guestrooms are decorated with taste and charm. The *Counting House,* on the main floor, was added during the British occupation of Newport in the 1770s. This suite features 18-foot ceilings, shell corner cabinets, a king-size four-poster bed, and a magnificent bathroom with a whirlpool tub. Many of the upstairs guestrooms have wood-burning fireplaces and views of either the gardens or the harbor; all are furnished with antiques, including four-poster beds. Pretty floral fabrics adorn the windows, beds, and chairs.

Guests are served a full breakfast in either the original formal dining room, where there is a Queen Anne mahogany table and yet another fireplace, or in the new dining room. The meal might include eggs Benedict, peach pancakes, pumpkin waffles, or raspberry crêpes.

The inn is within walking distance of antiques shops, boutiques, the *Newport Casino,* and the historic houses along Bellevue Avenue. Bicycling, boating, golf, and tennis can be found nearby. If you would prefer to stay put, there's a pretty enclosed courtyard in back with a fountain and benches.

FRANCIS MALBONE HOUSE INN 392 Thames St., Newport, RI 02840 (phone: 401-846-0392; 800-846-0392; fax: 401-848-5956). **This Federal house in the heart of historic Newport has 18 guestrooms with private baths, queen- or king-size beds, telephones, and air conditioning; 15 have fireplaces, 10 have TV sets. Open year-round. Rate for a double room (including full breakfast): $165 to $325 May through October; $135 to $295 November through April. Two-night minimum on weekends; three nights on weekends July through September. Major credit cards accepted. Not appropriate for children under 14. No pets. No smoking. Will Dewey, innkeeper.**

DIRECTIONS: From New York follow the directions to *Elm Tree Cottage* (see page 111) as far as America's Cup Avenue. Follow this road to the sixth light, turn right onto lower Thames Street at the *Perry Mill Market,* and drive three blocks. The inn is on the left. (To reach the private parking lot in back, turn left onto Brewer Street and into the first driveway on the right.) From Boston follow the *Elm Tree Cottage* directions to Route 138A south. At the second traffic light bear left and continue past the beaches and up the hill. At the fourth light (bottom of hill) turn left onto Thames Street, then follow directions above.

IVY LODGE

NEWPORT, RHODE ISLAND

Hidden behind a privet hedge, *Ivy Lodge*'s rather unassuming, gray-shingled exterior belies its elegant interior. Built in 1886, the house is much more conservative in style than the nearby summer "cottages" of the Vanderbilts and Astors, but it is nevertheless a stunner. The entry hall, with its carved solid-oak walls and elaborate 33-foot Gothic staircase with 365 spindles, sets the scene. There are fireplaces everywhere: in the entry hall, in the elegant pink reception room with its wicker and chintz, in the formal living room. Done in hunter green and cream, the latter has a grand piano (sometimes used for chamber music concerts) and bay windows overlooking the formal gardens. Open the French doors and step onto the wraparound verandah, outfitted with vintage wicker chairs.

Innkeepers Maggie and Terry Moy have furnished the bedrooms just as they have the common rooms—with museum-quality antiques. Maggie also has added decorative stenciling to the walls of some of the guestrooms. The *Library Room* has lace curtains on its bay windows and a sleigh bed piled high with pillows. Its wood-burning fireplace of blue Delft tiles sits

below a mantel with built-in bookshelves. The marble-and-tile bath has a Jacuzzi. The *Turret Room* (where Arnold Schwarzenegger and Maria Shriver once stayed) is done up with antique oak furniture, including a king-size bed, and has a private rooftop deck; its bath features a claw-foot tub and a pull-chain toilet. The *Ivy Room* is bright and fresh with a four-poster bed, a whitewashed antique pine vanity and mirror, and sea green carpeting.

The dining room is so large that the 21-foot cherry table fits comfortably. It's set with silver, bone china, and crystal for breakfast. Entrées may include Scotch eggs or Grand Marnier French toast stuffed with cream cheese.

Ivy Lodge is located in Newport's mansion area, near museums, beaches, tennis, golf, and the cliff walk.

IVY LODGE 12 Clay St., Newport, RI 02840 (phone: 401-849-6865). This lavish shingled inn has eight guestrooms with private baths (*Room No. 1*'s is off the hallway), twin, double, queen-, or king-size beds, and air conditioning. Closed Monday through Thursday from January through March. Rate for a double room (including full breakfast): $125 to $175. Two-night minimum stay on weekends. Major credit cards accepted. Not appropriate for children, although they will be accommodated. No pets. Kelly, a German shepherd, and Puff, a cat, in residence. Smoking permitted outdoors only. Maggie and Terry Moy, innkeepers.

DIRECTIONS: From New York follow the directions to *Elm Tree Cottage* (see page 111) onto Memorial Boulevard toward First Beach. At the next traffic light turn right onto Bellevue Avenue. Follow Bellevue to the first light, then turn left onto Narragansett Avenue. Clay is the first street on the left, and the inn is located two houses up on the right. From Boston take the *Elm Tree Cottage* directions "past the beaches and up the hill." Turn left onto Bellevue Avenue and follow the directions above.

Mid-Atlantic and Ontario

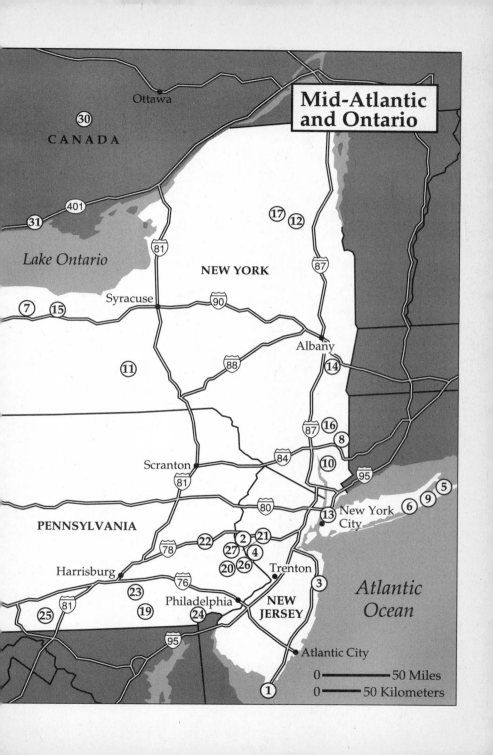

Mid-Atlantic and Ontario

New Jersey

MAINSTAY INN
CAPE MAY, NEW JERSEY

Located at the southernmost tip of New Jersey and surrounded by broad sandy beaches on the Atlantic Ocean, the Victorian town of Cape May was founded in 1848 and settled by people who came to enjoy the cool, salty air. Fortunately for today's visitors, the village eluded the trend toward urbanization and modernization that was so prevalent during the early 20th century. More than 600 Victorian structures still stand in Cape May, and the entire town has been designated a National Historic District.

When Tom and Sue Carroll bought the *Mainstay Inn* in 1976, they were in the forefront of the innkeeping industry in the US. Recognizing its uniqueness, the Carrolls sought to preserve the ambience of the elegant Italianate villa, built in 1872 as a gentlemen's gaming club. The structure still has many of its original features, including 14-foot ceilings, a huge chandelier in the dining room, and such furnishings as a 12-foot pier mirror in the entrance hall. Museum-quality antiques (in the dark, polished walnut so popular in the 19th century) and silk-screened wallpapers enhance the Old World charm of the common rooms. The broad front verandah provides the ideal spot to sip afternoon tea and listen to the sea breezes rustling through the giant sycamore trees that line the street, and the intimate belvedere, high on the roof, is a romantic place from which to watch the sun set.

The guestrooms are distributed among the main house, an adjacent *Summer Cottage,* and the *Officers' Quarters,* a former World War I navy officer's home across the street. Those in the main house and the *Summer Cottage* are furnished in a lavish style the Carrolls call "Renaissance Revival," featuring tall, carved walnut headboards, dressers, and armoires. The four suites in the *Officers' Quarters* are a bit more contemporary, boasting fireplaces and whirlpool tubs.

On summer mornings guests enjoy breakfast on the verandah—juice, fruit, fresh-baked breads and muffins, cereal, and yogurt. Throughout the rest of the year, a full breakfast is served in the formal dining room of the main house. The hearty entrées might include strawberry French toast, cheese-blintz soufflé, or an English muffin with a poached egg, tomato slice, and cheese sauce. Afternoon tea is also served.

Historic tours, bicycling, beaches, and bird watching are available nearby, and the village sponsors several special events, including a music festival in May and June, *Victorian Week* in October, and *Christmas in Cape May* throughout December.

MAINSTAY INN 635 Columbia Ave., Cape May, NJ 08204 (phone: 609-884-8690). This historic inn has 16 guestrooms and suites with private baths and double, queen-, or king-size beds; 10 rooms have air conditioning, four have telephones and TV sets. Wheelchair accessible. Suites in the *Officers' Quarters* open year-round; other rooms closed early January through mid-March. Rate for a double room (including breakfast and afternoon tea): $95 to $250. Three-night minimum stay requested June through September. No credit cards accepted. *Officers' Quarters* not appropriate for children under six; other rooms not appropriate for children under 14. No pets. Two cats, Boots and Bady, live on the grounds. No smoking. Tom and Sue Carroll, innkeepers.

DIRECTIONS: From Philadelphia take the Walt Whitman Bridge to the Atlantic City Expressway. After approximately 50 miles, take the Garden State Parkway south another 40 miles to Cape May. In Cape May, turn left at the first light onto Madison Street. Proceed 3 blocks and turn right onto Columbia Avenue. The inn is 3 blocks down on the right.

THE QUEEN VICTORIA

CAPE MAY, NEW JERSEY

Few people have arrived at innkeeping better prepared for the task than Joan and Dane Wells. Joan had been Executive Director of the Victorian Society of America and Dane was active in neighborhood revitalization in Philadelphia. Both were dedicated to achieving a meticulous restoration of their inn and to furthering the unique Victorian character of Cape May. Much of the town's attractiveness today is the result of their efforts.

With its picturesque turrets, bay windows, and gingerbread trim *The Queen Victoria* is a superb example of Cape May's Victorian architecture. Dane and Joan began restoring it in 1980. Since then, five buildings have

been added to the property. They range in style from *Regent's Park,* a charming little cottage, to *The Queen's Hotel,* which has rooms well-suited to business travelers and where breakfast is not included in the room rate. Other buildings include *Prince Albert Hall,* a former Victorian home that now contains rooms with whirlpool tubs, the *Carriage House,* and *The Queen's Cottage,* which has a pretty garden in the rear.

Each building (except for the *Carriage House* and *Regent's Park*) has its own parlor or common sitting area; some have two. Each also has a parlor stocked with coffee, tea, sodas, popcorn, and much more for guests' use. Hand-painted wallpaper embellishes the walls. When seated around the expansive tables in one of the dining rooms for breakfast or afternoon tea, guests often discuss Joan's collection of Van Briggle pottery, or the silver displayed in the cabinets, or even the impressive furniture.

Each guestroom has antique Arts and Crafts or Mission-style furniture. There are walnut and oak headboards, brass beds, and marble-topped dressers. Handmade quilts lend a country touch.

Breakfast might include such temptations as the inn's renowned granola, fresh-baked muffins and breads, fresh fruit and juice, and an entrée such as Aunt Ruth's baked eggs and cheese with savory sausage patties.

The ocean is only a block away, and guests often borrow the inn's bicycles to ride along the boardwalk. There are myriad activities in Cape May and at the inn throughout the year. During the first week in December, guests are invited to help decorate a variety of *Christmas* trees in typical Victorian styles. The *Dickens Extravaganza* open house and a series of musical events are also held at *Christmastime.*

THE QUEEN VICTORIA 102 Ocean St., Cape May, NJ 08204 (phone: 609-884-8702). This seaside collection of houses contains 23 guestrooms with private baths, queen-size beds, and air conditioning. Some have telephones, TV sets, whirlpool tubs, and/or fireplaces. Wheelchair accessible. Open year-round. Rate for a double room (including full breakfast and afternoon tea): $75 to $250. Two-night minimum on weekends November through March; three nights on weekends April through October. Prefer check or cash but will accept major credit cards. Children welcome. No pets. Two cats, Spats and Mugsy, live in owners' quarters. No smoking. Dane, Joan, and Elizabeth Wells, innkeepers.

DIRECTIONS: From the southern end of the Garden State Parkway, continue straight into town (just over a mile). The road merges with Lafayette Street. At the second stoplight, turn left onto Ocean Street. Go 3 blocks, inn is on the right.

CHESTNUT HILL ON THE DELAWARE

MILFORD, NEW JERSEY

For those who enjoy the exuberance of Victorian architecture, a visit to this historic inn is a must. Built in 1860 as a wedding present for a bride by her husband, the house, as well as an adjacent cottage, have been meticulously restored by innkeepers Linda and Rob Castagna.

The mansion and its little sister are painted to highlight individual architectural elements. The main house is pale green with accents of forest green and cranberry; a fanciful wrought-iron grapevine dances across the wraparound porch and down the pillars. The *Country Cottage* is painted a rich cream with taupe and teal trim. Both houses are steps away from the Delaware River and have magnificent views.

In the main house, the spacious entry hall with its cherry-and-oak parquet floor opens into the *Fireplace Room* on one side, decorated with an ornate painted mantel, and the spacious drawing room on the other, with a richly carved walnut fireplace. Spanning a wall in the drawing room is a black-walnut apothecary unit that serves as a lending library and gift shop. Both a pump organ and an upright piano are located here as well, although these instruments are no match for the clear, sweet trill of Keats the canary, in his antique brass cage. Mannequins dressed in lacy Victorian garb that once belonged to the house's original owner greet guests.

The decor of the guestrooms continues the Victorian theme. *Peaches and Cream* has a spindle spool bed with a key quilt and a black-walnut armoire; *Rose Garden* has a window seat from which to view the river, and a Jacuzzi; *Teddy's Place,* a third-floor suite with a splendid view of the Delaware, is home to more than 150 stuffed bears. The *Country Cottage* boasts a bedroom with a fireplace, a fully stocked kitchen, a private porch (on which an authentic hand-painted carousel horse resides), and views of the river from the queen-size bed. It's furnished in country French style.

Breakfast, including juice, fruit, fresh-baked bread and pastries, and perhaps French toast with bananas Foster or German apple-apricot pancakes, is served in the formal dining room on a black-walnut table.

For sheer relaxation, spend an afternoon in one of the large antique rockers on the verandah watching the Delaware River roll past. Nearby are river rafting, country fairs, antiques shops, a hiking trail along the old Delaware Canal towpath, bicycling, summer theaters, and musical events.

CHESTNUT HILL ON THE DELAWARE 63 Church St., PO Box N, Milford, NJ 08848 (phone: 908-995-9761). This Victorian mansion and cottage on the Delaware River offers six guestrooms (four with private baths) with double or queen-size beds and air conditioning; four have telephones. Open year-round. Rate for a double room (including full breakfast) in the main house: $85 to $125; in the *Country Cottage:* $140 per night or $750 per week. Two-night minimum stay on weekends and holidays. No credit cards accepted. Not appropriate for children under 10. No pets. A canary, Keats, in residence. Smoking permitted on outside porches only. Rob and Linda Castagna, innkeepers.

DIRECTIONS: From New York take I-78 west to Exit 11 (Pattenburg). Follow Route 614 for 8 miles south to Spring Hill. Turn left onto Route 519, and travel 3 miles south to Milford. In Milford turn right onto Bridge Street and then right onto Church Street. At the end of Church Street turn left; the inn's parking lot is straight ahead.

LA MAISON B & B AND GALLERY
SPRING LAKE, NEW JERSEY

Down by the seashore, the tiny community of Spring Lake boasts broad, tree-lined streets unencumbered by the fast food outlets and amusement centers associated with other Jersey Shore communities. Instead, it is a

serene oasis of wide, sandy beaches paralleled by a 2-mile boardwalk, elegant Victorian houses, and interesting shops and restaurants. Built in the late 1800s by wealthy Irish families from Philadelphia and New York, most of the original homes remain, their spacious lawns sloping to the street.

Although there are numerous inns and bed and breakfast establishments in town, petite *La Maison* stands out. Part art gallery (paintings line the hallways) and part French country inn (with French furnishings throughout), *La Maison* is a reflection of its charming innkeepers. Peter Oliver is a painter, and Barbara Furdyna studied French in college and is an inveterate Francophile.

There are pretty needlepoint pillows on the antique French armchairs in the parlor, exquisite Oriental rugs on the white wool carpets, and a formal dining room with a magnificent country French pine table and ladder-back chairs. In the guestrooms there are tall mirrored armoires, as well as antique sleigh beds, iron and brass beds, and fanciful Victorian beds, all with fluffy down comforters. Each bathroom is large and well-appointed. *Room No. 8,* for example, has a huge bath with a skylight and a two-person Jacuzzi tub.

The favorite retreat for honeymooners is the pretty, secluded rose-covered cottage in back. It has a living room with a cathedral ceiling and skylight, and a bath with a skylight over the clawfoot tub. A screened-in porch overlooks an English garden.

A full breakfast is served in the dining room every morning. The main dish might be Belgian waffles with strawberries and whipped cream or an omelette of *chèvre* and *herbes de Provence.* Mimosas or champagne accompany an array of fresh-baked breads, coffee, tea, cappuccino and espresso.

Visitors spend leisure hours bicycling, walking, or in-line skating along the boardwalk, or just lolling on the beach. In the village, there is a jogging and bicycling trail around Spring Lake, and a clutch of boutiques and antiques shops.

LA MAISON B & B AND GALLERY 404 Jersey Ave., Spring Lake, NJ 07762 (phone: 908-449-4860; 800-276-2088; fax: 908-449-4860). **An intimate village bed and breakfast establishment, this facility has eight guestrooms with private baths, queen-size beds, telephones, TV sets, and air conditioning; one with Jacuzzi. Wheelchair accessible. Open February through December. Rate for a double room (including full champagne breakfast): $110 to $220. Three-night minimum on weekends July and August; two nights on weekends rest of year. Major credit cards accepted. Children and small pets welcome in cottage. Two mini Schnauzers, Heidi and Shady, live in owner's quarters. No smoking. Barbara Furdyna and Peter Oliver, innkeepers.**

DIRECTIONS: Take the Garden State Parkway to Exit 98 and travel south on Route 34. At the first traffic circle, take Route 524 east. Go through three traffic lights and then cross the railroad tracks. At the second intersection, turn right onto Fourth Avenue and travel five blocks to Jersey Avenue. Turn right onto Jersey; the inn is the second house on the right.

WOOLVERTON INN

STOCKTON, NEW JERSEY

Just across the Delaware River from famed Bucks County, Pennsylvania, Stockton has a charm of its own. A park stretches along the banks of the river and interesting shops and restaurants line the downtown streets.

The *Woolverton Inn* is within walking distance of the village, but removed from it. The property comprises 10 peaceful acres, with a stately stone manor house, pastures and grazing sheep, a stone spring house, a picturesque barn (which may one day include guestrooms), and a carriage house.

The manor, with sweeping first- and second-floor verandahs, was built in 1792 and significantly enlarged in the mid-1800s by the inn's namesake, Maurice Woolverton. It has been offering overnight accommodations since 1980, but after being purchased by Elizabeth and Michael Palmer in 1993, it has taken on a whole new look.

One of the grandest rooms is *Amelia's Garden*. It has a four-poster cherry bed with a fishnet canopy, a fireplace, a dressing room, and a spacious bath. The walls are painted with flowers, and an Oriental rug rests on the pink tile floor. *Caroline's Balustrade* is a favorite because of its private entrance to the second-floor verandah; its bath, one of the prettiest in the inn, is across the hall. In addition to the eight rooms in the manor house, there are two more rooms in the carriage house.

The formal living room contains a grand piano, a game table, and English-style furniture comfortably arranged near a fireplace. The side porch, filled

with wicker furniture with colorful floral chintz cushions, provides a charming nook for curling up with a good book and looking out over the gardens.

Breakfast is served either in the formal dining room or in nice weather, on the stone verandah. The meal might start with a warm fruit compote, followed by whole wheat waffles or pocket French toast with strawberry sauce.

On the grounds of the inn, guests can enjoy a game of croquet or horseshoes. Nearby, the towpath along the Delaware River provides a languorous walking trail, and the river is popular with canoeists and rafters. Other possible diversions nearby include hot-air balloon rides and antiques hunting in local shops. The *James A. Michener Art Museum,* the *Bucks County Playhouse,* and the *Mercer Museum* are also nearby.

WOOLVERTON INN 6 Woolverton Rd., Stockton, NJ 08559 (phone: 609-397-0802; fax: 609-397-4936). This country manor house has 10 guestrooms with private baths, double, queen-, or king-size beds, and air conditioning; two have whirlpool tubs. Wheelchair accessible. Open year-round. Rate for a double room (including full breakfast): $95 to $180. Two-night minimum weekends; three-night minimum holiday weekends. Major credit cards accepted. Not appropriate for children under 13. No pets. One dog, Jane, and three cats, Willie, Nick, and Allie, at inn. No smoking. Elizabeth and Michael Palmer, innkeepers.

DIRECTIONS: From I-78 west, take Exit 29 to I-287. Take I-287 south to exit 13 to Route 202 south, taking the second Lambertville Exit onto Route 29 north to Stockton. Travel through the village to a fork in the road. Take the right fork onto Route 523 and travel ²⁄₁₀ of a mile. Turn left onto Woolverton Road. The inn is down the second driveway.

New York

BLUFF COTTAGE

AMAGANSETT, NEW YORK

Just down the hill and across the street from *Bluff Cottage,* the rolling surf crashes onto the white sand of Atlantic Beach. The inn's small second-floor balcony, with its comfortable wicker chairs, provides a popular viewing platform. From the broad front porch, furnished with more wicker and decorated with ferns and red and pink impatiens, guests enjoy a view of the lawns and colorful gardens, hidden from the street behind a clipped privet hedge.

With weathered shingles and white trim, this Dutch colonial house was built in 1892 by Dr. Rossiter Johnson, an editor at the New York publishing firm of Funk & Wagnalls. John Pakulek and Clem Thompson purchased it in 1971 and 21 years later opened their home as a bed and breakfast inn.

After many years of travel, Pakulek and Thompson had acquired some rare museum-quality antiques and, today, they happily share these treasures with their guests. The common rooms contain several interesting pieces. There's an ornately carved mahogany partners desk in the den. In the living room, an eight-foot country French fruitwood confessional dominates one corner, and a magnificent primitive painting hangs over the fireplace.

The four guestrooms are furnished in a style that combines elegance and comfort. The *Green Room,* for example, has forest green carpeting and walls; a plaid silk spread covers the Charleston rice four-poster bed. In the *Blue Room* is another four-poster, while the *Peach Bisque Room* has a canopy bed, an antique marble-topped Bombay chest, and an English fruitwood armoire.

A continental breakfast of juice, fruit, and fresh-baked muffins, croissants, and scones is served in the dining room. Here, the decor is highlighted by a lovely collection of rose medallion Chinese export china.

Bluff Road, with its vistas of grassy dunes and beaches, is a popular place for bicycling, jogging, walking, and in-line skating, especially on sunny afternoons. The inn also is near the *Amagansett Farmers' Market,* sailing, fishing, and nature preserves.

BLUFF COTTAGE 266 Bluff Rd. (mailing address: PO Box 428), Amagansett, NY 11930 (phone: 516-267-6172). This gray-shingled bed and breakfast establishment has four guestrooms with private baths, queen-size beds, and air conditioning. Closed November to *Memorial Day.* Rate for a double room (including continental breakfast): $210 to $230. Three-night minimum stay on weekends; four nights on holiday weekends. Major credit cards accepted. Not appropriate for children under 12. No pets. No smoking. John J. Pakulek III and Clement M. Thompson, innkeepers.

DIRECTIONS: Traveling east on Montauk Highway, continue through the village of Amagansett, turn right onto Atlantic Avenue (just before the fire station), and proceed 2 blocks. The inn is on the right, on the corner of Atlantic Avenue and Bluff Road.

BRIDGEHAMPTON INN

BRIDGEHAMPTON, NEW YORK

The Hamptons, on Long Island's eastern end, were first settled in 1640. Although the area remained largely agricultural, by the mid-1700s it had become a well-traveled pass-through to Connecticut; George Washington came this way when he traveled to Boston to receive his commission to lead the colonies' army in the Revolutionary War. Travelers needed places to stay, and many of the large homes took in boarders. The fine home that was built in 1795 and is now the *Bridgehampton Inn* was undoubtedly one of them.

A stately white clapboard with mullioned windows and a columned entrance, it was known as the *Boxwood Inn* during the 1980s. It fell on hard times, however, and had long stopped taking in travelers when it was purchased by Anna and Detlef Pump in 1993. After a massive renovation, the rechristened inn reopened in 1994.

This is not a fussy inn. The decor has a sophisticated elegance that's accented with clever artwork and extravagant floral displays in the common rooms. In the living room, filled with burnished antique chests, Victorian tables, and a pretty Victorian settee covered in forest green velvet, a fire glows in the hearth on cool days. Beyond the French doors, brick terraces with tables and chairs overlooking refined gardens offer quiet places to relax.

The room decor is crisp and serene, with beige wall-to-wall carpeting, hand-crafted four-poster beds, and antique dressers and tables. *Room No. 7* has a Victorian settee in a spritely red-striped twill and a polished antique chest with brass pulls. *Room No. 6* is furnished with a spectacular eight-piece antique Biedermeier suite. All the baths are outstanding. European in style, they are custom-designed in gray marble, with square sinks surrounded by broad gray counters, and enormous marble showers.

Breakfast is served on the terrace or in a sunny breakfast room decorated with antique blue-and-white china from Denmark, where Anna grew up. The continental breakfast, which is included in the room rate, features freshly baked muffins, scones, and croissants from *Loaves and Fishes,* the local catering firm also owned by the Pumps. A full breakfast is available for an additional charge.

In the heart of the hamlet of Bridgehampton, the inn is within walking distance of shops and fine restaurants. Recreational possibilities include bicycling, horseback riding, canoeing, fishing, antiquing, and sunning on the magnificent ocean beaches. Other activities include visits to local wineries and the *Corwith House* (a museum house), theater, concerts, and book readings.

BRIDGEHAMPTON INN 2266 Main St. (mailing address: PO Box 1342), Bridgehampton, NY 11932 (phone: 516-537-3660). This historic inn has six guestrooms and two suites with private baths, queen- or king-size beds, telephones, TV sets, and air conditioning. Open year-round. Rate for a double room (including continental breakfast): $185 to $290. Two-night minimum stay May through September; three nights on holiday weekends. Major credit cards accepted. Children welcome. No pets. No smoking. Anna and Detlef Pump, innkeepers.

DIRECTIONS: From New York City take I-495 (the Long Island Expressway) to Exit 70 (Manorville) and follow Route 111 south to Highway 27 (Sunrise Highway).

Take Highway 27 (which becomes the Montauk Highway) east for 25 miles to Bridgehampton. The Montauk Highway becomes Main Street as it reaches Bridgehampton. The inn is on the left, a half mile beyond the traffic light at the entrance to Bridgehampton Common shopping center.

ASA RANSOM HOUSE
CLARENCE, NEW YORK

In 1799, Asa Ransom, a young silversmith, saw an ad offering land in a wilderness area now known as Clarence to "any proper man who would build and operate a tavern upon it." Not one to let opportunity pass him by, Ransom bought the land and soon constructed a log home and tavern. In 1801, he added a sawmill and, two years later, a gristmill—the first in Erie County. These buildings did not survive, but the library, gift shop, and taproom of the present building date to 1853, and remnants of the grist-mill are visible.

Current innkeepers Bob and Judy Lenz purchased the white frame and brick farmhouse in 1975. They filled it with period antiques and Oriental rugs and added two dining rooms, in keeping with its architectural style. The property is on eight acres with flower gardens, a gazebo, and a pond.

Waverly fabrics in subtle colors accent the guestrooms and suites, all of which feature four-poster, canopy, iron-and-brass, oak, or carved mahogany beds and well-stocked, built-in bookshelves. Several also have fireplaces and balconies or porches overlooking the grounds.

Here, dinner, which consists of sophisticated country fare and British chophouse-style dishes, includes such entrées as shepherd's pie, Ransom mixed grill (lamb chops, chicken, mushrooms, bacon, and grilled tomatoes), and apple-cheddar chicken. Herbs from the inn's gardens flavor sauces and salads. In winter, a wood-burning fireplace warms the dining rooms, while, in summer, diners can enjoy a lovely view of the gardens along with their meal. On Wednesdays, lunch also is available; a delightful afternoon tea, complete with scones and clotted cream, finger sandwiches, and pastries, is served on Thursdays. A full breakfast of juice, muffins, French toast, soufflés, and crêpes is offered to guests each morning. The other meals attract locals as well as guests.

Golf, swimming, tennis, and fishing are available nearby, and there's a large antiques market in Clarence. The *Clarence Historical Society* maintains a museum nearby.

ASA RANSOM HOUSE 10529 Main St. (Rte. 5), Clarence, NY 14031 (phone: 716-759-2315; fax: 716-759-2791). Located 18 miles from Buffalo and 28 miles from Niagara Falls, this country inn has nine guestrooms with private baths, twin, double, queen-, or king-size beds, telephones, TV sets, and air conditioning. Wheelchair accessible. Inn closed Fridays and January; the dining room, which is closed for dinner Fridays, also serves lunch on Wednesdays and afternoon tea on Thursdays. Rate for a double room (including full breakfast and dinner): $145 to $260; bed and breakfast: $90 to $160. Discover, MasterCard, and Visa accepted. Quiet and well-supervised children welcome. No pets. No smoking. Robert and Judy Lenz, innkeepers.

DIRECTIONS: From the New York State Thruway west, take Exit 48A (Pembroke). Turn right onto Route 77 and right again onto Route 5. Travel 11 miles to Clarence, where Route 5 becomes Main Street. The inn is on the left. When traveling on the Thruway east, take Exit 49, turn left onto Route 78, turn right onto Route 5, and continue 5½ miles to Clarence.

OLD DROVERS INN

DOVER PLAINS, NEW YORK

Enter the low-slung doorway and duck under the ancient beamed ceiling. Pull a stool up to the old oak bar, close to the mammoth stone fireplace, and listen carefully. History is preserved so thoroughly at the *Old Drovers Inn* that you can almost hear the rough-tongued banter of the 18th-century drovers (cowboys who drove cattle along the old Post Road from upstate New York to the markets in New York City) who warmed up with hot buttered rum and gambled the night away here. The inn also has welcomed the likes of the Marquis de Lafayette, Elizabeth Taylor, and Richard Burton.

Nestled on 12 acres in the Berkshire foothills, this charming 1750 white clapboard colonial—frequently called the most romantic inn on the East Coast—is surrounded by majestic maples and landscaped flower gardens. Alice Pitcher and Kemper Peacock have owned the inn since 1989.

A dining room (also open to non-guests) takes over the first floor beyond the bar. With its dark paneling, intimate seating, and the glow from candles in massive, etched hurricane globes, it is the perfect place for a romantic meal for two. The menu features such regional American favorites as hearty cheddar cheese soup, turkey hash with mustard sauce, and double-

cut lamb chops with tomato chutney. There are also dishes with a French twist, such as breast of duckling with roasted pears in a claret sauce, and escalopes of veal with sautéed apples and calvados. Beware of the mixed drinks! They're served in double portions.

If you enter the inn from the rear parking lot, you will find yourself on the second floor where a broad central foyer includes a cozy corner with a fireplace. Here, you will fully appreciate the allure of this elegant country-house inn. To the right is the parlor, a room with comfortable sofas and chairs and an antique desk. Beyond, the library is reminiscent of the drawing room in an English manor, featuring chintz fabrics and a fireplace. A shell curio cabinet that stands in the corner originally had a mate in the parlor, but it now can be seen in the American Wing of New York City's *Metropolitan Museum of Art.* Breakfast is served in the *Federal Room* (located opposite the parlor), lined with historical murals of the area, painted in the style of the Hudson River School by Edward Paine in 1942. The meal is continental style on weekdays; a full breakfast is served on weekends.

Equally elegant are the four antiques-filled guestrooms (which are on the inn's third floor), three of which have fireplaces. One of our favorites is the *Meeting Room,* with a barrel-vaulted ceiling. Before it became a bedroom, this space served as a ballroom and as the town meeting hall.

Concerts are held on Sundays, in summer, in the inn's pasture, and there is much of interest in the surrounding area, including several wineries (one in the very handsome adjacent town of Millbrook), golf, hiking on the Appalachian Trail, and a riverside craft village nearby.

OLD DROVERS INN Old Rte. 22, Dover Plains, NY 12522 (phone: 914-832-9311; fax: 914-832-6356). This historic inn in the Berkshire foothills has four guestrooms with private baths, double or queen-size beds, and air conditioning. The restaurant is wheelchair accessible. Closed the first two weeks of January. Rate for a double room Sundays through Thursdays (including continental breakfast, taxes, and gratuities): $150 to $250; weekends and holidays (including full breakfast, dinner, taxes, and gratuities): $325 to $425. Two-night minimum stay if Saturday included. Diners Club, MasterCard, and Visa accepted. Not appropriate for children under 15. Pets welcome for a $20 additional charge and with prior permission. Three Yorkshire terriers, Goodness Gracious, Gordon Bennett, and Jeepers Creepers, in residence. Smoking permitted. Alice Pitcher and Kemper Peacock, innkeepers.

DIRECTIONS: Travel north on I-684 to Brewster and then take Route 22 north another 23 miles, watching for the sign on the right to the *Old Drovers Inn.* Turn right at the sign and travel a half mile. The inn is on the right.

CENTENNIAL HOUSE

EAST HAMPTON, NEW YORK

When David Oxford and Harry Chancey Jr. bought this property in 1988, they found a board the builder had signed in 1876. The serendipity of the house's having been built in America's centennial year inspired the new inn's name.

The house sits on on a slight knoll, well back from the road on more than an acre of land at the entrance to tony East Hampton. It is a classic Hamptons beach cottage of gray shingles and white trim with a porch across the front. Guests especially enjoy the seclusion of the side and back gardens with their beds of roses, dahlias, and climbing clematis. The gardens, as well as the inn's pool, are the perfect places to spend a lazy summer afternoon. To obtain a svelte beach physique, a fitness center is located in the barn. From the inn it's an easy 10-minute walk to the beach in one direction and the village in the other.

Inside, the atmosphere is suffused with English country-home gentility. The parlor has polished pine floors topped with Oriental rugs, floral chintz–covered sofas, a concert grand piano, and a fireplace. Two Czechoslovakian crystal chandeliers illuminate original oil paintings. The walls of the dining room are covered in a green floral Schumacher fabric; floor-to-ceiling bookshelves dominate one corner. Breakfast, including juice, fruit, home-baked breads, and an entrée such as sourdough French toast or eggs, is served on gilt-edged china at a mahogany table lighted by an antique French brass chandelier.

The guestrooms are as elegant as the public rooms. The *Rose Room* has a canopy bed, Oriental rugs, and a claw-foot bathtub in a curtained alcove. The *Bay Room* has a carved four-poster bed, wide-plank pine floors, and an English church pulpit that now contains a sink. The green-and-burgundy *Lincoln Room* has an ornate Victorian walnut bed, similar to the one in which President Lincoln died, and an armoire; there's a marble sink with brass legs in the bathroom. Droll *Spy* prints decorate the guestroom walls throughout.

Nearby attractions include swimming, bicycling, hiking, bird watching, ice skating in winter, numerous local museums, art galleries, the *John Drew Theatre, Bay Street Theatre,* and shopping for antiques.

CENTENNIAL HOUSE 13 Woods La., East Hampton, NY 11937 (phone: 516-324-9414; fax: 516-324-0493). A country inn in the heart of the Hamptons, it has five guestrooms with private baths, double, queen-, or king-size beds, telephones, TV/VCR sets, and air conditioning. Open year-round. Rate for a double room (including full breakfast): $125 to $375. Two-night minimum stay on weekends April through June and in September and October; three nights in July and August. MasterCard and Visa accepted. Not appropriate for children under 13. No pets. Two small dogs, Louis and Edwinna, in residence. No smoking. David A. Oxford and Harry Chancey Jr., innkeepers; Bernadette Meade, manager.

DIRECTIONS: From New York City take I-495 (the Long Island Expressway) to Exit 70 (Manorville) and follow Route 111 south to Highway 27 (Sunrise Highway). Follow Highway 27 (which becomes the Montauk Highway) east for another 32 miles to East Hampton. The inn is on the right, just before the light at the intersection of Main Street and the Montauk Highway. (If you pass Town Pond, you have gone too far.)

MAIDSTONE ARMS

EAST HAMPTON, NEW YORK

Steeped in history and tradition, the *Maidstone Arms* has been the heart of East Hampton village for more than 150 years. It is still the place where the entire village assembles every December for the lighting of the *Christmas* tree and the singing of carols, warmed by hot cider and freshly baked cook-

ies, and where the first signs of spring emerge in clusters of yellow daffodils on the front lawn. This historic Main Street house (parts of the foundation date to 1740) received a new lease on life in 1992, when it was purchased and restored by architect Coke Anne Saunders. It is ably managed by Christophe Bergen.

Located across from Town Pond, where swans regally float by, this is a classic village inn of white clapboard, blue shutters, flower-filled window boxes, a canopied porch, and a Greek Revival doorway. Inside, one of the most popular spots is the clubby *Water Room,* warmed in winter by a wood stove. Deep green walls, plaid cushions on chairs, antique duck decoys, wicker creels, and small tables with gameboard tops set the stage for animated conversation.

The guestrooms are uniquely decorated in a crisp but elegant style. Room No. 14 features an iron bed and French doors leading to a private porch overlooking the Town Pond. A dazzling red "Barnyard Toile" print by Brunschwig & Fils drapes the windows and bedskirt. Behind the main house are three cottages, all with fireplaces, VCRs, stereo systems, and private patios. The *Duplex Cottage* has whimsical "bookcase" wallpaper climbing the stairs to a mahogany sleigh bed; the *Studio Cottage* has a cathedral ceiling and a four-poster bed.

There are two dining rooms (open to non-guests), each with its own atmosphere but offering the same menu. The front room, with wood floors, a paneled fireplace, sailboat models and prints, and a bar in one corner, is cozy and intimate. The other is refined, with plaid carpeting, a classical fireplace, and pale yellow walls decorated with antique blue and white Staffordshire plates. In both, the food prepared by Chef William Valentine is exceptional. His contemporary American fare includes such offerings as marinated smoked salmon and East Hampton crab cake with rémoulade sauce and Colorado rack of lamb with ratatouille. Desserts include chocolate flourless cake with bananas Foster ice cream. The menu is complemented by an award-winning wine list that features more than 450 selections including a broad range of local wines.

The area offers many recreational activities, including swimming, beachcombing, golf, tennis, bicycling, hiking, and ice skating in winter. Cultural facilities include the *John Drew Theatre, Bay Street Theatre,* art galleries, boutiques, museums, and winery tours.

MAIDSTONE ARMS 207 Main St., East Hampton, NY 11937 (phone: 516-324-5006; fax: 516-324-5037). This village inn has 16 guestrooms and three cottages with private baths, twin, double, queen-, or king-size beds, telephones, TV sets, and air conditioning. Wheelchair accessible. Open year-round. Rate for a double room (including continental breakfast): $165 to $325. Two-night minimum stay on weekends; three nights on summer weekends. Major credit cards accepted. Children welcome. No pets. No smoking. Coke Anne Saunders, innkeeper; Christophe Bergen, managing director.

DIRECTIONS: Follow the directions to *Centennial House* (above) as far as East Hampton. At the entrance to the village is a traffic light, and Route 27 bears sharply left. Follow Route 27 for about 200 yards. The inn is on the left.

BIRD AND BOTTLE INN

GARRISON, NEW YORK

The history of this inn stretches back to 1761, when it opened as *Warren's Tavern,* a popular watering station on the New York–to–Albany stage route. Historians believe it was the site of the September 1780 meeting at which treacherous *West Point* commander Benedict Arnold agreed to reveal the secrets of *West Point's* fortifications to British spy Major John André for a handsome sum.

The white clapboard building, with double porches and a steeply pitched roof, welcomed travelers with food and drink until 1832, when steamboats on the Hudson River eclipsed the stagecoach business. For many years after, the property was the centerpiece of a prosperous farm owned by the Nelson family, who added a sawmill and gristmill (some of which still remains) and dubbed the site Nelson Corners. The old tavern was fully restored to its 18th-century ambience in 1940, when it reopened as the *Bird and Bottle Inn.* Ira Boyar has been the owner since 1982, now ably assisted by his daughter Jodi.

The inn is located on eight serene acres that include manicured lawns, magnificent maple, oak, and birch trees, pristine flower beds, and a babbling brook crossed by a romantic bridge, the site of many weddings. The main floor of the inn retains its colonial atmosphere with the smell of wood fires smoldering in the fireplaces; the play of candlelight across the low-beamed ceilings and paneled walls; the slanted wide-plank pine floors; and the wavy-paned windows. The *Drinking Room*, the inn's cozy bar, is a snug retreat with another fireplace.

There are four guestrooms, three upstairs in the original tavern and one in a cottage nearby. All boast colonial-style antiques, paneled walls, and fireplaces. The *Beverly Robinson Suite* has a canopy bed swagged in peach-and-beige damask, Oriental rugs, original oil paintings, and a deck. *Nelson Cottage*, decorated in shades of pink and cream with blue accents, has a carved four-poster.

The inn's noteworthy restaurant is dispersed among three rooms on the main floor, where dinner (also open to non-guests) is a four-course event. It may start with the inn's justifiably famous gorgonzola-and-mascarpone fritters with honey mustard sauce, followed by a salad, and such entrées as baked Norwegian salmon in a potato crust or roast pheasant (for two) served with pâté and a truffle sauce. For dessert, the choices may include chocolate ganache tart—a bitter chocolate and cream confection with a macadamia-nut crust and caramel sauce—or a sugar cone filled with fresh berries and served with *crème anglaise.* The outstanding wine list includes excellent local wines as well as rare vintages, and is remarkably well priced.

Golf, horseback riding, hiking in the adjacent *Fahnestock State Park*, and antiquing are popular pastimes, as are visits to *West Point,* Cold Spring, *Boscobel Restoration, Van Cortlandt Manor, Kykuit, Sunnyside, Lyndhurst,* and *Hyde Park.*

BIRD AND BOTTLE INN Nelson Corners, Rte. 9, Old Albany Post Rd., Box 129, Garrison, NY 10524 (phone: 914-424-3000; fax: 914-424-3283). This inn in the Hudson River Valley offers three guestrooms and one cottage with private baths, double or queen-size beds, and air conditioning. Open year-round; dining room closed Mondays and Tuesdays. Rate for a double room (including full breakfast and a $75 credit per couple toward dinner) Wednesdays through Sundays: $210 to $240; rate for a double room (with full breakfast) Mondays and Tuesdays: $135 to $165. Two-night minimum stay on weekends. Major credit cards accepted. **Not appropriate for children under 12. No pets. No smoking except in** *Drinking Room.* **Ira Boyar, innkeeper.**

DIRECTIONS: From New York City take the George Washington Bridge to New Jersey. Take the first exit off the bridge for the Palisades Parkway north. Continue on the Palisades Parkway to the exit for the Bear Mountain Bridge. Cross the Hudson River via the Bear Mountain Bridge. At the end of the bridge turn left onto Route 9D north. Continue for 4½ miles to Route 403 and turn right. Traveling east on Route 403, continue for 1 mile. Turn left on Route 9 and travel north for 4 miles to the inn.

ROSE INN

Ithaca, New York

The story of the completion of this inn is fairly incredible. Millwright Abram Osmun built the house between 1848 and 1851; it features heavy timbers, hand-carved doors of chestnut and butternut, and parquet floors of quarter-sawn oak. The centerpiece was to be a circular staircase of Honduras mahogany, but none of the craftsmen working on the original project was capable of executing the delicate design. Hundreds of feet of the priceless wood were put in storage—and remained there for more than 70 years. Then, in 1922, an itinerant tinker came to Ithaca looking for employment. Hearing of the unfinished staircase, he drove up to the house in his battered truck and went to work. Over the next two years he erected a magnificent circular staircase that extended from the main hall up through two stories to a cupola on the roof. The rail, constructed in a flowing triple curve, was so exquisitely fashioned that it seemed to be made of one solid piece of wood. When the job was done, the man left as mysteriously as he had arrived, leaving behind a legend and a lasting legacy.

Today, guests of the *Rose Inn* are treated not only to its lovely architecture but to the thoughtfulness of its owners, Sherry and Charles Rosemann. Friendly but thoroughly professional, Charles is a career hotelier with experience in Germany and the United States. Before opening the inn, Sherry was an interior designer, and her skill can be seen in the inspired decor and faithful re-creation of the period rooms. High ceilings, marble fireplaces, and antiques provide an elegant yet comfortable atmosphere in the guest and common rooms. Several suites have Jacuzzis.

The 17½-acre grounds include patios, a fish pond, a rose garden, abundant perennial flower beds, a vegetable garden, a huge raspberry patch, and a variety of fruit trees. An 1850s carriage house now contains a spectacular conference room.

A full breakfast is served to guests, including juice, a crystal bowl of fresh fruit and berries, and one of Charles's breakfast entrées. A particular favorite is the puffy apple pancake served with homemade apple butter or fresh raspberry sauce. Be sure to sample the fresh apple cider from the orchards and the variety of jams, all made from fruit grown on the property; they also are sold in the gift shop.

A prix fixe dinner is served in the inn's four dining rooms Tuesdays through Saturdays; guests are asked to select their entrées when they make their reservations. Choices might be chateaubriand with béarnaise sauce, rack of lamb, grilled salmon, or honey-almond duck.

Several lakes in the area are ideal for boating or swimming; guests also can visit the nearby *Corning Glass Museum*.

ROSE INN Rte. 34 N., Box 6576, Ithaca, NY 14851-6576 (phone: 607-533-7905; fax: 607-533-7908). A luxurious inn near *Cornell University,* it has 10 guestrooms and five suites with private baths, twin, double, queen-, or king-size beds, telephones, and air conditioning. Open year-round; dining room closed Sundays and Mondays. Rate for a double room (including full breakfast): $100 to $160; rate for suites (including full breakfast): $175 to $275. Two-night minimum stay, if Saturday included, *Easter* through *Thanksgiving*. MasterCard and Visa accepted. Not appropriate for children under 10. No pets. One dog, Brandi, in residence. No smoking. Sherry and Charles Rosemann, innkeepers; Patricia Cain, manager.

DIRECTIONS: The inn is 10 miles north of Ithaca. From the New York State Thruway take Exit 40 to Route 34 south and continue for approximately 39 miles. The inn is on the left before entering Ithaca. From Ithaca, head north on Route 34 and travel 6 miles to the intersection with a red flashing light. Turn right and continue for a half mile. At the fork in the road go left (onto Route 34, not Route 34B). The inn is 3½ miles farther on the right.

LAKE PLACID LODGE

Lake Placid, New York

As you awaken at *Lake Placid Lodge* to the lonesome cry of a loon and the smell of fresh pine in the air, you'll find it easy to understand why early industrialists were attracted to the haunting majesty and beauty of the Adirondack Mountains. Few places on earth can match the pristine clarity of the 2,300 lakes, the pounding water of the 31,500 miles of rivers and streams, or the grandeur of the 46 mountains in the 6½ -million-acre wilderness known as *Adirondack State Park.*

This lodge, overlooking Lake Placid and facing Whiteface Mountain, is the perfect place to enjoy the mountain scenery without sacrificing anything in the way of creature comforts. Composed of 22 rooms, suites, and cottages in six buildings built of rough-hewn cedar and spruce, the lodge has twig-framed porches offering glorious lake and mountain views. Inside, the decor continues the rustic Adirondack theme, but with more than just a touch of elegance and sophistication. Rooms with bark or bead-board paneled walls are furnished with overstuffed chairs covered in bright plaids and paisleys, painted wooden dressers, and coffee tables made of bark-covered logs. Most guestrooms have massive stone fireplaces with log mantels; the charming *St. Regis, Hawkeye,* and *Cascade Suites* each offer two fireplaces and two baths.

Every guest need has been anticipated. In every guestroom there are featherbeds and down pillows, monkeywood bowls of fragrant pine cones, and clever, fat pincushions made of bark and containing buttons, needles, pins, snaps, and spools of thread attached with hat pins.

Breakfast, lunch, and dinner are served in the dining room (also open to non-guests), which has an outside porch overlooking the lake, and the fare is equal in sophistication to the decor: A *confit* of roasted Muscovy duck is served with green lentils; poached salmon filet is served over stir-fried green vegetables with ginger and lime; and the dessert menu, which changes frequently, might include a summer pudding with raspberries or a classic lemon tart with *crème anglaise.* The extensive wine list is supplemented by brandies, ports, and liqueurs, which may be enjoyed in the cozy bar, the *Moose Room* (a lounge with a moose head over the fireplace), or in the guestrooms.

Among the multitude of facilities on the premises, guests enjoy an 18-hole championship golf course; four tennis courts; hiking trails; a sandy beach for lakeside swimming; a marina with canoes, fishing boats, paddleboats, and Sunfish; an open-decked sightseeing barge that offers a lake cruise every morning and a cocktail cruise every evening at sunset; mountain bicycles; and a ski-touring center. Downhill skiing, ice skating, and hunting are available nearby.

LAKE PLACID LODGE One Whiteface Inn Rd., Lake Placid, New York 12946 (phone: 518-523-2700; fax: 518-523-1124). This romantic 22-guestroom Adirondack Mountain retreat on the shores of Lake Placid offers private baths, twin, double, queen-, or king-sized beds, and telephones; 17 have fireplaces. Open year-round; dining room closed Tuesdays from *Labor Day* through *Memorial Day.* Rate for a double room (including full breakfast): $175 to $450. Two-night minimum stay on weekends; three nights on holidays. Major credit cards accepted. Children welcome. Pets permitted in two units at $50 per day. No smoking permitted indoors. Christie and David Garrett, owners; Kathryn Kincannon, managing director.

DIRECTIONS From I-87 take Exit 30 and travel northwest on Route 73 for 30 miles to Lake Placid. In the village take Route 86 for 1½ miles toward Saranac Lake. At the top of the hill, turn right onto Whiteface Inn Road. Follow the road for 1½ miles and turn right at the *Lake Placid Lodge* sign. Proceed through the golf course to the lodge.

BED & BREAKFAST ON THE PARK

NEW YORK CITY (BROOKLYN), NEW YORK

Prospect Park is one of the glories of New York City. Designed between 1866 and 1874 by Frederick Law Olmsted and Calvert Vaux (who also collaborated on *Central Park*), it contains 526 acres of lakes, meadows, statues, paths, quaint buildings, roads, and gardens. By the 1880s, sumptuous mansions had been built on the neighboring streets, and the area soon acquired such cachet that it was known as New York's Gold Coast.

Bed & Breakfast on the Park is in one of those mansions. A wide, gray limestone townhouse with tall windows and a traditional stoop, it was built in 1892 by George Brickelmeier, a liquor merchant. It was restored to a Victorian confection by innkeeper Liana Paolella (a former antiques dealer and real estate agent) and her daughter Jonna in 1985.

Oil paintings line the walls of the parlor-floor rooms and continue above the oak-banistered stairway. The front parlor, where guests are greeted today much as they were a hundred years ago, boasts exquisite African mahogany woodwork, a massive oil painting by Liana's step-father, William Earl Singer, tall windows softened with frothy lace curtains, and a Pairpoint lamp (whose blown glass is reverse-painted with poppies) on an antique table in the center of the room. An elegant powder room is hidden behind the foyer's carved oak walls. There's a second parlor with fringed sofas and chairs and elaborate, bead-fringed lamps, plus a dramatic, paneled dining room with Victorian fretwork, stained glass bay windows overlooking the back garden, and china cabinets filled with silver and china.

The guestrooms are also authentic Victorian re-creations. All but two have elaborate mantelpieces (over nonworking fireplaces). The *Park Suite,* overlooking *Prospect Park,* has an antique lace crown canopy and bedspread and a stunning stained glass window. A paneled dressing area with bird's-eye maple closets and mirrored doors includes a built-in vanity. The *Lady Liberty* room has a canopy bed, handsome marble-topped Victorian dressers, and a stairway to the stars—literally: French doors lead to a deck, where another staircase rises to the roof which has sensational views of New York's skyline, stretching from the Empire State Building, past the World Trade Center, to Lady Liberty herself.

Breakfast is served on gold-rimmed china with the finest Victorian silver and cut crystal. The meal includes fresh fruit, homemade breads, and such entrées as baked French toast with pecans and currants in a caramel sauce and sweet-potato frittata. The resident parakeet, Nonni-Nonni, entertains breakfasters.

Nearby attractions include the *Brooklyn Museum,* the *Brooklyn Botanic Garden,* the *Brooklyn Public Library*, and the *Brooklyn Academy of Music,* where dance performances, theater, and concerts are held. Other possibilities include riding the magnificent restored Victorian carousel in *Prospect Park,* bicycling, and antiquing in the numerous shops nearby. Manhattan is 15 minutes away by subway.

BED & BREAKFAST ON THE PARK 113 Prospect Park W., Brooklyn, NY 11215 (phone: 718-499-6115; fax: 718-499-1385). This Victorian townhouse has seven guestrooms (five with private baths) with twin, double, or king-size beds, TV sets, and air conditioning. Open year-round. Rate for a double room (including full breakfast): $100 to $250. Two-night minimum stay on weekends; three nights on holiday weekends. MasterCard and Visa accepted. Children welcome in two rooms. No pets. Shiva, a German shepherd, and Nonni-Nonni, a parakeet, in residence. No smoking permitted indoors. Liana Paolella and Jonna Paolella, innkeepers.

DIRECTIONS: Driving from Manhattan, take the Brooklyn Bridge to Brooklyn. After crossing the bridge continue straight ahead to Atlantic Avenue and take a left. Turn right at the intersection with Fourth Avenue. Continue for 1 mile, then turn left onto Fifth Street. At the end of the street, turn right onto Prospect Park West. Continue two blocks to the inn, which will be on the right.

INN AT IRVING PLACE

New York City (Manhattan), New York

Amid the hustle and bustle of Manhattan, *Gramercy Park* is a living reminder of old New York. The tree-lined streets retain many 19th-century brownstones and brick townhouses, and the park itself, sedately secluded behind its tall wrought-iron fence, offers flower-lined pathways and tree-shaded iron benches only to those fortunate enough to have a key. It's easy to imagine Elsie de Wolfe or Edith Wharton, former residents of the area, sitting here in the cool quiet with a book.

The *Inn at Irving Place* occupies two historic side-by-side townhouses and faces Irving Place, the primary commercial street in this genteel little neighborhood. It shares the street with a variety of fine restaurants, antiques shops, and boutiques.

Don't expect to see an identifying sign on the inn, as there is none. Just walk up the stairs and enter through the door, where you will be greeted by innkeeper John Simoudis, or one of his assistants. Perhaps you'll sit on

an antique sofa by a toasty fire and have a cup of tea before going to your room. You've left the rapid pace of 20th-century New York outside.

The guestrooms are spacious and elegant without being stuffy. Each has a fine antique bed, either in iron, brass, or carved walnut. There are elegant armoires, inlaid chests, Oriental and needlepoint rugs on hardwood floors, and oil paintings on creamy-white or pastel walls. The private baths have black-and-white tile floors, pedestal sinks, and all sorts of posh accoutrements.

Afternoon tea, evening drinks, and continental breakfast are served in *Lady Mendl's Tearoom,* which occupies one of the inn parlors. Reminiscent of a French *salon de thé,* the tiny boîte is furnished with Victorian cast-iron tables, colorful chairs, and wooden slat shutters covering the windows.

A fine restaurant, *Verbena* (under separate management), is located on the ground floor. Its entrance is so removed from that of the inn that few people realize it's in the same building. The decor is chic and simple with a fireplace in each of its two dining rooms and a spacious garden divided by planters of flowers, vegetables, and herbs. This is chef Diane Forley's domain. Her sophisticated menu features traditional American dishes prepared in unusual ways. Scottish red venison, for example, is served with with sweet potato compote, chestnuts, and huckleberries; seared sea scallops are accompanied by cauliflower soufflé and saffron-scented oyster stew. Desserts are equally spectacular; twin profiteroles are filled with black mission fig sorbet and pistachio ice cream.

Gramercy Park is within walking distance of Greenwich Village and SoHo, and midway between midtown and downtown. The *Theodore Roosevelt Birthplace,* the *Pierpont Morgan Library,* and the *Public Theater* are all nearby.

INN AT IRVING PLACE 56 Irving Pl., New York, NY 10003 (phone: 212-533-4600; 800-685-1447; fax: 212-533-4011). An urban bed and breakfast with 12 guestrooms with private baths, twin or queen-size beds, telephones, TV/VCR sets, air conditioning, stereos, mini-refrigerators, CD players, and fireplaces. Open year-round. Rate for a double room (including continental breakfast): $250 to $325. Major credit cards accepted. Not appropriate for children under 13. No pets. Smoking allowed; some rooms designated non-smoking. John Simoudis, innkeeper; Judy Darling and Stuart Lyons, managers.

DIRECTIONS: Irving Place is an extension of Lexington Avenue, separated from it by *Gramercy Park*. The inn is between East 17th and East 18th Streets.

INN NEW YORK CITY

NEW YORK CITY (MANHATTAN), NEW YORK

In 1989, Ruth Mensch and her daughter Elyn found themselves with a townhouse on Manhattan's residential Upper West Side, spare cash from selling their popular restaurant *Ruelles,* and no real plans for the future. They decided to turn to innkeeping—and succeeded beyond their wildest dreams, creating a homey place in the heart of the Big Apple where guests can snuggle in for weeks at a time (and many do just that).

A quintessential New York atmosphere pervades this four-story brownstone with ornate balustrades and a wrought-iron front door flanked by sandstone pillars. In the charming vestibule and front parlor are high ceilings, elaborate moldings, carved fireplaces, fine cabinetwork, inlaid hardwood floors, and crystal chandeliers.

Each suite is decorated with individual flair and each has a small kitchen. The *Parlor Suite,* for example, boasts 12-foot carved ceilings, an 18-foot living/dining room with a Baldwin piano, and an entryway with a spectacular stained glass ceiling. Its bedroom has a balcony, a fireplace, and a queen-size bed in which the headboard is outfitted with stained-glass cabinets; the bath features a pedestal sink and a Jacuzzi. The *Spa Suite,* which takes up an entire floor, is highlighted by a king-size bed with a headboard set into antique chestnut armoires. The pièce de résistance, however, is the spa-like bathroom, with a double Jacuzzi set on a platform, a fireplace with a carved mantel, an old barber's chair, a cast-iron foot bath, a Victorian dresser with a sink, a sauna for two, and a shower enclosed in glass blocks. All four suites feature such personal touches as private libraries, fresh flowers, and fluffy robes.

In the evening, the kitchens are stocked with fresh-baked muffins and scones, cereal, fruit, juice, coffee, and tea, giving guests the option of preparing it the next morning according to their own schedule.

The inn is convenient to many of Manhattan's prime attractions, including *Lincoln Center,* the *American Museum of Natural History,* the *New York Historical Society, Central Park,* and *Riverside Park,* as well as numerous restaurants and fine shopping.

INN NEW YORK CITY 266 W. 71st St., New York, NY 10023 (phone: 212-580-1900; fax: 212-580-4437). This brownstone has four suites with private baths, queen- or king-size beds, telephones, TV sets, kitchens, and air conditioning. Open year-round. Rate for a double room (including continental breakfast): $195 to $295. Two-night minimum stay; $35 additional charge for one-night stay except in the *Spa Suite* which has a one-night additional charge of $100. Major credit cards accepted. Not appropriate for children under 12. No pets. No smoking. Elyn Mensch and Ruth Mensch, innkeepers.

DIRECTIONS: The inn is located on the south side of West 71st Street, between Broadway and West End Avenue.

OLD CHATHAM SHEEPHERDING COMPANY INN

OLD CHATHAM, NEW YORK

If you treasure bucolic pleasures, if you long for freedom from the noise of airplanes and automobiles, if you remember fondly childhood days of walking barefoot through the grass, then head for this 500-acre farm nestled between the Berkshire Mountains and the Hudson River. Old Chatham is a sleepy little village just south of the New York State Thruway in Columbia County.

In 1993, Nancy and Tom Clark were interested in purchasing enough land to support a commercial sheep dairy. They found it, and as a bonus, the property included a stately manor house, picturesque outbuildings, and a museum with one of the most extensive collections of Shaker furnishings in the world. The Shakers established their first colony near here and the remarkable assemblage of artifacts in the museum was gathered over a 30-year period by John S. Williams, Sr., who also built the museum to house them. The Clarks purchased their farm from Mr. Williams's family.

The manor house is now the heart of this fine country inn. Guests enter a center hallway with polished wide-plank pine floors. There's a guestroom on the right and the office on the left. Straight ahead is the formal living room, which has a fireplace, elegant but comfortable sofas and chairs, bookcases filled with interesting books, and a game table set with a jigsaw puzzle. The mood is elegant but informal, much like an English country house. Beyond, there's a screened-in stone terrace, which provides the perfect spot to relax while gazing at the sunken garden and the sheep meadow beyond.

The guestrooms have polished English furniture and floral chintz fabrics. Nancy is an interior designer and an artist; she's decorated the inn with style and wit and her radiant watercolors are focal points in several rooms. There are fine antiques in all the rooms and each has a four-poster or canopy bed. *Suffolk* has a marvelous carved four-poster and a fireplace with a painted mantel. The baths are bright and spacious with hexagonal tile floors, old-fashioned pedestal sinks, and wainscoted walls; many have both a tub and a shower. Shaker baskets, towel racks, and boxes hold amenities. Two suites, located in a nearby cottage, are especially appealing. The *Cotswold Suite* has a fireplace, four-poster bed, private porch, and a loft, and the *Hampshire Suite* includes a whirlpool tub.

The dining room is exceptional in cuisine and decor. Tables are spread among three rooms and there are fireplaces and views across the fields. One of the rooms has a hunt scene mural. Whenever possible Chef Melissa Kelly (who is also co-manager of the inn), assisted by a pastry chef, incorporates sheep's milk, yogurt, and cheese into the dishes. One signature appetizer is grilled fresh sheep's cheese wrapped in grape leaves. Entrées may include pan-roasted striped bass with leeks, fennel, and baby spinach or rack of lamb with a fricassee of forest mushrooms, asparagus, and fava beans. The house-made creamy and light ice cream, accompanied by *tarte tatin,* is the ideal finale. Dinner and Sunday brunch are open to non-guests.

The inn organizes numerous guest activities on the premises. Everyone is encouraged to watch the twice-daily milking operation. In addition, there's sheep shearing in season, sleigh rides and cross-country ski trails in winter, nature trails to roam, and fishing in the Kinderhook Creek, which runs through the property. Lectures, teas, and theme dinners, such as those incorporating tastings of local wines, are held throughout the year. There's a freshwater pond for swimming, mountain bikes for riding, and a croquet course on the lawn. Tennis, horseback riding, and golf are nearby. The *MacHaydn Theater* in Chatham offers excellent summer musicals and *Tanglewood* is not far away.

OLD CHATHAM SHEEPHERDING COMPANY INN 99 Shaker Museum Rd., Old Chatham, NY 12136 (phone: 518-794-9774; fax: 518-794-9779). **This elegant country manor house on a 500-acre sheep farm has eight rooms with private baths, twin or queen-size beds, and air conditioning. Wheelchair accessible. Open year-round. Rate for a double room (including full breakfast except on Sundays): $150 to $325. Two-night minimum June through October; three nights on selected holiday weekends. Major credit cards accepted. Children welcome. No pets. No smoking. Nancy and Tom Clark, proprietors; George H. Shattuck III, innkeeper.**

DIRECTIONS: From I-90 take Exit B2 onto the Taconic Parkway south. Immediately after the toll booth, exit and go left at the end of the exit ramp; follow the signs to Route 295. Turn left onto Route 295 east and drive 1 mile into East Chatham. Turn left at the sign for Old Chatham onto the Albany Turnpike and go for approximately 3 miles into Old Chatham. In the village center, take a left onto Route 13 and continue for 1 mile to Shaker Museum Road. Bear right and follow this road for ½ mile to the inn, which will be on the left.

OLIVER LOUD'S INN

PITTSFORD, NEW YORK

In 1979, Vivienne Tellier acquired and extensively refurbished *Richardson's Canal House,* the oldest surviving tavern on the Erie Canal, and opened it as a superb restaurant. Then, in 1985, she learned that *Oliver Loud's Tavern,* an old stagecoach inn in the nearby hamlet of Egypt, was scheduled for demolition. Tellier rescued the structure from the wrecker's ball, moved it to its present site near *Richardson's,* fully restored its 1812 appearance, and began taking in overnight guests.

When refurbishing the inn, Vivienne painstakingly re-created many of the original refinements, including the buttercup yellow exterior, Federal moldings, French and English wallpapers, and wallpaper borders. She also used Loud's own "recipe for making any wood look like mahogany" to fashion the hand-grained pseudo-mahogany doors. Guestrooms, several with views across the canal, are appointed with antique and Stickley reproduction furniture, including either four-poster or canopy beds.

The original inn's warm hospitality has been faithfully reproduced as well. On arrival, guests receive a basket filled with fresh fruit, bread sticks, homemade cookies, and a bottle of mineral water. Continental breakfast comes in another charmingly outfitted basket, complete with *The Wall Street Journal.* On balmy summer mornings, guests may enjoy the repast in rocking chairs on the porch, watching the canal waters.

Dinner awaits at *Richardson's Canal House,* a few steps away. Built in 1818, it retains virtually all of its architectural details (it is listed on the National Register of Historic Places). There are two-story porches in the front and rear, a cooking fireplace in the kitchen, and Federal trim in the public rooms, which are stenciled and painted in the original colors of ocher and green. Oil paintings of stern-faced gentlemen and ladies and other period artifacts appear in all 10 dining rooms. (The *Porter Room*—painted with whimsical scenes of marching soldiers and playful bears by Ruth Flowers in the style of famed muralist Rufus Porter—is particularly interesting.) The multi-course, prix fixe menu features American fare prepared in innovative ways; dishes include terrine of rabbit and pistachio nuts on wild-berry *coulis* and orange-and-rosemary-glazed pork tenderloin.

The towpath on the grounds is great for running, biking, walking, and even cross-country skiing in winter. Nearby attractions include the *International Museum of Photography* at *George Eastman House* in Rochester and the scenic Finger Lakes.

OLIVER LOUD'S INN 1474 Marsh Rd., Pittsford, New York, 14534 (phone: 716-248-5200, inn; 716-248-5000, restaurant; fax: 716-248-9970). A historic inn on the banks of the Erie Canal, it has eight guestrooms with private baths, double or king-size beds, telephones, TV sets (on request), and air conditioning. Wheelchair accessible. Open year-round; restaurant closed *Memorial Day, Independence Day, Labor Day, Christmas,* and Sundays except *Easter* and *Mother's Day.* Rate for a double room (including continental breakfast): $125 to $155. Major credit cards accepted. Not appropriate for children under 14. No pets. Smoking permitted in some rooms. Vivienne Tellier, innkeeper.

DIRECTIONS: The inn is 3½ miles from the New York State Thruway. Traveling west, take Exit 45 to I-490 west. Then take Exit 27 (Bushnell's Basin), turning right onto Route 96 and then right again at the Marsh Road traffic signal. Turn immediately right again into Richardson's Canal Village.

BELVEDERE MANSION

RHINEBECK, NEW YORK

From a lofty perch above Route 9 and with a distant view of the Hudson River, *Belvedere Mansion* grandly surveys the countryside. This sparkling white Greek Revival mansion with fluted Corinthian columns opened as a country inn in 1995.

Guests who arrive in the afternoon are likely to find fellow lodgers reading in the open-air gazebo by the pond, swimming in the distant pool, sampling cheese and wine on the large outdoor deck or, if the weather is cool, in the cozy lounge with its hammered copper bar, or walking about the 10-acre property. Inside are a charming foyer with sponge-painted aqua walls, interesting hand-painted panels surrounding the fireplaces in the main-floor dining rooms, and a splendid carved staircase leading to a little private dining room with murals of colorful birds on lacy branches.

Innkeepers Nick and Patricia Rebraca also own *Cartouche,* an antiques shop in Rhinebeck that specializes in French furniture. The five guestrooms in the mansion are filled with elaborate silk and damask fabrics and French furniture culled from the shop's collection of beds, armoires, chests, tables,

and paintings. *Livingston*, for example, has a pair of French painted twin beds, a matching armoire, and a pretty antique desk in a nook. Blue-brushed walls show off ornate damask drapes. *Roosevelt* has chocolate-colored walls and a canopy bed draped in ruby silk damask. The elegant baths are finished in marble and tile and have pedestal sinks and, in some cases, clawfoot tubs.

Eight additional rooms are located in the carriage house. The decor here is less formal, but has its own whimsical appeal. Several rooms are tiny (Patricia calls these "cozies") but all have private baths. There are lacy iron beds, painted headboards, painted chests and dressers, and the walls are embellished with painted flowers and garlands. Several of the larger rooms have sitting areas and all have appeal for those who want a bit more privacy.

Each of the three dining rooms has a wood-burning fireplace and a view of the lawns and the Hudson River in the distance. Two have forest green walls; the third has red lacquered walls. Parquet floors add a warm glow. Tables are elegantly set with antique china and silverware in a variety of patterns. Entrées include such dishes as pan-seared breast of Muscovy duck with wild berries and red cabbage *confit*, or seared monkfish medallions with ragout of Tuscan beans and mushrooms. For dessert, there's *crème brûlée* and chocolate truffle cake with *crème anglaise*.

In addition to a pond and a swimming pool, the inn has a fitness center. This section of the Hudson River Valley has a wide variety of activities. *Hyde Park,* the home of Franklin and Eleanor Roosevelt, is nearby, as are the *Mills Mansion, Vanderbilt Mansion,* and the *Rhinebeck Aerodrome.* The *Culinary Institute of America* is also a popular destination. The Southlands Foundation, across the street, offers horseback riding and lessons.

BELVEDERE MANSION 10 Old Rte. 9 (mailing address: PO Box 785), Rhinebeck, NY 12580 (phone: 914-889-8000; fax: 914-889-8811). A country inn located in a mansion overlooking the Hudson River, with 13 rooms with private baths and twin, double, queen-, or king-size beds; six have air conditioning, three have fireplaces. Open year-round. Rate for a double room (including full breakfast): $85 to $195. Two-night minimum on weekends; three nights on holiday weekends. Major credit cards accepted. Not appropriate for children under 10. No pets allowed in inn, but a kennel is located next door. Smoking allowed in lounge only. Nick and Patricia Rebraca, innkeepers.

DIRECTIONS: From New York City take the Henry Hudson Parkway north to the Saw Mill River Parkway, following that north to the Taconic Parkway. Continue north to Route 55 and travel west to Poughkeepsie. In Poughkeepsie, take Route 9 north. The inn is 5 miles north of Hyde Park and 3½ miles south of Rhinebeck.

THE POINT
SARANAC LAKE, NEW YORK

Between the Civil War and the Great Depression, wealthy families built retreats in the wild Adirondacks as blessed escapes from big-city life. Careful to intrude on nature no more than was absolutely necessary, they built camps from logs and stones, twigs, branches, and slate on vast tracts of forested land; often, these massive complexes encompassed entire lakes.

When William Avery Rockefeller (great-nephew of John D.) built *Camp Wonundra* in 1933, he captured the character of the Adirondack camps with architecture that was considered to be the finest of its genre. Located on a 10-acre peninsula that pierces Upper Saranac Lake, it consisted of a main house and eight outbuildings. Unlike many of his friends, Rockefeller intended to use the resort year-round, so it was equipped for winter as well. This complex was converted to an inn to provide housing for visitors to the 1980 *Winter Olympics* at nearby Lake Placid.

The property comprises 11 guestrooms distributed among four log cottages. The buildings commune so completely with nature that it often seems there are no walls, making it that much easier to appreciate a lovely mist shrouding the lake at dawn, deer grazing in a nearby meadow, or a red fox darting through the trees. The rooms contain massive stone fireplaces, sturdy antique furnishings, sofas upholstered in rustic wool checks, moose and deer heads on the walls, and Oriental rugs on the rich hardwood floors; bay windows overlook the lake and the Adirondack wilderness.

The atmosphere is casual and welcoming, as though you're staying with friends. The day begins with a thermos of fresh-brewed coffee delivered to each room, followed by a tray laden with fresh fruit, juice, and hot or cold cereal; a heartier breakfast of eggs or pancakes may be eaten in the *Great Hall*. Lunch, dinner, and drinks also are included in the daily rate. Executive

Chef Sam Mahoney is classically trained. (His experience included an apprenticeship to Albert Roux at London's *Le Gavroche*.) Meals are formal affairs (jacket and tie required; black tie suggested Wednesday and Saturday nights) featuring such French dishes as roast sea bass *antiboise* (served on a bed of julienned vegetables with a tomato-herb sauce), roast rack of lamb with ratatouille, and baby chicken on a corn fritter. Be sure to leave room for the sinfully rich desserts, like white and dark chocolate mousse.

As the morning fog lifts, guests may choose to take out a small outboard for some lake fishing or water-ski behind the inn's Mastercraft speedboat. Other activities include hiking, tennis, sunset cruises, swimming, volleyball, badminton, bicycling, cross-country skiing, and ice skating. There are several museums in the area.

THE POINT HCR 1, Box 65, Saranac Lake, NY 12983 (phone: 518-891-5674; 800-255-3530; fax: 518-891-1152). An Adirondack retreat on the shore of Saranac Lake, it has 11 guestrooms with private baths and twin, queen-, or king-size beds. Wheelchair accessible. Closed mid-March to mid-April. Rate for a double room (including breakfast, lunch, dinner, drinks, and all activities): $900 to $1,200. Two-night minimum stay on weekends; three nights on holidays. American Express accepted. Not appropriate for children under 18. Pets allowed by prior permission only. Christie and David Garrett, owners; Jacques and Pamela Berry, general managers.

DIRECTIONS: Take I-87 north to Exit 30. Follow Route 73 north for 34 miles to Upper Saranac Lake. Detailed directions are given when reservations are confirmed and deposit received.

Pennsylvania

GLENDORN

BRADFORD, PENNSYLVANIA

Approaching Bradford, Pennsylvania, situated about 90 miles east of Erie and 90 miles south of Buffalo, it's startling to see oil rigs. But in 1859, before oil was found in Texas or Oklahoma, the first commercially productive oil well in the world was drilled not far from here in Titusville. The Dorn family began their enterprising oil business in Bradford by developing a method for coaxing additional oil from abandoned wells. In 1929, they began work on a family compound where several generations of family members were to spend their summers for the next 65 years. Today, the property is a dignified and secluded country inn.

Family members enjoyed a refined lifestyle on their 1,280-acre estate. They employed the finest craftsmen and artisans of the day and purchased exceptional materials for their use. There is exquisite built-in cabinetry throughout the common rooms, guestrooms, and cabins, all in beautifully grained woods. Drawers glide open as if oiled and, inside, are indentions which were made to hold specific spoons or fishing lures. But the wonder of *Glendorn* is that the silverware and the lures are still in place. The overwhelming impression is that you have arrived at the Dorn family compound in the 1930s to spend a quiet interlude among friends. Managers Gene and Linda Spinner are experts at enhancing the fantasy.

The *Big House,* an all-redwood lodge, has a two-story stone fireplace (so big it uses four-foot logs) in the cathedral-ceilinged *Great Hall*, which is large enough to accommodate a spacious dining area as well. There's also a *Pine Room* filled with games, books, tables, and sofas; a massive game room with billiard and pool tables; and a screened-in porch with a stone floor and wicker furniture.

There are two suites and two guestrooms in the *Big House,* the grandest of which is the luxurious *Dorn Suite,* with fireplaces in the living room and bedroom; built-in cabinets of white oak including walls of bookshelves, drawers of silverware; a TV; and an old console radio that's still in perfect condition. On a built-in dresser, a pair of Art Nouveau silver candlesticks is inscribed, "Ruth Dorn from Forest D. Dorn, Glendorn, Christmas 1938." The tile-floored sun room, with window seats under casement leaded windows, offers one of the nicest places to sit with a good book. You can hear the rushing stream nearby and prop your head on a cross-stitched or needlepointed pillow.

Jill's Cabin is a sprawling one-bedroom cottage paneled in chestnut, with a large dressing room and a fireplace. The most unique (and splendidly secluded) cottage is called *The Hideout.* It's reached by driving up a steep, half-mile-long forested drive to a mountaintop. Built of brick and sandstone, with a slate roof, the cottage is paneled in chestnut inside. There's a cozy fireplace, a kitchen, and a bedroom with two three-quarter beds built into twin alcoves. The family used to come here for treetop barbecues and a bank of ovens and grills still lines the flagstone patio. A mechanical shooting gallery is perched on a hillside.

Dinner at *Glendorn* is convivial yet formal. The meal starts with cocktails and hors d'oeuvres, giving guests an opportunity to become acquainted. The set menu begins with an appetizer, followed by a salad. The entrée might be grilled lamb with red wine, roasted garlic, and rosemary sauce, or a pecan-crusted fresh trout. For dessert, turtle cheesecake is popular.

The array of possible activities is staggering. There's a mosaic-lined pool near the house; several streams and creeks, as well as three lakes, contain an abundance of fish; there's a skeet- and trap-shooting range (with a private cabin where lunch can be catered); three tennis courts; a gymnasium with basketball hoops and a full range of fitness equipment; an archery range; and miles of marked trails for hiking and cross-country skiing. *Glendorn* also offers an excellent executive retreat. The *Playhouse,* once the exclusive sanctuary of the Dorn children (they played and ate here, as they were not allowed at the adult dinner table), is now equipped with a full range of meeting amenities, including sophisticated audiovisual facilities.

GLENDORN 1032 W. Corydon St., Bradford, PA 16701 (phone: 814-362-6511; 800-843-8568; fax: 814-368-9923). The exclusive retreat has 11 suites and guestrooms with private baths, twin, queen-, or king-size beds, and telephones; nine rooms and suites have TV sets, mini-refrigerators, and fireplaces. Wheelchair accessible. Open April through February. Rate for a double room (including full breakfast, lunch, dinner, all beverages and activities): $295 to $895. Two-night minimum July through October and on holiday weekends, as well as year-round for some cabins. No credit cards accepted. Children welcome in several cabins.

No pets. Smoking allowed, except in *Pine Room*. Gene and Linda Spinner, managers.

DIRECTIONS: From I-90 exit onto Route 219 in DuBois. Go north on Route 219 to Bradford. In Bradford, take the Elm Street exit. Follow Elm Street to Corydon Street. Travel for 5 miles to the *Glendorn* gate, which is just after a bright red barn. The complex is 1½ miles farther on a private paved road.

INN AT TWIN LINDEN

CHURCHTOWN, PENNSYLVANIA

When you enter Churchtown, you may feel as if you've stepped into the 19th century. Cars share the road with horse-drawn carts driven by men and women in traditional Amish dress. But even though this is the heart of Amish and Mennonite country, which is characterized by simple living, the *Inn at Twin Linden* has a sophisticated ambience.

In the center of this little town, guarded by 100-foot linden trees, stands the three-story white clapboard house, which was built in the 1840s by a local forge owner as a home for his daughter and her new husband. By the time current owners Donna and Bob Leahy came across it in 1987, however, the house had degenerated into a rather seedy apartment building. The Leahys had a hard task ahead of them, and despite Bob's other life (he's a nationally recognized underwater photographer and teacher at *Temple University*), they completed the task in three years and opened the inn with six rooms and one suite. It's set on two acres of lush gardens, complete with winding pathways and benches tucked into secluded corners, three porches, a brick courtyard, and an outdoor Jacuzzi.

The living room is decorated with comfortable chairs and sofas, plenty of books, and a fireplace; complimentary sherry and brandy are here for the sipping. A wicker-filled porch is a pleasant place to sit on hot days. The decor in the guestrooms is 19th-century traditional—oak beds with hand-crocheted canopies, stenciled walls, antique furnishings, and fresh flowers—but the bathrooms are completely modern.

Guests awaken to the aroma of hot-from-the-oven croissant cinnamon buns and coffee made from freshly ground beans. The full breakfast includes Donna's creative entrées. (Her raspberry croissant French toast with sausage and her dill crêpes filled with smoked salmon and eggs have even been featured on the "Today" show.) Afternoon tea is served, and on Friday and Saturday nights Donna prepares sumptuous dinners (also open to non-guests by reservation) that take advantage of the abundant local produce. Rack of lamb is a menu staple, but crab cakes with almonds also are popular. Be sure to save room for the fresh pear-lemon mousse. The inn has no liquor license, but guests may bring their own wine.

Activities in the area include antiquing and shopping at country auctions and farmhouse crafts stores (handmade Amish quilts are a particularly good find).

INN AT TWIN LINDEN 2092 Main St. (Rte. 23), Churchtown, PA 17555 (phone: 717-445-7619; fax: 717-445-4656). This inn has seven guestrooms with private baths, twin, double, or queen-size beds, TV sets, and air conditioning. Closed January 2 through 31; dining room also closed for dinner Sundays through Thursdays. Rate for a double room (including full breakfast and afternoon tea): $100 to $210. Two-night minimum stay if Saturday included. Major credit cards accepted. Children welcome on weekdays; children 10 and above welcome weekends. No pets. No smoking. Bob and Donna Leahy, innkeepers.

DIRECTIONS: From the Pennsylvania Turnpike take Exit 22 (Morgantown) to Route 10 south. Turn west onto Route 23 and travel for 4 miles into Churchtown. Route 23 becomes Main Street; the inn is in the center of town on the left.

HIGHLAND FARMS

DOYLESTOWN, PENNSYLVANIA

At *Highland Farms,* the longtime home of lyricist Oscar Hammerstein, it's easy to understand the inspiration for such classics as *Oklahoma, Carousel, The Sound of Music,* and *The King and I.* Gazing in summer from a window across the nearby planted fields, you too will see "the corn is as high as an elephant's eye," and you'll understand when you awake in his former bedroom why Hammerstein rejoiced, "Oh, what a beautiful morning." (In his youth, composer/lyricist Stephen Sondheim gained inspiration here as well.)

Innkeeper Mary Schnitzer has faithfully maintained the graciousness of this building, which is listed on the National Register of Historic Places.

Upon entering the 1740 stone-and-stucco house, guests find themselves in a grand foyer with oak floors and a massive mirror. The living room features a pastel Savonnerie rug and a 1700s lime-wood cabinet Hammerstein's wife, Dorothy, had built into the room. The lovely garden room has curlicued wicker furniture cushioned with Italian tapestry; the breakfast-room table is draped with a white, hand-crocheted linen bedspread dating from the 1800s. A massive brass chandelier illuminates the majestic dining room, with its Chippendale-style table, plum walls, saddle tan and cream woodwork, and an Oriental rug on a deep-hued oak floor. Upstairs, the library has a coffee table made from a sled and the walls are covered with sheet music from the master's musicals; a videotape collection of the shows is available for guests to view on the VCR.

Each guestroom has been named for one of Hammerstein's musicals and features unique touches. *The King and I,* Oscar and Dorothy's bedroom, contains a hand-painted fireplace mantel and a bed with a frothy white canopy. In the *Carousel* room, with another canopy bed, a fanciful carousel "rug" has been painted on the floor and carousel horses prance across the walls of both the bedroom and bath. The *Oklahoma* room is furnished with antique oak furniture, including a bed draped with a canopy crocheted by Mary's grandmother. Hand-painted magnolias border the ceiling and embellish the corner cupboard. The *Show Boat* room is decorated with 18th-century mahogany furniture (and shares a bath with *Oklahoma*).

Mary goes to great lengths to ensure guests' comfort. Her four-course breakfasts are painstakingly planned, with such treats as grapefruit marinated in blackberry brandy, homemade granola, fresh-baked popovers, mushroom tarts with chive cream, and freshly brewed coffee. In the afternoon she prepares canapés or finger sandwiches to enjoy with wine, lemonade, or iced tea. At night, when guests return to their rooms, they find a silver tray bearing sherry or blackberry brandy and a personal note from their hostess.

The five-acre grounds contain a tennis court, a pear-shaped swimming pool and cabana, grazing sheep, and a grape arbor where Henry Fonda got married. A baby elephant's bath is left over from an owner prior to Hammerstein who had a circus. Flower gardens, terraces, and a wraparound porch complete the picture.

Area attractions include the *Moravian Tileworks, Mercer Museum, James A. Michener Art Museum,* and *Pearl Buck Home,* as well as golf, cross-country skiing, bicycling, art galleries, and antiques shops.

HIGHLAND FARMS 70 East Rd., Doylestown, PA 18901 (phone: 215-340-1354). A country estate, it has four guestrooms (two with private baths) with double or queen-size beds and air conditioning. Open year-round. Rate for a double room (including full breakfast, afternoon refreshments, sherry, and brandy): $125 to $175. Two-night minimum stay on weekends; three nights on holidays. MasterCard and Visa accepted. Not appropriate for children under 13. No pets. A dog, a cat, and sheep in residence. No smoking. Mary Schnitzer, innkeeper.

DIRECTIONS: From New York take the New Jersey Turnpike south to I-78 west. Take Exit 29 to I-287 south, then Exit 13 to Route 202 south. Follow Route 202 across the Delaware River about 10 miles to Doylestown. In Doylestown cross Route 313, then take the second left onto East Road. The inn is the fourth driveway on the right. From Philadelphia take I-95 north to Route 332 west (Newtown). Follow this road for about 3½ miles, then take Route 413 north for about 10½ miles. At this point take Route 202 south to Doylestown and follow the directions above.

ISAAC STOVER HOUSE

ERWINNA, PENNSYLVANIA

The stately brick Isaac Stover house, circa 1837, has a mansard roof, ornate pillared front verandah, and black shutters. In 1988 it was purchased by Sally Jessy Raphael and her husband Karl Soderlund, who filled it with a variety of offbeat furnishings. Some items came from their travels around the world, some from flea markets and garage sales.

In 1995, however, Sally and Karl decided to give the house a makeover. Out went the garage sale decor—in came high-quality antiques spiced with lush fabrics, elegant stenciling, and oil paintings. A stylish white-on-white decor is warmed by polished, random-width, yellow pine floors, a marble fireplace, and crystal chandeliers. In the double parlors, French fauteuils and love seats are covered in creamy damask; plants bask in the sunshine that streams through uncurtained windows. Afternoon wine and cheese are offered in a Victorian taproom, which has a piano and paneling of rich pecan wood. Beyond, there's a spectacular kitchen that has become a popular gathering place to watch innkeeper Vinny Howe prepare breakfast or afternoon refreshments.

Upstairs, the guestrooms are welcoming and inviting. The room named *Blue and Cream* features French toile wallpaper, moire drapes, and a gorgeous antique bedroom suite in dark wood embellished with painted flowers. *Amore* has blue-and-white pinstripe paper and terrific views of the Delaware River, and the *Garden Room* contains wicker furnishings and also has a view of the water.

Since Vinny loves to cook, the breakfasts are a treat. He'll fix hot-from-the-oven muffins and breads, omelettes and home fries or eggs Benedict, accompanied by fresh fruits and juices, granola, and yogurt. In nice weather breakfast is served on the large covered front porch or slate patio; when it's cool, it's served in the taproom.

The inn is located on 10 acres and there are fields to walk through, a hammock under the trees to lie in, or the Delaware River towpath to meander along. Other popular local activities include boating, tubing, or fishing in the river, hot-air ballooning, visits to wineries, and bicycling. Nearby New Hope has numerous antiques shops and interesting boutiques, as does Frenchtown, New Jersey, just across the river. *Bucks County Playhouse,* interesting museums and art galleries, and several nightclubs are also in New Hope.

ISAAC STOVER HOUSE 845 River Road (Route 32), Erwinna, PA 18920 (phone: 610-294-8044; fax: 610-294-8132). This historic Bucks County bed and breakfast establishment has seven guestrooms, four with private baths and three with semi-private baths, double or queen-size beds, and air conditioning. Open year-round. Rate for a double room (including full breakfast and afternoon wine and cheese): $150 to $175. MasterCard and Visa accepted. Not appropriate for children under 13. Pets by prior permission. Smoking allowed in common rooms only. Vinny Howe, innkeeper.

DIRECTIONS: From New York City, take the New Jersey Turnpike south to Exit 14 and then take I-78 west to Exit 15 (Clinton/Pittstown). Turn left at the end of the ramp onto Route 513 south and go for 11 miles to the New Jersey town of Frenchtown. Cross the Delaware River on the Frenchtown Bridge and turn left onto Route 32 south. Follow Route 32 for 2 miles. The inn is on the right.

GLASBERN

FOGELSVILLE, PENNSYLVANIA

Glasbern sits on a 100-acre plot in a suburban setting where the atmosphere straddles both country and city. Built as a farm more than 150 years ago, the inn combines the feel of rural living with the contemporary amenities modern travelers expect. The oldest part of the farm is the Pennsylvania German bank barn, built into the bank of the hillside, with a ceiling that rises 26 feet to hand-hewn beams punctuated by skylights. In this *Great Room* rough shale walls contrast with the smooth, clean lines of the plaster fireplace and chimney. The corn crib remains from the days when this was a working barn, as do the ladders that lead to where the hayloft used to be. One wall consists almost entirely of windows and gave the inn its name (*glasbern* is a Middle English word meaning "glass barn").

Purchased in 1985 by Beth and Al Granger, the inn offers numerous creature comforts. The guestrooms, distributed among the barn, the original farmhouse, the carriage house, the gatehouse, and the garden cottage, are all equipped with modern amenities, including VCRs for use with the extensive video library. Some contain whirlpools and fireplaces; many are duplex suites with skylights and views of the countryside. Green plants, patchwork quilts, and Oriental rugs create an elegant yet country-style ambience.

At breakfast, served in the *Great Room* and the *Granary* (a small adjoining room), guests may choose to eat family-style at a large mahogany table or at individual tables. The hearty entrées might include French toast made with raisin bread, ham-cheese-and-egg strudel, or "egg blossoms in a silo" (eggs and phyllo dough baked in a muffin tin).

In the evening, the *Great Room,* the *Granary,* and the *Harvest Room* (in a wing off the *Great Room*) serve as dining rooms (open to non-guests). The menu features herbs and vegetables organically grown on the farm. Pork tenderloin medallions, encrusted with sesame seeds, sautéed and served with a salsa of mixed berries and accented with ginger and Grand Marnier, is one example of the inventive fare. Sunday brunch (also open to non-guests) is served here as well.

Tucked into a fold of rolling meadows and woods, the spacious grounds invite outdoor activities. There are trails for nature walks in mild weather and cross-country skiing in winter, flower beds filled to overflowing, and a pool surrounded by a flagstone patio. If you like, take apples from the orchard to feed Megan and Charlie, the inn's horses. Not far away, golf, hot-air balloon rides, and rafting are available.

GLASBERN 2141 Pack House Rd., Fogelsville, PA 18051-9743 (phone: 610-285-4723; fax: 610-285-2862). This inn has 24 guestrooms with private baths, queen- or king-size beds, telephones, TV sets, and air conditioning. Wheelchair accessible. Open year-round. Rate for a double room (including full breakfast, but not Sunday brunch): $100 to $300. Two-night minimum stay if Saturday included. MasterCard and Visa accepted. Not appropriate for children under 10. No pets. Several farm animals and one dog on the premises. Smoking permitted; some rooms designated non-smoking. Beth and Al Granger, innkeepers.

DIRECTIONS: Traveling from New York on I-78 west, take Exit 14B north onto Highway 100, turning left at the first light onto Old Route 22. Turn right onto Church Street and continue about a half mile. Turn right onto Pack House Road; the inn is on the right $^8/_{10}$ of a mile down.

SWISS WOODS B & B

LITITZ, PENNSYLVANIA

You might well ask, what's a Swiss chalet doing in Pennsylvania Dutch country? This one reflects the heritage of its owners: Lancaster native Debrah Mosimann and her Swiss husband, Werner. The Mosimanns have

combined their talents and cultures to offer American hospitality in a Swiss-German environment.

The chalet looks modern, and in fact it is: The Mosimanns built it in 1984. Construction was a family project. In the common room, called *Anker Stube* after the Swiss artist, is a massive sandstone fireplace; the mantel was hand-hewn by Debrah's father. Natural pine and cypress furniture, comfortable Biedermeier camelback sofas, and a profusion of cascading ferns create an inviting atmosphere. The seven guestrooms are decorated in the spare style that is very popular in Switzerland, with pine-framed beds (two are canopied) and fluffy European goose-down comforters. All have private patios or balconies; two have Jacuzzis.

Debrah makes good use of her degree in home economics when she prepares the inn's sumptuous breakfasts. Her raisin-bread French toast stuffed with strawberry cream cheese has become a local legend; another tasty entrée is eggs Florentine.

The inn is located on 30 acres overlooking Speedwell Forge Lake. Take a stroll through the extensive gardens, nurtured by agriculturalist Werner. Canoes are available for guests to use on the lake, and an extensive network of hiking trails laces the property. The area is also popular for bird watching. *Hershey's Chocolate World*, the *Hand-Twisted Pretzel Factory*, and a farmers' market are nearby.

SWISS WOODS B & B 500 Blantz Rd., Lititz, PA 17543 (phone: 717-627-3358; 800-594-8018; fax: 717-627-3483). A chalet-style inn, it has seven guestrooms with private baths, twin, queen-, or king-size beds, and air conditioning. Closed several days at *Christmas*. Rate for a double room (including full breakfast): $90 to $140. Two-night minimum stay on weekends; three nights on holidays. Discover, MasterCard, and Visa accepted. Children welcome. No pets. Dogs, cats, and rabbits on property. No smoking. Werner and Debrah Mosimann, innkeepers.

DIRECTIONS: From Lancaster travel north on Route 501 through Lititz for 11 miles. Turn left on Brubaker Valley Road and travel 1 mile to the lake, then turn right onto Blantz Road. The inn is down the first lane on the left.

FAIRVILLE INN

Mendenhall, Pennsylvania

Ole and Patricia Retlev began their innkeeping careers in New England, but in 1986 they moved to the lovely Brandywine River Valley. This picturesque area of winding country roads, massive estates, and extraordinary museums has been preserved on canvas by three generations of Wyeths. For their new inn, the Retlevs chose an 1826 Federal-style home with a covered porch. The inn, which had been enlarged in the Victorian era, sits on 3½ acres between *Winterthur* and *Longwood Gardens*.

Painted in soft shades of cream and white, the main floor of the inn contains a spacious living room accented with a copper coffee table, where afternoon tea is served. To accompany the tea, Patti bakes a variety of Swedish butter cookies, a recognition of Ole's Swedish background. A light and airy breakfast room is also located on the first floor. Here Patti sets out a continental breakfast of fruit, juice, and freshly baked scones, muffins, and sticky buns. Fresh flowers seem to be everywhere. There are bouquets in the living room, a single rose adorns each breakfast table, and the guestrooms have vases of fresh flowers as well. Most come directly from the inn gardens. Upstairs there are five guestrooms with canopy and four-poster beds and stylish furnishings.

After completing work on the main house, Ole and Patti began tackling the barn and carriage house. These now provide an additional 10 rooms and suites, which are also furnished with canopy or four-poster beds, period reproduction furniture, and pretty chintz fabrics. Larger than the rooms in the main house, they feature beamed ceilings, barnwood walls, and spacious and elegant baths. Seven have fireplaces and six have private decks, balconies, or terraces with flowering plants, where butterflies and hummingbirds provide fascinating diversions. The carriage house overlooks gardens and a pond.

Although the inn doesn't have a restaurant, historic *Buckley's Tavern* is a five-minute drive away. Here, in an atmosphere true to the tavern's 1817 origins, when it served as a stagecoach stop, there's an overhanging porch, low beamed ceilings, and paneled walls. The menu ranges from burgers and pastas to chicken and steak.

The inn is close to Wilmington and to the many attractions of the Brandywine River Valley. *Winterthur Museum, Garden & Library,* the premier museum of American decorative arts assembled by Henry Francis du Pont, should not be missed. There are 175 period rooms and almost 1,000 acres of gardens to explore. *Longwood Gardens* has more than 1,000 acres of horticultural exhibits connected by pathways and bordered by fountains, and 20 indoor conservatories. The *Brandywine River Museum* displays Wyeth paintings and the *Hagley Museum,* on the original du Pont estate, is a recreation of the Eleutherian Mills. *Brandywine Battlefield Park,* site of one of the most important battles of the American Revolution, is also nearby.

FAIRVILLE INN 506 Kennett Pike (mailing address: PO Box 219), Mendenhall, PA 19357 (phone: 610-388-5900; fax: 610-388-5902). This rural bed and breakfast establishment has 15 rooms and suites with private baths, twin-, queen-, or king-size beds, telephones, TV sets, and air conditioning; seven have fireplaces, six have porches or terraces. Wheelchair accessible. Open year-round. Rate for a double room (including continental breakfast and afternoon tea): $125 to $190. Two-night minimum on weekends; three nights on holiday weekends. Major credit cards accepted. Not appropriate for children under 7. No pets. No smoking. Ole and Patricia Retlev, innkeepers.

DIRECTIONS: From I-95 in Wilmington, Delaware, take Exit 7 and follow Route 52 north through Greenville and Centerville, across the Delaware/Pennsylvania state line to the village of Fairville in Mendenhall. The inn is on the right.

MERCERSBURG INN

MERCERSBURG, PENNSYLVANIA

The colonial village of Mercersburg, located in the beautiful Cumberland Valley at the foot of the Tuscarora Mountains, has maintained its historic architecture and small-town character since its founding in 1750. Later, it became a frontier trading post. Although Main Street was paved long ago,

it still is lined with buildings made of limestone, brick, or logs, many of which date to the 18th century.

Built in 1909, this estate was the creation of local businessman Harry Byron and his wife, Ione, who spared no expense in the construction of their dream home. The impressive three-story Georgian brick mansion has six massive columns at the entrance. Large double porches at either end overlook six acres of lawns and gardens. Transformed into an inn in the 1950s, the property gradually became run-down and was eventually abandoned.

In 1986, Fran Wolfe, an artist with more than 18 years of experience renovating buildings, purchased the dilapidated mansion and began an extensive restoration. Today her son, Chuck Guy, owns the inn. The grand entrance hall features a parquet floor, a fanlight over the broad doors, and polished chestnut paneling. The house's most unusual features are twin curving staircases wending their way to the second floor between two rose-colored faux marble columns. Serpentine banisters and elaborate wrought-iron balustrades add to the dramatic impact. On the landing above, sunlight filters in through stained glass windows.

The public rooms are as elegant as the entrance. The grand hall has four sets of French doors leading to various rooms. One of the most luxurious settings is the bright, airy sunroom, featuring a wallpaper pattern also used at *Monticello,* Thomas Jefferson's home. White wicker furniture and floral cushions on the window seats provide a comfortable spot in which to enjoy an iced tea laced with mint. The large windows afford a lovely view of grassy lawns in summer and pristine snow in winter. In the formal dining room a fireplace glows in chilly weather. The downstairs gameroom has an antique pool table, board games, a TV set, and a VCR.

The 15 guestrooms are furnished with canopied four-poster beds, cherry antiques, and floral fabrics. Several have fireplaces or balconies with views of Mercersburg, the Cumberland Valley, and the mountains in the distance. Original oil paintings and photographs by local artists grace the walls.

A full breakfast, featuring such treats as walnut sticky buns and egg casseroles, is offered to inn guests. Dinner (open to the public) is served on weekends. Such tempting continental fare as rack of lamb with dried cherry sauce and chocolate pâté with raspberry sauce are among the choices.

Attractions in the region include the birthplace of President James Buchanan, *Gettysburg National Military Park*, *Antietam*, Harpers Ferry, golf, and skiing at *Whitetail Ski Resort*.

MERCERSBURG INN 405 S. Main St., Mercersburg, PA 17236 (phone: 717-328-5231; fax: 717-328-3403). This mansion has 15 guestrooms with private baths, double, queen-, or king-size beds, telephones, and air conditioning. Open year-round. Rate for a double room (including full breakfast): $115 to $200. Two-night minimum stay on weekends in October and during ski season. Discover, MasterCard, and Visa accepted. Not appropriate for children under 10. No pets. Maggie, a Labrador retriever, in residence. No smoking. Chuck Guy, owner; John Mohr and Sally Brick, innkeepers.

DIRECTIONS: Traveling on I-81, take Exit 3, then go west on Pennsylvania Route 16 to Mercersburg, where it becomes Main Street. The inn is on the left.

MANSION INN

NEW HOPE, PENNSYLVANIA

For many years the fanciful Victorian mansion on New Hope's main street has attracted both the admiration and the dismay of passersby. You could not fail to be impressed by the arched windows and entrance doors, the elaborate gingerbread fretwork, and the domed cupola, but neither could you disguise your concern about their deteriorated condition. Fortunately, in 1995 the building obtained a new lease on life.

Built in 1865 by Charles Crook in a style whimsically described as Baroque Victorian of the Second French Empire, the house was embellished with a virtual catalog of fancy wooden trim. Even the wrought-iron fence in front is far from ordinary: A tangle of grapevines marches across the front on either side of an arched gate filled with clusters of grapes and anchored with gateposts of squiggly vines. Even the shingles on the mansard roof had a variety of shapes.

For some 60 years, the house was the home and office of Dr. Kenneth Leiby, who delivered many of the area's babies here. When he decided to sell, there were various proposals for its new use. None pleased him more, however, than the offer by Keith David and Dr. Elio Bracco to convert his home into a bed and breakfast establishment. During the restoration, workers found that whenever Dr. Leiby had made structural changes to the house, he left the original doorways and hardware inside the walls, hoping that a future owner might return it to its original state, and that's exactly what the partners did.

Today, the house glows in a soft buttercup yellow and the trim is painted a sparkling white, accenting the fancy carpentry. Inside, in the parlor and drawing room, Oriental rugs lie atop polished pine floors, crystal chandeliers illuminate elaborate moldings, and antique tables and chests are enhanced by upholstered velvet sofas and floral linen chairs and drapes. Oil paintings hang above arched marble fireplaces and sparkling cranberry and etched green glass are attractively displayed.

The guestrooms are equally refined, with canopy, iron and brass, and four-poster beds. Plush pillows are piled on top of white matelassé spreads. Starched and ironed Portault linens dress the featherbeds. *Hampton Court* is decorated in shades of sage and rose and has a magnificent marble bath with a bay window and an antique chandelier. *Windsor* has a canopy bed, a two-person Jacuzzi, and a gas fireplace, as well as antique tables and lamps and pretty boudoir chairs upholstered in pink. All baths offer the ultimate in comfort and style. Guestroom amenities include a tray with a decanter of sherry and stemmed glasses; fresh-baked cookies are offered bedside at night; bathrooms contain bath salts and oils.

Breakfast, served in a sunny room with linen-clad tables and wicker chairs, includes juice, fresh fruit, and baked goodies displayed on a handsome antique Dutch chest with massive brass hinges. An entrée, such as an omelette or stuffed croissant toast with raspberry sauce, is served at individual tables.

Behind the house, a pretty garden contains a gazebo. A swimming pool is located in a separate enclosure beside the private parking lot—a much-appreciated amenity in New Hope, where crowds of tourists throng the streets in summer and parking is often at a premium. New Hope is located along the Delaware River, where the old towpath is a popular walking trail. Barge rides along the picturesque canal are offered in summer. The village also contains numerous antiques shops, fine boutiques, and excellent restaurants. The *Bucks County Playhouse* offers distinguished performances with celebrity guest stars from March through December. Other attractions include the *James A. Michener Art Museum,* the *Parry Mansion Museum,* the *Pearl S. Buck House,* the *Mercer Museum,* the *Moravian Pottery and Tile Works,* and *Washington Crossing Historic Park.*

MANSION INN 9 South Main St., New Hope, PA 18938 (phone: 215-862-1231; fax: 215-862-0277). This village bed and breakfast establishment has nine rooms with private baths, queen-size beds, telephones, and air conditioning; seven with TV sets, five with fireplaces, and three with Jacuzzis. Wheelchair accessible. Open year-round except *Christmas Day.* Rate for a double room (including full breakfast): $160 to $250. Two-night minimum on weekends; three nights on holiday weekends. Major credit cards accepted. Not appropriate for children under age 14. No pets. No smoking. Keith David and Dr. Elio Filippo Bracco, proprietors; Susan Tettemer, innkeeper; Kimberly Woehr, manager.

DIRECTIONS: From New York City, take the New Jersey Turnpike south to Exit 14 and then take I-78 west to Route 202 south. After the Delaware River Toll Bridge, exit immediately onto Route 32 south to New Hope. At the traffic light (Bridge Street/Route 179), turn right. The parking entrance is on the left about three car lengths from the light.

WHITEHALL INN

New Hope, Pennsylvania

This stately inn, in a white clapboard plantation house built in 1794, is a very classy establishment. The setting is as bucolic as anyone could want— 13 acres, complete with an old barn, grazing horses, a rose garden, and a swimming pool. And if that weren't enough, there are the thoughtful innkeepers, Mike and Suella Wass, who go to great lengths to ensure their guests' comfort. From the number of repeat visitors they get, it seems the Wasses are succeeding admirably.

The Wasses' pampering is evident in the many small luxuries in each guestroom: fresh roses in a cut-glass vase, bottled water and glasses on a silver tray, burgundy velour bathrobes, Crabtree & Evelyn toiletries and specially milled soaps in the bathroom, and the nightly turndown service (complete with chocolate-raspberry truffles). Each guestroom is named for a former owner of the house and decorated with priceless colonial antiques. The *Gerald McGimsey Room* features a canopy bed with an ivory spread; the *Albert Hibbs Room* has a fishnet canopy bed and a fireplace; the *Phineas Kelly Room* has an antique brass-and-iron bed and a fireplace.

The public rooms are filled with family treasures. In the living room portraits of Mike's ancestors hang over the mantel. The Shaker cradle in this room was purchased by the Wasses just before their daughter was born, and Suella's exquisite needlework hangs on the walls. Other family relics include the upright piano on which Suella learned to play as a child and a side table that was handmade by Mike's father.

Breakfast is a major event here. Beckoned by the heady aroma of fresh-brewed coffee, guests congregate in the breakfast room/art gallery, and the multi-course feast begins. Freshly blended juice and bread or muffins hot from the oven comprise the first course, followed by an inventive fruit dish (perhaps a baked nectarine stuffed with almonds and served on a pool of vanilla custard). An appetizer comes next—maybe chilled strawberry-orange-champagne soup. The entrée could be a vegetable tart or Suella's special crêpes with apples, tangerines, dates, almonds, and cream cheese. If you aren't already bursting, you can finish the meal with a sweet. Then there's the formal afternoon tea, which might include poppyseed-orange scones with clotted cream and strawberry jam, finger sandwiches, fresh cherries, and butter cookies crusted with cinnamon.

With all this sumptuous food, you may want to work off some calories by hiking, bicycling, or playing golf (there are plenty of facilities in the area). Other activities include visiting the nearby *James A. Michener Art Museum, Washington Crossing National Park, Pennsbury Manor,* and the region's many antiques shops.

WHITEHALL INN 1370 Pineville Rd., New Hope, PA 18938 (phone: 215-598-7945; 888-37-WHITE). Set in the countryside, this manor house has six guestrooms (four with private baths) with double or queen-size beds and air conditioning. Open year-round. Rate for a double room (including full breakfast and afternoon tea): $140 to $210. Two-night minimum stay on weekends; three nights on holiday weekends. Major credit cards accepted. Not appropriate for children under 14. No pets. No smoking. Mike and Suella Wass, innkeepers.

DIRECTIONS: From New York take the New Jersey Turnpike south to Exit 10, then take I-287 north to Exit 13. Follow Route 202 south to Lahaska. Turn left onto Street Road in Lahaska and continue to the second intersection (a short distance beyond the railroad tracks). Bear right onto Pineville Road. The inn is 1³/₁₀ miles farther along on the right.

BRIDGETON HOUSE ON THE DELAWARE

UPPER BLACK EDDY, PENNSYLVANIA

Take one run-down 1836 terra cotta apartment house overlooking the Delaware River, combine it with the creativity and entrepreneurial daring of an enthusiastic couple, and what do you get? In the case of *Bridgeton House on the Delaware,* a unique inn characterized by youthful energy and style, and a bold, innovative decor.

Innkeepers Bea and Charles Briggs, working with Bea's cousin, artist Cheryl Raywood, have blended comfort and practicality with whimsy and artistry. After purchasing the building in 1981, Charles, who is a master craftsman, added windows and French doors along the back walls, to bring more light into the rooms, and built balconies that overlook the river. Each guestroom is painted in bold colors and decorated with imagination and flair. In one suite, for example, red plaid pillows accent the king-size bed and the walls are painted half yellow, half black-and-white checkerboard, with a molding dividing the two. Other features include a corner fireplace and a screened porch. The walls of another guestroom are fuchsia and gold; the bath is stenciled. Another room has a cobalt blue ceiling painted with gold stars. Several baths boast polished mahogany cabinets hand-crafted by Charles, and eight of the rooms have balconies or porches. One favorite is the cozy *Garrett Room,* with pink sponge-painted walls embellished with squiggles, a half-canopy bed, and a romantic porch.

The penthouse suite, by contrast, is positively restrained. Spanning most of the top floor, it features white walls, a 12-foot cathedral ceiling, and a fireplace of black-and-white marble. The king-size bed faces a wall of windows that affords unobstructed views of the river. There are black leather Barcelona-style chairs, an Art Nouveau hanging bar with stained glass doors that was crafted by Charles, and a huge bath with a marble floor, a pedestal sink, a deep tub surrounded by a marble border, and a separate shower.

The breakfast room is furnished rather simply and embellished with wall stencils. A full breakfast is served, here, each morning. The first course is a fruit dish, perhaps a baked apple with walnuts and raisins accompanied by fresh-baked bread; the entrée that follows might be orange-pecan waffles with cranberry-orange sauce, or an asparagus-cheddar omelette. An afternoon snack—featuring tea, sherry, and such sweets as lemon bars or chocolate chip cookies—also is offered.

This fanciful retreat is some 18 miles from the tourist traffic of busy New Hope, yet close enough so that guests can take advantage of the area's many fine restaurants and cultural attractions. The inn has a dock on the Delaware River that's convenient for boating, swimming, fishing, or canoeing; hiking and bicycling are available nearby.

BRIDGETON HOUSE ON THE DELAWARE 1525 River Rd. (mailing address: PO Box 167), Upper Black Eddy, PA 18972 (phone: 610-982-5856). On the banks of the Delaware River, this inn has 11 guestrooms with private baths, double or king-size beds, and air conditioning. Open year-round. Rate for a double room (including full breakfast and afternoon tea): $89 to $225. Two-night minimum stay on weekends; three nights on some holiday weekends. Major credit cards accepted. Children over 3 welcome midweek; those over 8 welcome weekends also. No pets. No smoking. Bea and Charles Briggs, innkeepers.

DIRECTIONS: From New York City, take the New Jersey Turnpike south to Exit 14 and then take I-78 west to Exit 15 (Clinton/Pittstown). Turn left at the end of the ramp onto Route 513 south and go for 11 miles to the New Jersey town of Frenchtown. Cross the Delaware River on the Frenchtown Bridge. The inn is on the left.

Ontario

LANGDON HALL COUNTRY HOUSE

CAMBRIDGE, ONTARIO

Elegance and grandeur characterize *Langdon Hall Country House* as much today as they did almost a century ago. Built in 1898 by Eugene Langdon Wilks, a direct descendant of John Jacob Astor, this Federal Revival brick mansion with a columned portico was a summer house in its early years, the site of numerous balls and theatrical presentations. Eventually Wilks's daughter and her family made it their full-time residence, remaining until 1982. In 1987 restoration architect William Bennett bought the magnificent house and began the long process of refurbishing it and turning it into an inn. Two years later, he opened *Langdon Hall* with his partner, Mary Beaton.

Today, it is the quintessential fine historic home. In the style of an English country-house hotel, it boasts eight formal common rooms, including the conservatory; the *Map Room* (named for the old map of *Langdon Hall* and the surrounding area that hangs on one wall), with a full-size pool table; the *Card Room,* with board games and decks of cards; and the *Red Room,* a sitting room with dark burgundy walls.

There are 41 guestrooms and suites distributed between *Langdon Hall* itself and *The Cloisters,* a newer house (featuring similar Federal Revival architecture) connected to the main building by an underground passage. All the rooms are decorated in subdued colors and furnished with lovely antiques (some of which belonged to the Astor family) and Oriental rugs on burnished wood floors. Many of the beds were hand-crafted by local artisans in the sleigh style that was a favorite of Wilks's daughter. The large baths boast luxurious appointments, including mahogany trim and separate dressing areas with makeup tables. Seven of the guestrooms have fireplaces, and twelve feature either a deck, a patio, or a balcony.

In the much-acclaimed restaurant (also open to non-guests), which overlooks the water garden filled with lilies, regional cuisine is prepared using fresh vegetables and herbs grown in the large kitchen garden. In the afternoons, watercress sandwiches, fresh-baked scones with clotted cream, and cakes are served on Limoges china, either in the glass-enclosed conservatory or on the verandah overlooking the *Cloister Gardens*. Vinegars, condiments, jams, honey, and herbed oils made on the premises are sold in the gift shop.

The inn is located in an area of Ontario known as Carolinian Canada, which enjoys an exceptionally mild climate. Bennett hired one of the province's foremost gardeners to re-create the estate's formal gardens, and tulip trees, sassafras, crab apple, bittersweet, and other trees and plants normally found much farther south all flourish here. The 40-acre grounds also offer a tennis court, a croquet lawn, a heated pool, a volleyball court, a fitness center, and a spa where guests can indulge in a variety of massages, facials, and beauty treatments.

Walking, jogging, and cross-country ski trails lace the adjacent 200 acres. Nearby attractions include several country markets (the inn lies at the heart of Ontario's Mennonite country), the *Seagram Museum* in Waterloo, and the *Stratford Shakespeare Festival* in summer.

LANGDON HALL COUNTRY HOUSE RR 33, Cambridge, ONT N3H 4R8, Canada (phone: 519-740-2100; 800-268-1898; fax: 519-740-8161). This country-house hotel has 41 guestrooms with private baths, queen- or king-size beds, telephones, TV sets, and air conditioning; 35 with fireplaces. Wheelchair accessible. Open year-round except first week of January. Rate for a double room (including continental breakfast): CN $195 to $290 (US $138 to $229 at press time). Two-night minimum stay on weekends from May through October. Major credit cards accepted. Children welcome. Pets permitted in some rooms. Two dogs, Leilah and Mousse, in residence. Smoking permitted in some public areas. William Bennett and Mary Beaton, innkeepers; Martin Stitt, general manager.

DIRECTIONS: From Toronto take Highway 401 west beyond Cambridge to Exit 275 (Homer Watson Boulevard and Fountain Street). Drive south on Fountain Street to Blair Road (the second road on the right) and follow the signs to Blair. Drive through the hamlet of Blair, pass the town tavern, and turn right onto Langdon Drive. After about 100 feet (30 meters), turn into the first driveway on the left, and follow the lane a quarter mile (0.4 km) to *Langdon Hall*.

ELORA MILL COUNTRY INN
ELORA, ONTARIO

Long before the British settled this area, the Native Americans thought Elora Gorge was a sacred place. Perhaps it is. Here, the waterfall cascading from 60-foot stone walls onto the rocks below is a spectacular sight.

In 1832, Captain William Gilkison purchased the land, naming it Elora after his brother's ship (which, in turn, had been named after the Ellora

Caves near Bombay). Other Scotsmen followed, and Elora quickly became a prosperous village of houses built from local stone. Perched on the edge of the limestone precipice, the five-story *Elora Mill* was erected in 1843 as the community's gristmill; several other buildings were constructed later. Its solid stone foundation and heavy wood beams are a testament to the expert work of the Scottish stonemasons. The complex of buildings was converted to an inn in 1976, and the current owners, Toronto natives Kathy and Tim Taylor, bought the place 10 years later.

The guestrooms are furnished with simple Shaker-style pine furniture, including four-poster beds, chests, and tables made for the inn by local craftspeople. Local Elora pottery was used for the bathroom sinks, while handmade quilts decorate the beds and wooden quilts (pieces of inlaid wood depicting scenes) grace the walls. Several of the rooms have fireplaces and balconies, and most overlook the gorge or the Grand River.

The balconied *Penstock Lounge,* in an old stable on a rocky outcrop, seems to be suspended over the falls. A jazz pianist entertains here on weekends; this is also the site of winter jazz weekends. The country-style dining room has stone walls and lofty beams. Breakfast, lunch, and dinner are served (also open to non-guests); entrées might include tweed of salmon Elora (a fresh salmon filet wrapped in spinach, encased in brie, and baked in puff pastry) or pork Wellesley (a stuffed tenderloin baked and glazed with apple-cider honey). Both Taylors are well-known oenophiles. The restaurant's award-winning wine list, 30 pages long, includes the area's largest selection of Ontario wines as well as some very rare imported vintages. The inn also has a small brewery that turns out Elora pale ale, and Kathy prepares the tasty jams featured at breakfast.

The inn sponsors several activities during the year, including *Octoberfest* and *Christmas* feasts. Nearby attractions include the *Elora Music Festival,* the *Guelph Spring Festival,* the *Theatre on the Grand,* and the *Wellington*

County Museum. Boutiques and antiques shops are also on site. Bicycling and hiking in the *Elora Gorge Conservation Area* are other popular pastimes.

ELORA MILL COUNTRY INN 77 Mill St. W., Box 218, Elora, ONT N0B 1S0, Canada (phone: 519-846-5356; fax: 519-836-9180). This historic inn has 32 guestrooms with private baths, twin, double, queen-, or king-size beds, telephones, TV sets, and air conditioning. Closed *Christmas* and the week following *New Year's Day.* Rate for a double room (including full breakfast): CN $135 to $220 (US $99 to $158 at press time). Two-night minimum stay on weekends. Major credit cards accepted. Children welcome. No pets. Restricted smoking. Kathy and Tim Taylor, innkeepers.

DIRECTIONS: Elora is 50 miles (80 km) west of Toronto and 180 miles (288 km) east of Detroit. From Toronto take Highway 401 west for 26 miles (42 km) to Highway 6 (Guelph). Travel north on Highway 6 for 10 miles (16 km) to Elora Road. Proceed 10 miles (16 km) to Elora and turn right into the business district. The inn is at the end of Mill Street. From Detroit cross the bridge to Windsor, Ontario, then take Highway 401 for 170 miles (272 km) to Highway 6. From there follow the above directions.

EGANRIDGE INN AND COUNTRY CLUB

FENELON FALLS, ONTARIO

Nestled in the hills of Ontario overlooking Sturgeon Lake, this bucolic retreat is part country club, part resort, and part inn. The young Victoria had just become Queen of England when the main house here, a 3,000-square-foot log building called *Dunsford House,* was built in 1838.

Dunsford House now contains six luxurious suites with spacious bedrooms and bathrooms featuring Jacuzzis. Two of these rooms have fireplaces; all have reproduction period furniture and are decorated with floral chintz fabrics. In addition, there are five newer cottages, each with a whirlpool and private deck. Common areas include a deck and a sunroom.

The dining room is in the original barn overlooking the lake; in warm weather many guests choose to eat on the screened porch. A continental breakfast of juice, fruit, coffee, tea, and muffins is served. Lunch and dinner are served here as well (also open to non-guests). Typical dinner entrées include roast rack of lamb with a glaze of mustard and fresh rosemary, and oven-baked chicken breast with calvados.

Set on 105 acres in the Kawartha Lakes region of Ontario, the inn has its own nine-hole golf course, tennis courts, a marina with 25 slips, and a lake beach with natural sand (a rarity in this part of Ontario). The *Eganridge Inn* also is popular with boating enthusiasts, thanks to the Treat Seven Waterway, a 240-mile (384-km) course that passes through a series of lakes, canals, and locks between Lakes Ontario and Huron. Sturgeon Lake is part of this system, and the world's largest lift locks are minutes from the inn. Many guests also enjoy strolling through the inn's landscaped gardens. Other attractions in the area include summer theater and fishing.

EGANRIDGE INN AND COUNTRY CLUB RR 3, Fenelon Falls, ONT K0M 1N0, Canada (phone and fax: 705-738-5111). A log manor house with adjacent cottages, it has 11 guestrooms with private baths, queen- or king-size beds, telephones, TV sets, and air conditioning. Wheelchair accessible. Closed November through April. Rate for a double room (including continental breakfast): CN $140 to $175 (US $111 to $138 at press time). Major credit cards accepted. Not appropriate for children under 18. No pets. Smoking permitted in cottages only. Patty and John Egan, innkeepers.

DIRECTIONS: From Toronto travel east on Highway 401 to Exit 436 in Newcastle. Pick up Highway 35/115 north, then take Highway 35 to Lindsay. At the light turn right onto Highway 36 and continue 26 miles (42 km) via Bobcaygeon to County Road 8. Turn left onto County Road 8 and watch for the *Eganridge* sign.

STE. ANNE'S COUNTRY INN AND SPA

GRAFTON, ONTARIO

The solid fieldstone buildings in this delightfully serene place are reminiscent of a monastery or cloister. Built in 1857 by a farmer named Samuel Massey, the estate was bought in 1939 by the Blaffer family of Texas. Adding turrets, archways, and walled gardens, the Blaffers used it as a summer home until 1975. The estate sat neglected and forlorn until 1981, when the Corcoran family purchased it with the idea of turning it into an inn. Four years later, after an extensive renovation, *Ste. Anne's* opened its doors.

The 12 spacious guestrooms and suites have fireplaces and private baths; six also feature Jacuzzis. The decor, with antiques and newer country-style furniture, is comfortable and unpretentious.

The inn serves well-prepared continental fare that is both tempting and healthful. Entrées may include poached Atlantic salmon and teriyaki chicken, accompanied in summer by fresh vegetables and herbs grown in the inn's garden. No liquor is served, but guests may bring their own. Every morning a full breakfast is offered; the menu changes daily but always includes juice, fruit, muffins, and an entrée such as pancakes or eggs.

Nestled on 560 acres of wooded hills, the estate overlooks shimmering Lake Ontario and meadows where herds of fallow deer graze. For the active, there are three clay tennis courts and a spring-fed swimming pool. More sedentary entertainment is available in the living room, with its stock of jigsaw puzzles, games, and books. There's also a spa that provides rejuvenating paraffin baths, reflexology, body polishing (scrubbing with a granular cream), flower-essence scalp treatments, and massage; there's a hot tub and sauna as well. Golf courses, fishing, *Presqu'ile Provincial Park,* and antiques shops are nearby.

STE. ANNE'S COUNTRY INN AND SPA RR 1, Grafton, ONT K0K 2G0, Canada (phone: 905-349-2493; 800-263-2663; fax: 905-349-3531). Set in the Northumberland Hills of Ontario, this property has 12 guestrooms with private baths, twin, double, queen-, or king-size beds, and air conditioning. Open year-round. Rate for a double room (including breakfast, lunch, and dinner, plus a $50 credit toward spa treatments): CN $350 to $410 (US $257 to $324 at press time). Two-night minimum stay on weekends. Major credit cards accepted. Not appropriate for children under 16. No pets. One dog and one cat in residence. No smoking. Jim Corcoran, innkeeper.

DIRECTIONS: From Toronto take Highway 401 east to Exit 487 (Grafton/Centreton). Travel north on Aird Street for 1 mile (1.6 km), then turn left at the top of the hill onto Massey Road. The inn is on the left.

Upper South

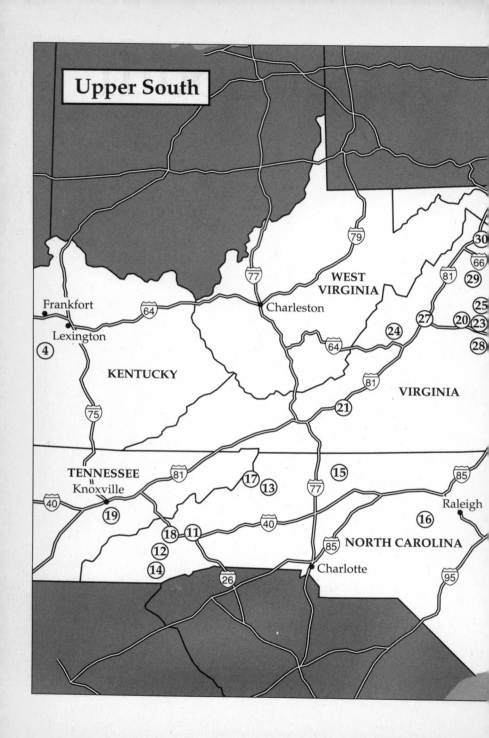

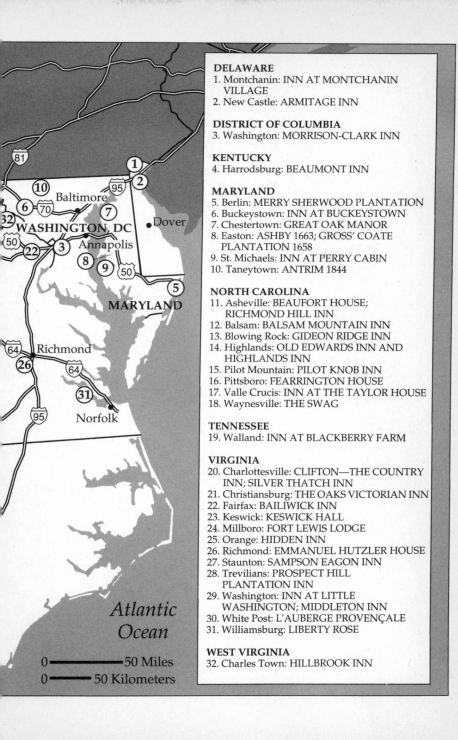

DELAWARE
1. Montchanin: INN AT MONTCHANIN VILLAGE
2. New Castle: ARMITAGE INN

DISTRICT OF COLUMBIA
3. Washington: MORRISON-CLARK INN

KENTUCKY
4. Harrodsburg: BEAUMONT INN

MARYLAND
5. Berlin: MERRY SHERWOOD PLANTATION
6. Buckeystown: INN AT BUCKEYSTOWN
7. Chestertown: GREAT OAK MANOR
8. Easton: ASHBY 1663; GROSS' COATE PLANTATION 1658
9. St. Michaels: INN AT PERRY CABIN
10. Taneytown: ANTRIM 1844

NORTH CAROLINA
11. Asheville: BEAUFORT HOUSE; RICHMOND HILL INN
12. Balsam: BALSAM MOUNTAIN INN
13. Blowing Rock: GIDEON RIDGE INN
14. Highlands: OLD EDWARDS INN AND HIGHLANDS INN
15. Pilot Mountain: PILOT KNOB INN
16. Pittsboro: FEARRINGTON HOUSE
17. Valle Crucis: INN AT THE TAYLOR HOUSE
18. Waynesville: THE SWAG

TENNESSEE
19. Walland: INN AT BLACKBERRY FARM

VIRGINIA
20. Charlottesville: CLIFTON—THE COUNTRY INN; SILVER THATCH INN
21. Christiansburg: THE OAKS VICTORIAN INN
22. Fairfax: BAILIWICK INN
23. Keswick: KESWICK HALL
24. Millboro: FORT LEWIS LODGE
25. Orange: HIDDEN INN
26. Richmond: EMMANUEL HUTZLER HOUSE
27. Staunton: SAMPSON EAGON INN
28. Trevilians: PROSPECT HILL PLANTATION INN
29. Washington: INN AT LITTLE WASHINGTON; MIDDLETON INN
30. White Post: L'AUBERGE PROVENÇALE
31. Williamsburg: LIBERTY ROSE

WEST VIRGINIA
32. Charles Town: HILLBROOK INN

Upper South

Delaware

INN AT MONTCHANIN VILLAGE

The gentle, rolling hills of the Brandywine Valley dip and fold like a drape of soft tapestry, revealing glimpses of fields of grazing cattle or a stone manor house at the end of an oak-lined drive. In one of those little hollows, in the 1800s, the duPonts built a tiny hamlet of houses, cottages, a blacksmith shop, and a school for workers in the nearby DuPont Gunpowder Company. This small cluster of charming buildings was renovated and opened as the *Inn at Montchanin Village* in 1996.

When local preservationists Missy and Daniel Lickle acquired the property, their primary concern was to find a use that would preserve the buildings in their original setting. The goal has been admirably achieved. The cluster of cottages and houses has been converted into enchanting accommodations that include antique four-poster and canopy beds, armoires, and painted blanket chests. The walls are sponged or faux painted, lavish fabrics drape the beds and windows, there are chain-stitched rugs on pine floors, wet bars in every room, and Frette sheets on the beds. Several have fireplaces and almost all have private gardens, porches, or terraces. The baths are done in marble and two include whirlpool tubs. Yet, for all their sophisticated amenities, they are decorated with such whimsy that the overwhelming feeling is one of supreme comfort instead of grand elegance. The tiny outhouses behind the cottages, for example, have been incorporated into private gardens; the lamplighted walkway to *Krazy Kat's* restaurant is called *Privy Lane*. Guestrooms throughout the inn contain examples of Missy's and Dan's collecting passions (he likes crows; she likes cows).

A massive post-and-beam barn with a stone foundation has been converted to a grand reception space for check-in. A monumental reading room has a cathedral ceiling and a giant fieldstone fireplace. Afternoon tea, as well as wine and cheese in the evening, is set out here.

Krazy Kat's restaurant, located in the former blacksmith shop, features New American cuisine with an emphasis on local products. Pan-seared scallops are wrapped with cured salmon and served with sautéed spinach and red potato rounds; Smithfield pork loin is sautéed and served with caramelized pearl onions, shiitake mushrooms, and Madeira, as well as rosemary sweet potato cubes. For dessert the Mount Rainier dried berry bread pudding with Wild Turkey sauce or the orange tartlet with ginger crisp and spicy honey sauce are excellent choices.

The variety of nearby activities is endless. There's golf, tennis, and bicycling, as well as visits to *Winterthur Museum, Garden & Library, Longwood Gardens,* and the *Hagley Museum.*

INN AT MONTCHANIN VILLAGE Rte. 100 and Rockland Rd. (mailing address: PO Box 130), Montchanin, DE 19710 (phone: 302-888-2133; 800-COWBIRD; fax: 302-888-0389). This country-inn complex has 22 guestrooms with private baths, twin, queen-, or king-size beds, telephones, TV sets, and air conditioning; eight have fireplaces and two have whirlpool tubs. Restaurant wheelchair accessible. Open year-round. Rate for a double room (including full breakfast): $125 to $350. Two-night minimum on weekends; three nights on holidays and special events. Major credit cards accepted. Children welcome. No pets. No smoking. Missy and Daniel Lickle, proprietors; Brooke Johnson, innkeeper.

DIRECTIONS: From I-95, take the Concord Pike/Route 202 exit. Travel north on Route 202 to Route 141. Turn left onto Route 141, continuing to the Rockland Road intersection. Turn right onto Rockland Road, passing the DuPont Country Club. Continue on Rockland Road over the Brandywine River and bear left at the fork, just past the river. At the corner of Rockland Road and Route 100, turn right onto Route 100 north. Travel approximately 500 feet and turn into the entrance of the inn at Kirk Road and Route 100.

ARMITAGE INN

NEW CASTLE, DELAWARE

New Castle is a little gift from the past—a former Dutch village as authentically colonial today as when it was laid out by Peter Stuyvesant in 1651. At night, after the shopkeepers have closed the doors to their antiques and

crafts shops, one walks on brick sidewalks under flickering gaslamps to the edge of the mighty Delaware where the only sounds are the soft lap of the water or, on foggy nights, the haunting sound of the foghorns.

When Zachariah Van Leuvenigh occupied his handsome brick house (he lived here from 1765 to 1789; his wife lived here until 1824) on *The Strand,* a grassy common park that borders the Delaware River, the little town was alive with commerce. Van Leuvenigh was the chief magistrate of New Castle, and since this was the height of the American Revolution, his home was often the unofficial town meeting hall, where post riders carrying news from the battlefields would rest before rushing on to Philadelphia. Today, overnight travelers receive the same gracious hospitality at his home—now known as *Armitage Inn.*

Stephen and Rina Marks restored the splendid Federal-style home in 1995. The house has a center hall with polished red-pine floors and a staircase sweeping to the second floor. To the right of the entrance is a formal dining room and to the left is a parlor with a fireplace and an extensive library. Beyond is the oldest room in the house (it probably dates to the 1600s), which still contains a mammoth cooking fireplace and beehive oven.

Upstairs are four spacious guestrooms. All have elegant marble and tile private baths, two with whirlpool tubs; conveniences include hair dryers. The guestrooms are furnished with canopy beds reached by little step stools, televisions inside period reproduction highboys, and armoires. Both the *White Rose Room* and the *Belle Fleur Room* have river views.

A formal breakfast is offered in the dining room each morning. The menu consists of juice, cereals, fruit, and breads, as well as a hot dish such as French toast or an omelette. The *Arsenal on the Green,* an 1809 building used to store munitions during the War of 1812, is now an excellent restaurant, merely three blocks away.

A screened porch and a walled garden provide warm-day retreats. Guests can walk along the riverbank and watch the Delaware River traffic or take a walking tour of the town. *Amstel House* and the *George Read House,* local museums, are open to visitors, and there are numerous cultural events in the summer. Wilmington is nearby as are *Winterthur Museum, Garden & Library* and *Longwood Gardens.*

ARMITAGE INN 2 The Strand, New Castle, DE 19720 (phone: 302-328-6618; fax: 302-324-1163). This charming bed and breakfast establishment has four guestrooms with private baths, queen- or king-size beds, telephones, TV sets, and air conditioning. Open year-round. Rate for a double room (including full breakfast): $95 to $135. Two-night minimum stay on weekends from April through June and in September and October. Major credit cards accepted. Not appropriate for children under 13. No pets. No smoking. Stephen and Rina Marks, innkeepers.

DIRECTIONS: From the north, take I-95 to Exit 5A and then take Route 141 south toward New Castle. Continue past the Routes 13 and 40 overpass. At Route 9, turn left (north) for half a mile. Bear right into historic New Castle via Delaware Street. Continue on Delaware Street through the village to the stop sign at The Strand. The inn is on the right. From the south on I-95, take I-295 toward New Jersey. Take Exit 5A onto Route 141 and follow directions above.

District of Columbia

MORRISON-CLARK INN

WASHINGTON, DC

Built in 1864 as two separate townhouses for businessmen David Morrison and Reuben Clark, the *Morrison-Clark* has undergone many changes over the years. Along the way, one of the houses even took on several distinctive Asian touches, including a Chinese Chippendale porch and a Shanghai roof. The two eventually were joined into one large house.

In 1923, the complex became the *Soldiers, Sailors, Marines and Airmen's Club,* and for 60 years it functioned as an inexpensive hostel for servicemen traveling to Washington, DC. During its peak, in 1943, some 45,000 servicemen, many fresh from the front, slept here. Traditionally, the club was under the wing of the First Lady, who held teas and benefits to raise operating funds. Mamie Eisenhower and Jacqueline Kennedy, in particular, expended considerable effort on its behalf.

Eventually it was sold and, some say, scheduled for the wrecking ball. In 1987, however, it was purchased by a group of local developers and, after a thorough restoration and a new addition, opened its doors the following year as the *Morrison-Clark Inn.* The preservation earned it a place on the National Register of Historic Places.

In the common rooms are original fireplaces with elaborately carved marble mantelpieces and mirrors that almost reach the 13-foot ceilings. The individually appointed guestrooms in the original Victorian houses have elaborate moldings, marble vanities in the baths, and ornately carved armoires. The decor ranges from antiques in the original Victorian houses to country French and neoclassical in the newer wing. Flowers adorn the inn, from the vibrant arrangement in the entranceway to the bouquets perched on the vanities in the bathrooms. Each room has two telephones, a dataport, desk, and a mini-bar.

The pastel-colored dining room is a romantic setting for chef Susan Lindeborg's delicious American menu, which has a Southern twist. Sample dishes include rabbit loin stuffed with pecan cornbread and Maker's Mark bourbon sauce; seared chicken breast with country ham, wide noodles, and tarragon; and red wine–and thyme-glazed baked salmon with potato gratin.

The inn is near Washington's *Convention Center,* midway between the *Capitol* and the *White House.* A fitness center is on site.

MORRISON-CLARK INN Massachusetts Ave. and 11th St. NW, Washington, DC 20001 (phone: 202-898-1200; 800-332-7898; fax: 202-289-8576). This Victorian inn has 54 guestrooms with private baths, twin, double, or queen-size beds, telephones, TV sets, and air conditioning. Wheelchair accessible. Open year-round. Rate for a double room (including continental breakfast): $125 to $195; corporate and weekend rates available. Major credit cards accepted. Children welcome. No pets. Smoking in some guestrooms; designated non-smoking rooms available; no smoking in dining room. William Petrella, general manager.

DIRECTIONS: The inn is in downtown Washington, DC, at the junction of Massachusetts Avenue and 11th and L Streets, just off Mount Vernon Place. An underground garage with valet parking is available (at additional charge).

Kentucky

BEAUMONT INN

HARRODSBURG, KENTUCKY

There's a gentleness to the landscape of Kentucky. In the heart of blue-grass country, where some of the world's most pampered horses graze, Harrodsburg—and the *Beaumont Inn*—exemplify this tranquillity.

The inn has had a distinguished history that predates the present structure. On the site was the boyhood home of John M. Harlan, who later became the chief justice of the *US Supreme Court*. In 1841 it was purchased by Dr. Samuel G. Mullins, who turned the old log homestead into the *Greenville Female Institute*. After a fire destroyed the building, he replaced it in 1845 with the magnificent Greek Revival brick mansion that is now the *Beaumont Inn* and listed on the National Register of Historic Places. With sturdy walls 18 inches thick and six Ionic columns at the entrance, it was built to last. Ancestors of the present innkeepers purchased the property in 1919; it's currently enjoying its fourth generation of management by the Dedman family.

Remnants of the old school are visible in many of the rooms. The current office was the school's library, and the original cherry bookcases are filled with books well-thumbed by students and teachers. The original fireplaces still grace the double parlors.

Dedman contributions to the inn are numerous. The embroidered cutwork linen curtains were custom-made for the family on the Portuguese island of Madeira in 1919. Crystal chandeliers, pier mirrors, a mahogany parlor-grand piano (given to Bessie Dedman in 1893), and the Empire and Victorian tables, chairs, and lamps have all been passed from generation to generation. Curio cabinets display collections of saltcellars, silver, and antique china.

Guestrooms are located in the *Main Inn* and in three other buildings, all within walking distance. Those in the former are furnished with antiques, including several highly decorated Victorian headboards, and cannonball, spool, and two-poster beds. There are additional rooms across the street in *Goddard Hall,* a pretty, white 1935 clapboard building with a covered verandah. The decor here is rich with family heirlooms, including portraits, four-poster beds, and decorative touches such as vintage clothing and antique lace tablecloths. Two units ideal for families are in *Bell Cottage,* a little 1921 house with a broad front porch. *Greystone House,* an imposing 1931 stone mansion built for May Lilly, niece of Eli Lilly of pharmaceutical fame, has four more large bedrooms.

The *Main Inn*'s gift shop presents a wide assortment of Kentucky crafts and food items. The parlors are well stocked with board games and books, and the porches are lined with split-hickory wicker chairs. The 33-acre property, shaded by more than 30 varieties of trees, holds two tennis courts, a swimming pool, a shuffleboard court, and several swings and benches that are just the thing on a lazy afternoon.

Breakfast, lunch, and dinner (all open to non-guests) are served in the dining room in the *Main Inn,* where fried chicken and locally cured ham are featured. Other typically Southern specialties, such as corn pudding and General Robert E. Lee orange-lemon cake, also are popular.

Among the attractions nearby are *Perryville Battlefield State Park*, superb antiquing, thoroughbred and harness racing, golf, and numerous historic museums, including the *Shaker Village of Pleasant Hill.* An outdoor drama reenacting the legend of Daniel Boone takes place every summer in Harrodsburg.

BEAUMONT INN 638 Beaumont Inn Dr., Harrodsburg, KY 40330 (phone: 606-734-3381; 800-352-3992; fax: 606-734-6897). This hotel has 33 guestrooms with private baths, double, queen-, or king-size beds, telephones, TV sets, and air conditioning. Closed January and February. Rate for a double room (including continental breakfast): $85 to $115. Major credit cards accepted. Children welcome. No pets. Smoking permitted; designated non-smoking rooms; no smoking in dining room. T. C. and Mary Elizabeth Dedman, owners; Chuck and Helen Dedman, innkeepers.

DIRECTIONS: Traveling east from Louisville on I-64, take Exit 48 to Kentucky Route 151 south, then take US Route 127 south for 15 miles to Harrodsburg. Beaumont Inn Drive is on the south end of town.

Maryland

MERRY SHERWOOD PLANTATION

BERLIN, MARYLAND

Eastern Shore Maryland is still as languid and peaceful as it was in 1859 when *Merry Sherwood* was built. Rural and remote, this gracious 8,500-square-foot, 27-room plantation home evokes a bygone era both in its exterior and interior demeanor. Approaching along a quiet country road, guests enter the 19-acre plantation through ornate gates along a drive lined with sugar maple trees.

The house has a classic Italianate style with Greek Revival, Greek, and Victorian influences, including a wraparound porch and an ornate cupola on top. Though years of neglect took their toll, the house was purchased in 1990 by local businessman Kirk Burbage, whose family has lived in the area for over 200 years. He spent two years restoring it to its former grandeur and opened it as a bed and breakfast establishment in 1992. Now painted a seafoam green, it has white trim and dark green shutters.

The interior architectural details are exceptional. Loblolly pine floors have a soft patina and there's a spectacular three-story mahogany staircase and rail. On the north, the grand former ballroom with its twin marble fireplaces is furnished with Victorian furniture upholstered in rich damasks. Among the treasures are a square grand piano and an ornately carved armchair, said to have been made for a scheduled visit to the United States by Queen Victoria (she never came). On the south side are a more intimate parlor, a library with paneled walls (ask to see the bookcase that opens to reveal a closet), and a formal dining room. The house has nine fireplaces. A sun porch with a tile floor contains pretty wicker and offers the best vantage point for viewing the gardens.

Upstairs, the bedrooms are furnished with museum-quality antiques. The *Harrison Room* has a Gothic Revival bed with a tall, carved headboard and footboard, as well as a Victorian fainting couch that can be transformed into a double bed. The *Purnell Suite* provides split-level accommodations with the bedroom and bath, which has a whirlpool tub, down several steps from the sitting room, which has a fireplace. The *Johnson Room* has an antique carved canopy bed and a mannequin wearing a Victorian morning dress in the corner.

A full breakfast is served in the formal dining room. Stacy offers fruit, juice, and fresh-baked breads, perhaps oatmeal-butterscotch muffins, followed by a hot dish such as *crème caramel* French toast. Don't miss the tiny gift shop arrayed on an ornate Victorian desk; one popular item is house-made vinegar in a pretty bottle.

The grounds of *Merry Sherwood* are being planted and restored with a grant from *Southern Living* magazine. Already there is a formal boxwood garden, a rose garden, and flower gardens profuse with color throughout the spring and summer. A fountain, statues, and a hammock and swing are hidden away among the massive trees. Numerous activities attract visitors. *Assateague Island National Seashore* is a mere 8 miles away, as is Ocean City. In Berlin, there are more than 12 historic houses and museums to visit and interesting antiques shops line the streets. Horseback riding, canoeing, and hiking are also possible pastimes.

MERRY SHERWOOD PLANTATION 8909 Worcester Hwy., Berlin, MD 21811 (phone: 410-641-2112; 800-660-0358). This grand plantation-style mansion contains eight guestrooms with double or queen-size beds and air conditioning; six have private baths, two share a bath. Open year-round. Rate for a double room (including full breakfast): $120 to $175. Two-night minimum on weekends. MasterCard and Visa accepted. Not appropriate for children under 8. No pets. No smoking. Kirk Burbage, proprietor; Stacy Kenny, innkeeper.

DIRECTIONS: From Baltimore/Washington, DC, follow Route 50 east across the Chesapeake Bay to the Eastern Shore and follow it to Berlin (about 150 miles). Exit onto Route 113 south and go 2½ miles. The inn will be on the right.

INN AT BUCKEYSTOWN

BUCKEYSTOWN, MARYLAND

The entire village of Buckeystown is listed on the National Register of Historic Places. Significant buildings—from early log cabins to brick and stone Federal homes and gingerbread Victorian mansions—line the streets.

The 1897 *Inn at Buckeystown* is among the most impressive Victorians, as is its sister property, *St. John's Reformed Church,* a restored 1884 Gothic-style brick church two blocks away. The inn has been owned and run by Daniel Pelz and Chase Barnett since 1980.

In the common rooms Oriental rugs grace polished wood floors and crystal chandeliers cast a soft glow on oil paintings. There are three working fireplaces. The five guestrooms in the main house are furnished with museum-quality antiques, including velvet-, mohair-, and satin-covered Victorian love seats and chairs, carved walnut headboards, and marble-topped shaving stands. Carved moldings trim the ceilings, and chintz fabrics cover the windows. *St. John's* boasts a two-level unit where the original stained glass casts multicolored light across the walls; the bedroom is in the choir loft! There's a fireplace and grand piano in the common area, and outside a private garden surrounds a hot tub. The one-story *Parson's Cottage,* near the former church, is a two-room retreat with a fireplace and its own kitchen.

Food is an important part of any stay here; both breakfast and dinner are included in the rate. Although the owners emphasize that "this is not a restaurant but an inn," dinner is offered to non-guests as well. The menu is continental and might include an appetizer of fried brie with fruit, followed by soup and salad. Popular entrées include honey-herb glazed breast of chicken on a bed of stuffing and garlic roast loin of pork. Desserts include blueberry purses and cranberry delight. The dining room is decorated in High Victorian style with Oriental rugs, carved oak sideboards, and a magnificent crystal chandelier. When the dinner bell rings, guests are seated at oak tables set with antique china, crystal, and silver.

The inn is located on 2½ acres of gardens, which can be viewed from chairs on the wraparound porch. Nearby are Civil War battlefields, the Appalachian Trail, and New Market, the antiques capital of Maryland.

INN AT BUCKEYSTOWN 3521 Buckeystown Pike (mailing address: c/o General Delivery), Buckeystown, MD 21717-9999 (phone: 301-874-5755; 800-272-1190). This historic inn has seven guestrooms with private baths, double or queen-size beds, and air conditioning; three with fireplaces and TV sets. Closed Mondays and Tuesdays. Rate for a double room (including full breakfast and dinner): $200 to $275. Major credit cards accepted. Not appropriate for children under 16. No pets. Two dogs, Chagney and Mr. Stubbs, and one cat, Melissa, on the property. No smoking. Daniel R. Pelz and Chase Barnett, innkeepers; Rebecca Smith, general manager.

DIRECTIONS: Traveling on I-270 north from Washington, DC, take Exit 26 (Buckeystown) to Route 80 west; continue for 5 miles. Turn right onto Route 85 north (Buckeystown Pike). The inn is a half mile farther on the right.

GREAT OAK MANOR

CHESTERTOWN, MARYLAND

From the famous to the infamous, *Great Oak Manor* has a rich story to tell. The brick Federal-style manor house was built on a 1,700-acre estate by Russell D'Oench, a W.R. Grace heir, in 1938. He employed the finest artisans of the day to install fine moldings and rich paneling, and to carve symbolic icons over the doors and fireplace mantels; one, in the mantel of the *Marmaduke* guestroom, refers to the D'Oenches's honeymoon in Sun Valley. In the 1950s, the estate was owned by a local character named Frank Russell, who turned it into an exclusive sportsmens' retreat. In addition to fishing and hunting, Russell offered high-stakes gaming. Celebrity guests during this period included Arthur Godfrey, Henry Ford, and Guy Lombardo.

Great Oak Manor, which now encompasses 12 acres, is encircled on three sides by the Chesapeake Bay and Fairlee Creek. It sits high on a bluff offering wonderful views of the water. Manicured lawns lead to a waterside patio, a screened-in gazebo, and lawn chairs and benches romantically placed along the ridge to offer vistas of the spectacular sunsets across the bay to Pooles Island.

Dianne and Don Cantor have owned the estate since 1993 and they've worked magic on transforming the rooms into the elegant country inn you see today. Dianne is an artist who works in stained glass and several of her pieces are displayed in the rooms.

The massive front-to-back entrance hall is distinguished by a graceful curved stairway to the second level. In the *Music Room,* with its fireplace and needlework painting by Don's grandmother, is a china cabinet that incorporates a dreamy pastel painting of Chestertown's pretty tiered foun-

tain. In the *Gun Room*, which has another fireplace, there's a hand-painted map of the original 1,700-acre estate on a pull-down panel that hides the bar. There's also a *South Sun Porch* with brick walls and floor and a *Library* with a paneled fireplace wall. Fine antiques, including an ornate tall-case clock and a burnished-wood armoire, are displayed throughout the house.

The guestrooms are equally interesting and five have working fireplaces. *Russell,* located in the former gambling hall, has pine paneling, a giant stone fireplace in a pine-paneled wall, and a towering cathedral ceiling. *D'Oench* also has a fireplace and a terrific view across the lawns to the bay.

A continental breakfast of fresh fruits, homemade muffins, and cereals is served in the dining room. On Sundays, Dianne adds an entrée such as pancakes or French toast. Every afternoon lemonade or tea and snacks (often homemade cookies) are laid out in the *Gun Room* as well.

The estate has a private beach where guests can swim, as well as flower gardens and a boxwood garden with hidden benches. The inn is adjacent to a quiet resort which has a nine-hole golf course, tennis courts, a swimming pool, and a marina, all of which can be used by guests of the inn. Guests can arrive by boat and fishing excursions can be arranged with advance notice. The flat, quiet country roads surrounding the inn are ideal for bicycling and walking.

GREAT OAK MANOR 10568 Cliff Rd., Chestertown, MD 21620 (phone: 410-778-5943; 800-504-3098; fax: 410-778-5943). This gracious country estate has 11 guestrooms with private baths, twin or king-size beds, telephones, and air conditioning; five with fireplaces, two with TV sets. Closed mid-February through mid-March. Rate for a double room (with continental breakfast and afternoon tea): $95 to $145; 20 percent discount midweek. Discover, MasterCard, and Visa accepted. Children welcome. No pets. One yellow Labrador, Beau, on the premises. No smoking in guestrooms; smoking permitted in designated areas. Don and Dianne Cantor, innkeepers.

DIRECTIONS: From Baltimore/Washington, DC, take Route 50 east to Route 301 north. Follow this to Route 213 north. Follow Route 213 for 18 miles to Chestertown. In Chestertown, follow Route 514 north for 1⁸/₁₀ miles (crossing Route 298) and turn left onto Great Oak Landing Road. Drive past the farm buildings, through a set of brick pillars, past a golf course (do not turn left into Great Oak Landing), and through a second set of brick pillars to the inn.

ASHBY 1663

EASTON, MARYLAND

When Cliff Meredith and Jeanie Wagner purchased the graceful white clapboard mansion with the grand columned Greek Revival entrance, it had been abandoned for several years, standing forlorn and empty on 23 acres bordering the Miles River. A realtor and contractor, Cliff was undaunted. After tackling the wiring, heating, and plumbing, he virtually rebuilt the house, including a spectacular new kitchen, a graceful stairway that sweeps up to the second and third floors, and walls of Palladian-style windows that open the house to views and light.

The common rooms are furnished with exquisite antique pieces. One enters a spacious entrance hall, which has heart-pine floors and archways leading to each of the adjoining rooms. The sunroom, with a fireplace at each end and Palladian-style windows across its width, contains coral-colored chintz sofas and polished antique chests and tables. French doors open to steps that lead to the pool, terrace, and spa; the Miles River is visible just beyond. There's also a dining room, a living room, and a screened porch, which has iron and wicker furniture and overlooks the formal gardens.

The guestrooms are so grand that one is tempted to snuggle in for the entire stay. The *Robert Goldsborough Suite* on the second floor contains a canopy bed lushly skirted, flounced, and covered in a rich peach and green fabric, a fireplace, and a wall of windows that overlooks the pool and the bay. The marble bath, however, is the pièce de résistance. Not only does it have a raised two-person whirlpool tub with a view of the bay from the floor-to-ceiling wall of windows, but also a fireplace to cast a seductive glow. The *Anne Buchanen Room,* with a canopy bed done in blue and rose floral fabrics, has a fireplace and a bath with a steam shower, a whirlpool tub, and a television set into the wall. Rooms are also located in the *Mary Trippe Place,* a separate cottage, and the *George Goldsborough House. Miles River Cabin,* a new building completed in 1996, borders the banks of the Miles River. It has five accommodations, each featuring a fireplace, private deck, whirlpool tub, and a view across the shimmering waters.

A full breakfast is served buffet-style in the dining room or on the screened porch. In addition to fresh-baked muffins and breads, fruit, juice, and cereals, there are such enticing entrées as asparagus in crêpes with hollandaise sauce and baked French toast with bananas and walnuts topped with maple syrup. In the evening, guests meet and greet while sampling offerings from the complimentary open bar and hors d'oeuvres tray.

The inn is located on a undulating piece of land that projects into the Miles River and provides half a mile of waterfront, as well as abundant gardens and century-old trees. In addition to the pool, there's a lighted tennis court, volleyball and badminton courts, bicycles for exploring the numerous nearby coves, and canoes and paddle boats at the dock for use on the river. Downstairs in the main house, where remnants of the original 1663 walls are visible, there's also an exercise room, a pool table, and a room with a mechanical massage table, sauna, and tanning bed. There are numerous restaurants nearby and the village of St. Michael's has interesting crafts and antiques shops. Golf, fishing, and boating are nearby.

ISHBY 1663 27448 Ashby Dr. (mailing address: PO Box 45), Easton, MD 21601 (phone: 410-822-4235; fax: 410-822-9288). This magnificent Eastern Shore estate has 13 guestrooms and suites with private baths, queen- or king-size beds, telephones, TV sets, and air conditioning; eight with fireplaces, nine with balconies or porches, and eight with whirlpool tubs. Open year-round. Rate for a double room (including full breakfast and evening drinks and hors d'oeuvres): $195 to $595. Two-night minimum if Saturday included. Major credit cards

accepted. Not appropriate for children under 12. No pets. No smoking. Clifford Meredith and Jeanie Wagner, innkeepers.

DIRECTIONS: From Washington, DC, take Route 50 across the Bay Bridge and follow it to Easton. At Airport Road turn right and travel to the stop sign. Turn right again onto Goldsborough Neck Road and continue past the "No Outlet" sign, bearing left at the fork and turning left again at the sign that reads "Ashby 1663." Continue on the paved road for ¾ mile to the inn.

GROSS' COATE PLANTATION 1658

EASTON, MARYLAND

Maryland's Eastern Shore is studded with gracious country estates hidden away down leafy lanes. At the confluence of the Wye River, Lloyd Creek, and Gross Creek, on a land grant that dates to 1658, is *Gross' Coate Plantation 1658.* The brick Georgian mansion and its numerous brick dependencies were built in 1760 by William Tilghman. The plantation contains 60 acres of lush gardens, verdant green lawns, and huge old linden, elm, and oak trees. It's surrounded by pastures containing thoroughbred horses, which owners Molly and Jon Ginn raise.

The manor house is entered from a broad porch supported by boxed columns that spans the front. A string of rockers is strategically placed for viewing the evening's light show as the sun sets over the Wye River. In the entrance hall, a collection of duck decoys rests on shelves. Throughout the numerous main-floor rooms, which all contain fireplaces, elegant antique furniture rests on priceless antique Oriental rugs and paintings with a sporting motif line the walls. There's a south parlor, a north parlor with a view across the lawns to the pool, which, in spring, is surrounded by vibrant iris and peonies, a loggia, a library with a complimentary cordial bar for inn guests, and a dining room.

All accommodations are in spacious suites. The *Master Suite* boasts two fireplaces, a bath with a whirlpool tub, and a view across the grounds. The *Gross Creek Suite* is decorated with a hunting theme; it features a canopy bed and a sitting area with a fireplace. The *Spring House Cottage,* in a separate building, has brick walls, a huge brick fireplace, and a beamed cathedral ceiling. The bath has pine-paneled walls, a steam shower, and a clawfoot tub, and there is a private garden with its own spa.

The main floor and guestrooms are adorned with fresh flowers from the inn's gardens and greenhouse. A pretty garden house with gingerbread overhangs (formerly the dairy) is festooned with dried flowers hanging from its rafters and bowls of petals with which Molly gives lessons in making potpourri. Guests are given a bag of potpourri or a bunch of dried flowers to take home. In the smokehouse, guests can, on occasion, smoke their own hams, and the former summer kitchen, which is now called *Ginn's Tavern,*

is a cigar-smoker's retreat with a separate bar and a wood-burning fireplace.

In the breakfast room, coffee, fresh fruit, and tea are available all day; there are also two fully stocked refrigerators in the house for guests to use. Typical breakfast fare includes fruit, apple crisp, cranberry temptation, apple walnut spice cake, muffins, sausage and cheese pie, and cereals, accompanied by champagne fruit punch or Wye River Mary (*Gross' Coate*'s version of Bloody Mary). In the afternoon, a lovely English tea includes such delights as raspberry creme pie, delicate lemon squares, brie cheese with cranberry-orange chutney, Maryland beaten biscuits with local honey, handmade chocolates, fresh lemonade, tea or coffee, and Plantation Sunset, a mixture of champagne, cranberry juice, peach schnapps, and Chambord.

Both children and pets are warmly welcomed. A swimming pool, croquet lawn, volleyball and badminton courts, bicycles, and a golf chipping range are all on the property. In addition, the *Wye River Fly Fishing School,* where expert instruction extends over a four-day period, is located here. The villages of St. Michaels and Easton offer numerous restaurant and shopping choices.

GROSS' COATE PLANTATION 1658 11300 Gross' Coate Rd., Easton, MD 21601 (phone: 410-819-0802; 800-580-0802; fax: 410-819-0803). This elegant country retreat has eight suites with private baths (some have two), twin, double, queen-, or king-size beds, and fireplaces; three with telephones, two with TV sets. Open year-round. Rate for a double room (including full breakfast, afternoon tea, and open bar): $295 to $495. Major credit cards accepted. Children and pets welcome. Dogs on property in separate area. Smoking allowed. Jon and Molly Ginn, innkeepers.

DIRECTIONS: From Baltimore and Washington, DC, take Route 50 east across the Chesapeake Bay Bridge and continue on Route 50 to Route 662 at mile marker 58. Go 1⁹⁄₁₀ miles and turn right onto Sharp Road, which later becomes Little Park Road. Continue straight for 3 miles to the stop sign. Turn right onto Todd's Corner Road. Go ³⁄₁₀ mile and bear left onto Gross' Coate Road. You will pass cottages and horse pastures. The inn is 1⁶⁄₁₀ miles away at the very end of a gravel lane.

INN AT PERRY CABIN

St. Michaels, Maryland

The long, rich history of the *Inn at Perry Cabin* begins with one Samuel Hambleton. During the War of 1812, Hambleton distinguished himself at the Battle of Lake Erie, where he served under Commodore Oliver Hazard Perry. On his retirement to St. Michaels in 1816, he built a manor house with a wing designed to look like Perry's ship cabin. In the middle of this century, the old house and surrounding estate were converted to a riding academy; then, in 1979, the owners of *Kentucky Derby* winner Spectacular Bid turned the property into an inn and restaurant. Ten years later, in his first venture into American innkeeping, Sir Bernard Ashley, co-founder of the Laura Ashley Company, purchased the 25-acre estate and created an American version of an English country-house hotel.

The numerous common rooms provide ample opportunity for relaxation. There's a wicker- and greenery-filled conservatory and an adjoining snooker room, with a massive table and fireplace. The meeting room beyond has the latest audiovisual equipment, and a tiled corridor serves as the gameroom, where chess and other board games share space with a buggy full of teddy bears. The morning room and the library with a piano both have fireplaces. There's also a fitness center and an indoor swimming pool.

The inn has 41 spacious guestrooms, several with balconies or duplex sitting rooms, and many with views of the Miles River. Not surprisingly, they are lavishly decorated with Laura Ashley fabrics, wallpapers, china, and furniture—canopied pine four-posters with spiral posts, soft down sofas strewn with bright pillows, and pine armoires. It's the perfect blend of elegance and comfort. The turndown service includes crisp, homemade oatmeal-raisin cookies delivered to each room.

Meals at *Perry Cabin* (also open to non-guests) are noted for their spectacular presentations as well as fine food. While guests peruse the menu, a plate of hors d'oeuvres is offered for nibbling. The appetizer might be creamy duck foie gras served with crisp brioches and grapes; the entrée, lightly grilled salmon served on a bed of shoestring potatoes. For dessert, raspberry bread pudding is dusted with powdered sugar and served in a pool of *crème anglaise.* The full breakfast, which is included, is equally delicious, with eggs Benedict, grilled kippers, French toast, muffins, and fruit on the menu. In the afternoon, guests are treated to tea and scones or pastries.

Located on Maryland's eastern shore, the inn has its own dock and boats, so guests can enjoy sailing and fishing. Antiquing and golf are nearby.

INN AT PERRY CABIN 308 Watkins La., St. Michaels, MD 21663 (phone: 410-745-2200; 800-722-2949; fax: 410-745-3348). This resort has 41 guestrooms with private baths, twin, queen-, or king-size beds, telephones, TV sets, and air conditioning; 34 have balconies, seven have fireplaces. Wheelchair accessible. Open year-round. Rate for a double room (including full breakfast and afternoon tea): $195 to $575. Major credit cards accepted. Not appropriate for children under 10. Pets permitted with prior permission. Smoking allowed except in the dining room. Sir Bernard Ashley, owner; Stephen Creese, innkeeper.

DIRECTIONS: From Washington, DC, take the Capitol Beltway to Route 50 east (John Hanson Highway), traveling across the Chesapeake Bay Bridge to Easton. From Route 50 turn right onto the Route 322/Easton bypass, then turn right again onto Route 33 and continue to St. Michaels. In St. Michaels take Talbot Avenue through town. The inn is on the right just outside of town.

ANTRIM 1844

TANEYTOWN, MARYLAND

Taneytown is tucked into the foothills of the Catoctin Mountains in the panhandle of Maryland, almost at the Pennsylvania border. Gettysburg is 12 miles to the north and Baltimore 45 miles to the southwest. The area is steeped in history. General George Meade, who assumed command of the Union Army on June 28, 1863, three days before the Battle of Gettysburg, headquartered at Antrim, then a 2,000-acre plantation. The manor house, once the hub of glorious social events, has now been meticulously restored by Dorothy "Dort" and Richard Mollett. Once again it is the scene of lively social engagements, as well as nightly dinners. And, in four plantation buildings on its 24 acres, *Antrim 1844* offers 14 rooms and suites for overnight guests.

The stately mansion, a white Federal-style gem with a colonnaded entry, is distinguished by ornate overhanging eaves and a cupola on top, from which General Meade watched troop movements. The spacious entry hall, which has 14-foot ceilings, leads to double drawing rooms with warm-toned peach walls, polished wood floors, twin fireplaces, and antique furnishings, including an ornately carved Knabe piano. On the opposite side of the entry, the library has walls lined with books, tufted leather sofas, another fireplace, and a red British telephone booth in one corner, where the guest telephone is located.

One of the favorite common rooms is the charming *Pub*, which has walls covered in red tartan, a plank floor, and a massive brick hearth. There's also a pretty enclosed verandah with glass-topped wicker tables and floral cushions on the chairs. One wall is of brick and the other has a bank of windows that overlook the gardens.

There are nine spacious guestrooms in the manor house, all with feather beds; those on the second floor have fireplaces. The *Boucher Suite* is spectacular: Its canopy bed faces a fireplace and two balconies; its marble bathroom features a cobalt-blue two-person whirlpool tub on a platform and two cobalt-blue sinks in a marble counter. The *Lamberton Room* has a 1790s canopy bed with turned posts, and the *Clabaugh Room* features walls of deep forest-green, a masculine Empire-style rosewood bed with a half-tester and bed coverings of rich polished chintz in burgundy and green. Additional rooms and suites with whirlpool tubs and fireplaces are found in the *Ice House,* the *Cottage,* the *Smith House,* and the *Barn.*

Early-risers are treated to a pot of coffee and a newspaper delivered to their room. A full breakfast—Belgian waffles or omelettes—is served either on the verandah or in the dining room. Tea is served every afternoon. A five-course prix-fixe dinner begins every evening at 6:30 PM in the *Pub;* dinner begins half an hour later in a restaurant carved out of the former slave kitchen, smokehouse, and summer kitchen. Chef Sharon Ashburn prepares regional American cuisine with a French twist. Following dinner, guests return to the *Pub,* where Richard will share his selection of Scotch malt whiskeys and cigars from his handsome humidor.

In addition to the extensive formal gardens, with a gazebo, the inn contains a swimming pool, tennis courts, a croquet lawn, putting green, horseshoes, volleyball, and badminton. A pavilion is frequently the scene of romantic weddings. Nearby, visits to *Gettysburg National Military Park* and the *Eisenhower National Historic Site* offer interesting historical excursions.

ANTRIM 1844 30 Trevanion Rd., Taneytown, MD 21787 (phone: 410-756-6812; 800-858-1844; fax: 410-756-2744). This gracious country estate contains 14 guestrooms with private baths, double, queen-, or king-size beds, and air conditioning; 10 have fireplaces and whirlpool tubs. Wheelchair accessible. Open year-round. Rate for a double room (including full breakfast): $150 to $300. Two-night minimum if stay includes Saturday. Major credit cards accepted. Not appropriate for children under 13. No pets. Smoking in *Pub* only. Dort and Richard Mollett, innkeepers; Stewart Dearie, manager.

DIRECTIONS: From Baltimore, take I-695 (Beltway) to Exit 19 and then follow I-795 north. Exit onto Route 140 west and follow this to Taneytown. Turn left onto Trevanion Road and proceed 150 feet to the inn, which is on the right. From Washington, DC, take I-495 to I-270 west to Frederick. In Frederick, take Route 15 north toward Gettysburg. In Emmitsburg, follow Route 140 to Taneytown. In Taneytown, go through the stoplight and over the railroad tracks. In ⅛ mile bear right onto Trevanion Road when the road splits. The inn is on the right.

North Carolina

BEAUFORT HOUSE

ASHEVILLE, NORTH CAROLINA

This charming pink 1894 Queen Anne Victorian confection looks almost good enough to eat—rather like a peppermint ice cream cone. Located on two acres in a residential area of majestic homes, it has a circular driveway that leads under oak, dogwood, magnolia, and maple trees and past a tea garden to the wraparound porch. Fancy gingerbread embellishes the porch and the gables on this house that's listed on the National Register of Historic Places. Robert and Jacqueline Glasgow opened it to guests in 1993.

Inside, all is serenity. Classical music plays softly. The Victorian parlors are furnished with museum-quality antiques; each has a fireplace. In one, a table is set with a child's tea set awaiting small guests. Up the stairway, with its ornate carved newel, a stained-glass window in shades of rose, blue, and gold casts jewel tones across the oak floors topped with Oriental rugs.

The guestrooms are equally ornate and utterly romantic. The *Rose Room,* featuring cabbage rose wallpaper, has a carved Victorian headboard and footboard and a lovely fireplace. A bay window makes this an especially light room. The huge marble bathroom has a claw-foot tub. The *Theodore Davidson Room* contains a carved four-poster rice bed, as well as a green tile bath with a Jacuzzi that has a view of the bedroom fireplace. In the *Sarah Davidson Suite* there are two bedrooms, one with a canopy bed. The entire suite is decorated with white Battenburg lace and the huge bath has a whirlpool tub.

A full breakfast is served in the elegant formal dining room set with white linens and fine china and silver. The meal will start with fresh fruit, juice, and homemade breads, muffins, and biscuits. Jacqueline and Robert prepare a variety of breakfast entrées. Among the most popular are the eggs Beaufort House (like eggs Benedict, except prepared with a thick slice of ham) and Belgian waffles.

A fitness center with a treadmill, Stairmaster, and free weights is available for guests to use, as are bicycles with which to explore the city. There are numerous visitor attractions in the Asheville area. The *Biltmore House and Gardens*, a fantastic, turreted former Vanderbilt castle, is located here as is the *Thomas Wolfe House*.

BEAUFORT HOUSE 61 North Liberty St., Asheville, NC 28801 (phone: 704-254-8334; 800-261-2221; fax: 704-251-2082). This in-town bed and breakfast establishment has 12 guestrooms with private baths, double, queen-, or king-size beds, telephones, TV/VCR sets, and air conditioning; five with fireplaces, and eight with whirlpool tubs. Wheelchair accessible. Open year-round. Rate for a double room (including full breakfast): $95 to $195. MasterCard and Visa accepted. Children welcome. No pets. One dog, Beaufort, in residence. No smoking. Robert and Jacqueline Glasgow, innkeepers.

DIRECTIONS: From I-40 take I-240 into Asheville. Take Exit 5A north onto Merrimon Avenue (Route 25). At the second light turn right onto Chestnut Street. At the next intersection, turn left onto North Liberty Street. The inn is in the second block on the right.

RICHMOND HILL INN

ASHEVILLE, NORTH CAROLINA

The fine Victorian mansion that is the centerpiece of the *Richmond Hill Inn* sits on 40 acres overlooking the French Broad River, with the lights of Asheville and the dusky mountains beyond. Built in 1889 for Richmond and Gabrielle Pearson—she a Southern belle and he a congressman and ambassador to Persia and Greece—the house's fine pedigree is evident upon walking into the grand entrance, *Oak Hall*. With its 12-foot paneled walls, exposed beams, and majestic stairway with twisted spindles and fluted columns, the hall embraces visitors in a warm, rich glow. Over the carved mantel hangs a portrait of Gabrielle, painted in Paris in 1888.

Dr. Albert (Jake) Michel, an avid preservationist, saw what had become a forlorn mansion one day in 1989. Unperturbed by the peeling paint, broken windows, and collapsing porches, he and his wife, Margaret, bought the estate and began the arduous restoration process. Once described by

North Carolina writer Thomas Wolfe as a "big, rambling, magnificent Victorian house," it is now listed on the National Register of Historic Places.

The mansion contains 10 large fireplaces with elaborate neoclassical mantels. The parlor is furnished with period pieces and accented with English garden prints. An ornate octagonal ballroom and a drawing room are used for meetings and receptions. This area of North Carolina has a rich literary tradition, and the library, which is paneled in pine painted to resemble walnut, houses an impressive collection of books about North Carolina and by authors with an Asheville connection.

Furnishings in the guestrooms are equally attractive. Canopy and four-poster beds, Victorian chairs and tables, Oriental rugs, and bathrooms with footed tubs are found throughout. Down pillows and fresh flowers add the finishing touches. The enormous rooms on the second floor of the main house are named for Pearson family members or close friends. The most lavish, the *Chief Justice Suite,* has a seven-sided bedroom, a sitting room, a wet bar, a whirlpool tub, and a fireplace. The *Gabrielle Pearson Room* has a canopy bed, richly curtained in a soft pink moire faille, and a fireplace. Rooms on the third floor are named for authors who lived or wrote in Asheville, such as F. Scott Fitzgerald and O. Henry, and contain a selection of their books.

Nine more rooms are in the yellow and green Victorian *Croquet Cottages,* which form a crescent adjacent to the croquet lawn. These elegant private retreats have bead board walls and ceilings, gas fireplaces, pencil-post beds, vibrant watercolors on the walls, and spacious baths. Individual porches provide popular places from which to watch a game of croquet or to view the surrounding mountains. A new Victorian-style building, *Garden Pavilion,* with a café and 15 more rooms opened in 1996. A peaceful mountain brook spills past the walkway that leads here from the main building and then tumbles into a pond below; the *Pavilion* wraps around a parterre garden. The guestrooms are more contemporary in style; all but one have fireplaces, four have private terraces, and two have whirlpool tubs.

Guests are treated to breakfast and an afternoon tea that includes scones, cookies, and drinks. Dinner (open to non-guests) is served at *Gabrielle's,* the inn's gracious restaurant. It's served either in the cherry-paneled dining room with a three-tiered brass chandelier, or on the sun porch with its wicker furniture, ceiling fans, abundant plants, and lavish view of the surrounding mountains. A pianist provides background music. Entrées might include grilled Carolina shrimp with sweet-potato hash or char-grilled lamb loin with potato–goat cheese mash and mushroom ragoût. The wine list is exceptional.

The inn is near the spectacular *Biltmore House and Gardens* (the George Vanderbilt mansion), *Chimney Rock Park,* and cultural attractions, including the *Thomas Wolfe House, Connemara* (the Carl Sandburg house), and the *Folk Art Center.*

RICHMOND HILL INN 87 Richmond Hill Dr., Asheville, NC 28806 (phone: 704-252-7313; 800-545-9238; fax: 704-252-8726). This Victorian hilltop retreat has 36 guestrooms with private baths, twin, double, queen-, or king-size beds, telephones, TV sets, and air conditioning; 27 have fireplaces and 13 have porches. Wheelchair accessible. Open year-round, except three weeks in January. Rate for a double room (including full breakfast and afternoon tea): $140 to $420. Two-night minimum stay on weekends. Major credit cards accepted. Children welcome. No pets. No smoking. Dr. Albert and Margaret Michel, owners; Susan Michel, innkeeper.

DIRECTIONS: The inn is 3 miles from downtown Asheville. From Asheville take I-240 west to the Route 19/23 (Weaverville) exit, then follow Route 19/23 north to Exit 251 (UNC-Asheville). Turn left at the bottom of the ramp. At the first light turn left onto Riverside Drive. Turn right onto Pearson Bridge Road and cross over the French Broad River. At the sharp curve turn right onto Richmond Hill Drive. The first driveway on the right leads to the inn.

BALSAM MOUNTAIN INN

Balsam, North Carolina

Located on 27 acres near the crest of the Great Balsam Mountains, the three-story *Balsam Mountain Inn* snuggles into a forested glen, surrounded by peaks that reach as high as 6,000 feet. This gracious Victorian gem first welcomed visitors back in 1908. It was the era of train travel, and the quaint Balsam depot on the *Western North Carolina Railroad* was the highest station east of the Rockies. Lured by the seven freshwater springs on the inn grounds and the bracing mountain air, city folks came to escape the heat of summer and to enjoy therapeutic walks.

When Merrily Teasley purchased the inn in 1990, she acquired a solid building with bead board walls throughout that had seen few cosmetic changes and even retained much of the original furniture. Extensive restora-

tion was necessary. Today, the massive building that once contained 100 tiny warrens has 50 spacious guestrooms (all with private baths), three common rooms, and three dining rooms.

The inn's old oak rockers, with handwoven seats and backs, welcome guests to "sit a spell" on the 100-foot, double-tiered front porch. Inside, the library boasts a collection of more than 2,000 volumes, while the game-room has puzzles and cards. The living room is charmingly decorated with chairs covered in bright chintz, Oriental rugs on heart-pine floors, twig furniture, an abundance of plants, and a double-sided fireplace. Antiques, including iron beds and wicker, are interspersed with twig beds and chairs made by a local craftsman; the wooden walls are painted vibrant colors such as turquoise with pink or plum trim. Many bathrooms have claw-foot tubs. Merrily created 16 new guestrooms on the inn's third floor in 1996; it's decorated with colorful quilts and repaired and repainted chairs and chests original to the inn.

The dining room offers hearty Southern fare: Local trout as well as an abundance of fresh produce are on the menu. A full country breakfast with fresh-baked muffins (maybe poppyseed-lemon) and an entrée (such as dilled scrambled eggs in a bread cup) is complimentary to inn guests. Breakfast, lunch, and dinner also are open to non-guests.

Mountain trails wind from the inn through acres of rhododendrons and fields of wildflowers, circling a freshwater pond, meandering along a stream, then stopping at a mountain ledge where hikers can view the brilliant sunsets. For those who want to explore the surrounding area, the Blue Ridge Parkway is a half mile away, and skiing, mountain biking, and whitewater rafting are nearby. Guests also can enjoy North Carolina's Mountains-to-Sea hiking trail, golf, horseback riding, trout fishing, and the *Biltmore House and Gardens* (the George Vanderbilt mansion) in Asheville.

BALSAM MOUNTAIN INN Seven Springs Road (mailing address: PO Box 40), Balsam, NC 28707 (phone: 704-456-9498; 800-224-9498; fax: 704-456-9298). This mountain inn has 50 guestrooms with private baths and double or king-size beds. Wheelchair accessible. Open year-round; restaurant closed for lunch weekdays November through May. Rate for a double room (including full breakfast): $90 to $150. Two-night minimum stay on holiday weekends, during fall foliage season, and during local college events. Discover, MasterCard, and Visa accepted. Children welcome. No pets. Two dogs in residence. Smoking permitted in lobby, some guestrooms, and a section of the dining room. Merrily Teasley, innkeeper.

DIRECTIONS: On the Blue Ridge Parkway, the inn is closest to milepost 443. From the parkway take the exit for Route 74/23 and turn south toward Sylva. About a quarter mile south of the parkway overpass, turn off Route 74/23 at a small green sign marking the village of Balsam. Make an almost immediate right up a hill, across the railroad tracks, and continue straight for another third of a mile. Drive across the tracks again, then turn into the inn's driveway.

GIDEON RIDGE INN

BLOWING ROCK, NORTH CAROLINA

Located in the heart of the Blue Ridge Mountains and just off the Blue Ridge Parkway, the village of Blowing Rock is named for an unusual rock formation that has the odd habit of returning light objects that are thrown toward it. The remote village, situated at 4,000 feet, enjoys crisp, cool mountain air.

From the stone terraces of *Gideon Ridge Inn*, the views across the valley can extend as far as 100 miles on a clear day. Stone walls gently rise to peaked gables and the flagstone terraces that circle the inn lead to abundant flower gardens. The original mansion was built in 1939 as a gentleman's retreat. It was opened as an inn by Jane and Cobb Milner Jr. in 1983. Today, their son Cobb Milner III and his wife Cindy share the innkeeping tasks.

The primary attraction of *Gideon Ridge* is the spectacular view. From the east the morning sun rises from behind Pilot Mountain; on the south, Mount Mitchell looms. On the stone terrace there are green wicker chairs with bright floral cushions to encourage guests to watch nature's awesome spectacle.

Indoors, the library, warmed by a fire in the huge stone fireplace in winter, is a comfortable haven with a tufted pigskin sofa, tapestry-covered chairs, a piano, and a multitude of books.

Most guestrooms have views and the furnishings incorporate a rustic mountain simplicity. The *Carriage Room* has a beautiful French sleigh bed, a marble whirlpool tub, a luxurious tile bath, and a spectacular view. The *Old Master Room* has a magnificent canopy bed and a woodburning fireplace; the *Colonial Room* has a four-poster bed, a fireplace, and French doors leading to a fantastic private terrace with a view.

Breakfast treats include fresh fruit, juice, and breads, as well as one of Jane's specialty entrées such as cornmeal pancakes with Smithfield ham and maple syrup, or blueberry-stuffed French toast with fresh fruit sauce. Tea—a selection of small sandwiches, cookies, and scones—is served every afternoon.

The inn is located on five acres laced with walking trails that lead to two pergolas and even to a cave. The town of Blowing Rock contains several fine restaurants as well as crafts and antiques shops. The *Blowing Rock Stage Company* performs seasonally, and *Appalachian Summer,* a series of cultural offerings under the auspices of Appalachian State University in nearby Boone, brings a variety of entertainment to the area. Hikers find abundant trails in the region; the Appalachian Trail and Grandfather Mountain are especially fine. Golf and tennis are also nearby.

GIDEON RIDGE INN 202 Gideon Ridge Rd. (mailing address: PO Box 1929), Blowing Rock, NC 28605 (phone: 704-295-3644; fax: 704-295-4586). This mountainside inn has 10 rooms with private baths and queen- or king-size beds; six with fireplaces, two with whirlpool tubs. Open year-round. Rate for a double room (including full breakfast and afternoon tea): $120 to $180. Two-night minimum on weekends. Major credit cards accepted. Not appropriate for children under 13. No pets. Two black Labrador retrievers, Scarlett and Melanie, and one cat, Miss Elizabeth, in residence. No smoking except on terrace. Jane and Cobb Milner Jr. and Cindy and Cobb Milner III, innkeepers.

DIRECTIONS: From I-40, take Exit 123 in Hickory to Route 321 and follow it for approximately 48 miles to Rock Road, which is 1½ miles south of Blowing Rock. Turn west onto Rock Road and at the fork, turn left onto Gideon Ridge Road. Go to the top of the ridge to the inn.

OLD EDWARDS INN AND HIGHLANDS INN

HIGHLANDS, NORTH CAROLINA

A spectacular drive through the Nantahala Range of the Great Smoky Mountains and Cullasaja Gorge, winding along a narrow two-lane road past dramatic cascades and waterfalls, leads to the beautiful mountain town of Highlands, where the *Old Edwards Inn* and the *Highlands Inn* have been welcoming guests for more than a century.

The Benton family has created a unique complex of these historic buildings, beginning with the 1981 purchase and renovation of the ca. 1878 *Old Edwards Inn.* They bought the adjacent *Central House* in 1983, turning it into a fine restaurant. In 1989 they added the 1880s *Highlands Inn,* across the street, to their collection. The *Highlands Inn,* larger and grander than the *Old Edwards Inn,* was originally known as the *Smith Hotel,* and was especially popular in the late 1800s, when the area's fresh mountain air attracted tourists. Today both inns are listed on the National Register of Historic Places.

Guestrooms feature numerous antiques—a "fainting" couch in one, and four-poster, sleigh, and canopy beds covered with down comforters and fluffy pillows throughout. The walls are stenciled. Several rooms have fireplaces and private porches, complete with rocking chairs.

In the parlor of the *Highlands Inn,* cushioned sofas and chairs are placed before the fire, providing inviting places to read one of the many books on the shelves. Just off the parlor is an enchanting garden room furnished in white wicker. This is also the room where guests gather for games of chess, Trivial Pursuit, and bridge. Downstairs is a masculine, paneled bar (county law permits the sale of wine only), added in 1994, which features a magnificent antique pool table, a polished mahogany bar, and hand-painted murals. A large-screen TV is a popular attraction, especially with sports fans. The *Old Edwards Inn's* parlor is called the *Moose Room* in honor of the massive head that hangs over the mantel.

A continental buffet breakfast—fresh fruit, fresh-baked breads or muffins, cereal, and juice—is served to guests every morning. Specialties of the *Central House* restaurant, a casual eatery, are local seafood and steaks, although lighter fare is available. The *Kelsey House,* a restaurant at the *Highlands Inn,* serves fine low-country fare. Entrées might include local rainbow trout, pan-seared pork tenderloins, and pan-fried Southern chicken. Both restaurants serve only wine, but guests may bring their own liquor and beer.

In addition to enjoying the breathtaking scenery and mountain air, guests may play golf, ride horses, and hike the Appalachian Trail. Within two blocks there is tennis, racquet ball, a swimming pool, basketball, and a fitness center. The inns are also near crafts outlets and boutique shopping.

OLD EDWARDS INN AND HIGHLANDS INN Main St. (mailing address: PO Box 1030), Highlands, NC 28741 (phone: 704-526-5036; fax: 704-526-5036, ext. 33). These inns have a total of 50 guestrooms with private baths, twin, double, queen-, or king-size beds, TV sets, and air conditioning. Closed December through March. Rate for a double room (including continental breakfast): $74 to $99. Major credit cards accepted. Children welcome in the *Highlands Inn.* No pets. Smoking permitted in designated public areas only. Rip and Pat Benton, innkeepers.

DIRECTIONS: From Asheville take I-28 south to Route 280. Follow Route 280 south to Rosman and then turn onto Highway 64, traveling west for 31 miles to Highlands. The inn is on Main Street at the intersection of Highway 64 and Route 28.

PILOT KNOB INN

PILOT MOUNTAIN, NORTH CAROLINA

The *Pilot Knob Inn* is in tobacco country, where the low, broad-leafed, green plants stretch in neat rows for miles along the roads. In the late 1800s, tobacco leaves were stored and dried in log sheds that have since been replaced by metal structures.

In 1987, inspired by the rustic old unused tobacco sheds scattered throughout the countryside, Jim Rouse purchased 50 acres on a wooded hillside of Pilot Mountain, complete with a 40-by-40-foot barn, and set about creating a romantic retreat. He dismantled five additional sheds, as well as a 160-year-old homesteader's cabin, and rebuilt them as individual cabins. Stones from the barn foundations became fireplaces, and tier poles used to dry the tobacco leaves became supports and railings for front porches.

Each of the three-room cabins is secluded in the woods. Although they contain all the creature comforts, they are decorated with cozy simplicity. The living room's massive stone fireplace might be flanked by tapestry love seats or wide-wale corduroy sofas, and the hardwood floors are covered

with carpets Jim collected on his world travels. In the separate upstairs bedrooms the beds are particularly unusual: The headboards and footboards
were crafted from the trunks of stripped juniper trees—some even include
attached limbs. Two-person Jacuzzis are a sybaritic note, while fresh flowers, fluffy bathrobes, and bowls of fruit are added indulgences. Each cabin's private porch contains rockers that Jim hand-crafted himself. This is
the place to listen to the call of the birds and to watch the numerous squirrels, raccoons, and other wildlife.

The property's original barn serves as the common meeting place. Strains
of classical music flow from the library, which has a vaulted ceiling, a 300-
year-old Italian marble fireplace, rich mahogany paneling (ca. 1790), and
old pine floors covered with a green floral Oriental rug. Games and books
are available here. In the morning, guests gather in the breakfast room for
homemade waffles, sausages, biscuits, muffins, coffee cake, and fresh fruit.

A swimming pool and deck are behind the large barn; there's a sauna
and a six-acre stocked lake where guests can fish for bass or bluegill. Hiking
trails lead to *Pilot Mountain State Park,* which borders the inn. The sunrise
view of the 115-foot, solid granite Pilot Knob, which takes on an orange
glow in winter, is unforgettable. Nearby attractions include hot-air balloon
rides at *Jomeokee Park* and visits to Winston-Salem, with its *Old Salem
Moravian Museum, Renolda House Museum of American Art* (the former
home of R. J. Reynolds), and tours of the Stroh Brewery.

PILOT KNOB INN PO Box 1280, Pilot Mountain, NC 27014 (phone: 910-325-
2502). This inn has six individual log cabins with private baths, double or queen-
size beds, telephones, TV sets, fireplaces, porches, whirlpool tubs, and air
conditioning. Open year-round. Rate for a double room (including full breakfast):
$105 to $125. MasterCard and Visa accepted. Not appropriate for children.

Smoking permitted. No pets. Four cats, Maggie, Maynard, Mildred, and Uncle Manly, on the property. Jim Rouse, innkeeper.

DIRECTIONS: From Winston-Salem take Highway 52 north to the *Pilot Mountain State Park* exit. At the bottom of the exit ramp, turn left, go 20 feet, and turn right onto small gravel road. Continue on this road, always bearing left, for about half a mile to the inn, which is at the end. (There is no sign at the entrance to the road. If you reach the entrance to the park, you've gone too far.)

FEARRINGTON HOUSE

PITTSBORO, NORTH CAROLINA

Fearrington Village, where the acclaimed *Fearrington House* inn and restaurant are located, is a picture-perfect planned country village. R. B. and Jenny Fitch boldly converted 65 acres of the 650-acre former Fearrington dairy farm into a old-fashioned rural village beginning in 1974. The original Fearrington home, built in 1927, now houses the acclaimed *Fearrington House* restaurant; the adjacent dairy barn is available for catered functions, and the granary is a busy country store with an upstairs café. There's also a well-stocked bookstore, pharmacy, garden shop, craft shop, and bank. The dairy's silo dominates the landscape, and cows still graze in the pastures.

In the heart of the village, next to the restaurant, the inn is built around an inner courtyard, its low-slung, white clapboard buildings punctuated by New England–style dormers. A kaleidoscope of flowers spills from planters along the slate pathways. The garden house and the sun room are relaxing hideaways where guests can congregate, but *Jenny's Garden,* just beyond the sun room, is the pièce de résistance. Bounded by white Victorian trellises and gazebos, it contains nearly 80 varieties of roses as well as herbs and other flowers. Nearby are a pool, tennis courts, and croquet and *bocci* lawns.

The guestrooms offer some delightful surprises. Nooks and crannies might hold antique desks or chairs. The bed may be an English antique pine four-poster, or the headboard might have been made from a church door. Original art graces the walls, and several units have fireplaces with hand-marbleized mantels. The lightly pickled pine flooring came from an 1850s British workhouse. Marble vanities and heated towel racks are featured in the bathrooms.

The *Fearrington House* restaurant, which opened in 1980, had a lot to do with elevating the concept of Southern cooking, and *The Fearrington House Cookbook,* which Jenny produced in 1987, brought its techniques into homes nationwide. Appetizers such as shrimp and grits with apple-onion vinaigrette and entrées such as roast lamb with bourbon-molasses sauce, showed the world that the local fare goes far beyond fried chicken and catfish. The restaurant offers a fine wine list, and its desserts, including ethereal soufflés, should not be missed. It's all served up with generous hospitality in a setting of candlelit tables, fresh flowers, original art, and antiques.

The inn is located in the Chapel Hill–Raleigh-Durham area, with golf, cultural events, antiquing, and boating nearby. Also in the area are *Duke University* and the *University of North Carolina.*

FEARRINGTON HOUSE 2000 Fearrington Village Center, Pittsboro, NC 27312 (phone: 919-542-2121; fax: 919-542-4202). This country inn has 28 guestrooms with private baths, double, queen-, or king-size beds, telephones, TV sets, and air conditioning; seven with fireplaces. Wheelchair accessible. Open year-round; restaurant closed Mondays, but dinner is available in the *Market Café.* Rate for a double room (including full breakfast and full English tea): $165 to $275. Three-night minimum during university graduations. Major credit cards accepted. Not appropriate for children under 13. No pets. No smoking. R. B. Fitch, owner; Richard Delany, manager.

DIRECTIONS: From Chapel Hill travel south on Route 15/501 for 8 miles to Fearrington Village. From Raleigh take I-64 west to Cary, and then Route 64 west toward Pittsboro. After 8 miles turn north onto Mt. Gilead Church Road to Fearrington.

INN AT THE TAYLOR HOUSE
VALLE CRUCIS, NORTH CAROLINA

A wooden sign showing a rooster greeting the sunrise hangs at the entrance to the *Inn at the Taylor House.* Located in the rural center of the Blue Ridge Mountains, the pristine two-story farmhouse was built in the early 1900s; with three large dormers and a broad, wraparound verandah, it is typical

of the period. An old-fashioned porch swing sways gently in the breeze, allowing guests to quietly listen to Dutch Creek rushing by.

The house was purchased in 1987 and converted to an inn by Carol "Chip" Schwab, a veteran of the hospitality business, who had owned a cooking school in Atlanta. She decorated the house with style and polish. Heart-pine floors gleam from beneath creamy Oriental rugs in the living room. Pale yellow walls provide a gracious backdrop for the white sofa piled with needlepoint pillows, an antique French commode, a fireplace, and Chip's collection of antique blue and white Chinese export china, inherited from her grandmother.

Guestrooms are decorated in an equally refined fashion. The *Luxury Suite,* reached by private staircase, has vaulted ceilings and a sitting room, lavishly adorned with Clarence House and Scalamandre botanical prints in green and rust tones. *Room No. 5,* a corner room, is light and breezy with white wicker furniture and balloon shades decorated with a lattice Waverly fabric. The *Red Cottage* is a charming accommodation carved out of a former barn. All rooms have featherbeds dressed with luxurious linens.

Breakfasts (open to non-guests) are renowned. Chip might prepare sour-cream pancakes topped with fresh strawberries or eggs Benedict. Seating in the cheerful yellow dining room is at glass-topped tables, enhanced by vases of bright flowers fresh from the gardens. The inn has a shop where fine-quality gifts, as well as canned and preserved foods, are sold.

The inn is located on 10 acres that include gardens with a gazebo. Massages can be arranged in the spacious, art-filled massage gallery. Nearby, the mile-high suspension bridge at Grandfather Mountain offers panoramic views. Additional hiking routes wind through the Blue Ridge Mountains, and the Appalachian Trail is not far away. Golfing, fishing, horseback riding, skiing, and canoeing also are nearby.

INN AT THE TAYLOR HOUSE Hwy. 194 (mailing address: PO Box 713), Valle Crucis, NC 28691 (phone: 704-963-5581; fax: 704-963-5818). This inn has eight guestrooms and suites (including one cottage) with private baths and double or king-size beds. Wheelchair accessible. Closed December through March. Rate for a double room (including full breakfast and afternoon refreshments): $120 to $235. MasterCard and Visa accepted. Children welcome with prior permission. No pets. A dog, Lulabell, cats, chickens, rabbits, guinea pigs, and pygmy goats on the property. Smoking on porch only. Carol Schwab, innkeeper.

DIRECTIONS: From Winston-Salem take Route 321 west to Boone, then take North Carolina Route 105 south for 5 miles to flashing yellow light. Turn right onto Route 1112 (Broadstone Road) and travel 2½ miles south to Valle Crucis. Turn left onto Higway 194. The inn will be on the right in ⁸/₁₀ of a mile.

THE SWAG

WAYNESVILLE, NORTH CAROLINA

As you make your way up a winding switch-back road—4 miles on a paved two-lane road and another 2½ miles on a private gravel road—you wonder if you'll ever arrive. Numerous waterfalls and rushing streams tumble down the mountain. As you reach an ear-popping 5,000 feet above sea level, the spruce, hemlock, and fir trees give way to open space—a bald mountain ridge (part of the Cataloochee Divide of the Great Smoky Mountains National Park) that affords vistas across Jonathan Valley for a distance of up to 50 miles.

Located on 250 acres of the ridge, *The Swag*'s buildings are as extraordinary as the site. The log structures were scouted by Dan and Deener Matthews and hauled, disassembled, to this mountaintop aerie. The complex was originally used as a family and church retreat (Dan is an Episcopalian minister), but it opened as an inn in 1981, and additions and improvements are made every year.

The heart of the *Main Lodge* is a former Baptist church from Tennessee that was dismantled and moved here. It has a massive stone fireplace and hand-hewn logs that create a cathedral ceiling. A player piano located here is often the scene of convivial sing-alongs following dinner. *Chestnut Lodge,* built of wormy chestnut in 1980, has a soaring cathedral ceiling, an antler chandelier, another huge stone fireplace, and an inlaid wood mural of mountains and pine trees. It houses both a book and a video library, a reading loft, and a room downstairs with a VCR.

The guest accommodations have stone walls, doors hewn from massive slabs of wood, and rustic furniture made by local craftspeople. The *Loft Room* has a pencil-post bed and a woodstove; the *Hideaway* has barnwood walls, a stone fireplace in the sitting area, a peeled-log bed, a private balcony, and a bath with a view from the whirlpool tub; the *Rock Room* has a

217

rock wall, a massive rock fireplace, a steam shower, a wet bar, and a stone slab verandah. Amenities include mini-refrigerators, hair dryers, and fresh coffee beans and coffee grinders for use in individual coffeemakers. The rooms lack TV sets and air conditioning, but you'll never miss them.

House guests enjoy three meals a day at *The Swag*. There are assigned seats at two communal tables, although individual tables can be arranged. A typical evening meal, lit by candlelight, will include chilled white corn soup, roast rack of veal with potato gnocchi, and a dessert such as hazelnut tart with chocolate sauce. (The inn is located in a dry county so guests are advised to bring their own liquor or wine, if desired.) A sit-down lunch is offered every day, although a picnic lunch can be provided.

The inn has an underground racquetball court, a sauna, a hot tub, badminton and croquet lawns, and hammocks tucked away among the trees. Special programs—ranging from fishing or hiking weeks to couples weekends—take place throughout the summer. The property has numerous hiking and walking trails. The most popular is the Waterfall Trail, which leads to a spectacular waterfall on Hemphill Creek. The inn also has a private entrance to the 500,000-acre *Great Smoky Mountains National Park* and the many trails within its boundaries.

THE SWAG Hemphill Rd. (mailing address: Route 2, PO Box 280-A), Waynesville, NC 28786 (phone: 704-926-0430; 800-789-7672; fax: 704-926-2036). This unique mountaintop retreat has 17 guestrooms with private baths and twin, double, queen-, or king-size beds, and telephones; 10 have fireplaces or woodstoves, 12 have private balconies. Wheelchair accessible. Open mid-May through October. Rate for a double room (including breakfast, lunch, and dinner): $200 to $400 (15 percent gratuity added; bring your own bottle). Two-night minimum required. Discover, MasterCard, and Visa accepted. Children welcome. No pets. One cat, Salt, outside. No smoking. Deener Matthews, innkeeper; Jennifer Walt, assistant innkeeper.

DIRECTIONS: From Asheville, travel west on I-40 to Exit 20. Go south on Route 276 for $2^{7}/_{10}$ miles and turn right onto Hemphill Road. Travel $1^{2}/_{10}$ miles to a stop sign. Turn right and follow this road for 3 miles to *The Swag* driveway on the left. Travel up the gravel road for $2^{1}/_{2}$ miles to the inn.

Tennessee

INN AT BLACKBERRY FARM

WALLAND, TENNESSEE

Located on 1,100 acres in the foothills of the Great Smoky Mountains, the *Inn at Blackberry Farm* is both park and inn. Jogging, bicycling, walking, and hiking trails lace the property. Singing Brook Trout Pond is stocked for anglers and perfect for canoeing, Pretty Place Loop has shady nooks with picnic tables for secluded afternoons, and there are tennis courts, a swimming pool, a basketball court, and shuffleboard.

The property consisted of the main house and a collection of outbuildings when Sandy and Kreis Beall purchased it in 1976. While Sandy was busy starting what became a chain of restaurants called *Ruby Tuesday's,* Kreis leased and managed a portion of the estate as an executive retreat, then expanded the use of the site for weddings and corporate functions. In 1989, the couple's passion for good food in elegant surroundings, a love of Tennessee, and a desire to share their cherished spot with others led them to open an inn. They added a *Guest House* with 11 rooms and converted *Cove Cottage* into three more rooms. There are now 29 guestrooms at *Blackberry Farm,* but the Bealls' hands-on attention makes it feel as if you're visiting friends.

Guestrooms are named after the abundant wildflowers that bloom in the fields. With names such as *May Apple, Foxglove,* and *Doll's Eyes,* they have a country ambience—from the flowered chintz draperies, quilted spreads, and English-style antiques to the four-poster and canopy beds, polished mahogany side tables, and plush sofas piled high with fringed pillows.

Oriental carpets cover oak floors in the living room of the *Main House* and the *Great Room* of the *Guest House.* There are two fireplaces in the *Great Room,* and original oils line the walls. A library is well stocked with books, but look closely before you grab one—there's also a trompe l'oeil wallpaper of books. The dining room affords panoramic views of *Great Smoky Mountains National Park*. Of all the public spaces, the favorite is the broad porch furnished with Tennessee rockers, where guests watch the pink and orange sun set behind the Smokies.

The couple's fondness for food is evident in the creative fare, which blends fancy and familiar in a style they call "foothills cuisine." At breakfast guests choose from a set menu, which might include fruit, fresh-baked muffins and scones, and Sally Lunn French toast or lemon soufflé pancakes. Dinner (also open to non-guests by reservation), served on Royal Worcester china with a blackberry motif, consists of four courses—perhaps onion soup followed by a salad of seasonal greens, cedar-planked grouper with hoppin' John and fried carrots or hickory-smoked loin of pork with buttermilk whipped potatoes, and banana pudding cheesecake with caramel sauce and homemade vanilla wafers. The inn is in a dry county, so guests are advised to bring their own wine and liquor.

The inn provides picnic lunches to complement the day's activities— perhaps a bicycle jaunt across the trails, a swim in the pool, a scramble across the rocks in Hesse Creek, or a rowboat outing on the three-acre bass and bream lake. The inn has plenty of fishing equipment, as well as a fleet of 20 mountain bikes, tennis racquets, walking sticks, binoculars, and nature reference books. If all this is not enough, head off the property: Hiking, golf, horseback riding, and *Dollywood* are nearby.

INN AT BLACKBERRY FARM 1471 W. Millers Cove Rd., Walland, TN 37886 (phone: 423-984-9850; 800-862-7610; fax: 423-681-7753). This country estate in the Smoky Mountains has 29 guestrooms with private baths, twin, double, queen-, or king-size beds, and air conditioning; 14 with telephones. Wheelchair accessible. Open year-round. Rate for a double room (including breakfast, lunch, dinner, and use of all equipment): $395 to $495 (package rates also available). Two-night minimum stay on weekends; three nights on holidays. Major credit cards accepted. Not appropriate for children under 10; children of all ages welcome during *Thanksgiving* and *Christmas*. No pets. Smoking permitted on the verandah only. Kreis and Sandy Beall, owners; Barry Marshall, innkeeper.

DIRECTIONS: From Knoxville take I-40 to the Airport/Smoky Mountain exit. Follow Highway 129 south for 12½ miles to *McGee Tyson Airport*. Past the airport, follow Highway 321 north 16 miles to West Millers Cove Road (a quarter mile beyond the Foothills Parkway entrance). Turn right onto West Millers Cove Road and go 3½ miles to *Blackberry Farm*.

Virginia

CLIFTON—THE COUNTRY INN

CHARLOTTESVILLE, VIRGINIA

The countryside surrounding Charlottesville is laced with historic estates, often hidden away along winding country roads that pass fields of grazing cattle and horses. Just outside the town proper, *Clifton* is announced by a discreet sign at the entrance to a tree-shrouded drive. The driveway leads through a historic 40-acre estate where Thomas Jefferson and other American luminaries were frequent visitors.

The manor house, a combination of Federal and Colonial Revival styles with a series of boxed columns across the front, was built in 1799 by Thomas Mann Randolph, who married Martha Jefferson, Thomas Jefferson's daughter. Randolph eventually became Governor of Virginia, a member of the Virginia House of Delegates, and a member of the US Congress. His grand house has been enlarged and embellished numerous times throughout the years, yet it retains its colonial ambience. The polished pine floors and the simple Federal fireplace mantels date to the late 1700s, while the fan- and sidelights are more recent additions. For comfort and style, however, the inn is strictly 20th century.

In the elegant entry, the walls are sponge-painted an apricot color and there's a massive floral display on a Federal sideboard. The drawing room has sofas and chairs grouped near a gracious fireplace and a grand piano, while the library is furnished with green leather chairs, another fireplace, and numerous books in built-in cases. Games are available here also for the enjoyment of the guests. To the rear, an enclosed stone terrace has an abundance of plants, iron tables and chairs, and a fireplace at one end. This is where breakfast is served, overlooking the formal gardens and a gazebo.

The guestrooms all have fireplaces and are furnished with antiques. *Room No. 5* has a windowseat overlooking the croquet lawn, a sofa in pink damask, and a pencil-post bed. The quaint rooms in the *Old Livery Building* overlook the lake. They have bead board walls and cabbage rose fabric covering sofas and chairs in the sitting areas, which also have fireplaces. Beds are located on raised platforms; baths have old-fashioned tubs with bead board surrounds, tiled showers, and built-in benches. Popular accommodations include the *Honeymoon Cottage,* which has an exposed beam ceiling and skylights, and the *Carriage House,* which contains a suite so large it has a grand piano in the sitting room.

The estate became an inn in 1987, but since Craig Hartman became the innkeeper in 1992 it's gained a wide following for its distinguished cuisine as well as its rooms. Craig has a notable restaurant background and he's a graduate of the Culinary Institute of America. He serves a multi-course dinner (open to non-guests) that starts with an appetizer, followed by a soup, then a salad (perhaps of assorted greens with a red grape dressing and *chèvre*), accompanied by sun-dried cherry bread. That is followed by a fresh fruit ice. There are two choices of entrées, perhaps a grilled rack of lamb served with mint vinaigrette and roasted garlic or oven-roasted North Atlantic salmon with a hot mushroom salad. Dessert may consist of a white-chocolate raspberry Bavarian torte served with a trio of sauces. A full breakfast and afternoon tea are also served.

The grounds meander down to the Rivanna River. There's a raised pool and a gazebo surrounded by shale, formal gardens, a tennis court, and winding trails through the trees to a lake. For off-property diversions, guests may bicycle to nearby *Michie Tavern,* or drive to *Monticello* or *Ashlawn.*

CLIFTON—THE COUNTRY INN 1296 Clifton Inn Dr., Charlottesville, VA 22911 (phone: 804-971-1800; 888-971-1800; fax: 804-971-7098). This country inn has 14 rooms and suites with private baths, double or queen-size beds, fireplaces, and air conditioning. Wheelchair accessible. Open year-round. Rate for a double room (including full breakfast and afternoon tea): $185-$245. Two-night minimum on weekends. MasterCard and Visa accepted. Children welcome. No pets. One cat, Marmalade, on premise. No smoking. Mitch and Emily Willey, proprietors; Craig Hartman, innkeeper.

DIRECTIONS: From I-64, take Exit 124 onto Route 250 east. Travel 2½ miles and then turn right onto Route 729. Turn left into the second driveway, in about ⅓ mile.

SILVER THATCH INN

CHARLOTTESVILLE, VIRGINIA

The *Silver Thatch Inn* has an unusual setting. This authentic country inn, parts of which date to 1780, is encircled by modern homes on spacious lots.

Nevertheless, they all blend harmoniously into a secluded little neighborhood, where the community swimming pool and tennis court are shared by inn guests.

The original part of the inn was built by German mercenaries who were captured in the Battle of Saratoga (New York) during the Revolutionary War and marched to Virginia. This section, now called the *Hessian Room*, is built of logs and mortar. In 1812, the center clapboard section was built to be used as a boys' school. Later, the house and its surrounding 300 acres were used as a tobacco or melon farm until, in 1984, it became an inn. Vince and Rita Scoffone have been owner/innkeepers since 1992.

Guests visiting the *Silver Thatch Inn* receive a warm welcome. A brimming plate of fresh-baked cookies awaits and either Vince or Rita is there to offer a refreshing glass of wine or beer in the inn's tiny bar, where the only TV set is located.

The guestrooms are charming; each is named for a president. Three are in the main building and four are in an adjacent cottage. In the main building, *Jefferson* has a four-poster canopy bed, a carved armoire, and a fireplace; *Madison* has a pencil-post canopy bed, a fireplace, and a lovely view across the courtyard. *Washington* is the grandest of the cottage accommodations, with a magnificent matching bedroom suite that includes a burled mahogany armoire, a marble-topped dresser, and an intricately carved mahogany headboard.

Dinner (available Tuesdays through Saturdays and open to non-guests) is served in three rooms; two of them have fireplaces and the third is the sunroom where breakfast is served. Typical dinner entrées may include a grilled rack of lamb with ginger and mint-apple honey accompanied by pecan rice pilaf or fresh fish of the day. For dessert, the triple-layered chocolate mousse, served in a stemmed glass, wins raves.

The Charlottesville area offers numerous opportunities for hiking, biking, horseback riding, golfing, fishing, and visiting wineries. The Blue Ridge Parkway and Skyline Drive are nearby, as are *Monticello, Ashlawn,* the *University of Virginia* (designed by Thomas Jefferson), and *Montpelier.*

SILVER THATCH INN 3001 Hollymead Dr., Charlottesville, VA 22911-7422 (phone: 804-978-4686; fax: 804-973-6156). This historic country inn has seven rooms with private baths, double or queen-size beds, and air conditioning; four have fireplaces. Open year-round. Rate for a double room (including continental breakfast): $110 to $150. Two-night minimum on weekends from April through June and from September through November. Major credit cards accepted. Children welcome. No pets. No smoking. Rita and Vince Scoffone, innkeepers.

DIRECTIONS: From I-64, take Route 250 west. Follow this to Route 29 north and proceed for 5 miles. Turn right at the traffic light (you'll see an inn sign) onto Route 1520. The inn is ⅓ mile up the hill. From I-66, take Route 29 south in Gainesville. Follow this 1 mile past the Charlottesville airport. Turn left at the traffic light onto Route 1520 and follow directions above.

THE OAKS VICTORIAN INN
Christiansburg, Virginia

Shaded by seven giant white oaks (one estimated to be more than 400 years old), this grand 1889 Victorian dwelling is situated on a knoll overlooking Main Street, amid manicured lawns, flower beds, and boxwood hedges.

The house is as romantic today as it was when it was built by Major William Pierce as a present for his bride, Julia. Even so, by the time Margaret and Tom Ray first saw it, the front door had fallen off and the basement was flooded. Now, after a meticulous restoration, it offers eight pristine guestrooms and is listed on the National Register of Historic Places. Along with nearby private homes, it also is part of the East Main Street Historic District of Christiansburg.

The spacious guestrooms are furnished with stunning antiques. The *Julia Pierce Room,* for example, has a carved Victorian bed, wicker chairs, and a polished cherry chest dating to 1820. Decorated in soft green and peach floral fabrics, it has a fireplace with hand-painted slate plus a five-window turret. All the rooms have private baths, and this one features a Jacuzzi for two. *Lady Melodie's Turret,* on the top floor, is decorated in rich blue and white Waverly fabrics and also has a fireplace, a canopy bed, and a sitting area with a sunset view. Every room has a refrigerator stocked with juice, soft drinks, and spring water; all but one have fireplaces. A decanter of sherry awaits guests' arrival.

The common areas are as wonderful as the guestrooms. A sunroom, a study, and a parlor offer a variety of retreats. The grand entry hall, with pine woodwork stained a rich oak hue and stained glass windows, comfortably accommodates a piano, an antique English writing desk, and a chiming clock. Soft music plays in the background. This is where five *Christmas* trees of varying sizes stand during the inn's celebrated Victorian-style holiday. The wraparound porch has Kennedy rockers and wicker chairs. On the grounds are gardens with a fish pond and fountain, a terrace, and a croquet lawn. Equally inviting are a hot tub tucked into a garden gazebo and a sauna in a garden cottage.

Breakfast in the stately dining room has won acclaim. The three-course meal is served by candlelight on fine china with sterling silver. Shirred eggs in spinach nests might be followed by whole-wheat–buttermilk pancakes in praline syrup with toasted pecans and maple cream, accompanied by meat or poultry, perhaps ginger-braised chicken breasts.

The inn is near *Virginia Tech.* Golf, horseback riding, tennis, winery tours, hiking on the Appalachian Trail, and biking on the Rails to Trails path are nearby. The inn arranges canoe rentals and river cruises on the *Pioneer Maid.*

THE OAKS VICTORIAN INN 311 E. Main St., Christiansburg, VA 24073 (phone: 540-381-1500; 800-336-6257; fax: 540-382-1728). This ornate Victorian inn has eight guestrooms with private baths, queen- or king-size beds, telephones, TV sets, fireplaces, and air conditioning; two with whirlpool tubs. Open year-round. Rate for a double room (including full breakfast and afternoon sherry, wine, or tea): $115 to $145; corporate rates for singles Sundays through Thursdays (including full breakfast): $75. Two-night minimum stay during special event weekends at *Virginia Tech* and *Radford University.* Major credit cards accepted. Not appropriate for children under 13. No pets. Two dogs—Kaile, a West Highland terrier, and Lulu, a Scottish terrier—in residence. No smoking. Margaret and Tom Ray, innkeepers.

DIRECTIONS: From I-81, take Exit 114. At the bottom of the ramp, turn right (if traveling from the north) or left (if approaching from the south) onto Main Street. Continue for 2 miles to the fork of Park and Main Streets, bear right onto Park, then turn left into *The Oaks*'s driveway. From the Blue Ridge Parkway, exit onto Route 8, which becomes Main Street in Christiansburg, and follow the directions above.

BAILIWICK INN

Fairfax, Virginia

Historic Fairfax has streets lined with Federal-style brick homes and a charming downtown of interesting shops and restaurants. The old courthouse (where George and Martha Washington's wills are on file) sits on a hill, and, across the street, stands a gracious home that Joshua Gunnell built sometime between 1800 and 1812 with bricks he imported from England. Significant additions were made to the house over the years, but it remains true to its Federal origins. The house, listed on the National Register of Historic Places, became the *Bailiwick Inn* in 1989.

No expense was spared when the building was converted to an inn. Decorators were hired to furnish the common rooms and the 14 guestrooms and baths in a style that would have been appropriate in the finest Federal homes. In the two parlors, Sheraton and Duncan Phyfe tables gleam and chairs and sofas are upholstered in raspberry and ivory damasks. Fires crackle in the fireplaces. It's been owned by innkeepers Bob and Annette Bradley since 1994.

The guestrooms are named for famous Virginians and are furnished as their own homes might have been. Each room has a book describing the life of its patron. *Patrick Henry* has an exquisite armoire inlaid with tiger maple and twin beds with delicately painted headboards that date to 1809. *Thomas Jefferson* is decorated in his favorite colors of red and gold and is modeled after his bedroom at *Monticello*. The *Antonia Ford* room has a sitting room with Chippendale furnishings, a bedroom with dormer windows, and a bath with a Jacuzzi; it's often requested as a honeymoon suite. Downy featherbeds and luxurious linens assure blissful sleep. Thoughtful little touches include a glass jar of freshly baked cookies on an upstairs chest and chocolates on the pillows at night.

Dinner (open to non-guests) is served Wednesdays through Sundays in the two-tiered dining room or, when the weather is nice, in the walled English courtyard with its bubbling fountain. The six-course repast includes a choice of salad or soup, entrée selections like roasted leg of lamb with lasagna of Provençale vegetables, or tournedos of salmon with ginger-glazed baby carrots, and dessert. Poached peaches with raspberry and glazed vanilla sabayon and a tower of bittersweet chocolate with brandied cherries are two of the possibilities. A full breakfast and high tea are also served to inn guests.

The inn provides access to a fitness center nearby. There's also an excellent walking tour of downtown Fairfax, the *Manassas Civil War Park* is nearby, and Washington, DC, is a 20-minute drive away.

BAILIWICK INN 4023 Chain Bridge Rd., Fairfax, VA 22030 (phone: 703-691-2266; 800-366-7666; fax: 703-934-2112). This elegant Federal-style inn has 14 guestrooms with private baths, twin, queen-, or king-size beds, telephones, and air conditioning; four with fireplaces, two with Jacuzzis; TV sets on request. Wheelchair accessible. Open year-round; dinner Wednesdays through Sundays. Rate for a double room (including full breakfast and afternoon tea): $130 to $295. MasterCard and Visa accepted. Children welcome. No pets. No smoking. Bob and Annette Bradley, proprietors; Stewart Schroeder, manager.

DIRECTIONS: From the Capital Beltway, take I-66 west to Exit 60 onto Route 123 south. The inn is located just past the fourth traffic light on the left.

KESWICK HALL

Keswick, Virginia

If you hear the cry of a bugle and an early-morning shout of "Tallyho," you're not dreaming. *Keswick Hall,* a 600-acre estate in the Virginia countryside, is adjacent to one of the oldest hunt clubs in America. (It's not open to inn guests, but it's fun to watch the riders charge by.)

Sir Bernard Ashley, co-founder of the Laura Ashley company, opened *Keswick Hall* to guests in 1993, completing his triple crown of Ashley House hotels (there's one in Wales and one in Maryland; see the *Inn at Perry Cabin,* above). The original estate, known as *Villa Crawford* and occupying the site of a pre–Civil War mansion, was built in 1912, and it's this imposing Italianate palace that Ashley expanded and converted to an impressive country-house hotel.

Elegant and sophisticated, the public areas at *Keswick Hall* combine period antiques and Laura Ashley fabrics. In the tile-floored *Great Hall,* stately columns define intimate seating areas about the fireplace. The *Crawford Lounge* is furnished with down-filled, yellow velvet sofas and needlepoint pillows. White predominates in the morning room, while the red snooker room offers a snooker table, a fireplace, Oriental rugs, and soft leather chairs. The inn also boasts an impressive collection of museum-quality oil paintings. A 30-foot-wide terrace offers treetop views of the rolling countryside and an outside fireplace. This is a popular evening retreat, when the only sound is the croaking of frogs in the nearby lake.

Guestrooms, lavishly decorated with more Laura Ashley prints, use prints and solid colors on the walls (forest green in one room; maroon in another). Wooden shutters filter the sun, upholstered window seats invite stargazing, and overstuffed chairs are accented with needlepoint pillows. The baths have tile floors and double pedestal sinks.

Guests are served a full breakfast that includes such British entrées as a mixed grill or smoked kippers and American standbys like Virginia ham with eggs and potatoes. Afternoon tea features fresh-baked scones with lemon curd and clotted cream, fresh berries, and cookies. The inn's accomplished chef also prepares lunch and dinner (open to non-guests), which are served in the elegant dining room on the lower level.

Light meals and snacks also are available at the members-only *Keswick Club.* Overnight guests may use its facilities, including the three outdoor tennis courts and the championship 18-hole golf course designed by Arnold Palmer. The *Pavilion Clubhouse* offers an indoor/outdoor pool, a fitness facility, an excellent gift shop, the *Bistro* restaurant overlooking the golf course, and the British-style *Pub,* complete with wooden floors, leather chairs, and ale on tap. Bicycles are available for touring the estate's miles of paved roads.

The inn is set amid the bucolic hills of Virginia hunt country near Charlottesville and about two hours from Washington, DC; *Monticello* and *Ashlawn* are nearby, as are wineries to visit.

KESWICK HALL 701 Club Dr., Keswick, VA 22947 (phone: 804-979-3440; 800-ASHLEY-1; fax: 804-977-4171). This country estate has 48 guestrooms with private baths, twin, double, queen-, or king-size beds, telephones, TV sets, and air conditioning. Wheelchair accessible. Open year-round. Rate for a double room (including full breakfast and afternoon tea): $195 to $645. Two-night minimum stay during special event weekends at the *University of Virginia.* Major credit cards accepted. Not appropriate for children under eight. No pets. Smoking permitted in designated public areas only. Sir Bernard Ashley, owner; Stephen Beaumont, general manager.

DIRECTIONS: From Washington, DC, travel west on I-66 to Route 29. Follow Route 29 south to the eastbound Route 250 bypass. Turn left onto Route 22, traveling east toward the towns of Cismont and Boyd's Tavern. After approximately 2 miles, turn right onto Route 744 (Hunt Club Drive). From the stop sign the gates of *Keswick Hall* are directly ahead.

FORT LEWIS LODGE

MILLBORO, VIRGINIA

The country roads on the way to *Fort Lewis Lodge* wind past a breathtaking view of Goshen Pass and may offer glimpses of deer feeding by a mountain stream. Turning onto the gravel lane that leads to the inn, you'll pass over a cattle guard and see a silo rising ahead and, down by the pond, a perfectly restored gristmill.

Snuggled into the Allegheny Mountains, *Fort Lewis Lodge* sits amid 3,200 acres of natural forests, meadows, and farmland that are laced with streams and hiking trails. In 1754 Colonel Charles Lewis built a stockade here to protect his family from Indian raids. Lewis died in 1774 at the Battle of Point Pleasant, considered by some historians to have been the first engagement of the American Revolution. Over its long history, the property has remained remarkably unchanged. In the 1950s, it was purchased by Robert Cowden as his retirement retreat, and he raised black Angus cattle on the land. Today, his son and daughter-in-law, John and Caryl Cowden, own and operate the property as a country inn.

Fort Lewis Lodge is anything but ordinary, and that's true of its owners as well. By anyone's standards, John is a master craftsman; the inn his masterpiece. He meticulously restored the 19th-century gristmill, with its two-foot-thick stone walls. It now serves as the dining room, where Caryl offers such hearty home-cooked dinners (open to non-guests) as a harvest roast with scalloped apples, fresh vegetables, homemade biscuits, and sinfully rich chocolate pie. Meals are served buffet-style and with complimentary wines. Guests may opt to sit at individual tables or at one of the large group tables. *Buck's Bar,* a screened porch overlooking the old millpond, is the place to get acquainted before dinner. In the evening, the old piano near the woodstove gets a workout during impromptu sing-alongs.

Guestrooms are scattered among several buildings and are furnished in Shaker-style simplicity with cherry, walnut, red oak, and chestnut furniture made by a local craftsman. John himself built the two-story cedar-shake lodge, right down to the milled pine floors, as well as the adjoining silo, which is an exact replica of the original that was here; it contains three guest-rooms with views across the fields. At the very top is an observation tower, reached by a spiral staircase. Two rustic log cabins (one dating from the 1860s, the other from the 1890s) were transported to the property in 1993 and now provide romantic retreats. They have stone fireplaces, front porches with rockers or a swing, patchwork quilts, and pioneer artifacts. The "Little House on the Prairie" ambience is conveyed by clothes pegs on the walls, patchwork quilts, and the simple but utilitarian bathrooms. On the other hand, few pioneers would have known what to make of the outdoor hot tub.

There's plenty of opportunity for hiking and exploring on the property. Down by the Cowpaster River a sturdy deck hangs over a swimming hole and a boat stands ready to use. For fisherfolk, the rainbow trout in the spring and smallmouth bass are legendary. The inn also caters to hunters in season—November through December. The lodge is near Warm Springs,

Fort Lewis Lodge

where Thomas Jefferson designed octagonal mineral baths and where evening concerts, championship golf courses, and shopping are available.

FORT LEWIS LODGE HCR3, Box 21A, Millboro, VA 24460 (phone: 540-925-2314; fax: 540-925-2352). This lodge has 13 guestrooms with private baths and twin, queen-, or king-size beds. Closed January through March; November and December are dedicated to hunters. Rate for a double room (including full breakfast and dinner): $140 to $190. MasterCard and Visa accepted. Not appropriate for children under five. No pets. A dog, Max, and a number of cats on the property. Smoking permitted in designated areas only. John and Caryl Cowden, innkeepers.

DIRECTIONS: Take I-81 or I-64 to Staunton. In Staunton take Route 254 west (at the railroad underpass) and follow the signs to Buffalo Gap. In Buffalo Gap turn south onto Route 42 and follow it for 29 miles to Millboro Springs (in Goshen the road becomes combined Routes 42 and 39). Follow Route 39 from Millboro Springs for three-quarters of a mile and turn right onto Route 678. Follow Route 678 for 10¾ miles, then turn left onto Route 625 and look for the inn sign on the left.

HIDDEN INN

ORANGE, VIRGINIA

It's easy to see how the *Hidden Inn* got its name. Although the inn is just off a busy highway in the center of Orange, it's tucked behind trees on eight acres in a glen that seems a world apart from the village that enfolds it.

The inn is made up of a collection of buildings that includes the *Main House*—a big, blue 1880s Victorian farmhouse with red shutters and a wraparound porch that was built by a descendant of Thomas Jefferson. In back are the skylighted *Garden Cottage* and the *Carriage House,* each of which has one guestroom overlooking the garden. Between them is a brick courtyard, bordered by herbs, with a fountain in the center and a gazebo. *Caroline House,* with two guestrooms, makes the perfect family retreat.

The *Main House* is the heart of Ray and Barbara Lonick's inn. The living room, with its formal fireplace, is painted a soft salmon with ivory accents and is furnished with floral wing chairs, a leather sofa, and an Oriental rug. A bowl of fresh-baked cookies welcomes guests, and afternoon lemonade, tea, and cakes are served here.

The owners want their guests to enjoy a memorably romantic interlude, and to that end, have created guestrooms that mix old-fashioned decor with up-to-date accoutrements. Lace curtains and beds with crocheted canopies capture the Victorian style. Handmade quilts, needlepoint and cross-stitch pieces made by Barbara, wicker and iron furnishings, and fresh flowers continue the theme. The bathrooms, however, are fully modern; four have whirlpool tubs.

A full breakfast—perhaps Ray's pumpkin pancakes, carrot-raisin muffins, chunky apple sauce, and juice—is served in the dining room. A five-course, set-menu dinner (for inn guests only by advance reservation) might include beef with tomato-garlic-brandy sauce or chicken breast stuffed with mushrooms in puff pastry with merlot sauce. Guests are seated at candlelit tables for two. Virginia is noted for its award-winning wines (the first grapes were planted by Jefferson), and guests gather in the living room to learn more about local wines from Ray, who is quite an expert. The Lonicks have their own vineyards on the property that produce 400 pounds of grapes annually for the inn's jellies.

A short distance from Orange is James Madison's lifelong home, 2,700-acre *Montpelier;* the *James Madison Museum* is in town. *Monticello,* the home of Madison's good friend Thomas Jefferson, is just a half hour away. Also nearby are historic battlefields, wineries, and tennis.

HIDDEN INN 249 Caroline St., Orange, VA 22960 (phone: 540-672-3625; fax: 540-672-5029). This inn has 10 guestrooms with private baths, twin, double, queen-, or king-size beds, and air conditioning. Closed *Christmas.* Rate for a double room (including full breakfast and afternoon tea): $79 to $159. Two-night minimum stay on weekends. Major credit cards accepted. Children welcome by prior arrangement only. No pets. Outdoor cats on the property. No smoking. Barbara and Ray Lonick, innkeepers; Chrys Dermody, manager.

DIRECTIONS: From Washington, DC, take I-495 to I-66 west to Exit 43A (Gainesville). Turn south onto Route 29 and go to Culpeper. Just outside Culpeper turn south onto Route 15 to Orange. Continue through the village of Orange. The inn is on the left, just past the Route 20 junction.

EMMANUEL HUTZLER HOUSE

RICHMOND, VIRGINIA

Richmond's Monument Boulevard is a handsome street, so broad that a grassy park, interspersed with magnificent monuments and statues (including those of Confederate heros Lee, Stuart, Jackson, Maury, and President Jefferson Davis) runs down its center, thus giving it its name. It's lined with arching old trees and stately 1900s mansions and townhouses, the *Emmanuel Hutzler House*, a beige brick, among them. It is located about 3 miles from downtown.

Richmond was the capital of the Confederacy during the Civil War. Both the State Capitol, which was designed in 1785 by Thomas Jefferson, and St. John's Church (built in 1775), where Patrick Henry declared "Give me liberty or give me death," are handsome 18th-century remnants.

The interior of the *Emmanuel Hutzler House* has a superb mahogany staircase and mahogany paneling in the living room that encompasses a fireplace mantel and bookcases. The elegant room, which also includes a coffered ceiling with dropped beams and leaded-glass windows, offers the perfect place to read a history of Richmond in front of the gas fireplace—that is if TC, the resident cat, agrees to yield a bit of space on the damask sofa.

The guestrooms upstairs are spacious and furnished with lovely antiques. All have fully modern baths. The *Robinette Suite,* a peach confection with creamy moldings, has a marble fireplace, as well as a four-poster bed and a cherry Sheraton dresser. The tiled bath has a Jacuzzi and a separate shower. *Marion's Room* has watermelon-toned walls, a brass-and-iron bed, and an antique English desk, while *Henrietta's Room* has hunter green walls, a decorative tiled fireplace, a bed with a cherry chairback headboard, and a Chippendale love seat.

A full breakfast is served in the formal dining room. Fare includes fresh fruit, cereals, muffins or breads, along with hot dishes such as French toast with bacon or scrambled eggs with sausage. For dinner, a multitude of fine restaurants are located nearby. Innkeeper Lyn Benson and her partner, John Richardson, will describe them and even make reservations for you.

Richmond's Shockoe Slip and Shockoe Bottom, where the town's original markets were located, are alive with shops, nightspots, and restaurants. Another charming area on West Cary Street, containing restored Victorian houses painted in an array of brilliant colors, houses crafts, antiques, garden, and clothing shops. Among Richmond's many cultural attractions are the *Richmond Ballet, Virginia Opera,* and *TheatreVirginia.* The *Richmond National Battlefield Park* is nearby.

EMMANUEL HUTZLER HOUSE 2036 Monument Ave., Richmond, VA 23220 (phone: 804-353-6900 or 804-355-4885; fax: 804-355-5053). An in-city bed and breakfast establishment on Richmond's historic Monument Avenue containing four rooms with private baths, queen-size beds, telephones, TV sets, and air conditioning; two with Jacuzzis. Open year-round except *Christmas* week. Rate for a double room (including full breakfast): $89 to $145. Two-night minimum on holiday and special-event weekends. Major credit cards accepted. Not appropriate for children under 13. No pets. No smoking. Lyn Benson and John Richardson, innkeepers.

DIRECTIONS: From Washington, DC, take I-95 south and follow signs to Petersburg/I-64 east (toward Norfolk and Williamsburg; do not follow signs to I-295). Take Exit 78, which is the exit for the *Travel Information Center* and Boulevard Street. Take a right onto Boulevard and follow it for 1 mile to Broad Street. Turn left onto Broad and go approximately half a mile past the *Science Museum* to Meadow Street. Turn right onto Meadow and go 2 blocks. Turn right onto Monument.

SAMPSON EAGON INN

STAUNTON, VIRGINIA

With a passion for collecting antiques and an equal devotion to history and historic preservation, Frank and Laura Mattingly have converted the 1840 Sampson Eagon house into a jewel of an inn. The cream-colored Greek Revival mansion sits on Staunton's Gospel Hill, across the street from Woodrow Wilson's birthplace.

Despite its classy decor, this is not a stuffy house. Comfort is the key, ensured by the innkeepers' Southern hospitality. In the peach-colored par-

lor are 12-foot ceilings, American antiques (including an 1840s butler's desk), oil paintings, and an Oriental rug on the pine floor. Guests enjoy walking through the flower-filled side garden and sitting on the side porch to read or sip a drink before going out to dinner.

The spacious guestrooms, each named for a figure who contributed to the history of the house, have either 12- or 10½-foot ceilings. The lovely antique furnishings span the house's long history, as each room matches the period of its namesake. The *Kayser Room,* for example, harks to the mid-1800s, when the Kayser family owned the home. It has a magnificent carved New York State four-poster Empire canopy bed draped with creamy damask and accented with teal blue. There's a two-tier crystal chandelier and an ornate mantelpiece with columns carved to match the bed. The mantel is topped by a late Victorian pier mirror. The *Holt Room* is furnished in Colonial Revival style, reflecting the taste of the Holt family, who lived here in the 1920s. The fireplace is surrounded by blue-and-white Delft tile; the four-poster mahogany bed and a matching highboy date to the 1930s. The room is lavishly swagged in cream-and-blue French toile. Thoroughly modern bathrooms include pedestal sinks; in *Tam's Room* the original brass-and-glass towel bars are still in place. Although most rooms have decorative mantels, the fireplaces are not functional, alas.

The dining room is furnished with a spectacular mid-19th-century Duncan Phyfe pedestal table, a Sheraton sideboard, and Chippendale chairs that date from 1760. In this grand setting, breakfast is served on antique Royal Doulton china, with family sterling and Waterford crystal. The Grand Marnier soufflé pancakes with strawberry sauce, accompanied by country sausage and homemade breads, are a popular way to start a day.

The inn is located in the Shenandoah Valley, near golf, tennis, swimming, hiking, horseback riding, and skiing, as well as the *Museum of American Frontier Culture* and the *Woodrow Wilson Birthplace and Museum.*

SAMPSON EAGON INN 238 E. Beverley St., Staunton, VA 24401 (phone and fax: 540-886-8200; 800-597-9722). This in-town mansion has five guestrooms and suites with private baths, queen-size beds, telephones, TV sets with VCRs, and air conditioning. Open year-round. Rate for a double room (including full breakfast): $89 to $109. Two-night minimum on some weekends. Major credit cards accepted. Not appropriate for children under 12. No pets. Jeepers Creepers, a Cairn terrier, in residence in the family quarters. Smoking on porch and in garden only. Frank and Laura Mattingly, innkeepers.

DIRECTIONS: From I-81 take Exit 222 and follow Route 250 west to Staunton. Turn right onto Route 11 (Coalter Street) and continue past the traffic light. The inn is on the left, at the corner of Coalter and Beverley Streets.

PROSPECT HILL PLANTATION INN

Trevilians, Virginia

Nestled into the rural countryside of Virginia, *Prospect Hill Plantation Inn* offers a 20th-century look at life on an 18th-century Southern plantation. With a reverence for the land and its history, Bill and Mireille Sheehan, who have owned the 40-acre property since 1977, converted the stately *Manor House* (ca. 1732) and its charming outbuildings into 13 spectacular guestrooms. The conversions were accomplished one by one and strictly adhered to the historic character of each building. The plantation is now listed on the National Register of Historic Places.

Prospect Hill is believed to include the oldest continuously occupied wood-frame plantation house in America. In 1699, Roger Thompson built the first log cabin; in 1720 he started construction on the *Manor House*. At one time 20 slaves tended the crops, the livestock, and the occupants of the *Manor House* on this self-sustaining plantation. The Overton family added several wings and began taking in guests after the Civil War. Today, the restored buildings surrounding the *Manor House* include *Sanco Pansy's Cottage* (last used as a henhouse); the *Coach House,* dating from 1880; the *Carriage House and Grooms Quarters* from 1850; *Uncle Guy's House* (the former slave quarters), ca. 1796; the *Overseer's Cottage,* the *Smokehouse,* and the *Summer Kitchen* (which still contains its brick fireplace) from 1720; and the *Boy's Cabin* (the original log cabin) from 1699.

Painted buttercup yellow with forest green shutters and white trim, the *Manor House* is a model of gracious hospitality. The living room, with its fireplace and plush sofas, opens to a verandah furnished with wicker and brightly colored cushions. The three dining rooms, which occupy the oldest part of the house, are rich in atmosphere. Old wide-plank floors are polished to a soft luster. Oriental rugs, a fireplace, Federal-style chairs, French toile wallpaper, and such antiques as a polished sideboard complete the decor. Downstairs, the brick-floored wine cellar displays the inn's impressive collection of vintages. Adjacent to the wine cellar is the *Board Room,* where leather chairs are pulled up to a fireplace for evening reading. Outside, a gazebo looks out over rolling pastureland, clipped hedges border flower beds, and a pool is surrounded by chaises, ready for sunny days.

Furnishings in the guestrooms include antiques compatible with their style. Some *Manor House* rooms, for example, have four-poster beds with lacy canopies and Federal antiques. The *Boy's Cabin,* with its beamed ceiling, log walls, and brick fireplace, has a simple bed with a quilt coverlet. All rooms have working fireplaces, and most have Jacuzzis.

For years, Mireille Sheehan, who was raised in Provence, France, was the chef at *Prospect Hill,* creating dinners that reflected her heritage. Today, her son Michael is both executive chef and innkeeper. In his first role, he oversees a full staff that continues to prepare robust Provençal dinners (also open to non-guests). The Sheehans take pride in serving local specialties, and wine is no exception. Guests find a half bottle of Virginia wine in their rooms, and there's a Virginia wine tasting before dinner every evening. A full breakfast, which might include a soufflé, is delivered to rooms every morning.

Located 15 miles east of Charlottesville, the inn is near the *University of Virginia, Monticello, Ashlawn,* and recreational activities such as hiking, golf, ballooning, and biking.

PROSPECT HILL PLANTATION INN 2887 Poindexter Rd., Trevilians, VA 23093 (phone: 540-967-0844; reservations: 800-277-0844; fax: 540-967-0102). This plantation inn has 13 guestrooms with private baths, double, queen-, or king-size beds, and air conditioning. Open year-round, except *Christmas Eve* and *Christmas Day.* Rate for a double room (including full breakfast and dinner): $245 to $325; bed and breakfast: $155 to $235. Discover, MasterCard, and Visa accepted. Children welcome. No pets. Horses on property. Smoking permitted except in the dining room. Sheehan family, owners; Michael and Laura Sheehan, innkeepers.

DIRECTIONS: From Charlottesville take I-64 east to Exit 136, and follow Route 15 to Zion Crossroads. Turn left onto Route 250 east. Go 1 mile to Route 613; turn left and drive 3 miles to the inn, which is on the left. From Washington, DC, take I-66 west to Gainesville. Take Route 29 south to Culpeper, then Route 15 south through Orange and Gordonsville to Zion Crossroads. Turn left onto Route 250 east and follow the directions above.

INN AT LITTLE WASHINGTON

WASHINGTON, VIRGINIA

This little inn neatly approximates the fine country-house hotels of England, yet for all its elegance, it is remarkably free of pretension.

Constructed as a nondescript garage, the building served as a country store, before owners Patrick O'Connell and Reinhardt Lynch turned it into a restaurant in 1978. Word of their exceptional fare spread, attracting diners from afar, so they added rooms to accommodate them.

If the decor and furnishings seem a bit dramatic, it's no accident. They were designed by Joyce Conway-Evans, a London theatrical designer, whose charming sketches for each of the rooms are framed in the upstairs hallway. Unusual touches include wallpaper with borders created by hand-cut paper flowers; the entryway ceiling is covered with a similarly spectacular collage. Fabric—used lavishly in window treatments and on canopy beds—swags the rooms. The bathrooms are a medley of brass and marble. Fresh flowers sit by the bed, on the desk, and in the bathroom, and a bowl of fruit awaits guests' arrival. Museum-quality antiques are found throughout.

The restaurant's decor is as stunning as that in the guestrooms, and since the restaurant was the raison d'être for the *Inn at Little Washington,* it would be a crime to miss dinner here. Self-taught Patrick is the acclaimed chef; Reinhardt the host. For first-time visitors, the tasting menu is an excellent choice, offering small portions of a broad variety of appetizers and entrées. On the other hand, since the menu changes every night to reflect the freshest local ingredients, it's impossible to go wrong. The cuisine can be described as classical French, but with the chef's own interpretations. An award-winning wine cellar contains more than 9,000 bottles. The pretty walled flower garden, with a terrace and reflecting pool, is a wonderful place for an aperitif or after-dinner coffee.

Continental breakfast is served to guests either in the garden or on an enclosed side verandah. It starts with juice, followed by a bowl of fresh fruit (strawberries or raspberries in season, topped with *crème fraîche*) and a basket of fresh-baked breads. For an additional charge a hot entrée is available.

The inn is located in the foothills of the Blue Ridge Mountains, an hour from Washington, DC. Hiking, horseback riding, wineries, and art galleries are all nearby.

INN AT LITTLE WASHINGTON Middle and Main Sts. (mailing address: PO Box 300), Washington, VA 22747 (phone: 540-675-3800; fax: 540-675-3100). This country inn has 12 guestrooms with private baths, queen- or king-size beds, telephones, and air conditioning. Restaurant is wheelchair accessible. Open year-round except *Christmas;* restaurant for dinner daily except Tuesdays (open Tuesdays in May and October only). Rate for a double room (including continental breakfast and afternoon tea): $240 to $490; $125 additional Saturday nights; $100 additional Friday nights, selected holidays, and in October. MasterCard and Visa accepted. Not appropriate for children under 10. Pets accepted by prior arrangement only; they must stay in a separate building. Two dalmatians, Rose and Desoto, in residence. Smoking permitted in guestrooms and lobby but not in the dining room. Patrick O'Connell and Reinhardt Lynch, innkeepers.

DIRECTIONS: From Washington, DC, take I-66 west for 22 miles to Exit 43A (Gainesville). Follow Route 29 south for 12 miles to Warrenton. In Warrenton take Route 211 west for 23 miles to Washington. Turn right onto Business Route 211 in Washington. The inn is a half mile down on the right, in the center of the village.

MIDDLETON INN

Washington, Virginia

Mary Ann Kuhn was a journalist with the *Washington Post,* as well as a TV producer for CBS News, before becoming an innkeeper. Now she's the lady of this gracious six-acre manor in the heart of Virginia's hunt country. Long a horsewoman herself, her property includes a barn, paddocks, and, of

course, horses. She happily tells her guests about the spring and fall point-to-point foxhunting races and will even prepare a tailgate picnic for them.

Just 65 miles west of Washington, DC, the tiny village of Washington, Virginia, is known as "Little Washington." There are two streets of 19th-century houses, an old post office, a library, and a few shops and galleries, but to all outward appearances, it's merely a small rural community. Nevertheless, there's an undercurrent of refinement that has made it a gastronomic and cultural jewel.

The centerpiece of the inn is an 1850s Federal brick house built by Middleton Miller, who designed the uniforms for the Confederate Army during the Civil War. It has an elegant center hall with tall ceilings. In the living room, which has daffodil yellow walls, a plaid sofa is placed to view the fire in the creamy marble fireplace. There are oil paintings of foxhounds and horses, as well as sporting prints, on the walls. The focal point is the magnificent 1830s square carved rosewood pianoforte in the corner, which, incongruously, has a sculpture of George Bush on top (Mary Ann will have to explain why). Wine and cheeses are set out here in the evening; in warm weather guests often nibble and sip their snacks on one of the broad porches.

The guestrooms are gorgeous; all have working fireplaces and either a porch or a verandah. The *Hunt Room,* with hunter green walls, has an antique carved four-poster bed, a unique French horn chandelier, and a marble bath. The *Ivy Room* has a rush sleigh bed and a needlepoint rug, while the *Men's Vanity* has a sleigh bed and a sink embedded in an ornate dresser. The former slave quarters have been turned into a charming private cottage. On the first floor there's a sitting room with shelves of books and a fireplace, and an upstairs bedroom has a sleigh bed and a marble bath with a Jacuzzi.

A full breakfast is served in the formal dining room, which has another fireplace. The tables are covered with dramatic linens and set with china displaying a bold green rim, as well as antique silver. The meal will consist of fresh fruit, juice, freshly baked muffins and perhaps raspberry pancakes or eggs Benedict made with smoked trout instead of Canadian bacon.

Activities in the area are plentiful. Hiking, bicycling, horseback riding, and enjoying the views and flowers along Skyline Drive, as well as watching performances at *Little Washington Theater,* are all possibilities.

MIDDLETON INN 176 Main St. (mailing address: PO Box 254), Washington, VA 22747 (phone: 540-675-2020; 800-816-8157; fax: 540-675-1050). This gracious horse farm includes five guestrooms with private baths, twin, queen-, or king-size beds, telephones, TV sets, fireplaces, and air conditioning; one with whirlpool tub. Open year-round. Rate for a double room (including full breakfast): $195 to $340. Two-night minimum in October and on holiday weekends. Major credit cards accepted. Not appropriate for children under 13. No pets. Two Labrador retrievers, Hannah and Gauge, and another dog, Charley, on premises. No smoking. Mary Ann Kuhn, innkeeper.

DIRECTIONS: From Washington, DC, take I-66 west for 23 miles to Exit 10A (Warrenton). Follow Route 29 south for 12 miles into Warrenton and turn right onto Route 211 west. Go 23 miles and turn right at the sign for Washington business. Turn left at the stop sign and go 2 blocks. The inn is on the left.

L'AUBERGE PROVENÇALE
WHITE POST, VIRGINIA

Tucked into Virginia's Shenandoah Valley, this little French *auberge* is just like the ones found in the countryside near Avignon—and that is no coincidence. Innkeeper Alain Borel was raised in Avignon, where he began acquiring his considerable culinary expertise at the age of 13 in his grandfather's restaurant. The inn's ambience is so thoroughly French that it's hard to believe it's really only 90 minutes from Washington, DC, and in a rural village with an all-American history: White Post got its name when a young surveyor, tramping these parts in the mid-18th century, set up a white marker post in town. His name was George Washington, and several other remnants of his early activities can be found nearby.

Set on nine acres and surrounded by flower and vegetable gardens, the inn occupies a stone manor house built as a private home in 1753. Borel's wife, Celeste, is responsible for the stunning French decor. Country French antiques are accented by bright, printed Provençal fabrics in the sitting area, the three dining rooms, and the guestrooms. There are pine canopy beds with turned posts, sleigh beds, and an antique cannonball bed; five rooms have fireplaces. The three guestrooms in the original 1753 manor house are among the largest, and all have fireplaces; the other rooms are in two wings that were added in 1983 and 1993. Guests find a platter of fresh fruit, homemade cookies, and chocolates awaiting their arrival.

Everyone looks forward to mealtimes at the inn—with good reason. One of Alain's fantastic breakfasts might start with a berry crêpe with *crème fraîche,* followed by poached eggs in a spinach nest. His dinners (also open to non-guests) are elaborate and inventive, using the freshest local ingredients and distinctive seasonings. Dinner is served in one of the manor house's three dining rooms, all of which are decorated with bright Provençal fabrics and French oils and prints. Be sure to note the original Picasso and Bernard Buffet.

The inn has a gift shop stocked with jam, honey, and vinegars made on the premises. It's also near golf, horseback riding, vineyards, and White Post Restorations, a high-quality restorer of classic cars.

L'AUBERGE PROVENÇALE Rte. 340 (mailing address: PO Box 119), White Post, VA 22663 (phone: 540-837-1375; 800-638-1702; fax: 540-837-2004). This country French inn has 10 guestrooms with private baths, double or queen-size beds, and air conditioning. Closed January except for *New Year's* weekend; restaurant also closed Monday and Tuesday dinner. Rate for a double room (including full breakfast): $160 to $250. Major credit cards accepted. Not appropriate for children under 10. No pets. One dog, Sparky, in residence. Smoking permitted in sitting room only. Alain and Celeste Borel, innkeepers.

DIRECTIONS: From Washington, DC, take I-66 west to Exit 23. Follow Route 17 north for 9 miles to Route 50. Turn left onto Route 50 and continue to the first traffic light—the intersection of Route 50 and Route 340. Turn left onto Route 340; the inn is on the right after 1 mile.

LIBERTY ROSE

WILLIAMSBURG, VIRGINIA

Liberty Rose offers its guests fantasy, illusion, and pure romance. Unlike most accommodations in Williamsburg, it is not decorated in colonial style, but in a lavish Victorian one. The charm and vivaciousness of the decor are matched by the same qualities in the innkeepers, Sandi and Brad Hirz. Although true Victorian decor tended to be dark and dismal, the colors and fabrics used here are light and refreshing.

From the outside, the inn appears to be a simple white clapboard house with a slate roof. Walk in the front door, and you're enveloped in a tasteful display of Victoriana. The parlor, with a fireplace, strategically placed comfortable chairs, and a grand piano, is restrained compared to the high-romantic air of the guestrooms.

Rose Victoria, for example, has elaborately draped bed coverings tied with fringed tassels, over an ornate French canopy bed in cherrywood. A TV set is hidden within an antique walnut French armoire and in the bath is an entire wall that was once part of a Victorian townhouse. A claw-foot tub and a shower enclosed in red marble complete the ensemble. As spectacular as *Rose Victoria* is, all the rooms contain interesting antiques. *Savannah Lace* has an ornately carved rosewood tobacco-post bed, and *Suite Williamsburg* has a carved ball-and-claw canopy bed with bed coverings of striped copper-colored silk and a duvet of rosy jacquard fabric. There's a working fireplace, as well as a bathroom with cherry paneling, a claw-foot tub, and a black Italian tile shower.

Brad and Sandi prepare elaborate breakfasts for their guests and serve it on the morning porch, which overlooks the gardens. There will be fresh fruit or berries, juice, muffins, and breads. For an entrée, Sandi may fix Granny Smith apple fritter hotcakes with roasted pecans accompanied by scrambled eggs topped with white American cheese and sausage patties. Guests will find freshly baked cookies waiting when they arrive and at night there will be another sweet on their pillow. Fine restaurants for dinner are nearby.

Located on a hill about 1½ miles outside of Williamsburg, *Liberty Rose* has a secluded patio under spreading oak, beech, and poplar trees. Williamsburg offers one of the richest and most diverse selections of attractions in the country. In addition to the many activities associated with *Colonial Williamsburg, Busch Gardens* and *Water Country*, both amusement parks, are nearby. Golfing, hiking, and bicycling are also popular.

LIBERTY ROSE 1022 Jamestown Rd., Williamsburg, VA 23185 (phone: 757-253-1260; 800-545-1825). This charming Victorian bed and breakfast establishment has four guestrooms with private baths, queen-size beds, telephones, TV sets, and air conditioning; one with a fireplace. Open year-round. Rate for a double room (including full breakfast): $125 to $195. Two night minimum. Major credit cards accepted. Not appropriate for children under 14. No pets. One cat, Mr. Goose, on premises. No smoking. Brad and Sandi Hirz, innkeepers.

DIRECTIONS: From I-64, take Exit 242A (Busch Gardens) onto Route 199. Follow Route 199 for 5 miles. Turn right onto Routes 31/5 east (Jamestown Road). Go ½ mile. The inn is on the left.

West Virginia

HILLBROOK INN

CHARLES TOWN, WEST VIRGINIA

At the *Hillbrook Inn*, you can drink water from the same springhouse that slaked George Washington's thirst. Its 17 pastoral acres were originally part of Washington's Rock Hall estate, and the springhouse still captures the crystal waters of Bullskin Run.

A half-mile drive leads to an English rock garden that skirts the walkway in front of the manor house, a rambling wood-frame and stucco Tudor. Built to resemble a small hillside village, the house was constructed in seven sections on 15 levels. From a picturesque limestone ridge, it overlooks rolling lawns and English gardens. The property contains two streams, each spanned by a bridge. The 12-foot-wide Bridge of Sighs, in a Chinese Chippendale design with ornate lions' heads, is particularly romantic.

In contrast to the dark woodwork and white walls of most Tudor houses, *Hillbrook*'s common rooms, with their 20-foot ceilings, offer the reverse—bright white woodwork set against deep terra cotta walls. Antique wooden tables, tapestry-covered easy chairs, and richly colored Oriental rugs are complemented by innkeeper Gretchen Carroll's eclectic collection of primitive and modern pottery and art treasures, which she gathered on her travels to Italy, Vietnam, Turkey, Thailand, and the Ivory Coast.

The house was built in 1922, around the frame of a 1700s log house, creating intriguing nooks and crannies, twists and turns in the guestroom configurations. The most sought-after room is *The Point,* with its mysterious tunnel entrance. Paisley linen on the double bed and dramatic wallpaper complement the European and Asian paintings and prints on the walls. *The Lookout,* tucked under a steeply slanted roof, has windows on three sides and overlooks the verdant countryside. A miniature teak Thai spirit house ensures safety and good luck.

Dinner (also open to non-guests) is served in the atmospheric dining room, with its brass chandelier made from antique oil lamps, and candles that cast romantic shadows on the fine crystal and antique tables. The seven-course meal might include sherried mushroom soup, grilled marlin with tarragon butter, and chocolate decadence. Generally, the morning meal—which may include pecan pancakes with ginger butter—is served on the glass-enclosed porch or on the terrace, as is lunch.

The inn is near *Harpers Ferry National Historic Park,* the *Antietam Battlefield,* whitewater rafting, the Charles Town races, and antiquing.

HILLBROOK INN Rte. 2, Box 152, Charles Town, WV 25414 (phone: 304-725-4223; 800-304-4223; fax: 304-725-4455). This Tudor-style mansion has six guestrooms with private baths, double or queen-size beds, telephones, and air conditioning; two with fireplaces. Open year-round, except *Christmas Eve* and *Christmas Day.* Rate for a double room (including full breakfast and seven-course dinner with wine): $198 to $450. Discover, MasterCard, and Visa accepted. Not appropriate for children under 16. No pets. One cat, Princess Fuzzy Butt, in residence, plus ducks and geese on property. Smoking permitted except in the dining room. Gretchen Carroll, innkeeper; Nadia Hill, manager.

DIRECTIONS: The inn is 70 miles west of Washington, DC. From Washington take I-270 to I-70 west, then Route 340 west past Harpers Ferry to the Charles Town Bypass, which is marked Route 340 south/9 east (Berryville/Leesburg). Go 4 miles and exit onto Old Route 340. Make an immediate left onto Huyette Road and drive almost 3 miles to a stop sign. Turn left, following Route 13 for just over a mile. The inn is on the left.

Deep South

FLORIDA
1. Amelia Island: ELIZABETH POINTE LODGE; FAIRBANKS HOUSE
2. Key West: THE GARDENS HOTEL; MARQUESA HOTEL
3. Orlando: COURTYARD AT LAKE LUCERNE
4. Seaside: JOSEPHINE'S FRENCH COUNTRY INN AT SEASIDE

GEORGIA
5. Newnan: PARROTT CAMP SOUCY HOME AND GARDENS
6. Palmetto: SEREN-BE B & B FARM
7. Savannah: BALLASTONE INN; MAGNOLIA PLACE INN
8. Senoia: THE VERANDA

LOUISIANA
9. New Orleans: HOTEL MAISON DE VILLE AND THE AUDUBON COTTAGES; HOUSE ON BAYOU ROAD INN; MELROSE MANSION
10. White Castle: NOTTOWAY PLANTATION

MISSISSIPPI
11. Jackson: FAIRVIEW INN
12. Natchez: BRIARS INN; MONMOUTH PLANTATION
13. Vicksburg: ANCHUCA; CEDAR GROVE MANSION INN

SOUTH CAROLINA
14. Beaufort: RHETT HOUSE INN
15. Charleston: BELVEDERE B & B; JOHN RUTLEDGE HOUSE INN; TWO MEETING STREET INN

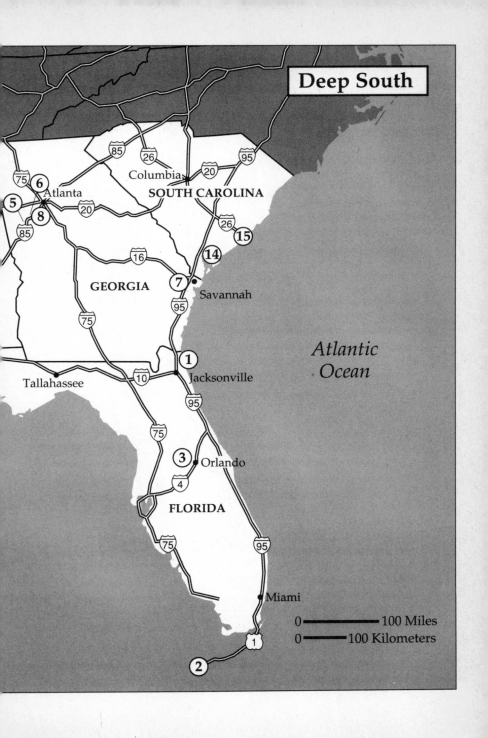

Deep South

Florida

ELIZABETH POINTE LODGE

AMELIA ISLAND, FLORIDA

A string of barrier reefs and islands stretches along the Atlantic Seaboard from New Jersey to Florida. On the ocean side are miles of sandy beaches, on the bay side, quiet harbors and sleepy villages. Florida's northernmost island, just across the border from Georgia, is Amelia Island, 13 miles long and 1½ miles wide, with sparkling white sands and broad beaches. Snuggled alongside the ocean is *Elizabeth Pointe Lodge,* a charming Stanford White–style Hamptons cottage of weathered shingles and white trim, fronted by a long oceanside porch with plenty of rocking chairs. It was designed and built in 1991 by long-time local innkeepers David and Susan Caples.

The inn's style is appropriately nautical. There are marine artifacts, boat models, paintings, prints, and photographs of the ocean, and an abundance of books about the sea on display throughout the inn. The common rooms invite relaxation. The library, with a massive stone fireplace and window seats with ocean vistas, has bookshelves stocked with puzzles, board games, and books. Lemonade and cookies are set out here throughout the afternoon, wine and hors d'oeuvres appear in the evening, and desserts are laid out for a late-night snack.

Each of the guestrooms has a crisp, trim decor and many have ocean views. White predominates, accented by sea greens and blues. There are turn-of-the-century furnishings, wainscoted walls, dark-stained pine floors, Oriental rugs, fresh flowers and green plants, armoires hiding television sets, and modern baths with black-and-white tile floors. *Room No. 3* has a four-poster bed covered with quilts and an antique wicker rocker. *Room No. 10* contains a sleigh bed, an oak table, and a bath with a hexagonal tile floor and brass fixtures. All rooms have marble tub surrounds and pedestal sinks; many have whirlpool tubs. There are 20 rooms in the main house and five more in adjacent buildings called *Harris Lodge* and *Miller Cottage.*

In addition to the rooms affiliated with the inn, the Caples offer a selection of houses and condominiums for vacation rental. For an absolutely unique experience, you can rent *Katie's Light*—a replica of a Chesapeake Bay lighthouse, which sits on stilts over the beach and has a deck that wraps around all six sides. This romantic hideaway has unbelievable views and was featured in the movie *Pippi Longstocking.*

A newspaper is delivered to guestrooms every morning. A full buffet breakfast—including juices, cereals, freshly baked muffins and breads, and probably eggs Victorian (a casserole of bread, sausage, eggs, and cheese)—is served to inn guests every morning. Light lunch and dinner fare is available until midnight.

The inn provides a fleet of bicycles, as well as beach chairs and umbrellas. Children are welcome and special youth activities are often planned. Sailing, deep-sea fishing, beachcombing, tennis, golf, and horseback riding are all available nearby, as are restaurants.

ELIZABETH POINTE LODGE 98 S. Fletcher Ave., Amelia Island, FL 32034 (phone: 904-277-4851; 800-772-3359; fax: 904-277-6500). This oceanside bed and breakfast establishment has 25 guestrooms and suites with private baths, twin, queen-, or king-size beds, telephones, TV sets, and air conditioning; 14 with whirlpool tubs. Wheelchair accessible. Open year-round. Rate for a double room (including full breakfast, afternoon snacks, wine, and hors d'oeuvres): $100 to $195. Major credit cards accepted. Children welcome. No pets. Smoking outside only. David and Susan Caples, innkeepers; Eric Moulton, manager.

DIRECTIONS: From I-95, take Exit 129 onto Route A1A east for 15 miles to Fernandina Beach. Cross the bridge onto the island and turn right at the second traffic light onto Sadler Road. Follow Sadler for 1½ miles to the ocean. Turn left onto Fletcher Avenue. The inn is on the right in exactly 2 miles.

FAIRBANKS HOUSE

AMELIA ISLAND, FLORIDA

The brick streets of Fernandina Beach, the pretty commercial center of Amelia Island, are lined with planters overflowing with flowers. Interesting shops abound—antiques stores, clothing boutiques, needlework and crafts shops, and art galleries. The busy harbor is home to a shrimp fleet and

excursion boats that take visitors to nearby islands. In the late 19th century, when the shrimp industry flourished, flamboyant Victorian homes—painted in sea-washed pastels—were built; of the many that remain, today, the *Fairbanks House* is among the grandest.

Built in 1885 by well-known architect Robert Schuyler, it has Italianate villa influences and is listed on the National Register of Historic Places. The house, painted a soft green with garnet trim, has three stories with a square central tower, an arched porch, and a square bay window. Inside, the polished heart-pine floors of the entrance hall are enhanced by Oriental rugs and rich Honduras mahogany paneling glows softly in the glow of the Victorian chandelier. Mary and Nelson Smelker, former IBM executives, purchased the rooming house in 1993 and, after a major renovation, opened it as a bed and breakfast establishment in 1994.

The rooms, appointed with antiques mixed with period reproductions, are spacious and have marvelous baths that include claw-foot or whirlpool tubs and hair dryers. *Room No. 3* has a fireplace, a bed with a padded headboard, a private porch, and a whirlpool tub. *Room No. 6* contains a four-poster bed, an antique dresser, a boxed window seat, and a whirlpool tub. There are eight guestrooms in the villa and three individual cottages, furnished with wicker in a more casual country manner, on the grounds.

Every evening guests congregate in the living room, with its wide ceiling moldings and fireplace, for wine and hors d'oeuvres; Mary and Nelson are on hand to suggest dining spots. In nice weather, the gathering takes place either on the wicker-filled piazza overlooking the courtyard or in the brick courtyard itself, which is surrounded by colorful flowerbeds.

Breakfast is served in the dining room or on the piazza. The menu consists of fresh fruits, juices, homemade breads, perhaps a chilled mixed fruit soup, and a hot entrée such as peach upside-down French toast or spicy breakfast bake (similar to a quiche).

The inn has a lovely swimming pool and the wide white-sand ocean beach is just a mile away (the inn will provide bicycles and beach chairs). An excellent restaurant in a fanciful Victorian building is just a block away and the village shops are a mere two-block stroll. Golfing and fishing are nearby.

FAIRBANKS HOUSE 227 S. 7th St., Amelia Island, FL 32034 (phone: 904-277-0500; 800-261-4838; fax: 904-277-3103). This village Victorian has 12 rooms with private baths, twin, queen-, or king-size beds, telephones, TV sets, and air conditioning; nine with fireplaces, six with whirlpool tubs. Wheelchair accessible. Open year-round. Rate for a double room (including full breakfast and evening wine and cheese): $95 to $165. Two-night minimum on weekends. Major credit cards accepted. Children welcome. No pets. One dog, Toby, on premises. Smoking outside only. Mary and Nelson Smelker, innkeepers.

DIRECTIONS: From I-95 take Exit 129 onto Route A1A east for 15 miles, crossing the bridge to Amelia Island and the village of Fernandina Beach. Stay on A1A to Cedar Street. Turn left onto Cedar and travel to 7th Street. Turn right onto 7th. The inn will be on the left.

THE GARDENS HOTEL
KEY WEST, FLORIDA

At *The Gardens Hotel,* you can tuck yourself away in a secluded cottage with a bright burst of bougainvillea cascading down a wall and sit in the shade of overhanging palm, croton, and jacaranda trees. You can delight in the beauty of orchids, hibiscus, and bromeliads, and savor the sweet smell of orange and jasmine. Peggy Mills, who owned the property from 1930 to 1979, was an extraordinary gardener, combining a palate of colors, shapes, textures, and scents in the gardens surrounding her home in Key West. It was once the largest private estate on the island, and still encompasses a quarter of a city block in the heart of the historic district. The complex, which is sequestered behind high walls, was deserted when it was purchased by world travelers Bill and Corinna Hettinger. They completed a major renovation and opened the buildings as an inn in 1993. The inn includes the 1870s main house with extravagant Victorian trim, a carriage house, a cottage built in 1850, and two new buildings. Cached away among the greenery of the gardens, guests will find a swimming pool, a spa, a tiered Georgian fountain, another Moorish-style tile fountain, four extremely rare earthenware jars called *tinajones,* ponds, garden benches, a garden bar, and a massive birdcage—home to Peggy, a brightly feathered macaw.

The common rooms, located in the main house, include an elegant lobby with a fireplace and a garden room solarium. A continental breakfast of fresh fruit (including papayas, mangos, bananas, and pineapples), juice, breads (Key lime beignets are favorites) and muffins is served here. An adjoining porch has tables for eating outside.

The guestrooms are breezy and sophisticated with polished oak floors and private porches. All are exceptionally spacious and furnished with

wicker chairs and iron beds. Armoires and desks are made of yew or mahogany; windows and beds are dressed in floral fabrics in soft tropical blues, yellows, roses, and greens. The marble baths are complete in every detail, including Jacuzzi tubs in all but two.

Duval Street, Key West's hot promenade of nightclubs, restaurants, galleries, and shops, is far enough away to ensure peaceful quiet and close enough to explore on foot. The *Ernest Hemingway House and Museum,* and the *Wrecker's Museum,* which is known as the oldest house in Key West, are interesting places to visit, but lively Key West always has numerous events taking place also. Photographers line the docks in the evening to take spectacular sunset shots. Sailing, snorkeling, diving, and deep-sea fishing are popular recreational activities.

THE GARDENS HOTEL 526 Angela St., Key West, FL 33040 (phone: 305-294-2661; 800-526-2664; fax: 305-292-1007). This small luxury bed and breakfast establishment in the heart of Old Town Key West has 17 rooms and suites with private baths, twin, queen-, or king-size beds, telephones, TV sets, air conditioning, and porches; 15 with whirlpool tubs. Wheelchair accessible. Open year-round. Rate for a double room (including continental breakfast): $155 to $625. Two-night minimum on weekends and for some special events and holidays. Major credit cards accepted. Children welcome. No pets. One macaw, Peggy, on premises. Smoking permitted outside only. Bill and Corinna Hettinger, innkeepers; Evelyn Baskin, general manager.

DIRECTIONS: Key West is 150 miles south of Miami on Route 1. Once in Key West, remain on Route 1, which becomes Truman Avenue. Continue to Simonton Street and turn right. After 3 blocks, turn left onto Angela Street. The inn is in the first block, on the left.

MARQUESA HOTEL
KEY WEST, FLORIDA

Built in 1884, the hotel spent most of its first hundred years as a blowsy boardinghouse. In 1987, however, partners Erik deBoer and Richard Manley invested $2 million and untold hours converting it to a small hotel. They were so successful that it's now listed on the National Register of Historic Places. Erik's wife, Carol Wightman, is the innkeeper, and Richard's wife, Pamela, a floral designer, is responsible for the fantastic flower arrangements found throughout the establishment. In 1993, deBoer and Manley purchased several adjacent Victorian houses and converted them to 12 more spacious rooms and suites, which they painted pastel aqua with white trim. Porches are furnished with wicker sofas and chairs dressed with tropical florals and are surrounded by lush gardens with brick walkways.

The *Marquesa* is stylishly sophisticated, with antique and high-quality reproduction furnishings, including pine sleigh beds and pine chests that hide the TV sets. Common areas such as the lobby, verandah, and sitting room have a Caribbean ambience, with wicker tables and chairs. Audubon prints and vintage photos of Key West adorn the walls. Many of the guestrooms have small balconies overlooking the little pool in back. All bathrooms are marble, with Italian chrome fixtures and Art Deco sconces. Nightly turndown service includes Godiva chocolates.

The pool is surrounded with a riot of color, including palm trees, birds-of-paradise, bougainvillea, acanthus, yew, ginger, and bromeliads. A profusion of pastel orchids and staghorn ferns climb a lattice wall.

Café Marquesa (which is open to non-guests at dinner) presents elegant meals in an airy, bistro setting with 15-foot-tall windows, gold-sponged plaster walls, and a grand mahogany-and-brass bar. A trompe l'oeil mural along one wall incorporates windows to the kitchen. Fresh local seafood is the specialty: Grilled shrimp in roast banana–red curry sauce comes with sweet-potato fritters and fresh mango relish; pan-seared yellowfin tuna in sun-dried tomato beurre blanc is accompanied by horseradish potatoes and roast green beans. For dessert, there's a sensational *crème brûlée* served with kiwi, starfruit, and fruit salsa.

In the heart of Key West's historic district, the hotel is near many major attractions: the *Key West Aquarium, Audubon House,* the *Ernest Hemingway House and Museum,* and the *Key West Lighthouse Museum.* Bicycling, ocean and gulf beaches, tennis, scuba diving, and fishing are among the recreational options.

MARQUESA HOTEL 600 Fleming St., Key West, FL 33040 (phone: 305-292-1919; 800-UNWIND-1; fax: 305-294-2121). This small hotel has 27 guestrooms with private baths, queen- or king-size beds, telephones, TV sets, and air conditioning. Wheelchair accessible. Open year-round. Rate for a double room: $120 to $280. Two-night minimum stay on weekends; three nights on holidays. Major credit cards accepted. Children welcome. No pets. No smoking in restaurant; smoking permitted in guestrooms. Carol Wightman, innkeeper.

DIRECTIONS: From US Route 1 turn right onto Simonton Street and continue for 5 blocks to Fleming Street. The inn is on the corner of Simonton and Fleming.

THE COURTYARD AT LAKE LUCERNE

ORLANDO, FLORIDA

Although visions of Orlando consist mainly of theme parks, there's much more to the town than Mickey and Pluto. *The Courtyard at Lake Lucerne,* a cluster of historic buildings on a dead-end street in the heart of the city, has private walkways that lead under a concrete freeway to paths that surround lovely Lake Lucerne.

A spacious brick courtyard with palm, magnolia, and banana trees, as well as colorful azaleas, impatiens, and birds of paradise, and an English fountain with koi, is the centerpiece that unites the three buildings of the inn. The first, the *Norment-Parry House,* is the oldest known house in Orlando, built by Judge Richard Norment in 1883. It was opened as an inn in 1986, the creation of antiques collector Charles Meiner. The house has a tiny lobby with heart-pine floors, a Victorian parlor, where afternoon wine is served, and six guestrooms upstairs. The *Honeymoon Suite* has a predominantly yellow theme, a massive walnut bed, and blue and white porcelain plates decorating the walls. *Room No. 104,* a cozy boîte painted in cardinal red with white trim, contains a carved walnut bed and a French armoire; the commode is tucked away in a minuscule closet and the sink is hidden behind a screen.

Directly behind the *Norment-Parry House* is the *I. W. Phillips House,* a gracious 1916 mansion with lustrous oak floors and stairway. When it was added to the inn, double verandahs—accessed by wide French doors—were installed across the front. In the broad reception hall, an 18th-century Flemish oil painting, a buffet table from Hungary, and Oriental rugs complement the splendor of a Tiffany morning glory window in the stairwell. Accommodations here comprise three magnificent suites, furnished with museum-quality Belle Epoque furniture, including a lovely chest and armoire in the *Honeymoon Suite.*

The third of the restored properties is the 1946 Art Deco *Wellborn* apartment building. True to its origins, the 13 suites here contain outstanding examples of Art Deco furnishings, as well as several that are more exotic. *Room No. 309,* for example, is a Thai room with an ornately carved Thai desk, elephant chairs, and a statue of a Buddhist monk.

A buffet breakfast is served in the *I.W. Phillips House* every morning. It includes fresh fruit, cereals, a selection of muffins and bagels, and juice.

In addition to *Walt Disney World, Epcot Center,* and *Universal Studios,* nearby attractions include the *Charles Hosmer Morse Museum of American Art* in Winter Park, which contains one of the nation's most impressive collections of Tiffany pieces. In addition, golf, tennis, and bicycling are possible diversions.

THE COURTYARD AT LAKE LUCERNE 211 N. Lucerne Circle E., Orlando, FL 32801 (phone: 407-648-5188; 800-444-5289; fax: 407-246-1368). This bed and breakfast establishment located in three historic houses in the heart of Orlando has 21 rooms and suites with private baths, double, queen-, or king-size beds, telephones, TV sets, and air conditioning; two with whirlpool tubs. Open year-round. Rate for a double room (including continental breakfast and afternoon wine): $69 to $165. Two-night minimum on some holidays. Major credit cards accepted. Children welcome in some rooms. No pets. Smoking allowed; designated non-smoking rooms. Charles, Sam, and Eleanor Meiner, innkeepers; Eleanor Meiner, manager.

DIRECTIONS: From I-4 north, exit at Anderson Street and travel west to Delaney. Turn right and go 2 blocks. Turn right onto North Lucerne Circle east. The inn is on the right. (There will be signs for the inn.) From I-4 south, exit at Gore Road and go west. Turn left onto Delaney and follow directions above.

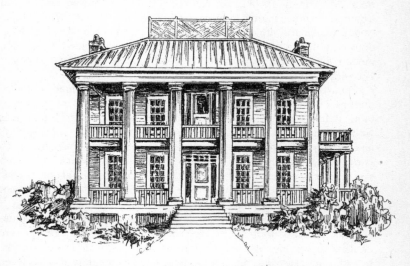

JOSEPHINE'S FRENCH COUNTRY INN AT SEASIDE

SEASIDE, FLORIDA

Nestled along the sheltered white sandy beaches of the Gulf Coast of Florida's panhandle lies a secret treasure: A Victorian village with fanciful houses painted robin's egg blue, seashell pink, and buttercup yellow has rose gardens and cloistered courtyards behind arched trellises and picket fences. There are brick-paved sidewalks for strolling, a theater, gazebos for band concerts, pavilions that act as gateways to the glorious expanse of uncrowded beaches, a shopping plaza with restaurants and a fancy food emporium, and an open-air bazaar where the Ruskin Artist Colony sells local crafts and hand-painted clothing. This masterfully planned new community, located between Panama City and Fort Walton Beach, was merely a stretch of ocean dunes 10 years ago, and it's still so new it often doesn't appear on maps.

Josephine's, which opened in 1991, is the clever work of a brother and sister team and their spouses and it provides the ideal environment in which to savor this idyllic retreat. The grand columned façade of this white

Victorian house has a broad verandah, brilliant with planters of ferns, petunias, gardenias, geraniums, and pansies; red roses wind along the white picket fence. The living room has a fireplace and pink walls that rise above white wainscoting and heart-pine floors rescued from a fallen plantation house. The dining room, where breakfast and dinner (open to non-guests) are served, has mahogany wainscoting, an antique marble-topped buffet, and tapestry-covered chairs.

Upstairs are seven guestrooms outfitted with wet bars, refrigerators, microwaves, coffee makers, and TV/VCRs; all except two have fireplaces. *Room No. 4,* in shades of green, has a private deck, a four-poster bed, and a bath with a green marble floor and walls. *Room No. 7* contains an antique carved headboard with a white cutwork duvet and a burgundy carpet. Next door is another house with four suites. *Suite No. 9* has pine floors, a full, modern kitchen with a separate dining room, a fireplace, and a four-poster bed with another cutwork duvet.

On arrival, guests receive a welcome basket of homemade cookies, muffins, or sweet breads, and cookies are set out in the afternoon for nibbling. A full breakfast, served daily, includes such offerings as pancakes with rum sauce and apples, Jody's strata, and eggs Mornay; on Saturdays and Sundays, champagne is included. At dinner, guests may enjoy such entrées as crab cakes, served on a bed of wilted spinach with a light cream sauce, and chargrilled rack of lamb marinated in rosemary and other herbs. Desserts include chocolate chip–raisin-walnut bread pudding with chocolate rum sauce and Key lime pie.

A secluded rooftop widow's walk affords views of the sparkling blue-green ocean across rooftops, and spectacular evening sunsets. Bicycles are available for touring along the village streets or down the quiet ocean byway. In addition to access to the glorious beach, the community also has three swimming pools, six tennis courts, a croquet lawn, a children's playground, shuffleboard, and numerous restaurants.

JOSEPHINE'S FRENCH COUNTRY INN AT SEASIDE 101 Seaside Ave. (mailing address: PO Box 4767), Seaside, FL 32459 (phone: 904-231-1940; 800-848-1840; fax: 904-231-2446). This village bed and breakfast establishment contains 11 rooms and suites with private baths, twin, queen-, or king-size beds, telephones, TV/VCR sets, and air conditioning; nine with fireplaces, two with whirlpool tubs. Wheelchair accessible. Open year-round. Rate for a double room (including full breakfast): $130 to $225. Two-night minimum on weekends and holidays March through October. Major credit cards accepted. Children welcome. No pets. Smoking permitted outside only. Jody, Sean, Bruce, Judy, and Peg Albert, innkeepers.

DIRECTIONS: Traveling east along Route 98, turn right onto Scenic Route 30A and travel to downtown Seaside. Enter Quincy Circle. *Josephine's* is on the east side. Traveling west along Route 98, turn left and proceed as above.

Georgia

PARROTT CAMP SOUCY HOME AND GARDENS

NEWNAN, GEORGIA

Newnan is only 30 miles south of Atlanta but it's a world away. Gracious homes in a potpourri of architectural styles border the tree-lined streets, and the town square, home to the stately brick courthouse, is lined with interesting shops and restaurants. It's a neat and compact town with broad sidewalks, numerous park benches, plenty of parking, and so many interesting houses that there are four National Historic Districts in town.

On a side street, the spectacular façade of the *Parrott Camp Soucy* frequently stops traffic. Built in a Greek Revival style, it was transformed into a Second Empire Victorian in 1890. Today, it's the square bay windows, ornate decorative work, and mansard roof topped with fanciful ironwork— all painted in shades of gray and white to accentuate the fancy details— that impress. A broad lawn bordered with boxwoods and azaleas leads to the wide verandah.

Inside, the house has 14-foot-high ceilings with elaborate moldings, accentuated by Bradbury and Bradbury wallpapers. The entry hall features intricate fretwork and a fireplace faced with tile. There's wood trim in quarter-sawn oak, black walnut, cherry, and maple, and a jewel-toned stained-glass window in the stairwell that casts a kaleidoscope of colors across the maple stair railing.

Helen and Rick Cousins, an enthusiastic young couple with backgrounds in computers, transformed the showplace private home into a bed and breakfast establishment in 1994. They have furnished the common rooms and guestrooms in appropriate high Victorian style. The *Ladies' Parlor* has another fireplace and the original wooden shutters, which still work. Oriental rugs cover the polished floors. There is also a library, where guests can browse through book, music, and video selections, and then enjoy them here by the fire.

The guestrooms are equally authentic. The *Regency Room,* on the first floor, has a bed with a lacy crown canopy, Oriental rugs, a fireplace, and separate "His" and "Hers" bathrooms, one with a sink in a carved cabinet, and another with a claw-foot tub placed before a fireplace. Upstairs, the sunny *Persian Room* contains a half-tester bed, a marble-topped chest, two ladies' boudoir chairs upholstered in fringed tapestry, and a bath with a claw-foot tub. The *Blue Room* has a full canopy bed, an antique dresser, and a bath with yet another claw-foot tub. There's a pull-chain commode across the hall.

Breakfast is served in the formal dining room and on the verandah. The menu includes fresh juice, a fruit dish (either fresh fruits, a fruit cobbler, or perhaps banana crêpes), and a hot dish. Helen often prepares a quiche with country potatoes or bruschetta.

There are four acres of formal gardens with flower beds and velvety lawns. Tucked among the trees are a gazebo, hammocks, a swimming pool, and a heated spa. Fine restaurants are located in town and there are walking tours along the streets. Many of Newnan's historic homes are open for tours.

PARROTT CAMP SOUCY HOME AND GARDENS 155 Greenville St., Newnan, GA 30263 (phone: 770-502-0676). This elaborate Victorian bed and breakfast establishment has four guestrooms with private baths, queen-size beds, fireplaces, and air conditioning. Open year-round. Rate for a double room (including full breakfast): $105 to $165. MasterCard and Visa accepted. Not appropriate for children. No pets. A terrier, Losty, on premises. No smoking. Helen and Rick Cousins, innkeepers.

DIRECTIONS: From Atlanta, take I-85 south to Exit 9 and turn right onto Highway 34 west. Travel about 4 miles to Route 29 south and follow this through Newnan. Route 29 becomes Greenville Street. The inn will be on the right.

SEREN-BE BED AND BREAKFAST FARM

PALMETTO, GEORGIA

Seren-be, a contraction of serenity and being, is a working farm of 284 acres with more than 90 horses, cows, chickens, goats, pigs, geese, turkeys, rabbits, a donkey, and cats in the various barns and pastures. The old farmhouse (now called the guesthouse), which dates to the 1930s, and several additional buildings were opened as a bed and breakfast establishment in

1995 by Marie and Steve Nygren, both of whom have extensive Atlanta restaurant backgrounds.

Although the surroundings suggest a rustic, simple, down-on-the-farm style, few farmhouses are decorated with such whimsical touches and in such an array of colors. There's all the sophistication of a big-city retreat combined with the tranquillity and casual ambience of the country.

Guests enter the inn from the wide screened-in back porch, which has two wide hanging sofa-swings and a floor painted to resemble a rug. A huge mercantile table with a heart-pine top is in the adjacent glassed-in porch, which is virtually surrounded by windows. Breakfast is served here.

There are guestrooms in the barn, as well as in several cottages. The *Gathering Room* in the barn has a stone fireplace, a pine armoire, and a great old woodstove that belonged to Steve's grandparents. The rooms are decorated with equal flair. *Room No. 1* has a white painted spool bed, twig furniture, a braided rug on the white wide-plank pine floor, a patchwork quilt hanging on the wall, and a private porch; the bath includes a sunken whirlpool tub and a pine dresser. *Room No. 2* has a floor painted in blue-and-white checks, three double beds, and a church pew painted white. *Room No. 3,* in the loft, is painted pure white—even the furniture is white—which contrasts with the glow of the natural heart-pine floors. There's an old chest and a reading nook full of bright pillows.

A few steps from the barn are a swimming pool, heated spa, and a tented cabana furnished with more great old painted furniture and another large swing. Beyond, a lane leads past an organic flower and vegetable garden to a guest cottage with views of the surrounding pastureland. It has two bedrooms, a full kitchen with a fireplace, and several sitting areas, including one with a second fireplace.

As one might expect of restaurateurs, a full Southern breakfast is served daily. Offerings include fresh fruit and juice, grits, an egg dish, bacon, biscuits, homemade jams and jellies, and perhaps pecan pancakes made with pecans from the farm's orchard, or a grits soufflé. Mostly it will depend on what's in season. In the afternoon, a sweet-mint Southern tea is served with hors d'oeuvres, perhaps cream cheese with pepper jelly and crackers. Sweets such as chocolate chip cookies, brownies, and gingerbread squares are set out at 9 PM when guests return from dinner at a local restaurant.

There are hiking trails across the property to a waterfall and a lake with canoes. In addition, guests are encouraged to bring their own horses or to rent several from the inn for a gallop across the fields. The many attractions of Atlanta are merely 30 minutes away.

SEREN-BE BED AND BREAKFAST FARM 10950 Hutcheson Ferry Rd., Palmetto, GA 30268 (phone: 770-463-2610; fax: 770-463-4472). This farm bed and breakfast establishment has four guestrooms with private baths, twin, double, or queen-size beds, and air conditioning; two with fireplaces, one with a whirlpool tub. Open year-round except one week at *Thanksgiving*, one week in March, and two weeks in the summer. Rate for a double room (including full breakfast and afternoon tea): $95 to $145. No credit cards accepted. Children welcome in the cottage. No pets. One standard poodle, Scarlett, in residence. Smoking outside only. Marie and Steve Nygren, innkeepers.

DIRECTIONS: From Atlanta, take I-85 south to Exit 16 and follow signs for Spur 14. Travel about 13 miles to the third stoplight and turn left onto Route 154. Go 3½ miles and turn right onto Carlton Road. Continue on Carlton Road for 1½ miles until Carlton Road dead-ends at Hutcheson Ferry Road. Turn right and continue for about 3½ miles to the farm, which will be on the right.

BALLASTONE INN

SAVANNAH, GEORGIA

Had Sherman ordered Savannah destroyed in 1864, as he did Atlanta, the 1838 townhouse now known as the *Ballastone Inn* would probably have been high on his list, as it was the home of his opponent at Fort McAllister, Major George W. Anderson. The home was subsequently sold to Captain Henry Blun who greatly enlarged it in the 1860s and lived there until 1910. But then it was strictly downhill for the house for some 50 years, becoming a boarding house, a bordello, and an apartment house until it was purchased in 1969 by the Girl Scouts of America for their national administrative offices. It was converted to a bed and breakfast establishment in 1980 and has been owned by innkeepers Richard Carlson and Timothy Hargus since 1988. It's named for the ballast stones (stones brought to Savannah in the holds of ships) with which the town is built.

The inn is in the heart of Savannah's historic district, one of the largest in America, encompassing some 1,100 structures. Hargus and Carlson have decorated their inn with traditional Savannah colors of green and deep red,

Scalamandre fabrics, and priceless period antiques. The gracious foyer has tall ceilings painted with a cloud-filled blue sky, oak paneling, a Victorian chandelier, and beautifully carved stairway spindles. To one side, a charming bar acts like a magnet. It has a wood-burning fireplace, royal blue moire walls, and sofas covered in blue toile. The gift shop, just inside the front door, is nearly as irresistible, containing a delicious array of gifts, books, and flowers. In the double parlors, both with fireplaces, there are wonderful Victorian collectibles. A pretty courtyard garden is a favorite spot to enjoy a refreshing drink on warm afternoons.

Dripping with romantic touches, the guestrooms are delightful retreats. *Victoria Suite,* for example, has a four-poster bed, a fireplace with its original columned mantel, and a lovely English-style chintz covering the bed and a chaise lounge. Victorian slipper chairs are covered in rose velvet. There's a whirlpool tub in the elegant bath. *Scarlett's Retreat* has a canopy bed, a fireplace, and another whirlpool tub. Even the smallest room, *Low Country,* is imbued with charm with its brick wall and beamed ceiling.

Cookies, fruit, tea, and coffee are set out for guests every afternoon, and sherry is offered on arrival. In the evening, brandy and chocolates are left in the room during turndown service. If you leave your shoes outside the door, they'll be polished during the night. Breakfast, which includes fruit and juice, muffins, croissants, and freshly baked breads, is brought to the room on a tray with fresh flowers and a newspaper every morning.

There are numerous historic attractions nearby. The *Juliette Gordon Low* (founder of the Girl Scouts) *Home* is next door; the *Green-Meldrin House,* General Sherman's headquarters during the Civil War, and the *Ownes-Thomas House* are nearby. Bull Street, with its eclectic collection of shops, and the Riverfront Plaza are easy walks.

BALLASTONE INN 14 E. Oglethorpe Ave., Savannah, GA 31401 (phone: 912-236-1484; 800-822-4553; fax: 912-236-4626). This elegant urban refuge has 17 guestrooms and suites with private baths, queen- or king-size beds, telephones, TV sets, and air conditioning; nine with fireplaces, three with whirlpool tubs. Open year-round. Rate for a double room (including continental breakfast and afternoon refreshments): $100 to $215. Three-day minimum over *St. Patrick's Day.* Major credit cards accepted. Not appropriate for children under 13. Small pets permitted in courtyard-level rooms. Smoking permitted. Timothy Hargus and Richard Carlson, innkeepers; Jessie Balentine, manager.

DIRECTIONS: From I-95 take I-16 into Savannah. At the second traffic light, turn right onto Oglethorpe Avenue. Proceed 5 blocks. The inn will be on the left.

MAGNOLIA PLACE INN

SAVANNAH, GEORGIA

Savannah is a lovely town of tree-lined streets intersected by park squares filled with flowers, commemorative statues, and benches. It's a walker's town, offering numerous opportunities for admiring the historic architecture (or to search out landmarks from the movie *Forrest Gump). Forsyth Park* is Savannah's great green common, where walkers, runners, and dog walkers enjoy the live oak trees dripping with moss and the abundant flowering magnolia and dogwood trees. But the favorite time of year is early spring when the azaleas weave a web of red and pink along the pathways and photographers, garden enthusiasts, and most of Savannah's citizenry come to savor the beauty.

Magnolia Place Inn, a true Southern belle, sits opposite *Forsyth Park* in a lush garden of her own. Walk through the ornate iron gate, past palmetto palms, and listen to the softly splashing fountain. Continue beneath the huge namesake magnolia tree and up the broad stairs to the sweeping front porch framed by wrought-iron columns. This is old Savannah at its best— a great 1878 Victorian confection claiming its place among Savannah's premier hostelries.

Vanessa Howle-Brooke and Witter Brooke have decorated their inn in an opulent but not fussy style. The entry hall has intricate inlaid floors, inlaid paneling, and tall ceilings, while the parlor has a fireplace, a grand brass chandelier, fine English antiques, and 12-foot-high windows draped in a rosy faille; a bay overlooks a small courtyard.

The guestrooms, which are painted in bright, high-fashion colors like ruby and persimmon, are large and decorated with antiques and period reproduction pieces. There are canopy and four-poster beds, fireplaces, and huge marble baths with whirlpool tubs surrounded by lush green plants. *Andrew Jackson,* on the courtyard level, contains a massive armoire, a fireplace, and a whirlpool tub surrounded with marble that projects into the

huge room. There's a curved wall of frosted windows with greenery beyond and pots of ficus trees and philodendrons.

Tables in the parlor are dressed with lacy cloths and set with fine china. At breakfast, a selection of fresh fruit and juice, croissants, muffins, and cereals are set out on an antique table. Tea and wine are available in the afternoon and at turndown you'll find a praline on your pillow and a glass of Madeira.

A daylight walk or jog through the park should be on every agenda, while restaurants and Savannah's many historic attractions are nearby. The *Georgia Historical Society* is next door. The *King-Tisdale Cottage,* a pretty Victorian with dormer windows, elaborate gingerbread, and a picket fence, tells an enthralling story of Savannah's African-American history.

MAGNOLIA PLACE INN 503 Whitaker St., Savannah, GA 31401 (phone: 912-236-7674; 800-238-7674; fax: 912-236-1145). This graceful Victorian jewel offers 13 guestrooms with private baths, queen- or king-size beds, telephones, TV sets, and air conditioning; 11 with fireplaces, six with whirlpool tubs. Open year-round. Rate for a double room (including continental breakfast and afternoon tea and wine): $100 to $195. Two- or three-night minimum over *St. Patrick's Day*. Major credit cards accepted. Children welcome. No pets. One cat, Flannery, on premises. Smoking permitted. Vanessa Howle-Brooke and Witter Brooke, innkeepers; Robin Laverty, manager.

DIRECTIONS: From I-95, exit onto I-16 and follow it to its end at the Savannah Civic Center. Turn right onto Liberty Street. Go to the next light and turn right onto Whitaker Street. The inn is the second building on the right after the Gaston Street traffic light.

THE VERANDA

Senoia, Georgia

The sleepy little town of Senoia (pronounced Se-*noy*) could have been taken straight from the pages of the novel, *Fried Green Tomatoes*. The streets are lined with graceful vintage homes, all preserved in a setting of Southern gentility. Most of the town is included on the National Register of Historic Places, including *The Veranda*.

Originally the *Hollberg Hotel*, the inn was built in 1906, when Senoia was still a prosperous cotton town. Over the years, numerous famous people have graced its doorstep. In 1908, William Jennings Bryan stayed here while campaigning for the presidency against William Howard Taft. Margaret Mitchell visited to interview Civil War veterans when she was writing her great American novel. In 1985, Jan Boal and his wife, Bobby, purchased and refurbished the hotel, adding private baths and air conditioning. It was after this restoration that Jessica Tandy and Kathy Bates were guests while filming *Fried Green Tomatoes* in town.

The inn is a white clapboard house, its Doric-columned, wraparound verandah lined with rocking chairs and swings. Several rooms have original pressed-tin ceilings and stained-glass windows. This was one of the first commercial establishments in the area to use electricity, and many of the original light fixtures are still in use. The common rooms and guestrooms are literally filled with various collections. Don't expect priceless antiques with "don't touch" signs; you are invited to examine and enjoy the treasures. In the front parlor a pair of antique bookcases that once belonged to President William McKinley dominates the room. They contain a priceless collection of books, including such rare volumes as a 1789 10-volume commentary on the Old Testament and *Hume's History of England,* published in 1795.

Across the hall is a gift shop with tall shelves and cabinets laden with games, gifts, dolls, and kaleidoscopes. Fifteen minutes here will yield a keepsake treasure for every grandchild. Examples of the inn's collection of more than 400 kaleidoscopes are found in every room of the house, and most are for sale. A kaleidoscope is even placed on each guest's pillow during the nightly turndown service.

The guestrooms have an old-fashioned ambience; each is filled with family heirlooms and collections based on given themes. The *Walking Stick Room,* for example, contains more than a hundred canes collected by Bobby's father (and some made by him). The *Historic Room* is notable for its original bathroom with its claw-foot tub and pedestal sink, as well as the dollhouse and furniture made by Jan for the couple's daughters. The *Mystery Room* contains several hundred paperback mysteries.

It's hard to imagine more pampering innkeepers. Both breakfast and dinner turn into special events and give Jan and Bobby—she's an exceptional cook—an opportunity to tell their guests about their town (there's a movie studio here) and to help guests become acquainted with one another. Breakfasts are so extensive and delicious that lunch is generally unnecessary, if not impossible. Dinner (for house guests only) might begin with a fresh seasonal fruit salad accompanied by homemade crackers, followed by French onion soup with Swiss cheese under a puff pastry dome, then seafood cocktail. Entrées might be baked sesame chicken served with rice, or veal Ione with a sweet-potato puff. Desserts are equally inventive.

Guests may stroll the grounds, with a rock garden, flagstone pathways, and the *Hollberg Hotel*'s original fountain. And don't miss the old-fashioned hardware/country store or the *Buggy Shop Museum* just across the street. Golf, tennis, fishing, historic walking tours, festivals, and antiquing are all nearby.

THE VERANDA 252 Seavy St. (mailing address: PO Box 177), Senoia, GA 30276 (phone: 770-599-3905; fax: 770-599-0806). In a village 36 miles south of Atlanta, this inn has seven guestrooms with private baths, queen- or king-size beds, and air conditioning. Wheelchair accessible. Open year-round. Rate for a double room (including full breakfast): $100 to $125. Major credit cards accepted. Children welcome with prior permission. No pets. Smoking permitted on the verandah only. Jan and Bobby Boal, innkeepers.

DIRECTIONS: From Atlanta take I-85 south to Exit 12 and turn left onto Route 74. Drive approximately 16½ miles, then turn right onto Rock-a-Way Road. Follow Rock-a-Way Road into Senoia. Turn left at the traffic light onto Seavy Street. *The Veranda* is on the left.

Louisiana

HOTEL MAISON DE VILLE AND
THE AUDUBON COTTAGES

New Orleans, Louisiana

The historic preservation movement in the United States first flowered in the Vieux Carré (the French Quarter) of New Orleans. Once a neighborhood of gracious homes with lacy wrought-iron balconies and hidden gardens and courtyards, the section had deteriorated, becoming overrun by honky-tonk bars and fortune-tellers' storefronts. In 1936, the historic district was created, showcasing the advantages of preserving America's heritage.

The 1742 *Hotel Maison de Ville* is in the heart of the Vieux Carré and it captures the Quarter's very essence. It was here that onetime owner Dr. Peychaud added a dash of bitters to brandy, using an egg cup (or *coquetier*) as a measure, thereby inventing the cocktail. And Tennessee Williams rewrote *A Streetcar Named Desire* on the wrought-iron tables in the sequestered courtyard with its three-tier, cast-iron fountain splashing. Perhaps he was thinking about the *Maison de Ville* when he wrote that Blanche Dubois loved her languid "afternoons in New Orleans when an hour isn't just an hour—but a little piece of eternity dropped in your hands."

Another visitor was John James Audubon, who stayed in one of the cottages when he painted the Louisiana portion of *Birds in America.*

Guestrooms in the original townhouse are formal and plush, decorated with antique canopy and four-poster beds, marble fireplaces, needlepoint chairs, gilt-framed mirrors, and swagged silk draperies with matching bedcovers. French doors lead to balconies overlooking a flower-filled stone courtyard, cooled by overhanging palm trees. Four more guestrooms are in the converted slave quarters on one side of the courtyard, the stucco exteriors painted a soft watermelon color. These actually predate the main building by about 50 years, making them (along with the *Ursuline Convent*) the oldest buildings in New Orleans. They have beamed ceilings, brick walls, and fireplaces, and are less formal than those in the mansion.

The seven *Audubon Cottages* are several blocks away, secluded behind a stucco wall. A brick pathway leads from the gate to the charming cottages, each with a large private courtyard, filled with flowers and a fountain behind high brick walls. Beamed ceilings, brick walls, and floors of brick or slate covered by Oriental rugs characterize the interiors. Antiques are used throughout, and the baths are spacious and modern. At the center of the cottage complex is a swimming pool flanked by greenery overseen by a statue and tall palm trees. For serene privacy in the heart of the French Quarter, the cottages are ideal.

Continental breakfast and fresh flowers arrive at guestroom doors on a silver tray. Guests are welcome to carry it to the courtyard. *The Bistro,* a popular French restaurant under the same ownership, is located next door. It's open to the public for lunch and dinner. In a setting as engaging as the inn, it has mahogany paneling below mirrored walls and lazy ceiling fans. Entrées include plantain-crusted mahi-mahi with basil couscous and vanilla-rum essence and cassoulet Rue Toulouse with duck *confit,* mesquite-smoked pork loin, and sausage. For dessert, the chocolate *crème brûlée* is outstanding. There's an excellent aperitif, wine, and liqueur list.

The inn is close to the city's many museums, shops, restaurants, and galleries.

HOTEL MAISON DE VILLE AND THE AUDUBON COTTAGES 727 Toulouse St., New Orleans, LA 70130 (phone: 504-561-5858; 800-634-1600; fax: 504-528-9939). This historic inn has 23 guestrooms with private baths, double, queen-, or king-size beds, telephones, TV sets, courtyards or balconies, and air conditioning; two with whirlpool tubs. Open year-round. Rate for a double room (including continental breakfast, sherry, and port): $165 to $205. Two-night minimum stay on weekends. Major credit cards accepted. Not appropriate for children under 13. No pets. A turtle, Bistro, on premises. Smoking permitted in courtyard only. Jean-Luc Maumus, manager.

DIRECTIONS: In New Orleans's Vieux Carré, Toulouse Street is between St. Louis and St. Peter Streets; the inn is on Toulouse between Royal and Bourbon Streets.

HOUSE ON BAYOU ROAD INN

New Orleans, Louisiana

When this Creole house was built in 1798 it was the centerpiece of a 3,200-acre indigo plantation and Bayou Road was the main route between the Mississippi River and Bayou St. John. The streets in this little enclave just off Esplanade are still paved in cobblestones, and other gracious antebellum mansions are nearby, but the *House on Bayou Road* is unique. Rather than emulating its plantation cousins that rise to several stories, this house is a low-slung two-story place with dormer windows in its overhanging roof. It's painted a soft pink; white accents its columns, railings, and trim. Set well back from the road, it's entered through a garden gate. A pathway leads guests past a garden with a fountain, variegated camellia and gardenia bushes, and a towering magnolia tree. Sprawling behind the charming house are two additional acres of lawns, gardens with banana trees and elephant ears, a courtyard, a pool and spa, two cottages, and even a barn. Although in the heart of the city, about half a mile from the French Quarter (it's not recommended to walk it, however), this is a world unto itself—one cleverly created by owner Cynthia Reeves for her guests' pleasure and comfort.

The house is filled with lovely antiques and decorated with style. The foyer, with its dark polished cypress floors, has a collection of French military medals on display; a double parlor has watermelon-colored walls, a fireplace, and white sofas piled high with needlepoint pillows. There are bouquets of fresh flowers on tables and classical music plays softly in the background.

The guestrooms are equally delightful. *Bayou Self,* a small romantic cottage, has two fan windows, a cathedral ceiling with a collection of baskets atop the beams, and walls of unpainted bead board. The bath has a pine floor, a whirlpool tub, and two arched stained-glass windows. There's a four-poster bed piled high with pillows and antique clocks on the wall. In the anteroom to the closet, there's a wet bar and a refrigerator stocked with soft drinks and wine. Stemmed glasses and dishes are on shelves; a coffee maker sits on a counter beside a basket of coffees and teas. A private porch has cedar furniture painted a sparkling white. *Bayou St. John,* in the original library, has olive walls, a fireplace, floor-to-ceiling bookcases, a four-poster rice bed, an armoire, and an Oriental rug on the pine floor. There are four rooms in the main house and three in the *Victorian Cottage,* plus the individual cottage. Private parking is located behind locked gates in the rear.

In chilly weather, breakfast is served in a dining room, which is furnished with a pine sideboard and a massive buffet table. Muslin curtains are tied back with gossamer gold French ribbon. Generally, however, it will be served at umbrella-topped tables by the pool. The breakfast is as extraordinary as the decor. It may start with a baked apple garnished with pecans, followed by scrambled eggs in a pastry shell topped with hollandaise sauce, and end with a light bread pudding soufflé with blueberry sauce. Mimosas or champagne are offered Saturdays and Sundays and guests often linger on the wicker-filled screened porch overlooking the courtyard.

Cynthia also conducts a popular cooking school here, *Cuisine Eclairée Ecole de Cuisine.* When the school is in session, participants can take lessons during the day, sample New Orleans's distinctive cuisine in the evening, and sleep in luxury at night—all at one inn. And there's still time to enjoy all the history and charm of New Orleans. *Restaurant Indigo* was scheduled to open as this book went to press.

HOUSE ON BAYOU ROAD INN 2275 Bayou Rd., New Orleans, LA 70119 (phone: 504-945-0992; 800-882-2968; fax: 504-945-0993). This charming in-city bed and breakfast establishment has eight rooms and suites, six with private baths (two share a bath), double, queen-, or king-size beds, telephones, TV sets, and air conditioning; two with fireplaces, one with a whirlpool tub. Open year-round. Rate for a double room (including full breakfast and many extras): $115 to $300. Two-night minimum on weekends. Not appropriate for children under 13. No pets. Siamese cats, Ping Pong and Samson, in residence. Smoking outside only. Cynthia Reeves, innkeeper; Karon Baudouin, manager.

DIRECTIONS: From the west on I-10, exit at the Metairie Road/City Park exit. Turn left back under I-10 and proceed to City Park Avenue. Follow City Park Avenue for 1³/₁₀ miles to a traffic light at Carrollton Avenue. Turn left, go about 100 yards, and turn right across the bridge over Bayou St. John onto Esplanade Avenue. Follow Esplanade for ⁸/₁₀ mile. Cross through the traffic light at Broad Street. Take the third left onto North Tonti. Take an immediate left again onto Bayou Road. The inn is behind a picket fence on the right. From the east on I-10, pass through town (about 3 miles), get off at the Metairie Road/City Park exit and follow directions above.

MELROSE MANSION

New Orleans, Louisiana

Esplanade Street borders the French Quarter. Yet, in mood and style, it's worlds apart. The narrow warren of treeless streets, narrow sidewalks, and side-by-side townhouses in the Quarter gives way here to broad tree-lined streets and large single homes on spacious lots.

The grand white clapboard home now called *Melrose Mansion* was built in a Second Empire Victorian style in 1884. It has a double set of porches across the front embellished with fluted columns topped with Corinthian capitals and a square turret on one side. Arched windows, elaborate brackets under the eaves, and numerous bays and projections give the house a distinctive architectural style. Its magnificent restoration was the painstaking accomplishment of Melvin and Rosemary Jones in 1990.

The parlor glows with Lancaster white walls, a lustrous red heart-pine floor covered with an Oriental rug, and damask-covered chairs and love seats. A glittering crystal chandelier, hanging from a 14-foot ceiling, illuminates polished antique tables and chests. Ornate moldings surround the room. Adjacent to the parlor is a verandah with white rocking chairs and a side porch with wicker chairs and bright floral cushions.

The guestrooms are elegant. *Miss Kitty's Room,* for example, has champagne-colored walls, a lovely antique quilt on an iron bed, an antique armoire, and access to a secluded balcony. The most acclaimed accommodation is the *Donecio Suite,* which has a four-poster rice bed with a crocheted lace coverlet, an antique armoire, a Persian rug on the red heart-pine floor, and a love seat in the square turret. Lace curtains and drapes soften the windows and French doors lead to a private balcony with wicker furniture.

On the third floor, a fitness center and retreat are housed in the *Sol Owens Suite.* There's a treadmill, Lifecycle, Stairmaster, and free weights. A wet bar is handy and there's a television as well. In the turret, a reading area with wicker furniture provides a quiet treetop retreat. Tucked between the main house and the carriage house is a pool, surrounded with lush roses, camellias, hydrangeas, and palm trees.

Melvin and Rosemary's pampering care begins with limousine service to and from the airport. Numerous little pleasures await at the inn: cocktails and hors d'oeuvres in the evening; hair dryers and thick terry robes in the baths; bouquets of flowers perfuming the air; whirlpool tubs and decanters of Courvoisier in the suites.

Breakfast, which can be delivered to the room or perhaps to the verandah, includes hazelnut coffee, fresh fruits and juices, and an entrée of perhaps eggs Benedict or maybe a frittata with eggs, onions, potatoes, peppers, and mushrooms. The breakfast dessert may be a peach cobbler pie or bread pudding with whiskey sauce.

The innkeepers are pleased to tell their guests about their favorite shops, the best restaurants, and excursions to plantations, museums, and even to New Orleans's unique cemeteries.

MELROSE MANSION 937 Esplanade Ave., New Orleans, LA 70116 (phone: 504-944-2255; fax: 504-945-1794). This grand in-town mansion has eight rooms and suites with private baths, twin, queen-, or king-size beds, telephones, TV sets, and air conditioning; four with whirlpool tubs. Open year-round. Rate for a double room (including full breakfast and limousine transfer to and from airport): $225 to $425. Two-night minimum on weekends; more for special events. Major credit cards accepted. Limited facilities for children. No pets. Limited smoking permitted; designated non-smoking rooms. Melvin and Rosemary Jones, innkeepers.

DIRECTIONS: The inn is across the street from the French Quarter on the corner of Burgundy Street and Esplanade Avenue.

NOTTOWAY PLANTATION

WHITE CASTLE, LOUISIANA

During the period between 1820 and the Civil War, numerous mansions were built along the roads bordering the Mississippi River between New Orleans and Baton Rouge. They were the centerpieces of sugar or cotton plantations and had numerous outbuildings for the managers and slaves. Dependent on the river for transportation, they were built with sweeping

verandahs and tall windows to capture river breezes and views. Today, many of these grand houses are gone and the riverbanks are peppered with the sprawling stacks of giant factories, brightly lighted at night.

Nottoway Plantation, one of the remaining mansions (the town was named for it), is listed on the National Register of Historic Places and is majestic in all respects. Boasting 53,000 square feet and 64 original rooms, furnished as they must have been when the estate was the scene of grand balls and parties, this is the largest surviving antebellum mansion in the South. A total of 22 massive two-story square columns surrounds the exquisite house.

Guests enter the estate through a simple gate and driveway to a parking lot. A pavilion contains a reception desk and a gift shop. Ahead, the house looms. Along the pathway is a parterre garden behind a picket fence and an old brick cistern; in spring, the grounds are ablaze with azaleas.

The main house was built in 1858 by John Hampden Randolph, a wealthy sugar planter, on an estate that eventually grew to 7,436 acres. Every detail was meticulously planned, using the finest construction techniques, artistry, and woods. Ornate decorative cast-iron grillwork with wood railings is unique to the house; the chocolate mahogany stair railings, newels, and balusters are elaborately carved, and the white ballroom has a maple floor, grand arches, and fluted columns with lacy Corinthian capitals. Eleven Randolph children were raised here; six daughters were married in the ballroom.

Although the house is open for tours during the day, in the evening, guests have it to themselves. They can sit in the *Gentleman's Study* with its Italian black marble fireplace mantel and rich green velvet drapes. Oil portraits of the Randolph family line the walls of the halls and rooms. From the *Ancestral Hall* guests can reach the front verandah which has a view of the river.

Guestrooms are luxuriously furnished: The *Randolph Suite,* a large third-floor room, contains a four-poster bed draped in ivory damask. The adjoining morning room, which is part of the suite, is furnished with the room's original lacy wicker. There's a bath with a claw-foot tub and pedestal sink. The *Master Suite,* which has a half-tester rosewood bed, also has a matching armoire, bureau, and dresser. The walls are a pale blue with ivory trim. These two suites are part of the house tour; therefore, guests staying in them are asked to leave the rooms unoccupied between 9 AM and 5 PM. Other rooms in the main house are equally elaborate and also have canopy beds and modern baths. There are additional rooms in the *Overseer's Cottage,* a separate building that's 20 years older than the mansion. Guests may check into all the other rooms after 2:30 PM. When they do, they will find sherry and nuts on a bureau or table.

The romantic and elegant restaurant, *Randolph Hall,* is open for lunch and dinner. Decked out with pink walls, blue ceiling, crystal chandeliers, candlelight, and silver, the room is further enhanced by soft piano music played on the carved concert grand piano. There's a dance floor in the middle. Guests might start the meal with a mint julep or planter's punch. Typical entrées feature Creole cuisine such as blackened fish Nottoway and crawfish *étouffée.* For dessert, there's bread pudding with rum sauce and plantation pecan pie.

Coffee, juice, and sweet potato muffins are available to guests at 7 AM, and a full breakfast is served in the dining room of the main house between 8 and 9:45 AM. Offerings include a traditional *pain perdu* (Southern-style French toast) or waffles with sausage. These are accompanied by an egg dish, fresh fruit, and grits.

A lovely swimming pool is located in an enclosed courtyard behind a brick wall and guests are welcome to explore all 35 acres of grounds and gardens.

NOTTOWAY PLANTATION Mississippi River Rd. (mailing address: PO Box 160), White Castle, LA 70767 (phone: 504-545-2730; fax: 504-545-8632). This grand antebellum mansion has 13 rooms and suites with private baths, twin, double, or queen-size beds, telephones, TV sets, and air conditioning; seven with fireplaces, and one with whirlpool tub. Wheelchair accessible. Rate for a double room (including full breakfast and sherry): $125 to $250. Major credit cards accepted. Children welcome. No pets. Peacocks, Napoleon and Josephine, on property. No smoking. Cindy Hidalgo, manager.

DIRECTIONS: From New Orleans, take I-10 west and exit onto Route 22. At the junction with Route 70 turn left and follow the signs across the Mississippi River on the Sunshine Bridge. Turn west onto Route 1 and follow it for 14 miles through Donaldson to Nottoway. From Baton Rouge, cross the Mississippi River on I-10 and exit onto Route 1. Follow Route 1 south for 18 miles through Plaquemine to Nottoway.

Mississippi

FAIRVIEW INN

JACKSON, MISSISSIPPI

Jackson, founded in 1821, is the capital of Mississippi and its largest city. Located on the Pearl River, it is named for Andrew Jackson. Almost destroyed during the Civil War, today it is a lovely town of quiet streets and gracious homes. Its peaceful atmosphere has long attracted artists and writers; Eudora Welty lives here.

On a residential street of stately homes on spacious lawns, a curving driveway leads to *Fairview Inn,* a Colonial Revival home built in 1908 and occupying nearly two acres. With a series of two-story rounded columns supporting a porch, it offers an impressive façade. On the National Register of Historic Places, the house is in its second generation of Simmonses, who have owned it since 1930. Bill and Carol Simmons have operated the house as a bed and breakfast establishment since 1993.

As impressive as the exterior of *Fairview Inn* is, the interior is even more so. Guests enter a classic foyer with a green-veined marble floor, oak columns, a tiered crystal chandelier, a vaulted ceiling, and a carved marble mantel. A round table just inside the entrance is extravagantly swathed in four luxurious fabrics ranging from a plaid taffeta to red velveteen and topped by a raw silk in reds and greens. An adjacent library has walls and floor of lustrous quarter-sawn oak, oak shelves filled with leather-bound volumes on the Civil War, and a fireplace surrounded by an oak mantel with noble columns surmounted by carved Corinthian capitals. An Oriental rug, a tufted oxblood leather sofa, and drapes and upholstery in a bright red-and-blue geometric pattern complete the picture. The conservatory has tapestry-covered love seats. Outside, there's a brick courtyard. A garden room serves as a grand ballroom for receptions and parties.

The guestrooms, located in the main house and in an adjacent carriage house, are equally exquisite. The *Natchez Room,* for example, has a bed with a crown canopy, yellow floral wallpaper, sage-colored damask drapes tied with an elaborate fringe, and a tile bath with a whirlpool tub. The tile-floored *Tack Room,* complete with a sitting room, has a king-size bed of inlaid woods and is dressed mostly in black. A leopard rug adds accent. When the beds are turned down at night, a sweet pirouline, a crisp, rolled, light chocolate pastry made locally, is left on the pillow.

A multi-course dinner (open to non-guests by reservation) is served in a variety of locations, depending on the number of guests. The set menu consists of an appetizer, salad, first course (perhaps a pasta), an entrée such as grilled Atlantic salmon with grilled fennel and braised chickory or beef tenderloin with roasted new potatoes and fresh asparagus, and dessert choices like dark-chocolate soufflé crêpe with white-chocolate sauce or caramel custard with Grand Marnier. Appropriate wines accompany each course.

Breakfast, equally elaborate, starts with fresh fruit, juice, cereal, and fluffy biscuits. An entrée, perhaps French toast served with ham and sausage, eggs, and cheese grits, follows.

Formal gardens extend the ambience. There are two large redwood decks with benches under the shade of a magnificent magnolia tree. A formal boxwood garden contains statues and benches.

FAIRVIEW INN 734 Fairview St., Jackson, MS 39202 (phone: 601-948-3429; fax: 601-948-1203). The luxurious in-city inn has eight rooms and suites with private baths, queen- or king-size beds, telephones, TV sets, and air conditioning; two with whirlpool tubs. Wheelchair accessible. Open year-round. Rate for a double room (including full breakfast): $95 to $165. Major credit cards accepted. Well-behaved children welcome. No pets. No smoking. Carol and Bill Simmons, innkeepers.

DIRECTIONS: From I-55, take Exit 98A onto Woodrow Wilson Boulevard. At the first traffic light turn left onto North State Street. Go 1 block past the second traffic signal and turn left onto Fairview Street. The inn is the first house on the left.

THE BRIARS INN

NATCHEZ, MISSISSIPPI

Natchez—one of the state's most beautiful and historic towns—sits high on a bluff above the Mississippi River. Founded in 1716 by the French, the city has flown the flags of England, Spain, the Confederate States, and the

United States. It enjoyed commercial prosperity during the steamboat era when side-wheelers and stern-wheelers stopped here on their travels between New Orleans and St. Louis. The romance of riverboat gamblers, dark-haired beauties in hoop-skirted dresses, and antebellum homes is still alive in Natchez.

The Briars Inn, an 1814 Southern plantation-style house, played its own role in history. The main house was the site of the marriage of Jefferson Davis (later to become President of the Confederacy) to Varnia Howell in 1845. The *Parlor* where the ceremony took place is as gracious today as it was then with cypress floors topped with Oriental rugs, antique desks and tables, an Adam-style fireplace, oil paintings, and a Waterford crystal chandelier. The 48-foot-long *Drawing Room* contains twin staircases and a series of arches that define a gallery along one wall. Antiques, abundant plants, and sofas covered in pale damasks create private sitting areas. Down the hall is an 80-foot-long verandah, filled with white wicker, with lovely views across the gardens to the river. A bar in the glassed-in porch has walls lined with riverboat prints.

Outside, garden paths lead past noble magnolia trees, bright pink and red camellia bushes, and azaleas (there are more than 1,000 bushes). There are fountains, several gazebos, covered walkways, a pond, and a swimming pool. The river views from the gardens, and also from some of the guestrooms, are breathtaking.

The rooms are located in the main house, a schoolhouse, a guesthouse, and upstairs in the dining pavilion. Innkeepers Robert Canon and Newton Wilds are both interior designers and the antiques-filled guestrooms attest to their skill. *Room No. 4* has an antique four-poster bed and a fireplace. *Room No. 6,* in a charming old schoolhouse, has a gas fireplace, a beamed ceiling, and a lovely antique dresser. *Room No. 11* contains a four-poster bed, an antique dresser and side table, a sparkling crystal chandelier, and windows on three sides offering expansive river views.

A five-course breakfast—served in the dining pavilion every morning—includes homemade biscuits, fig muffins, fresh juice and fruit, grits, and perhaps herbed eggs in a crêpe with blueberry chutney, or *grillards* (a Creole dish of turkey breast, peppers, and onions).

In addition to Natchez's numerous antebellum homes that are open for tours (especially during Pilgrimage), there are carriage rides downtown and steamboat rides and casino boats on the Mississippi. Visitors to the area should plan to drive at least part of the beautiful 450-mile-long Natchez Trace Parkway; maintained by the National Park Service, this route follows an ancient Native American path and colonists' trail and extends from Natchez to Nashville, Tennessee.

THE BRIARS INN 31 Irving La. (mailing address: PO Box 1245), Natchez, MS 39120 (phone: 601-446-9654; 800-634-1818; fax: 601-445-6037). This historic in-city bed and breakfast establishment has 14 rooms and suites with private baths, twin, queen-, or king-size beds, telephones, TV sets, and air conditioning; eight with fireplaces. Wheelchair accessible. Open year-round. Rate for a double room (including full breakfast): $130 to $145. Major credit cards accepted. Not appropriate for children under 13. No pets. Smoking in public areas only. Newton Wilds and Robert Canon, innkeepers; Nancy Diehl and Christine James, managers.

DIRECTIONS: Traveling east from Louisiana on I-84, cross the Mississippi River to Mississippi and stay on the I-65/I-84 Natchez Bypass. Turn right to the Ramada Inn in approximately 200 yards. Access to the inn is through the Ramada Inn parking lot. Traveling west, take the I-75/I-84 Natchez Bypass and turn left at the Ramada, just before the bridge across the Mississippi River.

MONMOUTH PLANTATION

NATCHEZ, MISSISSIPPI

Southern hospitality is in full flower at *Monmouth Plantation,* one of the South's finest antebellum homes. Amid 26 acres of live oak trees dripping with Spanish moss, banks of azaleas in bright reds and pinks, magnolia trees, and camellia bushes rises a grand 1818 Greek Revival mansion. This was the home of General John Quitman, an early governor of Mississippi, and his family, from 1826 to 1925. It's now on the National Register of Historic Places and has been lovingly restored by Ron and Lani Riches.

Guests can rise early to the trill of a mockingbird and sit in the brick courtyard with its black wrought-iron furniture. A walk along the pebble paths of the garden reveals a lion's head fountain, a rose garden, a pond stocked with fish and crossed by a bow bridge, a gazebo, a croquet lawn,

and a pergola covered with wisteria. The pretty gift shop, located in the former summer kitchen, is a destination unto itself. It's stocked with a range of gifts from books, vases, plants, and seeds to clothing.

The spectacular common rooms are open for tours during the day. Nevertheless, only one guestroom is on the regular tour and any of the other rooms that are occupied are off-limits to sightseers. Overnight guests can take their own private tour of the mansion at 9:30 AM before the day-trippers arrive. They'll see the main hall with its allegorical 1836 mural French Zuber woodblock wallpaper (there's a duplicate in the White House), a side parlor with swagged blue damask drapes and fringed tufted chairs, and a music room with a needlepoint rug and a harp and concert grand piano. A grand verandah sweeps across the front overlooking sloping lawns. A downstairs parlor is filled with Quitman family books, paintings, and photographs, as well as Civil War mementoes.

Guestrooms are located in the main house, the slave quarters, separate cabins, and the carriage house. They're filled with period antiques, including tester, canopy, and four-poster beds, dressed with elaborate drapes, skirts, and curtains. The *Plantation Suite* has an elaborately carved canopy bed swagged in peach and green silk. *Room No. 30* has a carved headboard and a marble-topped dresser. The bed and window curtains are lavishly draped in tawny beige and bronze fabrics.

A five-course dinner (open to non-guests) is served in the formal dining room, under an ornate gilt gas chandelier on an antique Empire mahogany table set with fine china, silver, and crystal, and adorned with bouquets of fresh flowers. There's a gilt mirror over a marble mantel and Oriental rugs soften the heart-pine floors. Heavily fringed rose velvet drapes puddle on the floor. The menu includes soup, salad, sorbet, yeast rolls, and such entrées as filet of beef with Dijon mustard sauce or red fish Perez. For dessert, there might be a lemon chess pie or a white-chocolate bread pudding.

Breakfast is served in a separate pavilion with Wedgwood blue walls and a fireplace. Linen napkins rest in silver holders and silver vases hold fresh flowers. A buffet of fresh fruit, cereals, and sweet breads, such as lemon poppyseed, is at one end. A hot dish, perhaps scrambled eggs with ham, accompanied by grits and cream biscuits, will be served. Tea or lemonade and pralines are offered when guests check in, while mint juleps and hors d'oeuvres are served before dinner. At night, a chocolate waits on the soft pillow.

Guests may play croquet and fish on the property and there are also numerous activities in Natchez year-round. During Pilgrimage in the spring and fall many of Natchez's private homes are open to visitors. In addition, the *Natchez Opera Festival* and the *Natchez Little Theatre* mount productions annually, and numerous activities take place during *Mardi Gras*.

MONMOUTH PLANTATION 36 Melrose Ave., Natchez, MS 39120 (phone: 601-442-5852; 800-828-4531; fax: 601-446-7762). This grand antebellum mansion has 27 rooms and suites with private baths, twin, double, queen-, or king-size beds, telephones, TV sets, and air conditioning; 17 with fireplaces, most with private porches, seven with whirlpool tubs. Wheelchair accessible. Open year-round; restaurant open for dinner Mondays through Saturdays. Rate for a double room (including full breakfast and afternoon refreshments): $115 to $215. Major credit cards accepted. Not appropriate for children under 14. No pets. No smoking. Ron and Lani Riches, proprietors; Jim Anderson, innkeeper.

DIRECTIONS: From Baton Rouge, take I-110 and exit onto Route 61 north into Natchez. At the fifth traffic light, turn left onto the Melrose-Montebello Parkway. Go past the next stop sign and then turn left at the next intersection. The inn is on the corner.

ANCHUCA

VICKSBURG, MISSISSIPPI

Anchuca is a Choctaw word meaning "happy home," and as you enter the brick courtyard, you know it's true.

The gracious yellow brick 1840 Greek Revival house with its imposing two-story columns stands high above the street, offering views of the Mississippi River from its broad verandah. On the second floor is a balcony where Confederate President Jefferson Davis once gave a speech. By the time May Burns purchased the mansion in 1979, however, it had been an apartment house for some time. She accomplished a major restoration and opened it as Vicksburg's first bed and breakfast establishment. Filled with magnificent period antiques, it affords guests an authentic pre-Civil War ambience.

In the *Gentlemen's Parlor,* for example, there's a stunning Waterford crystal chandelier hanging from an elaborate medallion, as well as opulent

drapes, and a huge gilt-framed mirror over the white marble fireplace. The *Ladies' Parlor* contains a magnificent square rosewood grand piano, a red moire chaise lounge, another white marble fireplace, and original oil paintings. There are fine Oriental rugs on polished wood floors, and bouquets of fresh flowers abound.

The guestrooms are equally faithful to the period. In *Room No. 10* there's a spectacular built-in tester bed with elaborate side drapes in a blue Waverly fabric, wine velvet chairs, and a Victorian dresser with a marble top. The elegant bath includes a bidet. The *Anchuca Suite* is a medley of pinks: An antique apostle's bed (a four-poster canopy) is swagged with pink fringed solid and floral fabrics; matching pieces include a dressing table, an armoire, and a dresser; there's another Waterford crystal chandelier; and the huge bath/dressing room has a pink rug on a slate floor. There are two rooms in the main house and four in the *Guest Cottage.* (Although tours are conducted through the house, any rooms that are occupied are strictly off-limits.)

Breakfast is served in the dining room, on a mahogany Sheraton table under a Waterford crystal chandelier, amid fine silver, crystal, and china. A collection of silver napkin rings hold linen napkins. The Southern breakfast includes fresh fruit, cream biscuits or poppyseed bread, grits, and an entrée of an egg and cheese dish or waffles, accompanied by bacon or sausage.

Beyond the brick courtyards, there's a swimming pool and a spa. A cabana and chaise lounges provide a secluded retreat surrounded by flower gardens and magnolia, oak, and Oriental cherry trees.

ANCHUCA 1010 First East St., Vicksburg, MS 39180 (phone: 601-631-6800; 800-469-2597; fax: 601-630-4121). This gracious Southern antebellum mansion has six rooms and suites with private baths, queen-size beds, telephones, TV sets, and air conditioning; three with fireplaces. Open year-round. Rate for a double room (including full breakfast): $85 to $300. Major credit cards accepted. Not appropriate for children under 12. No pets. No smoking. May C. Burns, innkeeper.

DIRECTIONS: From I-20, take Exit 4B onto Clay Street. Continue on Clay for about ten minutes. Turn right onto Cherry Street and go for 5 blocks. Turn right onto First East; the inn will be on the right.

CEDAR GROVE MANSION INN
Vicksburg, Mississippi

Vicksburg is steeped in Civil War history. With its strategic location on a bluff overlooking the confluence of the Mississippi and Yazoo Rivers, Union General Ulysses S. Grant knew that the capture of Vicksburg was essential to winning the war. Northern troops besieged the city for 47 days before the valiant citizens surrendered. Fortunately, many of Vicksburg's fine antebellum mansions survived and are open for visits today.

Cedar Grove Mansion Inn saw its share of action in the Battle of Vicksburg, a fact amply illustrated by the cannonball lodged in the parlor wall. Built in a Greek Revival style by John Klein in 1840, and located on four acres, the brick mansion was used as General Grant's headquarters during the siege, while the Klein family (Mrs. Klein was a cousin of General Sherman) continued to live upstairs. Many of the original family furnishings are still in the house.

In the parlor, there are original oil paintings, blue tufted furniture, and blue damask drapes. The grand ballroom contains a carved square grand piano and a harp. Most of the books in the library were here when the Kleins were in residence, and even the antique wicker in the *Wicker Room* is original to the house. The *Garden Room,* where breakfast and dinner are served, is charming, with a fireplace, a wall of windows that look across the gardens, antique furniture, and a brick floor. A pretty little bar, a few steps above the dining room, also has a brick floor, and leads to an outside porch.

The guestrooms are sumptuous. Some are located in the mansion, others are in the *Carriage House,* the pool-side *Guest House,* or across the street in *Cottage Suites.* The *Grant Room,* in the mansion, has an elaborate antique tester bed elegantly draped with gold brocade; this is believed to be the bed General Grant slept in. Other furnishings include an Oriental rug on heart-pine floors, a carved armoire, and a marble fireplace mantel. *Aunt Pitty Pat's Suite* in the *Carriage House* has an antique canopy bed, a marble-topped dresser, two fireplaces, a whirlpool tub, and a private brick courtyard with black wrought-iron furniture. The rooftop garden, atop the main house, boasts a sun deck with a great river view.

Dinner (open to non-guests) is served in the *Garden Room* or on the *Courtyard.* Typical entrées include New Orleans catfish with Cajun crawfish *étouffée* and yellowfin tuna with Creole seasonings. The brandy bread pudding is especially popular for dessert. A full Southern breakfast of fresh fruit, scrambled eggs with sausage patties, and cheese grits is served.

The grounds include formal gardens, several courtyards, a pool surrounded by a brick courtyard, a spa, a fountain, a croquet lawn, and a tennis court. Bicycles are available. Visitors to Vicksburg will want to visit the *Vicksburg National Military Park,* as well as several of the other antebellum mansions. The *Biedenharn Museum of Coca-Cola Memorabilia* is in the original building where Coca-Cola was bottled in 1890. It includes a reproduction of the bottling works, and you can buy floats, cherry cokes, and ice cream from a 1900s soda fountain as well as candy from a restored 1890 candy store. Casino gambling has come to Vicksburg in a big way.

CEDAR GROVE MANSION INN 2200 Oak St., Vicksburg, MS 39180 (phone: 601-636-1000; 800-862-1300; fax: 601-634-6126). This antebellum mansion has 34 rooms and suites with private baths, double, queen-, or king-size beds, telephones, TV sets, porches or courtyards, and air conditioning; three with fireplaces, 16 with whirlpool tubs. Wheelchair accessible. Open year-round. Restaurant closed for dinner on Mondays. Rate for a double room (including full breakfast and afternoon refreshments): $85 to $165. Major credit cards accepted. Children welcome. No pets. A standard poodle, Goobah, on premises. Smoking permitted; some designated non-smoking rooms. Ted and Estelle Mackey, proprietors; Ann Holland and Peggy Spring, innkeepers.

DIRECTIONS: From I-20 take Exit 1A (Washington Street) north for 2 miles. The inn is bounded by Washington, Klein, Speed, and Oak Streets.

South Carolina

RHETT HOUSE INN

BEAUFORT, SOUTH CAROLINA

This inn, originally the home of Thomas Rhett and his wife, Caroline Barnwell, is typical of the grand plantation houses built during the 1820s. Corinthian columns support a classic two-story verandah that loops around both sides of the house. The gardens are rich with pink and red azaleas, roses, and salvias growing beside a splashing fountain.

The mansion has been artistically decorated by owners Steve and Marianne Harrison, refugees from fashion and textile careers in New York City. Polished pine floors and pristine white walls are complemented by Oriental rugs, antique furnishings, floral fabrics, and original artwork. In the sun-drenched living room guests relax on sofas before the Adam-style mantelpiece. Family photographs add a personal touch.

The spacious guestrooms are furnished with English and American antiques, carved Charleston rice beds (four-posters with a rice-grain pattern), armoires, and crystal chandeliers among them. Some rooms have fireplaces, and two of the baths have Jacuzzis.

Afternoon tea and cookies are served in the parlor, as is an evening snack of fruit and cheese. A full breakfast of fruit, muffins, and perhaps French toast made with cinnamon-raisin bread and topped with fresh strawberries is included in the room rate. Dinner (also open to non-guests) is served in a smart black-and-white room, which has a fireplace and access to the verandah. The menu features such regional items as crab cakes and fresh fish, accompanied by vegetables and herbs from the inn's gardens.

The inn is in downtown Beaufort near historic sites and the Intercoastal Waterway. Bicycles are provided to guests who want to tour the town. Swimming, golf, fishing, and tennis are nearby.

RHETT HOUSE INN 1009 Craven St., Beaufort, SC 29902 (phone: 803-524-9030; fax: 803-524-1310). This elegant antebellum mansion has 10 guestrooms with private baths, queen- or king-size beds, telephones, TV sets, and air conditioning; four with fireplaces, two with whirlpool tubs. Open year-round; restaurant open Wednesdays through Sundays. Rate for a double room (including full breakfast, afternoon tea, and evening fruit and cheese): $125 to $225. Two-night minimumon some weekends and holidays. Major credit cards accepted. Not appropriate for children under five. No pets. Smoking permitted on verandah only. Steve and Marianne Harrison, innkeepers.

DIRECTIONS: Traveling south on I-95, take Exit 33, then follow the signs to Beaufort. In Beaufort follow Bay Street along the waterfront, turning right onto New Castle Street. The inn is on the corner of New Castle and Craven Streets.

BELVEDERE B & B

CHARLESTON, SOUTH CAROLINA

This is not the first house in Charleston that David Spell has turned into a bed and breakfast establishment. His first project was *Two Meeting Street,* overlooking the Battery, which is now owned by his brother and family.

Belvedere is in a residential area adjacent to Colonial Lake and enjoys fine views from the grand curving double piazzas across the front of the house. Although this unique Colonial Revival house was built in 1900, some of its most unusual features predate the house by 100 years. When the circa-1800 Belvedere Plantation on the nearby Cooper River was being torn down, the carved door and window surrounds, fireplace mantels, wainscoting, and transoms were salvaged and installed here. The quality of this fine Adam-style woodwork is remarkable.

David has matched the grandeur of the woods with equally fine antiques. In the den, in addition to a TV and VCR, are bookshelves filled with blue and white Canton china. In the living room, which has a marvelous fireplace and a tiered crystal chandelier, there are elegant chairs, and Scalamandre drapes on the windows. Oriental rugs cover oak parquet floors with mahogany borders. The commodious second-floor stairway landing is furnished with sofas and chairs, creating another living room. In the afternoon, sherry, light hors d'oeuvres, and sweets are set out on a handsome buffet. From this room, a door leads to the second-floor piazza.

The guestrooms are equally grand. Each is named for its predominant color or colors: *Blue, Pink Raspberry,* and *Blue and Yellow.* There are canopy or four-poster beds in all rooms. Baths are thoroughly modern; two have deep soaking tubs and all have decorative fireplaces.

Continental breakfast—juice, fresh seasonal fruit, and pastries—is offered every morning.

There's a lovely courtyard in back graced with flowers. A wrought-iron trellis features climbing Confederate jessamine and trumpet vine, while the fence is ablaze with climbing roses.

Either David or Rick Zender, the full-time manager, will help with restaurant reservations or touring advice. Charleston is a great walking city and those who like to jog will find lots of company around the lake across the street. In addition, there are numerous historic houses open for tours. The *Spoleto Festival, USA* is held in the spring.

BELVEDERE B & B 40 Rutledge Ave., Charleston, SC 29401 (phone: 803-722-0973). This grand in-town mansion has three rooms with private baths, queen-size beds, TV sets, and air conditioning. Open February through November. Rate for a double room (including continental breakfast): $125. Two-night minimum on weekends; three nights on holiday weekends. No credit cards accepted. Not appropriate for children under 9. No pets. Black toy poodle, Beauregard, on premises. No smoking except on piazzas. David Spell, innkeeper; Rick Zender, manager.

DIRECTIONS: From I-26, exit onto Meeting Street and continue to Wentworth Street. Turn right onto Wentworth and travel 8 to 10 blocks to Rutledge Avenue. Turn left onto Rutledge and go about 2 blocks. The inn is on the left.

JOHN RUTLEDGE HOUSE INN

CHARLESTON, SOUTH CAROLINA

John Rutledge played a key role in the shaping of the United States: He was one of the signers of the Constitution, and he later became Chief Justice of the Supreme Court. He built this handsome brick townhouse for his bride in 1763; a rough draft of the Constitution was written here in his parlor. In 1989, hotelier Richard Widman restored the house and turned it into a bed and breakfast establishment. It is now on the National Register of Historic Places.

The three-story house has a split stairway with elaborate wrought-iron lace railings across the second-floor piazza. Added in 1853, the railings have patterns of palmetto palms and eagles symbolizing Rutledge's contributions to his state and nation. The interior has 14-foot-high ceilings and is noted for its intricate wood floors, added in the 1850s.

You will want to arrive in time for afternoon tea in the spectacular second-floor ballroom. In the evening, wine, sherry, and port are set out here in decanters on a silver tray. This gracious room is one of the most romantic in Charleston—tall windows, marble mantels, and crystal chandeliers.

The guestrooms are equally elaborate. To the left of the entrance, the *William Moultrie Suite* is a grand space with two carved marble fireplaces, a canopied rice bed, and an elegant bath. On the second floor, the Rutledges' library is now part of the *John Rutledge Suite*. The remaining rooms in the main house also have canopy or four-poster beds, fireplaces, and antique furnishings. They are unusually large (three suites are 850 square feet) and have tile baths. Additional rooms are located just across the courtyard garden in twin carriage houses. The rooms here have arched windows, repro-duction canopy beds, and large, modern baths.

A continental breakfast of coffee or tea, juice, and a pastry is delivered to the rooms. Hot entrées such as eggs Benedict, eggs seafood, and shrimp and grits are available for an additional charge.

The inn is within a block of fine restaurants (be sure to try Charleston's she-crab soup, supposedly introduced at a dinner party at the *John Rutledge House*). There are exceptional antiques and crafts shops, and boutiques about three blocks from the inn on famous King Street.

JOHN RUTLEDGE HOUSE INN 116 Broad St., Charleston, SC 29401 (phone: 803-723-7999; 800-476-9741; 803-720-2615). This historic townhouse in the heart of Charleston has 19 rooms and suites with private baths, double, queen-, or king-size beds, telephones, TV sets, and air conditioning; eight with fireplaces, three with whirlpool tubs. Wheelchair accessible. Open year-round. Rate for a double room (including continental breakfast and afternoon tea): $140 to $200. Major credit cards accepted. Children welcome. No pets. Smoking permitted; some designated non-smoking rooms. Richard T. Widman, proprietor; Linda Bishop, innkeeper.

DIRECTIONS: From I-26 take the King Street exit. Turn right onto King Street and then turn right after about 20 blocks onto Broad Street. The inn is the fourth building on the right. Off-street parking is provided.

TWO MEETING STREET INN

CHARLESTON, SOUTH CAROLINA

A lavish Queen Anne Victorian mansion with fish-scale shingles on the tur-rets, bay windows, and a broad, curved porch supported by double-columned arches, *Two Meeting Street Inn* was built in 1892 as a father's wedding pre-sent to his daughter. The exceptionally beautiful stained-glass windows by Louis Comfort Tiffany, depicting iris and dogwood and magnolia trees, in the parlor were another present from the bride's father. There are nine stained-glass windows in the house, including a sunburst design in the din-ing room that measures six feet across at the bottom. The entrance hall has carved English oak paneling, 12-foot ceilings, a Czechoslovakian cut-crys-tal chandelier, and seating around a fireplace.

The house was purchased from the original family in 1946 by the Spell family, who have run it as an inn ever since. The inn is furnished with fam-ily antiques and photographs, original artwork, and fine silver.

In the guestrooms are Charleston rice canopy beds as well as armoires, marble-top chests, and Oriental rugs. All rooms are spectacular but the *Blue Room* is particularly notable. It was the original master suite and has a balcony overlooking the gardens, a window seat in the rounded turret window, a wood-burning fireplace, a carved tester bed, and an ornate

mahogany secretary. Oriental rugs cover the polished oak floors, and fabric in various shades of blue lavishly drapes the bed and windows. The bath in the *Pink Room,* originally the mother-in-law room, retains its original ornate marble sink with its attached mirror and the ball-and-claw tub. The third-floor rooms were recently renovated in a pretty blue and white color scheme and given bright new baths.

Continental breakfast is served in the dining room, in the courtyard, or perhaps on the verandah—and always on family china and silver. Guests can expect giant homemade muffins (orange-cranberry and fresh strawberry are among the varieties), juice, and luscious, locally grown fresh fruit. Afternoon tea also is served, perhaps accompanied by a spot of sherry.

From rockers on the porch, guests look across to *White Point Gardens* and the harbor on Charleston's historic Battery. Located in the historic district, the inn is close to all the city's main attractions, including the *Dock Street Theatre* and the *Spoleto Festival, USA.* Nearby are the *Middleton Place* and *Magnolia Gardens* plantations, beaches, tennis, and golf.

TWO MEETING STREET INN 2 Meeting St., Charleston, SC 29401 (phone: 803-723-7322). This inn has nine guestrooms with private baths, double or queen-size beds, TV sets, and air conditioning; three with porches, two with fireplaces. Closed December 24 through 26. Rate for a double room (including continental breakfast and afternoon tea): $130 to $235. Two-night minimum on weekends; three nights on holidays. No credit cards accepted. Not appropriate for children under 13. No pets. Smoking permitted outside only. Spell family, owners; Karen Spell Shaw, innkeeper.

DIRECTIONS: From I-26 south, take the Meeting Street exit south. The inn is on the corner of Meeting Street and South Battery at *White Point Gardens.*

Midwest

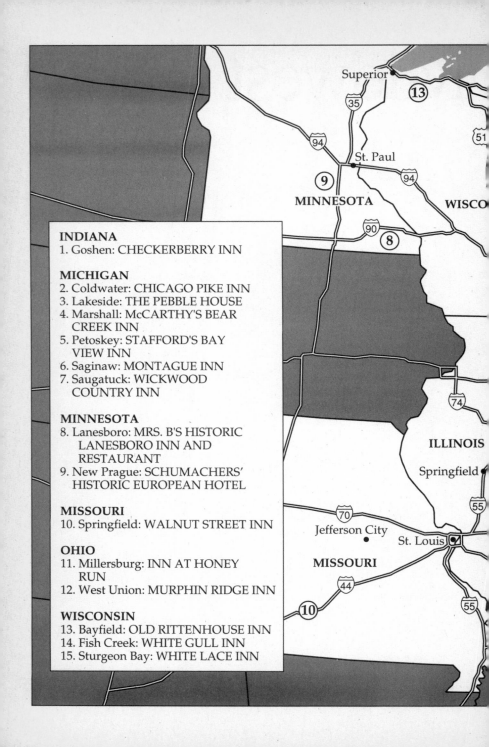

INDIANA
1. Goshen: CHECKERBERRY INN

MICHIGAN
2. Coldwater: CHICAGO PIKE INN
3. Lakeside: THE PEBBLE HOUSE
4. Marshall: McCARTHY'S BEAR
   CREEK INN
5. Petoskey: STAFFORD'S BAY
   VIEW INN
6. Saginaw: MONTAGUE INN
7. Saugatuck: WICKWOOD
   COUNTRY INN

MINNESOTA
8. Lanesboro: MRS. B'S HISTORIC
   LANESBORO INN AND
   RESTAURANT
9. New Prague: SCHUMACHERS'
   HISTORIC EUROPEAN HOTEL

MISSOURI
10. Springfield: WALNUT STREET INN

OHIO
11. Millersburg: INN AT HONEY
    RUN
12. West Union: MURPHIN RIDGE INN

WISCONSIN
13. Bayfield: OLD RITTENHOUSE INN
14. Fish Creek: WHITE GULL INN
15. Sturgeon Bay: WHITE LACE INN

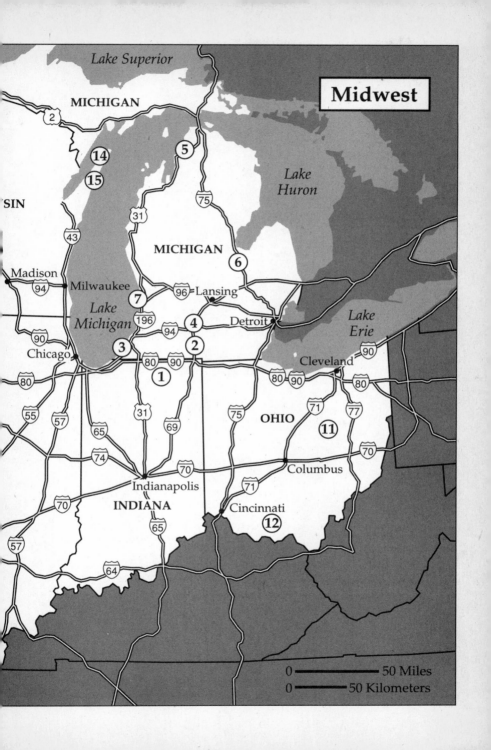

Midwest

Indiana

CHECKERBERRY INN

GOSHEN, INDIANA

Located on a 100-acre farm in Indiana's Amish country, the *Checkerberry Inn* offers sheer tranquillity. Along the 6-mile road from Goshen to the inn, the only other travelers you're likely to pass will be driving simple Amish buggies.

John and Susan Graff decided to open an inn after renovating the 1880s farmhouse here, but rather than expanding the house (which had become their residence) they built a three-story, butter-colored Georgian house across the road. Black shutters frame the windows, and an expansive verandah with white wicker furniture extends the length of the building. Tennis courts, a pool, and a croquet lawn are incorporated into the gardens, which are vibrant with colorful blooms. At the inn's entrance, purple chrysanthemums and pink and red geraniums spill from earthenware pots.

Inside, the inn has a European ambience, enhanced by John's photographs of the Bordeaux region of France. An interior decorator, Susan has used traditional and contemporary furnishings, from country French to Amish, rustic to Chippendale. There's a pine-paneled library with a fireplace that invites curling up with a good book and French doors that lead to the gardens. All the spacious guestrooms, named for flowers found in the yard, have views across the farmland. One has a sitting room with fireplace and a bath with Jacuzzi; another contains a secretary from the 1850s. Still another room has black Amish hats hanging over the bed. All the baths are well appointed.

The buffet-style continental breakfast might include Susan's special blend of granola or fresh-baked muffins. Lunch (served Wednesdays, June through August only) and dinner are offered as well, and the dining room is popular with non-guests as well as those staying at the inn. A favorite luncheon dish is tomato pie: beefsteak tomatoes layered with cheese and baked in a pastry crust. For dinner Amish chicken breast is stuffed with brie and caramelized onions and served with an apple cider cream sauce.

The inn is near *Notre Dame University, Amish Acres* (a re-created village), antiques and crafts shops, theaters, and museums.

CHECKERBERRY INN 62644 County Rte. 37, Goshen, IN 46526 (phone and fax: 219-642-4445). This country inn has 14 guestrooms with private baths, twin, queen-, or king-size beds, telephones, TV sets, and air conditioning; one with a fireplace; two with whirlpool tubs. Wheelchair accessible. Closed January; dining room open for dinner Fridays and Saturdays in February and March; Tuesdays through Saturdays from April through December; lunch served only on Wednesdays from June through August. Rate for a double room (including continental breakfast): $100 to $375. Major credit cards accepted. Not appropriate for children under 13. No pets. No smoking. John and Susan Graff, innkeepers; Sheila Reed and Linda Vicary, managers.

DIRECTIONS: The inn is 10 miles from I-80/90 (Indiana Toll Road). Take Exit 107 (Middlebury) south onto State Route 13. Drive through Middlebury west to Route 4. Turn right (west) onto Route 4 and travel a half mile to County Route 37. Turn south onto County Route 37 and travel 1 mile. The inn is on the right.

Michigan

CHICAGO PIKE INN

COLDWATER, MICHIGAN

Four American flags fly from massive columns at the entrance to the *Chicago Pike Inn*. Located on the old Chicago Turnpike (now US 12), the well-traveled route between Chicago and Detroit, the 1903 mansion served for many years as the home of the Clarke family. Intricate gingerbread trim and a wide verandah across the front of the inn contrast with the clean lines of the pale yellow clapboard exterior.

The Schultz family, who have owned the house since 1987, have lavished attention on its renovation and decor. Below a beamed ceiling, the reception room contains a spectacular, sweeping, polished cherry stairway and fireplace, said to have been fashioned from trees cut from the Clarkes' orchard. The room has been decorated in a canine theme, with a collection of Staffordshire dogs on a double mantel poised below a choice collection of pottery. Fine fabrics by Schumacher and Waverly cover the walls. From above the landing, a stained-glass Palladian window casts brilliant colors across the parquet floors.

In the library, a collection of raspberry glassware and the white woodwork of the bookshelves contrasts with the dark paneling found throughout the rest of the house. A Victorian love seat near the fireplace provides a rainy-day retreat, and Jane Schultz's three-tiered Victorian candy table is always filled with delectable goodies. Tea and scones are served here, in the afternoon.

The lace-curtained guestrooms are named for Clarke family members. *Miss Sophie's Suite* includes a private balcony filled with wicker furniture and a sitting room highlighted with period antiques. *Ned's Room* has the feel of a gentlemen's club, with a brass bed and an antique oak chifforobe. Two quarters in the *Carriage House*—the rose-and-ivy *Garden Room* and the black-trimmed *Stableman's Room*—offer Jacuzzis, refrigerators, and private balconies, plus room service for breakfast, if desired.

The dining room boasts cherry-paneled walls and a built-in cherry buffet. Breakfast is served here at a large polished walnut table, which has elaborately carved chairs with needlepoint cushions. It may include an apricot Victorian (a frozen mix of apricot purée and preserves), as well as deviled eggs and ham served on toasted English muffins. A set dinner menu for house guests only (served Fridays from January through March and Thursdays from June through August) might include mandarin salad, marinated chicken with wild rice, and a dessert of raspberry trifle. Guests may bring their own wine.

A Victorian gazebo in the yard beckons on summer afternoons and guests who call ahead can book a ride in the inn's own horse-drawn carriage. Bicycles are available for guests who want to pedal around the village. Other activities in the area include *Tibbitts Opera House,* fishing, boating, and browsing through the nearby antiques center in Allen and the Amish areas of northern Indiana.

CHICAGO PIKE INN 215 E. Chicago St., Coldwater, MI 49036 (phone: 517-279-8744; 800-471-0501; fax: 517-278-8597). This Victorian inn has eight guestrooms with private baths, twin or queen-size beds, and TV sets. Limited wheelchair accessibility. Open year-round; dinner served Fridays January through March, Thursdays June through August. Rate for a double room (including full breakfast): $80 to $165. Major credit cards accepted. Not appropriate for children under 12. No pets. One dog, Sophia, on premises. Smoking permitted in the library and reception room only. Harold and Jane Schultz, owners; Rebecca Schultz, innkeeper/manager.

DIRECTIONS: Coldwater is midway between Chicago and Detroit on the old Chicago Turnpike (Route 12). From I-94 take the exit for I-69 south. Follow I-69 to Exit 13 (Coldwater), turning right onto US Highway 12, which is Chicago Street. Go to the second traffic light. The inn is on the next corner on the right, across from a hospital.

THE PEBBLE HOUSE

LAKESIDE, MICHIGAN

In the early 1900s, the Arts and Crafts movement influenced architecture, furnishings, fabrics, pottery, jewelry, book design, and the fine arts. It rejected Victorian excess and the cookie-cutter designs made possible by the Industrial Revolution. It is considered the first truly American style. *The Pebble House* incorporates the best of this movement, as well it might:

Owners Jean and Ed Lawrence, authorities in the field, are researching a book on the subject and operate an antiques shop that specializes in Arts and Crafts pieces; they seek out the finest examples for their personal collection and for their inn. Jean, herself an artist, has taught a course on the Arts and Crafts movement at *Indiana University* and regularly conducts seminars. With Ed, she founded the *Midwest Arts and Crafts Society,* and they sponsor special weekends at the inn, to discuss the philosophy of the period.

Set on a one-acre plot directly across from Lake Michigan, the inn's main building is a 1912 Arts and Crafts–style house that had been abandoned before the Lawrences purchased it in 1983. The outside walls, as well as the fence posts at the entrance to the driveway, are constructed of blocks embedded with thousands of beach pebbles, giving the inn its name. Wooden walkways connect the *Main House* to the outbuildings: the *Coach House,* with two suites and a guestroom, and the *Blueberry House,* a separate cottage.

Jean designed everything in the inn—from dried arrangements of herbs and wildflowers from her gardens to the rooms themselves. Each has either a deck or a balcony. One is decorated with Victorian pieces, but the rest are furnished in American or European Arts and Crafts style, as are the common rooms. For example, the living room features a Stickley buffet and a Charles Limbert settle, gateleg table, and buffet. From the Lawrences' wide selection of books on the subject, guests enjoy learning more about the Arts and Crafts movement while they are surrounded by examples of it.

A bountiful Scandinavian-style breakfast buffet, served in the dining room, includes juice, fruit, breads, cereal, and a hot entrée—perhaps Finnish pancakes with a fresh fruit sauce or baked apple pancakes. There's often a big bowl of oatmeal, studded with apples, raisins, nuts, brown sugar, and cinnamon.

The inn, which has a tennis court, is 90 minutes north of Chicago on Lake Michigan, with the beach just across the street and two marinas nearby. Also in the area are *Warren Dunes State Park,* art galleries, and antiques shops.

THE PEBBLE HOUSE 15093 Lakeshore Rd., Lakeside, MI 49115 (phone: 616-469-1416; fax: 616-469-8170). This Craftsman-style inn has seven guestrooms and suites with private baths (one is across the hall), queen- or king-size beds, decks, and air conditioning; three with fireplaces, one with a TV set; telephones available. Wheelchair accessible. Open year-round. Rate for a double room (including full breakfast): $90 to $150. Two-night minimum stay on weekends; three nights on holiday weekends. MasterCard and Visa accepted. Not appropriate for children under 10. No pets. One cat, Timothy, in residence. Smoking permitted on decks and balconies only. Jean and Ed Lawrence, innkeepers.

DIRECTIONS: From Chicago take I-94 north to Exit 6 (Union Pier) and turn left at the end of the ramp. Go about 200 feet to the stop sign and turn left onto Lakeside Road. Continue for 1½ miles, crossing over the Red Arrow Highway and passing through the town of Lakeside, to the stop sign at Lakeshore Road. Turn left and travel about half a mile. The inn is on the left. From Detroit, take I-94 to Exit 12 (Sawyer Exit) and turn left at the end of the ramp. Turn left onto Red Arrow Highway and travel 5 miles to Lakeside Road. Turn right onto Lakeside Road and follow the directions above.

MCCARTHY'S BEAR CREEK INN

MARSHALL, MICHIGAN

On a knoll 2 miles west of the National Historic District town of Marshall, *McCarthy's Bear Creek Inn* is surrounded by fieldstone fences enclosing 14 acres of green lawns, rolling meadows, century-old oak trees, and fields whose mowed paths are ideal for summer hiking and winter cross-country skiing. There's also a footbridge crossing a gurgling creek that wends below the cream-colored brick, Cape Cod–style *Main House,* built in 1948 by Robert Maes, a wealthy inventor, who patented the first automatic milking machine. In back is a 1930s slate-roofed, stone-and-wood dairy barn, called the *Creek House.*

The property was purchased in 1986 by Beth and Michael McCarthy, who converted it to an inn. Michael is a woodcraftsman, and examples of his work are found throughout the inn. He built the *Creek House*'s Shaker-style pencil-post beds, blanket chests, and moldings, as well as the cupola on top. The seven rooms here have French doors leading to private balconies and five have views of the creek, which often attracts deer at dawn. Favorites are the *Reed Room,* with its hand-crafted log bed, and the *Stone Room,* which has washed pine and wicker furnishings; both feature rock foundation walls. Rooms in the *Main House* are decorated with iron, brass, four-poster, and Jenny Lind beds (twins with spindles on the head- and footboards). The favorite here is the *Library Room,* which has a fireplace, a brass bed, and a bow window overlooking Bear Creek.

The inn offers several comfortable common rooms. In the *Main House,* reading chairs are set by the living room fireplace. In the *Creek House,* there's a meeting room with views of the creek and fields. Deer, black squirrels, raccoons, and even a fox or a blue heron might be spotted.

A breakfast buffet is set up in the dining room, a sunny enclosed porch with a slate floor highlighted by a millstone. On the menu are fresh fruit, cereal (from the nearby Kellogg plant), breads (including chocolate bread and Michael's fresh-baked blueberry or raspberry muffins), and a baked egg-and-cheese dish.

Marshall's downtown is a National Landmark Historic District with more than 1,200 homes built before 1900 and five museums describing its history. Quaint antiques, crafts, and specialty shops abound. In *Schuler's Restaurant,* a town landmark established in 1909, the walls are hung with photographs of Marshall's historic buildings; the menu specializes in prime rib.

MCCARTHY'S BEAR CREEK INN 15230 C Dr. N., Marshall, MI 49068 (phone: 616-781-8383). This country inn has 14 guestrooms with private baths, twin, double, or queen-size beds, and air conditioning; nine with balconies or decks, TV sets on request. Limited wheelchair accessibility. Closed December 23 through *Christmas Day.* Rate for a double room (including full breakfast): $65 to $98. Major credit cards accepted. Children welcome. No pets. A chocolate Labrador, Jake, in residence. Smoking permitted in guestrooms. Beth and Michael McCarthy, innkeepers.

DIRECTIONS: From I-69 take Exit 36 to Marshall and turn west onto Michigan Avenue. The inn is a quarter mile down on the left, at the junction of Michigan Avenue and C Drive North.

STAFFORD'S BAY VIEW INN

PETOSKEY, MICHIGAN

Petoskey is located on Little Traverse Bay, south of the Straits of Mackinac. The section of town known as Bay View was founded as a Chautauqua summer campground in 1876 (Helen Keller and William Jennings Bryan were once guests). Some 500 Victorian cottages and campus buildings remain, and Bay View is now on the National Register of Historic Places.

Stafford and Janice Smith met as college students while working at the old *Bay View Inn.* Just before their wedding day, the winter hotel where Stafford worked was sold, and he lost his job. Aware that the *Bay View Inn* was for sale, he boldly inquired about buying it. The owner agreed to set him up in business, and the 22-year-old newlyweds found themselves the proud owners of a 63-room summer hotel with only seven baths. Now, more than three decades and three children later, through careful renovation they have pared down the inn to 31 rooms, all with private baths and many with such luxurious appointments as gas fireplaces and whirlpool tubs. Today a new generation of Smiths carries on the family innkeeping tradition—son Reg and his wife Lori are now the innkeepers here and daughter Mary Kathryn is at *Stafford's Perry Hotel* in downtown Petoskey.

Constructed in 1886, *Stafford's Bay View Inn* is a High Victorian building with a mansard roof, turret, and grand front porch. The interior is embellished with gingerbread woodwork and fireplaces. In the forest green sunroom, guests can relax on antique wicker furniture, while sipping early-morning coffee. A library on the second floor offers board games and a cozy spot for reading.

The guestrooms contain a variety of antiques, with a full range of beds: two- and four-posters, canopy, brass, and sleigh. Amish quilts gathered on family outings to Ohio and Pennsylvania accent the modest cottage-style furnishings in the *Primrose Rooms*. The *Trillium Rooms* are larger and have views of the manicured lakeside gardens, while the popular *Forget-Me-Not Spa* rooms have fireplaces and whirlpool tubs; four have decks and some have views.

Stafford's is a full-service inn, offering breakfast, lunch, and dinner daily in the summer and weekend dining in the winter. A full breakfast is complimentary for inn patrons; the popular buffet-style Sunday brunch attracts between 600 and 700 people each week. *Stafford's* roast turkey, smoked ham, and famous malted waffles are favorites. The dinner menu features such local specialties as Great Lakes whitefish and local brook trout. Bay View, located on "Methodist land," is a dry community by tradition; the inn observes the local custom and does not sell alcohol, although it provides a bottle of wine for guests to enjoy in their rooms or with dinner in the dining room.

Take a walk along the many trails that wind through the property, or borrow a bicycle for a ride along the shore. Play a game of croquet, badminton, or *bocci* on the grounds, or walk across the street to watch the spectacular sunset across Little Traverse Bay. In winter, there's skiing, ice fishing, and rides on sleighs pulled by the inn's matched Percheron horses. In July and August, Chautauqua programs continue to attract visitors to Bay View, with lectures, Sunday worship services, adult education, and a variety of recreational activities. The *Bay View Conservatory* frequently holds concerts and noted artists come to perform and teach. The gaslight shopping district of Petoskey is nearby. For sports enthusiasts, there are opportunities for golf, boating, tennis, fishing, hiking, and swimming in the area.

STAFFORD'S BAY VIEW INN 613 Woodland Ave., PO Box 3, Petoskey, MI 49770 (phone: 616-347-2771; 800-258-1886; fax: 616-347-3413). This lakefront hotel has 31 guestrooms with private baths, twin, double, queen-, or king-size beds, and air conditioning. Limited wheelchair accessibility. Closed mid-March to *Mother's Day;* restaurant open May through October. Rate for a double room in summer (including full breakfast): $128 to $228; in winter (including continental breakfast midweek): $79 to $185. Major credit cards accepted. Children welcome. No pets. No smoking. Stafford and Janice Smith, proprietors; Reginald and Lori Smith, innkeepers.

DIRECTIONS: From Detroit take I-75 north to the Gaylord exit, then follow Michigan Route 32 to Route 131 north to Petoskey. In Petoskey take Route 31 north to Bay View, where the road becomes Woodland Avenue. The inn is on the right.

MONTAGUE INN

SAGINAW, MICHIGAN

After settling comfortably, aperitif in hand, onto a love seat in the sunny library at the *Montague Inn,* glance around the book-lined walls to see if

you can locate the hidden panel. When the Georgian-style mansion was built by Robert Montague in 1929, Prohibition was the law of the land and many citizens went to elaborate lengths to conceal their contraband alcohol. One of the bookcases here is cleverly hinged to conceal a closet where liquor was stored; today it holds jars of house-made Dijon cherry mustard and red raspberry preserves.

Robert Montague, a Saginaw community leader, was a pioneer in the local sugar beet industry who also developed a soaps and cosmetics business that he eventually sold to the Jergens Company. After Mrs. Montague died, the mansion was empty for several years before being used as the Saginaw City Hall. When the city moved out in the mid-1970s, the property was abandoned once again. In 1986, four local couples purchased it, restored it to its former beauty, and opened it as an inn.

Today, the *Montague Inn* is surrounded by eight acres of velvety lawns and gardens that sweep down to Lake Linton, a lagoon that separates it from *Ojibway Island,* a city park. Its leaded-glass and paneled front doors and its side porte cochère lead to an elegant foyer with a majestic curved staircase. Furnished with Oriental rugs, oil paintings, and fine Georgian-style antiques, the richly appointed common rooms have numerous fireplaces and bay windows with inviting nooks tucked into stair landings.

The guestrooms also contain antique furnishings, and several have four-poster or canopy beds. The *Montague Suite* and the *Mary Sage Room* are especially popular. The original Arts and Crafts–era tiles from Detroit's famed Pewabic Pottery have been preserved in the bathrooms.

The dining room is an inviting place with a massive brass chandelier and a bay window overlooking the lawns to the lake beyond. The inn has a well-deserved reputation for fine fare. A buffet breakfast is served daily; lunch and dinner (open to non-guests) are prepared Tuesdays through Saturdays. Dinner entrées might include rack of lamb with pesto cream or baked

Norwegian salmon stuffed with shrimp and brie and served with an orange beurre blanc.

The inn is in a parklike setting in the Grove area of Saginaw, with fishing and ice skating nearby. The *Children's Zoo* is just south.

MONTAGUE INN 1581 S. Washington St., Saginaw, MI 48601 (phone: 517-752-3939; fax: 517-752-3159). **This Georgian mansion has 18 guestrooms (16 with private baths) with double, queen-, or king-size beds, telephones, TV sets, and air conditioning; three with fireplaces. Wheelchair accessible. Open year-round. Rate for a double room (including continental breakfast): $72 to $165. Major credit cards accepted. Children welcome. No pets. Smoking permitted in the library only. The Kinney, Acker, Tincknell, Kiefer, and Ideker families, owners; Janet Hoffmann, innkeeper.**

DIRECTIONS: From I-75 take the Route 46 exit (Holland Avenue), bearing right onto Remington Avenue. Turn left onto Washington Avenue and continue to the inn, which is ¹/₁₀ mile on the right.

WICKWOOD COUNTRY INN

SAUGATUCK, MICHIGAN

Can you take a cookbook author out of the kitchen? Not unless it's to run a country inn, and even then, Julee Rosso Miller, innkeeper of the *Wickwood Country Inn,* has managed to write more cookbooks.

Julee's saga began in 1977, when she and Sheila Lukins opened a tiny food shop called the *Silver Palate* on Manhattan's Upper West Side. Soon, they were bottling and packaging their sauces, vinegars, and chutneys (eventually 150 items) and distributing them to some 5,000 outlets across the United States. The culinary duo followed up with a cookbook in 1982, another in 1985, and a third in 1989. Eventually, however, they sold the business, and Julee returned home to Michigan. There she became reacquainted with, and later married, Bill Miller.

In 1991, the couple purchased the *Wickwood Country Inn,* the first bed and breakfast establishment in Saugatuck—a village on the shores of Lake Michigan that now calls itself the "bed and breakfast capital of the Midwest." Julee, who began her New York career by working for several textile designers, brought an inspired array of color, texture, and design to redecorating the inn. Floral chintzes, bold checks, and tartan plaids combine to create an eclectic but sophisticated decor. There are paneled walls and cozy fireplaces, accented by an abundance of original paintings and sculptures, some of which are for sale. Feather beds are dressed with stunning canopies, or have brass-and-iron headboards. The *Master Suite,* for example, has a cherry canopy bed with drapes and a duvet of navy-and-white Fragonard French toile, plus a bedskirt and pillow shams in red, white, and blue plaid taffeta. It's piled high with antique lace pillows.

And true to form, Julee's seldom out of the kitchen. While working on her fourth cookbook, *Great Good Food,* which came out in 1993, and her fifth, *Fresh Start,* which was published in 1996, she frequently would zip through the common rooms, dispensing samples of cookies or candies to guests. Breakfast, served during the week in an elegant buffet-style in the garden room, includes fresh juices, fruit salad, homemade granola, and fresh-baked berry muffins or cinnamon-pecan coffee cake; brunch is served on weekends, including perhaps a ham-and-pesto strata, a baked egg dish, or blueberry French toast. Every evening, an array of hors d'oeuvres is set out in the library, which looks like an English gentlemen's club. Guests may bring their favorite wine along (the inn doesn't serve liquor).

The inn is in the heart of town, with golf, tennis, boating, sailing and windsurfing on Lake Michigan, and crafts and art galleries nearby.

WICKWOOD COUNTRY INN 510 Butler St., PO Box 1019, Saugatuck, MI 49453 (phone: 616-857-1465; fax: 616-857-4168). This bed and breakfast establishment has 11 guestrooms with private baths, queen- or king-size beds, and air conditioning. Open year-round except *Christmas Day.* Rate for a double room (including continental breakfast weekdays, brunch weekends, plus evening hors d'oeuvres): $150 to $190. Two-night minimum stay on weekends. MasterCard and Visa accepted. Not appropriate for children under 13. No pets. No smoking. Bill and Julee Rosso Miller, innkeepers.

DIRECTIONS: From I-196 take Exit 41 and go west on A2 (also called Blue Star Highway). Follow "Saugatuck Business Route" signs to Butler Street. Turn left onto Butler; the inn is one block down, on the corner of Mary Street.

Minnesota

MRS. B'S HISTORIC LANESBORO INN
AND RESTAURANT

LANESBORO, MINNESOTA

Set amid Minnesota's farm country, Lanesboro village is also surrounded by 400,000 acres of hardwood forests and high bluffs. A fork of the Root River meanders through the center of town, where trees and 19th-century buildings line both sides of wide streets.

Mrs. B's, a native limestone structure, was built as a furniture shop in 1872, and the storefront looks the same now as it did then, except for the awning shading the entrance. In back, the land drops away to the river; two levels of decks with rocking chairs overlook the river, whose banks have been landscaped with split-rock terraces and gardens.

Inside, the ceilings are high; the decor, country Victorian. In the lobby, where afternoon coffee and tea are served, overstuffed chairs and a sofa are grouped near the piano and fireplace. Stenciled borders line the hallway to the 10 guestrooms. The rooms feature canopy beds, pine furniture, and quilts that create a cozy, rather than elegant, feeling. Two of the rooms have fireplaces; all have either balconies or decks; two have views of the river.

Food is one of the highlights of a stay at *Mrs. B's.* A full breakfast—perhaps including oatmeal-buttermilk pancakes with blueberries and hot syrup—is served to guests in the cheerful breakfast room. Dinner (also open to non-guests) is a five-course meal that changes daily and uses fresh vegetables, herbs, and raspberries from the garden in season. Popular specialties include a wildflower salad with honey-rhubarb vinaigrette, a warm vegetable strudel appetizer, and pork loin stuffed with dried-fruit compote and crusted with peppercorns. Desserts tempt even the diet-conscious, and "Mrs. B's Bedtime Bump," a concoction of milk, eggs, brandy, chocolate, and "secret ingredients," sends even the most stress-ridden off to a sound sleep.

The paved 45-mile Root River Trail, an outstanding bicycle, hiking, and cross-country ski route, passes the inn. The Root River is also noted for its trout fishing and canoeing. Other options nearby include guided tours of caves, wineries, Amish country, and a tour of a commercial shiitake mushroom operation.

MRS. B'S HISTORIC LANESBORO INN AND RESTAURANT 101 Parkway N. (mailing address: PO Box 411), Lanesboro, MN 55949 (phone: 507-467-2154; 800-657-4710). This inn has 10 guestrooms with private baths, twin or queen-size beds, balconies or decks, and air conditioning. Wheelchair accessible. Open year-round; dining room open for dinner Wednesdays through Sundays; for lunch Saturdays and Sundays only. Rate for a double room (including full breakfast and afternoon tea, coffee, and sherry): $50 to $95. No credit cards accepted; personal checks welcome. Children welcome with prior permission. No pets. No smoking. Bill Sermeus and Mimi Abell, innkeepers.

DIRECTIONS: From Minneapolis/St. Paul traveling south, take Minnesota Route 52 through Rochester to Fountain. Turn left onto County Road 8 to Lanesboro. Once in town turn north onto Parkway and proceed to the inn.

SCHUMACHERS' HISTORIC EUROPEAN HOTEL

NEW PRAGUE, MINNESOTA

The *Broz Hotel* was a very fashionable edifice when it was built in 1898. Cass Gilbert, who also designed the *Woolworth Building* in New York City the *Supreme Court Building* in Washington, DC, was one of the finest Beaux Arts architects of his day. When he designed the *Broz Hotel,* now called *Schumachers' Historic European Hotel,* he created a relatively straightforward building, quite unlike some of his frothier confections.

After John and Kathleen Schumacher purchased the hotel in 1974, they masterminded its conversion into a European–style inn. There are ornately carved Bavarian cuckoo clocks, 150-year-old Bavarian pine wainscoting imported from Europe, and carved German chairs. Bavarian folk artist Pipka painted the distinctive furniture throughout the inn.

The guestrooms, which have the same Old World ambience, are named for the months of the year (since there are only 11, there is no July). *May* has a canopy bed with a hand-painted design; *August* features an elaborate hand-painted armoire and a gas fireplace. Each room has a double whirlpool tub, and a complimentary bottle of wine awaits guests.

People come from miles around for the food. John is a master chef who received his training at the *Culinary Institute of America*. His distinctive fare—which borrows heavily from Czech, Austrian, and German cuisine—has earned numerous awards. There's Wiener schnitzel, sauerbraten in gingersnap sauce, and such accompaniments as *spätzle, knedlicky* (a Czech potato dumpling), and red cabbage. For dessert, don't miss John's torte, made with meringue, whipped cream, nuts, and chocolate, or the *kolache* bread pudding, made with Czech sweet rolls. In the hunting-style pub, German and Czech beers are on tap, and additional brands are available by the bottle. Breakfast, which is not included in the room rate, features a special omelette of the day.

The inn's extensive gift shop specializes in handcrafted imports, particularly unusual *Christmas* nutcrackers and ornaments. A casino, golf, tennis, and cross-country skiing are nearby, and the *Mall of America* is 42 miles away.

SCHUMACHERS' HISTORIC EUROPEAN HOTEL 212 W. Main St., New Prague, MN 56071 (phone: 612-758-2133; fax: 612-758-2400). This European–style hotel has 11 guestrooms with private baths, double, queen-, or king-size beds, telephones, whirlpool tubs, and air conditioning; seven with TV sets and fireplaces. Restaurant is wheelchair accessible. Closed *Christmas Eve* and *Christmas Day.* Rate for a double room: $107 to $165. Major credit cards accepted. Not appropriate for children under 18. No pets. Smoking permitted in bar only. John and Kathleen Schumacher, innkeepers.

DIRECTIONS: From Minneapolis/St. Paul take I-35 south to Exit 76 (Elko/New Market), then turn right (west) onto County Road 2. Continue for 10 miles to Highway 13. Turn left (south) onto Highway 13 and follow this road for 2 miles to the New Prague exit (Highway 19 west). The hotel is 4 miles farther along, on the south side of Main Street.

Missouri

WALNUT STREET INN

Springfield, Missouri

Built in 1894 by Charles McCann for his 18-year-old bride, the *Walnut Street Inn* features 21 hand-painted Corinthian columns, delicate leaded-glass windows, a grand verandah, and Victorian roof gables. Once a gracious family home, today it is a romantic bed and breakfast establishment.

The inn even embraces the separate carriage house; dirt floors and horse stalls have been replaced by luxurious suites, complete with four-poster beds, European antiques, double Jacuzzi tubs, fireplaces, and fully stocked bars. The *Rosen Room,* for example, has burgundy paisley-print wallpaper and white lace curtains, a forest green chaise with colorful pillows tucked into its corners, and a gilt-framed mirror. The guestrooms also boast skylights, private gardens, balconies, or fireplaces.

The common rooms are as charming as the guestrooms. The living room has pale peach walls accented with touches of teal and gold, a rosewood piano, and leaded-glass windows. In the *Gathering Room* a fireplace warms those who nestle in the wing chairs with a book from the room's shelves. The *Walnut Street Inn* may be located in the heart of the Springfield Historic District, but the amenities are thoroughly up-to-date. There's a computer, a fax machine, a spacious writing desk, and other services required by business travelers.

Breakfast, which is served in the dining room, on the deck, or in the guestrooms, might include Ozark "feathercakes" or raspberry blintzes, a fresh-fruit soup, and black-walnut bread or persimmon muffins.

Guests enjoy tennis, golf, boating, and spelunking nearby. Also in the area is *Wilson's Creek National Park*. The music shows in neighboring Branson are particularly popular.

WALNUT STREET INN 900 E. Walnut St., Springfield, MO 65806 (phone: 417-864-6346; 800-593-6346; fax: 417-864-6184). This Victorian inn has 14 guestrooms with private baths, double or queen-size beds, telephones, TV sets, and air conditioning. Wheelchair accessible. Open year-round. Rate for a double room (including full breakfast and wine and cheese): $80 to $150. Major credit cards accepted. Not appropriate for children under 10. No pets. No smoking. Gary and Paula Blankenship, innkeepers.

DIRECTIONS: From I-44 take Highway 65 south. Turn west onto the Chestnut Expressway and drive for about 2 miles. Turn left onto Sherman Avenue (John Q. Hammons Parkway). Go three blocks to Walnut Street. The inn is on the southeast corner of Hammons and Walnut. Off-street parking is located behind the inn.

Ohio

INN AT HONEY RUN

MILLERSBURG, OHIO

Innkeeper Marge Stock's dream was to create an inn that would comple-ment the forest and fields surrounding it, and she has succeeded. The *Inn at Honey Run*—60 acres of pastures and woods, laced with nature trails—is a treasure. Though relatively new, it blends beautifully into the forest of maple, ash, oak, poplar, black walnut, butternut, and hickory trees.

The goal of the inn is to enhance guests' enjoyment of nature. The decks actually reach into the forest, and there are bird feeders everywhere. A six-acre orchard has been planted with 450 trees—14 varieties of apple, peach, cherry, and plum. Floor-to-ceiling windows bring the outdoors inside.

The main house has 25 contemporary rooms decorated with furniture made nearby in Holmes County, as well as local art. This is Amish coun-try, and many of the colorful quilts that cover the walls and beds were made by local craftspeople. The spectacular freestanding fireplace in the living room is made of native sandstone.

Some of the most popular accommodations are in the *Honeycomb*, a building tucked into the hillside so discreetly that azaleas, junipers, and heather almost hide it. The *Honeycomb*'s lobby soars 30 feet, and skylights add to the sense of spaciousness. Marge believes this is the first earth-shel-tered building with public accommodations in the country. As in the rest of the inn, the furnishings are contemporary: In each guestroom a massive fireplace wall of native sandstone has a niche for a TV. Beyond the sliding doors, the private patio is literally in a wildflower meadow. These rooms face east, so guests are treated to fantastic sunrises.

Two additional cottages are hidden in the woods. Each has a stone fire-place, a living room with a skylight, a Pullman kitchen, and a bedroom up a short flight of stairs. *Trillium Guesthouse* has a private hot tub.

Lunch and dinner (open to non-guests) are prepared using regional bounty such as trout and chicken. The drink of choice is local grape or peach juice. (In deference to the religious beliefs of the Honey Run Valley, the innkeeper does not allow alcoholic beverages in the public areas of the inn.) A bountiful continental breakfast served buffet-style is complimentary to inn guests; a full breakfast also is available. On Sunday nights, when the dining room is closed, guests are invited to a "raid the kitchen supper." The *Inn at Honey Run* is much more than a place to stay and eat. Marge cares deeply about the environment, wildlife, and local crafts; on Sunday nights in the winter, she sponsors a fireside talk or symposium where there might be a speaker discussing Amish recipes, a musical program, a nature slide show, or a photography demonstration.

The inn is in north-central Ohio, home to the world's largest Amish population. Local crafts shops specializing in quilts and cheese are especially popular with visitors. Also nearby are golf, canoeing, and performances of the *Ohio Light Opera* in Wooster.

INN AT HONEY RUN 6920 Country Rd. 203, Millersburg, OH 44654 (phone: 330-674-0011; 800-468-6639; fax: 330-674-2623). This contemporary inn has 41 guestrooms with private baths, twin, queen-, or king-size beds, telephones, TV sets, and air conditioning; 18 with private balconies or patios, 12 with whirlpool tubs, three with fireplaces. Wheelchair accessible. Closed the first two weeks of January as well as *Christmas Eve* and *Christmas Day*. Rate for a double room (including continental breakfast): $79 to $275. Two-night minimum stay on weekends. Major credit cards accepted. Not appropriate for children under 18. No pets. Two dogs, Luke, a Walker coonhound, and Sandy, a beagle, plus a cat, Honey, share the property with sheep and goats. Smoking permitted in designated guestrooms and all public areas except the dining room. Marjorie Stock, innkeeper; Margret Schlichting, manager.

DIRECTIONS: From Millersburg take East Jackson Street (Routes 39 and 62) past the courthouse and gas station on the right. At the next corner turn left onto Route 241. After almost 2 miles turn right immediately around the small hill onto Route 203 (it's not well marked). After about 1½ miles turn right at the inn sign. (Beware of slow-moving Amish buggies on the road in this area.)

MURPHIN RIDGE INN

WEST UNION, OHIO

Surrounded by towering maples, the *Murphin Ridge Inn*—with its unique combination of old and new architecture—presides over 717 acres of woods and farmland. Only an hour east of Cincinnati, this quiet haven offers not only serenity and comfort, but excellent regional cuisine as well.

In 1990, owners Bob and Mary Crosset began serving food in the original 1810 brick farmhouse that serves as the inn's *Dining House.* Four months after the restaurant opened, the new, separate guesthouse was completed, and the Crossets were in business.

The three small dining rooms in the *Dining House* are simply furnished with Shaker-style polished tables and plank chairs. Borrowing from the local Amish culinary heritage and adding some Swiss and Southern-style dishes, Bob and Mary created what they call "folk cuisine." Murphin Ridge meat loaf, a hearty mix of pork, beef, onions, and spices served with orange-tomato mayonnaise, is especially appealing, as is the Cedar Run salmon—grilled salmon with a cracked black pepper–and–orange juice sauce. The full breakfast may include homemade Danish and scones, fresh fruit, and cottage-cheese pancakes with local maple syrup.

The simple guesthouse was built of materials compatible with the custom-designed, Shaker-inspired furniture of David T. Smith, a local craftsman specializing in 19th-century reproductions. Two of its 10 guestrooms have fireplaces, two have porches with views of the woods and fields, and most are furnished with trundle beds.

The inn's common rooms include a *Gathering Room* in the guesthouse and two galleries in the *Dining House,* which display the work of local artists. Among the items exhibited, and for sale, are paintings, sculpture, furniture, baskets, dolls, quilts, and ceramics. The inn also sponsors a popular *Art Fair.*

Extensive gardens, a patio, and porches are welcome spots to relax, while a pool and a tennis court beckon more energetic guests. The inn maintains 8 miles of hiking trails and has shuffleboard, croquet, horseshoes, miniature golf, and a basketball court. Amish farms, shops, quilt auctions, *Nature Conservancy* preserves, and the *Serpent Mound Historic Site* are all nearby.

MURPHIN RIDGE INN 750 Murphin Ridge Rd., West Union, OH 45693 (phone: 513-544-2263). This inn has 10 guestrooms with private baths, twin, double, or queen-size beds, telephones, and air conditioning; two with fireplaces and two with porches. Wheelchair accessible. Closed January through mid-February, and Mondays and Tuesdays throughout the year. Rate for a double room (including full breakfast): $84 to $94. No credit cards accepted. Children welcome. No pets. A dog, Honey, and five cats on the property. No smoking. Robert and Mary Crosset, innkeepers.

DIRECTIONS: From Cincinnati take Ohio Route 32 east to Unity Road (about 60 miles). Turn right onto Unity, go under a grove of maple trees and continue on Unity to the left and up the hill to Wheatridge Road in the village of Unity. Turn left onto Wheatridge Road and travel 3 miles to Murphin Ridge Road. Turn left onto Murphin Ridge Road and continue for less than 1 mile to the inn, which is on the right.

Wisconsin

OLD RITTENHOUSE INN

BAYFIELD, WISCONSIN

The quaint village of Bayfield is tucked away on a little wing of land that extends into Lake Superior, in the northernmost reaches of Wisconsin. Nearby is the *Apostle Islands National Lakeshore,* a group of 22 islands teeming with birds, including Canada geese, loons, and eagles; here, too, deer, bear, raccoon, and beaver make their homes. Whitefish and lake trout are plentiful in this anglers' and boaters' paradise.

Sleepy Bayfield was originally a fishing and logging port, and many Victorian homes built in its heyday still grace its streets. The *Old Rittenhouse Inn* is an impressive Queen Anne Victorian mansion that sits high on a knoll above the town and shoreline. The house has four stories of decorative gingerbread and a wide verandah that wraps around the front and side. Hanging baskets spilling over with flowers and white wicker tables and chairs add to the charm. Owners Jerry and Mary Phillips also have added three additional historic houses to the inn complex, *Le Château Boutin,* the *Fountain Cottage,* and the *Grey Oak Guest House,* all nearby.

Jerry and Mary pride themselves on the fine antiques that fill the inn's common areas and guestrooms. There are walnut, cherry, and mahogany dressers and beds, brass beds, and Victorian tables and lamps. All the rooms have romantic touches, including wood-burning fireplaces. There is a Victorian *Parlor Room* in the *Grey Oak Guest House,* and the entire first floor of *Le Château Boutin* is a sitting area, also furnished with Victorian pieces.

The *Old Rittenhouse Inn* offers fine dining in three intimate, interconnected rooms, each with a fireplace. A six-course dinner (also open to nonguests) starts with a choice of three soups or, in summer, a fruit salad of homegrown raspberries, blueberries, or apples. Local whitefish or trout might be on the menu, accompanied by fiddlehead ferns or mushrooms. In the fall, the Phillipses stage concerts featuring the *Rittenhouse Chamber Singers,* who entertain dinner guests with choral chamber music.

In addition to their innkeeping endeavors, the Phillipses have a thriving gourmet food business. Jams, jellies, marmalades, candies, and fruitcakes are among the items sold at the inn's shop and by mail.

Guests may enjoy magnificent views of Lake Superior from the porch of the *Old Rittenhouse Inn;* or, on the two-acre grounds of *Le Château Boutin,* play croquet or relax to the sounds of a splashing fountain in the formal gardens. Hiking, sailing, and bicycling are available, and many festivals are held in the vicinity.

OLD RITTENHOUSE INN 301 Rittenhouse Ave. (mailing address: PO Box 584), Bayfield, WI 54814 (phone: 715-779-5111; fax: 715-779-5887). **This Victorian inn has 22 guestrooms with private baths and queen- or king-size beds. Wheelchair accessible. Open year-round. Rate for a double room (including continental breakfast): $99 to $229; with full breakfast: $5 additional. Two-night minimum stay on weekends. MasterCard and Visa accepted. Children welcome. No pets. No smoking. Jerry and Mary Phillips, innkeepers.**

DIRECTIONS: This inn is approximately 85 miles east of Duluth. From Duluth take Route 53 south across the bridge to Superior, Wisconsin. Turn east onto Route 2 and travel some 60 miles to Ashland. Turn north onto Highway 13 to Bayfield. Highway 13 becomes Rittenhouse Avenue in Bayfield. The inn is right in the town, which is only 5 blocks long.

WHITE GULL INN

FISH CREEK, WISCONSIN

The Door County Peninsula, which thrusts into Lake Michigan some 80 miles north of Green Bay, offers miles of shoreline and is a popular summer recreational magnet for boaters and anglers. On the west bank of the peninsula is Fish Creek, a village with a turn-of-the-century flavor.

The *White Gull Inn* has been hosting visitors here since 1896, when it was part of a bustling summer resort run by local doctor Herman Welcker. He created the property by having houses moved intact across ice-covered Green Bay—a less expensive procedure than constructing new ones. The complex catered to guests who came by steamboat from Chicago and Milwaukee. Andy and Jan Coulson have been running the *White Gull Inn* since 1972.

The white clapboard, New England–style inn is informal—a place to kick off your shoes and relax. The Coulsons have improved the main lodge over the years, adding to the many antiques that were in the inn when they bought it. In addition, there are five cottages with one to four bedrooms each. These are rented to families or groups. *Cliffhouse,* yet another building, has four suites. Eight of the guestrooms and all the cottages have fireplaces. One of the suites has a whirlpool.

The inn has long been famous for its Door County fish boil—the local version of a New England clambake—which takes place every Wednesday, Friday, Saturday, and Sunday in summer (Wednesdays and Saturdays in winter). The master boiler starts a wood fire outside under a cauldron filled with water, then places chunks of fresh whitefish (probably caught only hours earlier) and new potatoes in the pot. At just the right moment he tosses kerosene on the flame, and the sudden burst of heat causes the water to boil over. This eliminates the fish oil from the water's surface and adds a dramatic finale to the cooking. In the dining room, guests eat the light, flaky fish with melted butter, coleslaw, and sweets bread (similar to pumpkin bread). A piece of homemade Door County cherry pie, and the meal is complete. A more traditional dinner is served the rest of the week.

Breakfast and lunch are served daily (all meals are open to non-guests). Among the interesting breakfast items are cherry-stuffed French toast and eggs Benedict. Locally raised produce and products made in Wisconsin are used liberally in all the inn's dishes. Among other thoughtful touches, hot cider, popcorn, and cookies are set out in the lobby on winter afternoons; coffee and newspapers are delivered to the rooms every morning.

The inn's location near Lake Michigan means guests can enjoy swimming, boating, fishing, and the natural beauty of the Door Peninsula. Also available are music festivals, summer-stock theater, antiques shops, art galleries, golf, and cross-country skiing.

WHITE GULL INN 4225 Main St. (mailing address: PO Box 160), Fish Creek, WI 54212 (phone: 414-868-3517; fax: 414-868-2367). This village inn has 14 guestrooms and cottages with private baths, twin, double, or queen-size beds, telephones, balconies or porches, TV sets, and air conditioning; 13 with fireplaces, one with whirlpool tub. Restaurant is wheelchair accessible. Closed *Thanksgiving* and *Christmas*. Rate for a double room: $90 to $175. Two-night minimum stay on weekends; three nights for cottages in July and August. Major credit cards accepted. Children welcome. No pets. Smoking permitted on porches and patio only. Andy and Jan Coulson, innkeepers.

DIRECTIONS: From Milwaukee take I-43 north. Before reaching Green Bay, take Highway 57 north in Manitowoc to Sturgeon Bay. In Sturgeon Bay take Highway 42 north to Fish Creek. Once in the village turn left at the bottom of the hill. Drive three blocks; the inn is on the left.

WHITE LACE INN

STURGEON BAY, WISCONSIN

When Bonnie and Dennis Statz purchased the turreted *Main House* of the *White Lace Inn* in 1982, it was decidedly down-at-the-heels. After repairing, painting, and decorating it, however, they created one of the most delightful Victorian inns in Wisconsin. And this energetic couple never slowed down. The inn now has rooms in three other houses, all connected by brick pathways bordered by colorful flower beds.

The *Main House* was built in 1903 and is notable for its broad porch and ornate oak interior, a highlight of which is the mantelpiece in the parlor. The exterior is done in tints of rose, ivory, and raspberry. The *Garden House* next door, an 1880s country Victorian with long, inviting porches, is painted different shades of green with pink trim, while the *Washburn House* is butter yellow with blue gingerbread trim. The latest addition is the *Hadley House,* an 1880s Italianate-style house, which opened in 1996. It features a pale blue exterior with raspberry trim.

Guestrooms in all four buildings are furnished with lovely antiques or high-quality reproductions. There are handsome four-poster canopy beds, brass beds, and a spectacular 1880s Victorian Renaissance bed. Fabrics are coordinated with wallpapers in Laura Ashley or Ralph Lauren prints. All of the rooms in the *Garden House* have fireplaces, and several in the *Main House* have double whirlpool tubs; those in the *Washburn House* and *Hadley House* have both. Every guest need has been anticipated. The baths are tiled; the towels are thick; the linen is of high quality; and games, puzzles, and books about local history are available.

The continental breakfast features fresh-baked breads such as cherry-orange-walnut scones, lemon-herb bread, or bran muffins, supplemented

by a Scandinavian fruit soup or creamy rice pudding with apricots. In the afternoon, Bonnie fixes lemonade, iced or hot tea, and cookies.

More than 6,000 daffodils bloom in the garden, in spring, and from early spring to late fall the perennial gardens are full of lilacs, phlox, peonies, and mums. A Victorian gazebo and Adirondack chairs placed about the garden are scenic spots for relaxation.

The inn is near Sturgeon Bay's historic district, the *Door County Historical Museum,* cultural events, boating, fishing, beaches, cross-country skiing, and unique crafts, art, and gift shops.

WHITE LACE INN 16 N. Fifth Ave., Sturgeon Bay, WI 54235 (phone: 414-743-1105). This Victorian inn has 19 guestrooms with private baths, double, queen-, or king-size beds, and air conditioning; 17 with TV sets, 14 with fireplaces, 11 with whirlpool tubs. Wheelchair accessible. Open year-round. Rate for a double room (including continental breakfast and afternoon refreshments): $75 to $190. Two-night minimum stay on weekends; three nights on holiday weekends and weekends during the fall festival (late September to early October). Major credit cards accepted. Not appropriate for children under 12. No pets. Smoking permitted on porches only. Bonnie and Dennis Statz, innkeepers.

DIRECTIONS: From Milwaukee take I-43 north. Before reaching Green Bay, take Highway 57 north in Manitowoc to Sturgeon Bay. In Sturgeon Bay follow Business Route 42/57 across the bridge into town. You will be on Michigan Street. Follow Michigan to Fifth Avenue and turn left. The inn is on the right.

Southwest, Plains, and Rocky Mountains

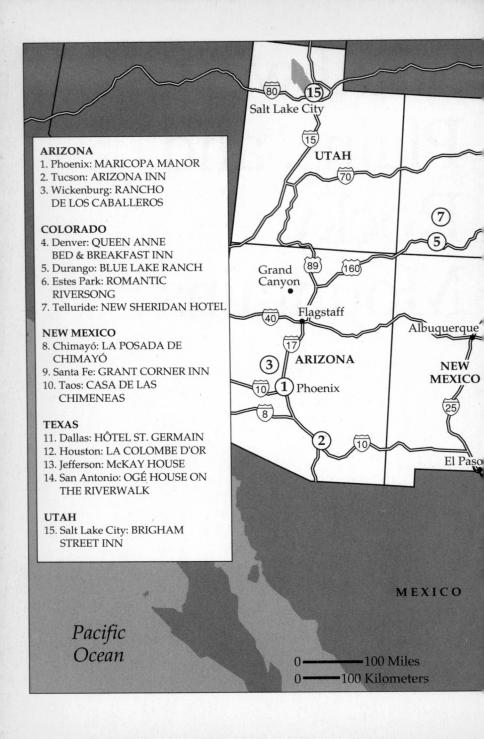

ARIZONA
1. Phoenix: MARICOPA MANOR
2. Tucson: ARIZONA INN
3. Wickenburg: RANCHO
   DE LOS CABALLEROS

COLORADO
4. Denver: QUEEN ANNE
   BED & BREAKFAST INN
5. Durango: BLUE LAKE RANCH
6. Estes Park: ROMANTIC
   RIVERSONG
7. Telluride: NEW SHERIDAN HOTEL

NEW MEXICO
8. Chimayó: LA POSADA DE
   CHIMAYÓ
9. Santa Fe: GRANT CORNER INN
10. Taos: CASA DE LAS
    CHIMENEAS

TEXAS
11. Dallas: HÔTEL ST. GERMAIN
12. Houston: LA COLOMBE D'OR
13. Jefferson: McKAY HOUSE
14. San Antonio: OGÉ HOUSE ON
    THE RIVERWALK

UTAH
15. Salt Lake City: BRIGHAM
    STREET INN

Salt Lake City

UTAH

Grand
Canyon

Flagstaff

Albuquerque

ARIZONA

**NEW
MEXICO**

Phoenix

El Paso

MEXICO

*Pacific
Ocean*

0 ——— 100 Miles
0 ——— 100 Kilometers

Southwest, Plains, and Rocky Mountains

⑥ 〔25〕

④ Denver

COLORADO — 〔70〕

Colorado Springs

〔160〕

⑩

⑧

〔25〕

⑨ Santa Fe

〔40〕

〔40〕

Topeka

〔70〕

〔135〕 〔35〕

KANSAS

OKLAHOMA

〔44〕

〔40〕

Oklahoma City

〔35〕

Dallas 〔30〕

⑪ 〔20〕 **⑬**

〔20〕

TEXAS

〔35〕

〔10〕

〔45〕

Houston

Austin **⑫**

San Antonio **⑭**

〔35〕

Gulf of Mexico

Southwest, Plains, and Rocky Mountains

Arizona

MARICOPA MANOR

PHOENIX, ARIZONA

In 1970, Paul and Mary Ellen Kelley purchased the one-acre compound now known as *Maricopa Manor* (named for the Maricopa Indians who once lived here) because it was large enough to house their three children, eight foster children, and visiting exchange students, as well as Mary Ellen's mother and Aunt Jeannette. Aunt Jeannette is still living there, but as the last of the fledglings left the nest, the Kelleys expanded their hospitality to the general public, opening their home as an inn in 1990.

When the buildings were constructed in 1928, they were beyond the city limits. In the ensuing years the city spread out, so now the inn is close to many attractions. Built in Spanish Revival style, the main house and adjacent *casita* have been renovated and modernized. Red tile roofs and white stucco walls reflect the intense Arizona sun. In the courtyard, water splashes in the fountain. An outside hot tub is surrounded by a latticed gazebo and palm trees. In the gardens behind the house, a pool with fountains and waterfalls is surrounded with Mexican tile and murals.

The inn has five suites, each decorated in a different style. In the main house, the *Library Suite* has a king-size bed with a brilliant blue canopy. Bookshelves are filled with some of the Kelleys' leather-bound collection. The *Victorian Suite* evokes romance with its antique mirrored armoire and accents of satin and lace. The two-bedroom *Palo Verde Suite* has antique furniture, including a carved spool bed with a lace canopy in one room and a king-size canopy bed and Franklin stove in another. The guesthouse has two more suites. *Reflections Past*, whose name comes from its wall of antique mirrors, has a canopy bed, rich tapestries, and a fireplace. *Reflections Future* is in contemporary black and white with Art Deco touches and a sunroom.

The common rooms in the main house are equally inviting. The *Gathering Room* has white sofas and wing chairs; a massive antique hutch occupies one wall. The music room, with its dark oak floors and a pale blue Oriental rug, boasts an Irish harp, a dulcimer, and an organ. The more formal living room has a fireplace and antique love seats.

Breakfast—fresh juice, fruit, homemade breads, and an egg dish (perhaps three-cheese quiche)—is delivered to each suite in a basket.

The inn is near tennis, golf, horseback riding, the *Phoenix Art Museum*, and shopping.

MARICOPA MANOR 15 W. Pasadena Ave., PO Box 7186, Phoenix, AZ 85013 (phone: 602-274-6302; 800-292-6403; fax: 602-266-3904). This Spanish-style inn has five suites with private baths, queen- or king-size beds, telephones, TV sets, and air conditioning; three with fireplaces, two with whirlpool tubs. Open year-round. Rate for a double room (including full breakfast): $89 to $179. Major credit cards accepted. Children welcome. No pets. Smoking permitted only in designated areas outside. Paul and Mary Ellen Kelley, innkeepers.

DIRECTIONS: The inn is located in north-central Phoenix. From I-17 take the Camelback Road exit to Third Avenue. Turn left onto Third and travel 1 block, turning right onto Pasadena Avenue. The inn is on the right.

ARIZONA INN

Tucson, Arizona

The *Arizona Inn* has an unusual history. Shortly after World War I, when many veterans moved to Arizona for health reasons, philanthropist Isabella Greenway opened a furniture factory to provide employment. The furniture they crafted by hand, which included spool beds and spindle-back chairs with rush seats, was sold through major outlets in New York. When the Depression hit, the retail market dried up, but rather than close the factory, Greenway started buying the furniture herself. Soon, she had warehouses full of it. Then she had another idea: Her East Coast friends loved to visit Arizona, so she built an inn for them, giving her furniture a permanent home. Today, her granddaughter Patty Doar is the innkeeper.

When Isabella built the inn, she gave it a typical Southwestern look with pink adobe walls. Despite the heat, the 14 acres of landscaped grounds are lush with green lawns, stone fountains gushing water, and flower gardens bright with bougainvilleas, zinnias, lilianthus, and daisies.

The 83 rooms at the *Arizona Inn* are noted for their privacy. Most have patios secluded by trees, creating personal hideaways. Several also have fireplaces for the cool months. The original furniture remains, maintained by a carpenter shop on the grounds.

The common rooms, decorated with ornate family antiques, include a classics-filled library with a beamed cathedral ceiling and hand-pegged mahogany floor; the *Audubon Lounge,* where bird lithographs hang on the walls and piano music is played nightly; and two dining rooms, one of which is decorated with lithographs by George Catlin. There's also an outside terrace. Dining is traditional at the inn, which specializes in filet mignon and broiled salmon. Both a continental and a full breakfast are available to guests; dinner is open to non-guests as well.

Amenities include a 60-foot swimming pool bordered by snapdragons, poppies, and anemones, Ping-Pong, croquet, an exercise room, and tennis on two clay courts. Thanks to its location near downtown Tucson, there are many things to do and places to go. Golf, horseback riding, hiking in the Sabino Canyon, skiing, the *Arizona-Sonoran Desert Museum,* the *Tucson Museum of Art,* the *Saguaro National Monument,* and Colossal Cave are all nearby.

ARIZONA INN 2200 E. Elm St., Tucson, AZ 85719 (phone: 520-325-1541; 800-933-1093; fax: 520-881-5830). This luxury hotel has 83 guestrooms with private baths, twin, double, queen-, or king-size beds, telephones, TV sets, and air conditioning; 66 with patios, 14 with fireplaces. Wheelchair accessible. Open year-round. Rate for a double room: $82 to $240. Major credit cards accepted. Children welcome. No pets. Smoking permitted everywhere except the lobby and library. Patty Doar, president and general manager.

DIRECTIONS: From I-10 take the Speedway exit. Travel 2 miles east on Speedway to Campbell Avenue. Turn left onto Campbell and proceed to the first traffic light. Turn right onto Elm Street and travel 3 blocks. The inn is on the right.

RANCHO DE LOS CABALLEROS

WICKENBURG, ARIZONA

The very name *Rancho de los Caballeros* (Ranch of the Gentlemen on Horseback) conjures up romantic images, and the setting—20,000 acres in Arizona's high country north of Phoenix—doesn't disappoint. A working cattle ranch when the Gants began welcoming guests in 1948, this elegant guest ranch (we used to call them dude ranches) is still run by the same family.

So many horseback-riding trails wind through here, that it's possible to go out twice a day for a week and never take the same one. In addition to riding, there are four tennis courts, an 18-hole golf course, a pool, and a range for skeet and trap shooting. Baby-sitters are provided for infants, and counselors will supervise children ages five through 12 on daytime rides, swims, and hikes, and keep them occupied with games in the evening. They even accompany children to all three meals in a special dining room, if desired. For families who'd rather play together, the inn will arrange family rides or a friendly game of tennis with the resident pro.

Most of the accommodations are built around a cactus garden and putting green. Each of the brick *casitas* has two or three guestrooms and a private patio. The *Sunset* and *Bradshaw Mountain Rooms* have wood-burning fireplaces and views of either the Sonoran Desert (with spectacular sunsets) or the golf course with its Bradshaw Mountain backdrop. The decor reflects the colors of the desert: soft earth tones of beige, brown, and yellow accented with bright Southwestern colors and dark wood furniture. Twelve new suites opened in 1995. The generous *Maricopa Suites* are decorated with bright Southwestern fabrics and have king-size beds, *kiva* fireplaces, wet bars, and sizeable bathrooms with custom tilework and whirlpool tubs.

Dinner is served in the dining room, where gentlemen are asked to wear jackets or Western vests. Meals typically begin with a green salad and hot homemade yeast rolls, followed by such entrées as roast rack of lamb, fresh mahi mahi, and broiled New York sirloin steak. For dessert there might be mocha fudge cake or bread pudding with whiskey sauce. Wednesday is generally cookout night, and there's a buffet lunch every day.

RANCHO DE LOS CABALLEROS 1551 S. Vulture Mine Rd., Wickenburg, AZ 85390 (phone: 520-684-5484; 800-684-5030; fax: 520-684-2267). This guest ranch in the Sonoran Desert has 77 guestrooms with private baths, double, queen-, or king-size beds, telephones, TV sets, patios, and air conditioning; 12 with whirlpool tubs. Wheelchair accessible. Closed mid-May through September. Rate for a double room (including breakfast, lunch, dinner, and most facilities):

$254 to $499; supplemental charge for golf, horseback riding, and skeet shooting. No credit cards accepted. Children welcome. No pets. Smoking permitted except in the dining room. Dallas Gant and family, owners/innkeepers.

DIRECTIONS: Leave Phoenix Airport westbound via the 24th Street exit and follow signs to I-17. Take I-17 north for 29 miles to State Route 74 (Carefree Highway). Continue on State Route 74 for 30 miles to US Route 60. Turn right (northwest) onto Route 60 and travel 12 miles through Wickenburg to the second traffic light, which is at the intersection with Vulture Mine Road. Go south on Vulture Mine Road for 1½ miles to the ranch. The trip takes about 90 minutes.

Colorado

QUEEN ANNE BED & BREAKFAST INN

DENVER, COLORADO

In Denver's Clements Historic District, these two Queen Anne-style houses (dating to 1879 and 1886) bracketing a pretty garden are listed on the National Register of Historic Places. Built by noted architect Frank Edbrooke (who also designed Denver's Brown Palace hotel), the 1879 property has stained-glass windows, a grand oak staircase, and a three-story turret. In 1992, Tom King purchased it, and the following year acquired and restored the 1886 house with its 35-foot turret.

Guestrooms in both houses are furnished with Victorian antiques—a canopied four-poster bed in one; a carved king-size bed and cherry armoire in another; a walnut-and-ash armoire in a third. The highlight of the *Aspen Room* is a hand-painted wraparound mural of an aspen grove that extends 12 feet into the turret peak, making the room itself a work of art, and there's a view of the city. Four spectacular suites are named for King's favorite artists—Alexander Calder, Frederic Remington, Norman Rockwell, and John James Audubon—each featuring artwork by its namesake. The *Frederic Remington Suite* has bronze statues, Native American art, a claw-foot cast-iron tub, a barbershop-style washbasin, and a private porch with a hot tub; the *Norman Rockwell Suite* features a sitting-room view of pretty *Benedict Fountain Park* just across the street and large bay windows in the bedroom. Two of the rooms have Jacuzzis, and all have fresh flowers and speakers that pipe in soothing classical music. Most of the guestrooms overlook the mountains, the Denver skyline, or the garden. But up on the roof, there's a private deck with a two-person outside spa and a spectacular downtown view.

A buffet breakfast is laid out each morning: juice, fruit, muffins, croissants, granola, and a hot entrée such as spinach-mushroom quiche or perhaps an apple or strawberry strudel. In the afternoon, Colorado wine and cheese are served in the dining room.

Sitting in the quiet interior courtyard, it's hard to believe that you're in the heart of one of America's largest cities. In fact, this inn's location near Denver's business district and many of its major attractions makes it a popular choice with both businesspeople and vacationers. Nearby are a fitness center, golf, tennis, and the *Denver Art Museum, Museum of Western Art, Colorado History Museum,* and *Governor's Mansion.*

QUEEN ANNE BED & BREAKFAST INN 2147-2151 Tremont Pl., Denver, CO 80205 (phone: 303-296-6666; 800-432-INNS outside Colorado; fax: 303-296-2151). Near Denver's business district, this inn offers 14 guestrooms with private baths, twin, double, queen-, or king-size beds, telephones, and air conditioning; six with TV sets, four with whirlpool tubs, one with balcony and fireplace. Wheelchair accessible. Open year-round. Rate for a double room (including full breakfast and afternoon wine and cheese): $75 to $165. Two-night minimum stay on some holiday weekends and *New Year's Eve.* Major credit cards accepted. Not appropriate for children under 12. No pets. Smoking outside only. Tom King, owner; Chris King, innkeeper.

DIRECTIONS: From I-70 go to I-25 south. Follow I-25 to the Colfax Avenue exit and go east on Colfax. At Logan Street, turn left (north) and drive to the end, where it will dead-end at *Benedict Fountain Park.* Turn left onto 20th Street and then immediately take 2 right turns to get around the Park. The second right will be Tremont. The inn is on the left.

BLUE LAKE RANCH

DURANGO, COLORADO

Homesteaded by Swedish immigrants in the early 1900s, Blue Lake remained a ranch until 1982, when David and Shirley Alford bought the place and turned it into a flourishing bed and breakfast inn. Surrounded by an Indian reservation and a 6,000-acre agricultural station, the 100-acre grounds include a lake filled with rainbow trout and a magnificent, uninterrupted view of La Plata Mountains, part of the Rockies. In spring and summer, bright colors blanket the hills—purple lupines; pink, red, and yellow Indian paintbrush; and blue columbine.

Today the original homestead, painted yellow with white trim and green shutters, has four charming guestrooms filled with family antiques. The *Garden Room* contains a Louis XV armoire and is accented by a green car-

pet and curtains in a pink-and-green floral fabric. A French chaise and sofa snuggle beside the fireplace, and French doors lead to a private deck overlooking the lake. The elegant bath has double sinks set into a green marble counter, a soaking tub, and a "living wall" of cedar with clusters of small orchids growing out of it. A spiral staircase leads to the lovely *Rose Room,* where the highlight is a marvelous 360° view of the inn's hills and gardens. The walls are faux terra cotta, and a mural over the bed depicts a garland of flowers held by two birds.

The inn also offers a variety of accommodations in five cottages. *Cabin on the Lake* was designed to resemble a Swiss chalet: Geranium-filled window boxes line the exterior, and there's a little balcony overlooking Blue Lake. Located on La Plata River, *River House* is an old Indian hunting lodge that has been turned into a two-bedroom, one-bath cottage—ideal for families. *Mountain View Suite,* with two bedrooms and two baths, overlooks the iris field and has uninterrupted mountain views. *Cottage in the Woods* boasts a hot tub and its own picnic area by the lake.

Large flower gardens surround the main house—the source of the brilliantly colored arrangements throughout the inn. Adirondack chairs are scattered on the grounds to encourage quiet communion with nature.

A buffet breakfast, consisting of hot croissants, tamales, corn bread, various cheeses, cereals, and fresh fruit, is served in the main house; tea is served on the patio in the afternoon.

Blue Lake Ranch is about 16 miles west of Durango in the San Juan Range of the Rocky Mountains. Trails leading from the ranch can be used for hiking in warm weather and cross-country skiing in winter. Nearby, in *Mesa Verde National Park,* the *Mesa Verde Cliff Dwellings* reveal intriguing artifacts left by the Anasazi, who occupied these cliffs more than 1,200 years ago.

BLUE LAKE RANCH 16000 Hwy. 140, Hesperus (Durango), CO 81326 (phone: 970-385-4537; fax: 970-385-4088). This inn offers nine guestrooms and cottages with private baths, twin, double, queen-, or king-size beds, telephones, and TV sets; five with fireplaces, three with whirlpool tubs. Wheelchair accessible. Open year-round. Rate for a double room (including buffet breakfast and afternoon refreshments): $85 to $245. Two-night minimum stay. No credit cards accepted. Children welcome. No pets. One cat, Fuzzy, on property. No smoking. David and Shirley Alford, innkeepers.

DIRECTIONS: From Durango take Highway 160 west for 12 miles. Turn right at Highway 140 in Hesperus and travel about 6½ miles south. The entrance to the ranch is on the right.

ROMANTIC RIVERSONG

ESTES PARK, COLORADO

In 1986, Gary and Sue Mansfield traded their house in Denver for a 27-acre property in this Rocky Mountain region of Colorado. They also exchanged their careers (Sue had been a wholesale tour operator, Gary a real-estate broker) for the challenging task of running an inn. *Romantic RiverSong* is aptly named: Its warm, intimate ambience and lovely nature setting make this a perfect love nest. (You even can get married here—Gary, a mail-order minister, has officiated at many wedding ceremonies at the inn itself or on a nearby mountaintop.)

Elegant comfort and rustic charm characterize the inn's atmosphere and decor. The massive living room has a floor-to-ceiling river-rock fireplace and a wall of windows affording a splendid view of the Continental Divide. Many guests like to spend an afternoon or evening in this room, thumbing through the diverse selection of books on the shelves.

Family heirlooms and antiques grace both the guestrooms and common areas. For example, the eight-foot headboard in *Forget-Me-Not* once belonged to Sue's grandmother. The *Chiming Bells Suite* has a brass bed, a rock fireplace, a skylit cathedral ceiling, and a bath with both a sapphire blue recessed tub and a redwood-paneled shower with another skylight. The most unusual guestroom, however, is *Indian Paintbrush,* a separate cottage ringed by pine trees and decorated in a Southwestern theme. A rose tiled fireplace warms the room, Indian pottery and baskets provide accents, and there's a swinging bed suspended from the ceiling by heavy white chains. Five rooms have baths with heated marble floors.

A full breakfast is served each morning. It might include fresh peaches with banana blizzard (yogurt and bananas spiked with lemon zest), Irish potato pancakes with garlic and green peppers, a fresh pineapple-banana smoothie (a drink made with yogurt, juice, and fruit), or John Wayne chili pepper–cheese casserole served with apple-cinnamon tortillas. Dinner is available by prior arrangement.

The inn's surroundings are unsurpassed in their natural beauty, and there are plenty of opportunities for outdoor activity. The house sits amid a cluster of pines, with the Little Thompson River running alongside the road. A gazebo by the river, with an old stone fireplace, is a romantic place to sit and enjoy the peace and quiet, as are the numerous two-person swings hidden among the trees. There's excellent fly-fishing in the river and the many ponds on the grounds. Guests can hike the trails around the inn as well as those in nearby *Rocky Mountain National Park,* with its abundance of wildflowers and mountain peaks that are snow-capped throughout the year. Deer, bighorn sheep, chipmunks, squirrels, and raccoons frequently can be seen, and if you're lucky, you may spot an elk. Cultural events in the area include several art and music festivals in summer and the popular Irish-Scottish Festival in September.

ROMANTIC RIVERSONG 1765 Lower Broadview Rd. (mailing address: PO Box 1910), Estes Park, CO 80517 (phone: 970-586-4666). This mountain retreat offers nine guestrooms with private baths and double or queen-size beds, and fireplaces; seven with decks or patios, six with whirlpool tubs. Wheelchair accessible. Open year-round. Rate for a double room (including full breakfast): $135 to $205. Two-night minimum stay; three nights on holidays. Not appropriate for children under 12. No pets. Smoking permitted outside only. Sue and Gary Mansfield, innkeepers.

DIRECTIONS: From Denver take I-25 north to the Highway 36 exit toward Boulder. Continue on Highway 36 to Estes Park, where Highway 36 becomes Main Street. Continue on Main Street to the traffic light at Mary's Lake Road. Turn left and go half a block; cross a bridge and immediately turn right onto an unpaved country road. This ends at the inn.

NEW SHERIDAN HOTEL

TELLURIDE, COLORADO

Telluride, located at 8,745 feet in a remote section of the San Juan Mountains (a western range of the Rockies), was settled in 1887. When prospectors shouted, "Thar's gold in them hills," they meant it—and silver as well. The little town boomed with fancy restaurants and hostelries and gained distinction for more than its mines: Butch Cassidy robbed his first bank here and William Jennings Bryan delivered his famous "Cross of Gold" speech in front of the *New Sheridan* in 1903. All but deserted after the mines closed, the town saw an influx of hippies in the 1960s. Coming full circle, Telluride is now one of the hottest new upscale resorts in the West. Even so, it's a mellow, laid-back style along with its Old West fixtures of board sidewalks and false-fronted wooden buildings. The entire town is on the National Register of Historic Places.

The *Sheridan Hotel,* a three-story wooden structure, was built in 1887. When it burned down in 1894, the substantial three-story brick building that rose in its place was named the *New Sheridan Hotel.* At the turn-of-the-century, the hotel was the town's social center and its dining room, the *American Room,* set the standard for fine, and very private, dining. Adorned with a massive oil painting of a voluptuous naked woman, this males-only bastion had velvet-curtained booths equipped with telephones so diners could call for service when, and if, they desired it. The *American Room* is now used for breakfast, but it retains all of its old charm, including the booths and the painting. Eventually the hotel deteriorated and by the early 1990s it needed a major renovation. Purchased by a group of investors, it underwent a $1.5 million restoration and reopened in 1995.

The lobby, richly paneled in warm cherry wood, is much the same as it was in its heyday. The adjoining library, with its stone fireplace, is an inviting après-ski gathering spot where wine and hors d'oeuvres are set out in the afternoon. The decor of the *New Sheridan Bar* has remained essentially unchanged—an intricately carved cherry back bar, which was imported from Austria, a mahogany front bar, wooden paneling and room dividers enhanced by beveled- and leaded-glass panels, and Victorian light fixtures.

The guestrooms and suites continue the Old West mood with oak, canopy, brass, and iron beds, and TV sets hidden from view in Victorian-style armoires. Many rooms have views (and they all have teddy bears). Baths are new and modern with tile or pine floors. Twenty-one of the rooms are located in the original hotel and five more (with whirlpool tubs) are in a new attached wing. Six luxury accommodations, the *Colorado Suites,* are located in a building three blocks away. These are complete with kitchens and tile baths, and are ideal for families.

Breakfast includes juice, bagels and cream cheese, a fresh-baked pastry (such as an apricot Danish), and an entrée (perhaps a vegetable frittata). The new wing holds the *New Sheridan Restaurant,* where the dinner menu includes exotic items like grilled kangaroo loin and grilled ostrich filet, as well as more traditional entrées like pan-roasted veal chop with sweet garlic and sage Marsala, and grilled chicken breast with fresh fruit salsa. More than 100 wines are available and dessert offerings include such temptations as chocolate-chocolate Grand Marnier cake and Creole bread pudding with whiskey sauce.

Among the inn's amenities are an elevator to reach the top floors, and a ski storage room on the main floor.

Nearby activities include golfing, hiking, fishing, tennis, horseback riding, mountain climbing, and cross-country skiing. The Oak Street Lift and Coonskin Lift, downhill ski slopes, are mere blocks away. In addition, numerous festivals—from bluegrass to chamber music and from film festivals to wine tastings—take place in town.

NEW SHERIDAN HOTEL 231 W. Colorado Ave.(mailing address: PO Box 980), Telluride, CO 81435 (phone: 970-728-4351; 800-200-1891; fax: 970-728-5024). This historic hotel in the heart of town has 32 rooms and suites, 24 with private baths and all with queen- or king-size beds, telephones, and TV sets; five with whirlpool tubs. Wheelchair accessible. Open year-round. Rate for a double room (including full breakfast and afternoon wine and hors d'oeuvres): $65 to $185. Major credit cards accepted. Children welcome. No pets. No smoking. Four Sisters Inn, managers; Tom Taylor, innkeeper.

DIRECTIONS: From Denver, take I-70 west to Grand Junction (about 250 miles). In Grand Junction take Route 50/550 south through Montrose to Ridgeway (93 miles). Then take Route 62 west to Placerville (23 miles). In Placerville turn left and follow Route 145 another 16 miles to Telluride. A regional airport is located just outside Telluride.

New Mexico

LA POSADA DE CHIMAYÓ

CHIMAYÓ, NEW MEXICO

Route 76 winds between Española and Taos along a stretch of mountain road known as the "High Road." Although the portion to Chimayó is mostly alongside farmland, beyond Chimayó it dips and turns, offering breathtaking views of the Sangre de Cristo mountains. Along the way it passes tiny old towns with pretty churches, art and crafts galleries, and stunning hilltop views of the valley.

Chimayó, about 25 miles north of Santa Fe, is a tiny Spanish colonial village that traces its history to the 16th century. The village has gained international recognition for the magnificent blankets and rugs woven here by Spanish families who trace their craft back many years.

Sue Farrington came to New Mexico in 1973 after a stint with the Peace Corps in South America. In 1981, she built *La Posada de Chimayó*, a two-suite guesthouse to accommodate guests who came to visit the weavers, and New Mexico's first bed and breakfast establishment. In 1992, Sue renovated a hundred-year-old adobe farmhouse to create two additional rooms. This wonderfully relaxing inn is located on a dirt road beyond the village.

The property features adobe-style buildings with 20-inch-thick walls, *kiva* (rounded stucco domes) fireplaces, hand-loomed Mexican rugs, brick, tile, and adobe floors, and *viga* (hand-hewn beams) ceilings, and an abundance of Mexican art. In front of the guest house is a rustic *ramada* (a separate pavilion-like structure with a roof made of twigs); in the back there's a porch, outfitted with swings, that runs the length of the house. The farmhouse porch overlooks the orchard and rustic grounds where, in the fall, the cottonwood trees turn to gold. A common room, located in the farmhouse, has built-in seating, a *kiva,* a refrigerator stocked with wine, a telescope, which guests use to scan the crystal-clear night sky, and lots of books and games to occupy guests on a rainy day.

The two suites in the original guesthouse are called *Chicken* and *Duck;* the two rooms in the farmhouse (which are actually a bit more luxurious) are called *Turtle* and *Lizard.* The largest is *Lizard,* which has peach-colored walls, two double beds, and a Mexican fire-pot (a large pot used as a fireplace). The rooms are furnished with *equipal* furniture (rustic Mexican furniture with pigskin seats, backs, or tabletops, and cross-hatched cedar frames); most of the beds have iron frames and are covered with handwoven spreads. The baths contain modern fixtures accented by beautiful Mexican tiles.

A full breakfast is served in the dining room and may include either French toast stuffed with cream cheese and topped with apricot syrup, scrambled eggs and sausages, or *chiles rellenos* with ham and toasted rolls, all accompanied by juice, coffee, and tea.

In town is *Rancho de Chimayó,* a legendary New Mexico restaurant with a terraced patio, the *Chimayó History Museum,* and the weaving shops where one can meet the weavers and watch them work. The serene *Santuario de Chimayó* church, dating from the early 1800s, is filled with Spanish colonial folk art; in a small back room there's a hole in the floor where dirt said to have miraculous healing powers may be scooped up. Nearby are six Native American pueblos and the archaeological sites of Bandelier, Poyé, and Tsankawi, which offer fascinating insights into the life of the ancient Anasazi people. In addition, there are numerous hiking trails in the area.

LA POSADA DE CHIMAYÓ (mailing address: PO Box 463), Chimayó, NM 87522 (phone: 505-351-4605). This rural adobe inn has two rooms and two suites with private baths, double or queen-size beds, porches, and fireplaces. Open year-round. Rate for a double room (including full breakfast and wine): $80 to $100. Two-night minimum on weekends; up to four nights during some fairs and holidays. Discover, MasterCard, and Visa accepted for advance reservations only. Not appropriate for children under 12. Pets by prior arrangement. A mellow chow, Rufus, and a feisty cat, Little, on property. Smoking outside only. Sue Farrington, innkeeper.

DIRECTIONS: From Santa Fe take Route 68/285 north to Española. In Española take Route 76 east for 8 miles to Chimayó. Turn left onto County Road 88 (a dirt road) and go for 1 mile, always staying to the right. The inn will be on the left.

GRANT CORNER INN

SANTA FE, NEW MEXICO

The architecture of the *Grant Corner Inn* is different from most others in the "City Different." Instead of a low-slung adobe building, it's a handsome 1906 three-story, camel-colored Victorian with a wraparound verandah, sheltered by overhanging willow trees and surrounded by a white picket fence. The verandah has white iron furniture and there's a brick courtyard in the front.

Owned by Louise Stewart, an interior designer whose father owned Scottsdale's famed *Camelback Inn,* this inn reflects the marriage of her decorating wizardry with her knowledge of caring hospitality. The decor showcases lovely European and American pine and oak antiques, including several drawleaf tables. A magnificent floral needlepoint hangs in the entryway. Walls are wedgwood blue with white trim and polished oak floors sport Oriental rugs. In the evening, wine and cheese are set out in the lobby or on the patio, providing an opportunity to become acquainted with other guests and for Louise to make dinner recommendations. On the third floor is a lounge with books, games, and puzzles for rainy-day pursuits. Just off the foyer, a tiny shop offers stuffed animals, jewelry, books, jams, and jellies for sale.

The guestrooms contain antique furniture and Oriental rugs on polished wood floors, yet each has a unique style: one features antique quilts, another Native American weavings; others have photographs of the previous owners of the house and of Louise's family; one room has a lovely hand-painted armoire from Holland. There are iron and brass beds, a pine pencil post bed with muslin curtains, and one with a hand-knotted canopy. Whimsical touches include a collection of dolls in one room, bunnies in another, and bears in a third. A two-story hacienda in back has two bedrooms (one with a fireplace; one with a four-poster *latilla*, a bed of unpeeled, rough posts) and two baths, as well as a kitchen and a living room with another fireplace. The good-sized baths are all tiled.

Breakfast is served in the combination living and dining room or on the patio. Offerings may include such unusual items as blueberry blue-corn pancakes, Italian eggs Benedict (made with eggplant and mushrooms), and a bountiful basket of freshly baked breads, perhaps coconut tea cakes and orange muffins. Tables are set with lovely china, silver, and fine linens; guests may sit at a communal table or by themselves. On Sunday, brunch is open to the public.

Santa Fe is a marvelous walking town. The inn is two blocks from the plaza and close to the art galleries of Canyon Road. Many artists' studios are open to visitors by advance reservation; Louise will be pleased to make the arrangements. Nearby are Native American pueblos, the *Santa Fe Opera,* hiking, river-rafting, and horseback riding.

GRANT CORNER INN 122 Grant Ave., Santa Fe, NM 87501 (phone: 505-983-6678; fax: 505-983-1526). A Victorian-style inn located in downtown Santa Fe with 12 rooms and suites, 10 with private baths, all with twin, queen-, or king-size beds, telephones, TV sets, and air conditioning; three with balconies, one with a fireplace. Wheelchair accessible. Open year-round. Rate for a double room (including full breakfast): $70 to $155. Two- to three-night minimum on holiday weekends. MasterCard and Visa accepted. Not appropriate for children under eight. No pets. No smoking. Louise Stewart, innkeeper.

DIRECTIONS: Take I-25 to the St. Francis Drive exit and then travel north and turn right onto Alameda Street. Turn left onto Guadalupe Street, then turn right onto Johnson Street. The inn is 2 blocks in, on the corner of Johnson and Grant Streets.

CASA DE LAS CHIMENEAS

TAOS, NEW MEXICO

In Spanish, *chimeneas* means "chimneys," and true to its name, the adobe *Casa de las Chimeneas* has at least one *kiva* fireplace in each room (some have two). The beehive-shaped *kivas,* based on a centuries-old Pueblo Indian design, are embellished with hand-painted Mexican *talavera* tiles, as are the elegant bathrooms. The four spacious guestrooms also have *viga* (beamed) ceilings, hand-carved furniture, and luxurious extras such as sheepskin mattress pads and down pillows. Tiled counters serve as bars, and mini-refrigerators are stocked with juices and mineral water. Each guestroom has a private entrance off the terrace.

Framed by dark wooden *vigas* and twisted pillars, the living room has creamy-white adobe walls enlivened by plants and and regional artwork in

radiant fiesta colors. A comfortable sitting area, bright with pillows, surrounds the living room fireplace.

Innkeeper Susan Vernon has created a garden oasis surrounding the inn, with seasonal blooms of irises, tulips, daffodils, roses, daisies, pansies, columbine, lilies, and poppies. A manicured lawn and a seven-foot-high wall separate the property from the street. Cottonwoods, elms, and a massive willow tree ring the one-acre grounds. Two fountains serve as playgrounds for neighborhood birds, and there are paths for strolling.

A full breakfast might include enchiladas, blue-corn pancakes with fresh berries, or French toast made with whole-wheat-orange-date-nut bread; pears baked with maple syrup and cinnamon in a pastry crust or an individual strawberry-rhubarb cobbler; and an iced fruit frappé. In the late afternoon, guests snack on hors d'oeuvres or sweets, perhaps while soaking in the outdoor hot tub. One favorite is moonshine cake, filled with fruit that has been steeped in liquor for a month; in winter the array will include a hot dish such as chile con carne or a crock of green chile corn chowder.

In the heart of Taos, the inn is within walking distance of Taos Plaza and a short drive from the Native American *Pueblo de Taos,* which is a thousand years old and still occupied. Hiking, skiing, fishing, excellent museums, and numerous art galleries and shops are also in the area.

CASA DE LAS CHIMENEAS 405 Cordoba Rd. (mailing address: Box 5303), Taos, NM 87571 (phone: 505-758-4777; fax: 505-758-3976). This luxurious adobe inn has four guestrooms with private baths, twin, queen-, or king-size beds, telephones, *kivas,* patios, and TV sets. Limited wheelchair accessibility. Open year-round. Rate for a double room (including full breakfast and afternoon snack): $125 to $150. MasterCard and Visa accepted. Children welcome. No pets. Smoking permitted outside only. Susan Vernon, innkeeper.

DIRECTIONS: From Santa Fe, travel north on Paseo del Pueblo Sur to Taos. At the traffic light at the intersection of Paseo del Pueblo Sur and Los Pandos Road, turn right onto Los Pandos. Go 1 block and turn right again onto Cordoba Road. Look for the inn sign on the adobe wall on the left.

Texas

HÔTEL ST. GERMAIN

DALLAS, TEXAS

Dallas is an anomaly. Although it was originally settled in 1841, its style is much more modern city than Wild West. Yet though the downtown is a forest of glass-and-steel skyscrapers, there are still little pockets—not exactly neighborhoods—that retain a semblance of their turn-of-the-century ambience. One of those sections is Oak Lawn-McKinney where the streets are lined with refurbished Victorian cottages and turreted mansions, freshly painted in bright colors, housing fashionable boutiques, antiques shops, and restaurants.

In their midst stands the majestic *Hôtel St. Germain.* Painted a patrician white, the inn has ornate black wrought-iron railings sweeping around two curved verandahs, a gabled roof, numerous columns, fanlight windows, and a sweeping circular driveway. It wasn't always this way, however. When Claire Heymann purchased the 1906 building, it was abandoned and in deplorable shape.

Claire has turned the *Hôtel St. Germain* into a refined retreat, reflecting the romantic styles of New Orleans, where she spent her childhood, and of France, where she once lived. As you enter the foyer you are swept into a sophisticated 19th-century French townhouse with 14-foot ceilings, Persian carpets on maple floors, gold crackle moldings, and spectacular antiques. Soft classical music plays. The tiny front parlor has a marble fireplace mantel, European oil paintings, a lovely Aubusson screen, a Kerman carpet, damask-covered chairs, and velvet-covered sofas. The library, with floor-to-ceiling bookcases, is illuminated by an Empire chandelier. At the end of the hall is a magnificent Mallard armoire, and a rich red-toned Sarouk rug carpets the stairway that leads from the hall, past a multi-paned window, up to the bedroom floors.

The elegantly appointed accommodations are all suites, each with a fireplace, a feather bed, fine linens, bouquets of fresh flowers, and fine antique furniture. *Suite 4* has a Mallard half-tester bed draped in cream and taupe silk and covered with a lace bedspread and piles of lace-covered pillows; other furnishings include a burl veneer armoire and a table draped with an antique cutwork cloth. *Suite 5* has a French Lit Polonaise brass bed and access to a wraparound balcony with views of the city. *Suite 7* seems to be plucked straight from Malmaison: It has a Napoleonic sleigh bed and a gorgeous walnut chest dating to the 1700s; its hideaway location under the gabled roof and its sumptuous wine damask and French toile fabrics make it one of the most seductive suites in the house. All baths are appointed with black-and-white tiles, pedestal sinks, and, in three cases, Jacuzzi tubs.

A five-course prix-fixe dinner is served in the dining rooms on Thursday, Friday, and Saturday nights to house- and outside guests. The setting is spectacular, highlighted by a magnificent 19th-century crystal basket chandelier and an 1800s Aubusson tapestry. The tables are set with fine linens, elegant silver, lush floral arrangements, and 100-year-old gold-rimmed Limoges china. Entrées change frequently, but such dishes as veal tenderloin served with a walnut-and-roquefort-cheese stuffed bosc pear with *cognac crème demi-glace* are typical.

Guests may take continental breakfast in their rooms, in the dining room, or in the New Orleans–style walled courtyard. The menu is composed of freshly baked pastries, breads, fruit, juice, and coffee or tea. In order to ensure her guests' every comfort, Claire provides valet parking, nightly turn-down service with a chocolate confection, a full-time butler, business services, room service, a 24-hour concierge, and evening bar service. Hors d'oeuvres and a glass of champagne are presented to guests on arrival.

Across from the *Crescent Complex* with its tiers of shopping, and located in a delightful area of boutiques, art galleries, and bookstores, the inn is great for those who like to buy or browse. In addition, a pool, spa, and multi-story fitness center are nearby. Dallas has a wealth of other activities ranging from visits to the *Dallas Museum of Art* to watching the Dallas Cowboys play.

HÔTEL ST. GERMAIN 2516 Maple Ave., Dallas, TX 75201 (phone: 214-871-2516; 800-683-2516; fax: 214-871-0740). This sumptuous French-inspired all-suite inn located in a Dallas neighborhood has seven suites with private baths, twin, queen-, or king-size beds, telephones, TV sets, fireplaces, and air conditioning; three with Jacuzzis, two with balconies. Restaurant wheelchair accessible. Open year-round except the first week of August. Rate for a double room (including continental breakfast, glass of champagne and hors d'oeuvres): $225 to $600. Children welcome. No pets. Smoking permitted. Claire Heymann, innkeeper.

DIRECTIONS: Heading south toward downtown on the Dallas North Tollway, exit at Wycliff Avenue. Turn right onto Wycliff. At the first stoplight turn left onto Maple and continue for 10 to 12 blocks. The inn is on the left just past Cedar Springs Road.

LA COLOMBE D'OR

HOUSTON, TEXAS

In a cosmopolitan city of glass-sheathed skyscrapers, *La Colombe d'Or* is a pleasant departure. Located about five minutes from downtown Houston, on a full city block in a residential area near the *Museum of Fine Arts* and *Rice University,* this former mansion has been restored and converted to a fine inn and restaurant. With only six exquisitely appointed suites, *La Colombe d'Or* is a jewel.

When owner Steve Zimmerman first saw this splendid but run-down home, he knew it had possibilities. It had been built in 1923 by the founder of Esso (now Exxon) and offered spacious rooms with oak floors, high ceilings, dark woodwork, numerous fireplaces, plus a regal stairway. Today, the main floor contains four luxurious dining rooms, a European-style bar, and a library. The bar is especially lively on weekends, when it attracts those visiting the nearby museums. Outside are a terrace and sculpture garden.

Each of the suites is furnished with either Victorian or contemporary pieces, and original art decorates the walls. Oriental rugs cover the floors, and vases of fresh flowers seem to be everywhere. The *Penthouse Suite* occupies the entire top floor and has a Jacuzzi with an expansive treetop view. The baths, finished in marble and brass, are almost as large as the bedrooms. One unusual feature is the private dining room in each suite, where guests frequently entertain friends; they are also romantic spots for special-occasion dinners.

Some people compare *La Colombe d'Or* to an *auberge* in the south of France; certainly, the acclaimed restaurant compares favorably with that country's finest. It has received many awards for its distinctive cuisine—roasted redfish with caramelized carrots and rack of lamb are examples—and is renowned for its "Oil Barrel Baron Special," a three-course lunch which costs the same as the day's price for a barrel of West Texas crude. Breakfast is available to guests; both the restaurant and bar are open to non-guests for lunch and dinner.

The inn is in the heart of Houston's museum district, not far from the *Astrodome.*

LA COLOMBE D'OR 3410 Montrose Blvd., Houston, TX 77006 (phone: 713-524-7999; fax: 713-524-8923). The inn has six suites with private baths, king-size beds, telephones, TV sets, and air conditioning; one with whirlpool tub. Open year-round. Rate for a double room: $195 to $575. Major credit cards accepted. Children welcome. Small pets allowed. Smoking permitted. Steve Zimmerman, innkeeper; Blaze Mustache, manager.

DIRECTIONS: From downtown Houston take Main Street north to Elgin Street. Go west on Elgin, which becomes Westheimer after 2 blocks. At Montrose Boulevard turn left and travel 1½ blocks to the inn.

MCKAY HOUSE
JEFFERSON, TEXAS

Located on Big Cypress Bayou, Jefferson was a boom port town in the mid-1800s when trade goods from the East and settlers from New Orleans arrived here by steamboat. The refined Southern families built grand plantation-style houses imitating those they left behind. Jefferson is now a National Historic District and in recent years many mansions have been restored, making it one of the best places to see and visit antebellum homes.

The *McKay House,* built in 1851, is a classic Greek Revival cottage surrounded by a broad verandah with swings, a bench, and rockers. It was built by Daniel Alley, a co-founder of the town, but named for a later resident, Captain Hector McKay. McKay looms large in Jefferson history. A lawyer, he prosecuted the notorious Abe Rothchild for the murder of Diamond Bessie, the daughter of a New Orleans diamond merchant and Jefferson's best-known madam. Rothchild was finally acquitted, after an incredible seven years of trials and retrials; the saga is reenacted every year in May.

In 1984 Tom and Peggy Taylor restored the *McKay House* and the *Sunday House,* on either side of a pretty, shared garden. The *McKay House,* studded with period antiques, contains a fantastic 1880s pine-and-cypress staircase with carved spindles that was salvaged from an old building, a stained-glass skylight, and heart-pine floors, and five guestrooms. The *Sunday House* has an additional two rooms. On summer afternoons, both the garden and the porch provide shady spots in which to enjoy a cool lemonade and shortbread cookies; in winter, the *McKay House* fireplace makes a cozy spot.

The guestrooms feature Victorian antiques and, to thoroughly immerse themselves in the era, guests are encouraged to don the Victorian nightgowns and nightshirts that are provided in each room. The *McKay Room* has a four-poster bed and also some of the original documents from the trial; the *Garden Suite* has two back-to-back claw-foot tubs. In the *Sunday House,* the *Keeping Room* has an iron bed covered with an Amish quilt and shams, a fireplace, an 1860s claw-foot tub, and a mock indoor privy. The baths are spacious and charming.

A full breakfast is served in the plant-filled conservatory, at a 12-foot dining table made of old pine flooring planks salvaged from a local warehouse. An entrée (perhaps orange-pecan French toast with bacon) is accompanied by fresh fruit, juice, and freshly baked muffins.

The charming host and hostess and their long-time innkeepers know Jefferson well. They will suggest activities, steer guests to the best antiques shops, and make dinner reservations at one of the town's excellent restaurants. The *Jefferson Historical Museum,* located in the 1888 Federal Courthouse, contains interesting exhibits about the town's early days. Many historic homes are open to visitors, especially during the annual historical Pilgrimage. It's also fun to take the riverboat or steam train tours of the area. Both Caddo Lake and Lake O' the Pines offer swimming, fishing, and boating.

MCKAY HOUSE 306 E. Delta St., Jefferson, TX 75657 (phone: 903-665-7322; fax: 903-665-8551). This delightful Victorian cottage in a historic East Texas town has seven rooms and suites with private baths, double or queen-size beds, telephones, TV sets, and air conditioning; five with fireplaces. Open year-round. Rate for a double room (including full breakfast and afternoon refreshments): $90 to $145. Major credit cards accepted. Children welcome. No pets. Smoking outside only. Tom and Peggy Taylor, proprietors; Alma Anne and Joseph Parker, innkeepers.

DIRECTIONS: From I-20 exit onto Route 59 north in Marshall. Travel 19 miles north to Jefferson. At the traffic light in Jefferson, turn right onto Broadway and go 3 blocks. Turn right onto Alley Street and go 4 blocks to Delta. Turn right onto Delta and the inn will be on the left.

OGE HOUSE ON THE RIVERWALK

SAN ANTONIO, TEXAS

The city of San Antonio is one of the treasures of the United States. The first of five Spanish missions was built here in 1718 and the area was Mexican territory until after the Battle of the Alamo in 1836. It became part of the Republic of Texas and remained so until 1845, when Texas joined the United States. A decidedly Mexican atmosphere still prevails here, especially along the enchanting *Riverwalk,* a 2½-mile-long flagstone pathway lined with shops and restaurants that meanders through town along both sides of the San Antonio River. In *La Villita,* the original Mexican village, adobe houses have been restored and now house artists' workshops and galleries. *El Mercado,* the old open-air marketplace, is the largest market of its kind outside Mexico.

Located on one and a half acres in the King William Historic District right on the *Riverwalk* is *Ogé House,* a lovely Southern mansion with double verandahs in a neoclassical style. It was built in 1857 for use as an arsenal, which accounts for its 16- to 18-inch-thick stone walls. It was purchased by Patrick and Sharrie Magatagan in 1992 and converted to a luxury bed and breakfast establishment.

The huge 15-by-45-foot foyer, with a 12-foot-high ceiling and a graceful curved stairway leading to a bowed landing, is furnished with European antiques, gilt-framed paintings, and Oriental rugs on Texas pine floors. Beyond is a library and a long verandah with a view of the river. The grounds include massive oak and pecan trees, an extensive herb garden (from which herbs are sold to local restaurants), and a gazebo, which is an ideal spot for surveying the passing river scene. Bring a bottle of wine and the stemmed glasses from your guestroom for a totally romantic experience.

The guestrooms, furnished with French and English antiques, are spacious and elegant. There are French armoires and magnificent beds, including one of carved and inlaid satinwood, one of French maple, and a carved rosewood set of bed and matching armoire. The *Riverview Room* has a King William II–style bed and a private balcony overlooking the river. The luxurious, tiled baths have tubs *and* showers, all with brass fixtures. Most rooms have fireplaces; all have little refrigerators. Guests find luscious chocolates in the room at turndown time.

A full breakfast—cereal, pastries, fresh fruit and juice, and a hot entrée, such as a breakfast taco and biscuits and gravy—is served in the dining room or on the verandah. Tables are adorned with fresh flowers, and the meal is served on Wedgwood china with fine linen, silver, and crystal. Fresh-baked cookies and a bowl of fruit are available in the library throughout the day.

Pat and Sharrie have a selection of menus from area restaurants and they are happy to make suggestions. Among the many attractions of San Antonio, the *San Antonio Museum of Art, La Villita,* and *El Mercado* should be high on the visitor's list.

OGE HOUSE ON THE RIVERWALK 209 Washington St., San Antonio, TX 78204 (phone: 210-223-2353; 800-242-2770; fax: 210-226-5812). This gracious historic in-town mansion located on the *Riverwalk* has nine rooms and suites with private baths, queen- or king-size beds, telephones, TV sets, and air conditioning; seven with fireplaces, six with porches or verandahs. Open year-round. Rate for a double room (including full breakfast): $135 to $195. Two-night minimum on weekends; three nights on holidays and during *Fiesta.* Major credit cards accepted. Not appropriate for children under 16. No pets. Smoking permitted outside only. Patrick and Sharrie Magatagan, innkeepers.

DIRECTIONS: From Route 281 take the Durango-Alamodome exit. Turn right onto Durango. Go through three stoplights (the last is St. Mary's Street) and turn left onto Pancoa Street (immediately after St. Mary's Street). The inn is the first house on the right. There's a large parking lot hidden from the street by a hedge.

Utah

BRIGHAM STREET INN

SALT LAKE CITY, UTAH

In 1982, Nancy Pace was looking for a house to use as a designers' show-house to benefit the Utah Heritage Foundation, on whose board she served. She came across a red brick Victorian mansion, built in 1896 by a wool merchant and located on the same street where Mormon leader Brigham Young had lived. Although the house was extremely dilapidated, Nancy recognized its potential. She bought the place, and after the showhouse was over, she gave it new life as the *Brigham Street Inn.*

The common rooms reflect the character of a grand, late-19th-century mansion. There are eight working fireplaces, some with original tile facings; warm woods are found throughout. Golden oak wainscoting highlights the entry, and bird's-eye maple was used for the mantel of the tiled fireplace in the parlor. Nancy's extensive collection of paintings by local artists can be seen throughout the inn. Guests may play the Steinway grand piano in the gracious music room, with its dramatic black walls, white woodwork, and richly carved mantel. A 17th-century Tibetan tapestry graces one wall of the dining room, where guests enjoy continental breakfast each morning.

Each of the nine guestrooms was decorated for the showhouse by a different local designer in a different style—Victorian, colonial, Asian, contemporary, and so on. Several have fireplaces, and one room *(No. 4)* has a balcony.

Salt Lake City has all of the historical and cultural attractions of a state capital. *Temple Square,* the heart of the Mormon church, is near the inn, as are the *University of Utah,* performances by the *Mormon Tabernacle Choir, Ballet West,* and the *Utah Symphony,* and several museums. In addition, several ski areas are within a half-hour drive of the city. If you need guidance, Nancy, who now works for the *Salt Lake County Convention and Visitors Bureau,* has plenty of information.

BRIGHAM STREET INN 1135 E. South Temple, Salt Lake City, UT 84102 (phone: 801-364-4461; 800-417-4461; fax: 801-521-3201). An elegant bed and breakfast mansion in the heart of downtown Salt Lake City, it offers nine guestrooms with private baths, twin or queen-size beds, telephones, TV sets, and air conditioning. Open year-round. Rate for a double room (including continental breakfast): $115 to $175. Major credit cards accepted. Children welcome. No pets. Smoking permitted in guestrooms only. Nancy Pace, innkeeper; Sandy Scott, manager.

DIRECTIONS: From the airport travel east on North Temple Street to *Temple Square* (where North Temple intersects South Temple). From there turn left and travel 11 blocks on South Temple to the inn.

California

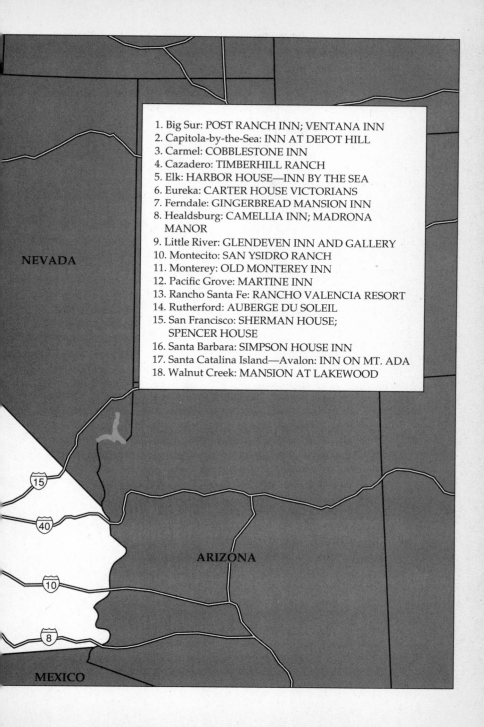

1. Big Sur: POST RANCH INN; VENTANA INN
2. Capitola-by-the-Sea: INN AT DEPOT HILL
3. Carmel: COBBLESTONE INN
4. Cazadero: TIMBERHILL RANCH
5. Elk: HARBOR HOUSE—INN BY THE SEA
6. Eureka: CARTER HOUSE VICTORIANS
7. Ferndale: GINGERBREAD MANSION INN
8. Healdsburg: CAMELLIA INN; MADRONA MANOR
9. Little River: GLENDEVEN INN AND GALLERY
10. Montecito: SAN YSIDRO RANCH
11. Monterey: OLD MONTEREY INN
12. Pacific Grove: MARTINE INN
13. Rancho Santa Fe: RANCHO VALENCIA RESORT
14. Rutherford: AUBERGE DU SOLEIL
15. San Francisco: SHERMAN HOUSE; SPENCER HOUSE
16. Santa Barbara: SIMPSON HOUSE INN
17. Santa Catalina Island—Avalon: INN ON MT. ADA
18. Walnut Creek: MANSION AT LAKEWOOD

NEVADA

ARIZONA

MEXICO

California

POST RANCH INN

BIG SUR, CALIFORNIA

The air is clear and the smell of redwood and sage hangs heavy on the breeze. At night a million stars dance across the sky and the crash of the sea mingles with the call of birds. Few places on earth provide such repose for the soul as Big Sur. In the heart of it, *Post Ranch Inn* settles quietly into the landscape and provides a place for humans to enjoy nature's gifts.

In 1860, W.B. Post staked his claim in the hills here; his property eventually grew to 1,640 acres of cattle range and apple orchards. Through the years, the Posts built primitive little cabins on remote acreage and packed paying guests in for a week or two at a time; eventually, they also operated a roadside restaurant called *Sierra Mar*.

Post Ranch Inn, on 98 acres of Post's former property, is a blend of earth and ocean. Built by Michael Freed and Myles Williams, buildings are constructed of untreated redwood, gently weathering to a bark color, and steel that is taking on a rusty tinge. Each is designed to protect and blend with the terrain. Seven *Tree Houses* are built on stilts to preserve the sensitive roots of the native redwood trees. Five *Ocean Houses* are built into earth berms with wildflowers growing on the roof; guests who wake early are often rewarded with the sight of deer grazing on the roof. The houses seem to hang directly over the ocean, with wraparound windows that jut into space like the prow of a ship. Accommodations in the *Mountain House* and *Coast House* are equally dramatic.

Guestrooms have warm redwood walls, twig chairs with luxurious honeycomb leather seats, headboards and cabinetry of *bubinga* (richly colored African hardwood), and etched-glass room dividers designed to resemble waterfalls. The beds have denim spreads and woven geometric-patterned pillows, which bring the blue of sky and sea directly into the rooms. Each room has a massage table, a fireplace, a two-person jetted tub (cleverly designed to give the illusion of being outside), or a hot tub on the deck. And each has a astonishing view of the mountains or the ocean. Baths have counters of polished granite and walls of raja slate that turns to gold and bronze in the light of the setting sun.

Each unit is built to ensure privacy; few guests bother to cover the windows. Throughout the inn, curved walls are complemented by contoured sofas; there are skylights, and sofas near the fireplaces. From *Sierra Mar,* the glass- and-redwood dining room, the view is breaktaking at sunset. A prix-fixe dinner menu is offered (open to outside guests), with the sodium, fat, and calorie content of many dishes specified. Typical entrées include grilled yellowtail rockfish with papaya, cilantro, clams, and mussels, and grilled filet of beef with chive-potato cake and tomato relish. There's a 20-page wine list. Dessert choices include chocolate truffle cake and ginger-pear napoleon.

The houses are connected by trails that also lead to a fern grotto, a lagoon, past a wildflower meadow, to a pond surrounded by sculptures, and through the redwood forest. Among the facilities are a lap pool and a basking pool, a fitness center with treadmills, stairs, a weight machine, and free weights. Personal fitness training is available, as are yoga instruction and specialty massages, including Swedish, aromatherapy, body polish, and herbal wraps. There are daily escorted hiking expeditions.

POST RANCH INN Highway 1 (mailing address: PO Box 219), Big Sur, CA 93920 (phone: 408-667-2200; 800-527-2200; restaurant: 408-667-2800; fax: 408-667-2824). This ecologically sensitive inn on the California coast has 30 rooms with private baths, king-size beds, telephones, fireplaces, terraces, jetted or hot tubs, and air conditioning; one with a TV set. Wheelchair accessible. Open year-round. Rate for a double room (including continental breakfast): $285 to $545. Two-night minimum on weekends; three nights on holidays. Major credit cards accepted. Children not encouraged. No pets. A cat, Marcella, on premises. No smoking. Larry Callahan, manager; Jamie Short, innkeeper.

DIRECTIONS: From San Francisco, follow Highway 101 south to the Monterey Peninsula exit (about 2 hours). Take Highway 156 west to Highway 1 (about 10 minutes). Follow Highway 1 south through Monterey/Carmel to Big Sur (about 45 minutes). Watch for the sign to *Ventana Inn* on the left. The entrance to *Post Ranch Inn* will be on the right.

VENTANA INN

BIG SUR, CALIFORNIA

The surf pounds against the rocks and salt spray fills the air as guests drive along Highway 1 toward the *Ventana Inn,* 28 miles south of Carmel. On the other side of the road, rolling hills are covered with oak, redwood, and bay laurel trees, and meadows are blanketed in wild poppies.

Located on 243 acres atop a bluff on the opposite side of the road from the perpetual drama of the ocean (*ventana* means "window" in Spanish), the inn was built in 1975. Preservation of the natural environment has been a keystone of the *Ventana* philosophy from the beginning, and although the inn is now owned by the Transamerica Corporation, that philosophy remains an important part of the operation. It has a complete recycling program, practices organic gardening, encourages water and energy conservation, and features indigenous plants on its grounds.

The inn's 12 cedar-sided buildings boast 59 guestrooms; there is also one private cottage. On entering the main lodge, new arrivals may find a fire crackling in the massive stone fireplace, as guests gather for afternoon wine, fruit, and cheese. Picture windows overlook the mountains meeting the sea.

Ventana is a casual, relaxed resort, and in keeping with the informality, furnishings are simple yet stylish. Rattan chairs are cushioned in striped fabrics; headboards, end tables, and chests are custom-made of cedar. Walls are finished in cedar as well, giving them a fresh-from-the-woods smell. Most of the rooms have stone fireplaces, with an ample supply of logs provided. All have large, private decks; some feature private hot tubs. Windows overlook either the ocean, the Santa Lucia Mountains, or the forest.

The inn is also a spa. Its complete fitness center is equipped with treadmills, bicycles, and weights, and there are two heated swimming pools, a sauna, and communal Japanese hot tubs. Trained practitioners offer a complete line of spa services. The screened sun deck is a clothing-optional area.

With a romantic view of the coast, the restaurant (also open to nonguests) is decorated with parquet cedar floors and redwood tables. The food is California style, with an emphasis on fresh local seafood prepared in an uncomplicated manner. Whole rainbow trout may be accompanied by a salad of baby chicory; vegetarian plates are made to order. A buffet breakfast of fruit and fresh-baked breads is available to inn guests in the lobby or delivered to the room.

Pathways lead from the inn through the woods, down to the beach, and across the meadows. Boutiques and hiking trails are nearby.

VENTANA INN Hwy. 1, Big Sur, CA 93920 (phone: 408-667-2331; reservations: 800-628-6500; fax: 408-667-2419). This oceanfront resort has 59 guestrooms with private baths, queen- or king-size beds, telephones, balconies, TV sets, and air conditioning; 49 with fireplaces. Wheelchair accessible. Open year-round. Rate for a double room (including continental breakfast and afternoon wine and cheese): $195 to $440. Two-night minimum stay on weekends and holidays. Major credit cards accepted. Not appropriate for children under 18. No pets. No smoking in public rooms; smoking permitted in 12 guestrooms only. Randy Smith, general manager; Lisa Mitchell, inn manager.

DIRECTIONS: The inn is 152 miles south of San Francisco. From San Francisco, follow Highway 101 south to the Monterey Peninsula exit. Take Highway 156 west to Highway 1. Follow Highway 1 south through Monterey/Carmel to Big Sur. Watch for the sign to *Ventana Inn* on the left.

INN AT DEPOT HILL

CAPITOLA-BY-THE-SEA, CALIFORNIA

At one time, this Southern Pacific depot, a 1901 train station on the bluffs above the village of Capitola and Monterey Bay, was a stop on the "Suntan Special" route from San Francisco to Salinas. In 1990, innkeepers Suzie Lankes and Dan Floyd bought the structure and transformed it into Capitola's first bed and breakfast establishment. (Suzie's grandfather was an architect for the Southern Pacific.)

The inn retains much of the old railway station's romantic aura. Doric columns (some new ones hand-milled to match the originals) support the eaves surrounding the simple tan-and-white building, and the bay window in the dining room was originally the ticket window. The parlor/library has a baby grand piano, a gilded Venetian glass chandelier, a fireplace, and an

abundance of railroad memorabilia; books about trains fill the bookcases. A wrought-iron gate opens to a red brick courtyard and, around back, a garden patio is bordered by beds of climbing roses, trumpet vines, and azaleas.

In keeping with the travel theme, the 12 guestrooms are named after locations around the world and decorated accordingly. The *Delft Suite,* for example, is decorated with delftware and has a fireplace faced with blue-and-white tiles, a wrought-iron bed with floor-to-ceiling drapes in blue-and-white chintz, and lace curtains at the windows. Planted with pink and white tulips, the suite's private garden boasts an outdoor Jacuzzi. All of the guestrooms have fireplaces, and most have either four-poster or canopy beds and balconies or patios. In-room extras include VCRs (there's a lending library of tapes), dual shower heads, and fresh flowers.

In 1996 four new guestrooms were completed. One of them, *The Library,* is a three-level suite with two bedrooms. Guests enter a room with floor-to-ceiling bookshelves and a trompe l'oeil mural which creates an illusion that the room extends beyond the walls. Down several stairs, there's a bedroom with a fireplace. Several steps up from the entrance is a loft with a bed enclosed in gold velvet drapes similar to those in an elegant Pullman car. More trompe l'oeil paintings add to the railroad motif.

A full breakfast—juice, fruit, croissants, cinnamon rolls, and an entrée—is served to inn guests on a unique three-legged, paw-footed table in the dining room. Entrées, based on the cuisine of different countries (such as Belgian waffles or Mexican quiche), change daily. In the afternoon, hors d'oeuvres and wine are set out, and following dinner at a local restaurant, guests may indulge in one of the inn's desserts—coconut-nut tart and lemon-yogurt cake head the list.

Inn at Depot Hill is near beaches, golf, shops, art galleries, and museums.

INN AT DEPOT HILL 250 Monterey Ave., Capitola-by-the-Sea, CA 95010 (408-462-3376; 800-572-2632; fax: 408-458-2490). This inn has 12 guestrooms with private baths, queen- or king-size beds, telephones, fireplaces, and TV sets; 10 with patios, seven with whirlpool tubs. Wheelchair accessible. Open year-round. Rate for a double room (including full breakfast, wine and hors d'oeuvres, and evening dessert): $175 to $350. Two-night minimum on holidays and if stay includes Saturday. Major credit cards accepted. Not appropriate for children under 13. No pets. Smoking permitted outside only. Suzanne Lankes and Dan Floyd, innkeepers; Inez Marshall, manager.

DIRECTIONS: From Highway 101 or I-280 south, take the exit to Highway 17/880 toward Santa Cruz. Pass the Soquel/Capitola exit and take the Monterey/Watsonville exit onto Highway 1, which parallels the coast. Leave Highway 1 at the Park Avenue/New Brighton Beach exit and proceed 1 mile to the T-intersection with Monterey Avenue. Turn left and immediately left again into the driveway of the inn, which is at the corner of Park and Monterey Avenues.

COBBLESTONE INN

Carmel-by-the-sea, California

Regardless of its celebrity status (Clint Eastwood has been its mayor), Carmel-by-the-Sea remains a small town. There are no house numbers and residents make daily pilgrimages to the post office for mail and gossip. Its storybook cottages, many built by artists, poets, and writers in the 1920s, have tiny gardens with abundant flowers. Ocean Avenue, the main street, and the little warren of pathways and courtyards that thread from it, are filled with art galleries, upscale boutiques, crafts shops, fancy food and wine markets, and interesting restaurants. The town's historic district ordinance prohibits obtrusive signs and requires adherence to strict design codes.

In the heart of it all is the *Cobblestone Inn.* Located just a few blocks from Ocean Avenue, this charming two-story, horseshoe-shaped inn has smooth Carmel River rock covering the first story, giving it the appearance of a romantic English Cotswold inn. Inside, there's a lobby with a carousel horse and a cookie jar that is always full. The living room features a large stone fireplace and plush gingham- and plaid-upholstered sofas; a pine hutch showcasing pottery, stuffed animals, and jams for sale; and a breakfast area.

The guestrooms—each with a stone fireplace—are equally charming. Ranging from cozy and tiny to spacious, the rooms are decorated in an English country manner with pine furniture, overstuffed chairs, and Battenburg lace bedcovers. The corner rooms and the *Honeymoon Suite* (with a pencil-post canopy bed) have wet bars and separate sitting rooms. Most rooms have small refrigerators. The tile baths are complete in every detail, although some are quite small. At night guests will find a red rose and a Godiva chocolate on their pillow.

In the morning, a breakfast buffet is set out and guests help themselves to coffee cake, quiche, fresh fruit, homemade muffins and pastries, and cereal. If the weather is nice, breakfast can be enjoyed at tables in the sun-splashed courtyard. In the afternoon, wine, a tray of cheeses, and fresh vegetable crudités are set out for nibbling.

The inn provides bicycles for pedaling to the ocean or for excursions through town. In addition to ocean beach sunbathing, there are numerous shops and restaurants to explore. Monterey is a scenic 17-mile drive past Pebble Beach and its famous golf course; its numerous attractions, including the *Monterey Bay Aquarium,* are located along famed *Cannery Row.* Big Sur, offering breathtaking panoramas of ocean views, is 45 minutes south.

COBBLESTONE INN Junipero Street (mailing address: PO Box 3185), Carmel, CA 93921 (phone: 408-625-5222; 800-833-8836; fax: 408-625-0478). This English-style bed and breakfast establishment has 24 rooms with private baths, queen- or king-size beds, telephones, TV sets, and fireplaces; 20 with mini-refrigerators. Open year-round. Rate for a double room (including full breakfast and afternoon refreshments): $95 to $170. Major credit cards accepted. Children welcome. No pets. No smoking. Four Sisters Inns, proprietor; Suzi Russo, innkeeper.

DIRECTIONS: From San Francisco, follow Highway 101 south to the Monterey Peninsula exit (about 2 hours). Take Highway 156 west to Highway 1 (about 10 minutes). From Highway 1 south, take Ocean Avenue. As you enter town, turn left onto Junipero. The inn is between 7th and 8th Streets on the right.

TIMBERHILL RANCH

CAZADERO, CALIFORNIA

Winding up the coastal highway toward *Timberhill Ranch* and then wandering through its 80 acres, you'll pass meadows peppered with wild flowers and groves of blood-red madrona, oak, and fir trees standing beside majestic redwoods. Horses, llamas, sheep, and goats graze beside the road. The ranch sits in a clearing 1,000 feet above the Pacific Ocean's coastal fog and wind. Although located in Sonoma County, it is separated from the Sonoma Valley by a range of low mountains. In the 1800s, the Pomo Indians chose this sheltered slice of northern California coast for their winter home. Today, the serenity here is a balm for modern jangled nerves.

On arrival at the ranch, you will be greeted by one of the four owners, Tarran McDaid, Michael Riordan, Barbara Farrell, or Frank Watson, all of whom left high-pressure corporate jobs in San Francisco for the peace and quiet of these hills. They live on the ranch and share many of the innkeeping duties.

A working ranch in the 1930s, then a school, the main house was restored in 1984. Its cedar-shake exterior may look rustic, but the interior will immediately dispel any worries about "roughing it." Beneath a vaulted ceiling guests relax on comfortable sofas before a large fieldstone fireplace.

Each guestroom is located in a separate cottage with cedar-log walls, beamed ceilings, and a wood-burning fireplace. The furniture is hand-crafted in pine and walnut; colorful patchwork quilts, handmade by local artisans, cover the beds. A private deck affords views of the surrounding landscape, spectacularly enhanced in the evening by sunsets. Privacy is paramount at *Timberhill,* and even turndown service, which includes a small bouquet of flowers and chocolates placed on each pillow, will be withheld on request.

In the morning, continental breakfast is delivered to each door (a full breakfast is available for a supplemental charge). Lunch, which some guests choose to take in a picnic basket, also is available daily for an additional fee. In the candlelit dining room, the six-course evening meal (open to non-guests by reservation only) begins with a selection of appetizers and progresses through soup, salad, sorbet, entrée, and dessert. The menu might include roast Petaluma duckling with sun-dried figs or grilled Pacific salmon with tomatillo *coulis*. All breads and desserts are made on the premises, and there's a full bar in addition to a fine selection of California wines.

Bordered by the 317-acre *Kruse Rhododendron Reserve* and 6,000-acre *Salt Point State Park,* the ranch offers miles of hiking trails. Also on the grounds are a heated swimming pool, a hot tub, and two tennis courts. Ocean beaches, golf, and art galleries are only 4 miles away; a 60-mile drive leads to the Sonoma Valley wineries.

TIMBERHILL RANCH 35755 Hauser Bridge Rd., Cazadero, CA 95421 (phone: 707-847-3258; fax: 707-847-3342). This ranch has 15 cottages with private baths and twin or queen-size beds. Wheelchair accessible. Closed weekdays in January. Rate for a double room (including continental breakfast and dinner) weekdays: $325; weekends: $365. Two-night minimum stay on weekends; three nights on holidays. Major credit cards accepted. Not appropriate for children under 14. No pets. Dogs, cats, llamas, sheep, goats, and horses on the property. Smoking permitted in designated cottages only. Tarran McDaid, Michael Riordan, Barbara Farrell, and Frank Watson, innkeepers.

DIRECTIONS: The ranch is 96 miles north of San Francisco. From San Francisco take Highway 101 north for 5 miles past Santa Rosa. Turn west onto River Road and continue through Russian River to Jenner. Follow Highway 1 north for 5 miles beyond Jenner, then turn right onto Meyers Grade Road and ascend to the ridge. Continue on this road for 13¾ miles (its name changes to Seaview, then to Hauser Bridge Road). Continue three-quarters of a mile past Seaview Plantation Road to the ranch.

HARBOR HOUSE—INN BY THE SEA

ELK, CALIFORNIA

In this part of the world the sea in its many moods dominates the scenery. Waves wash ashore in a never-ending rhythm, great rock formations seem to have been thrown helter-skelter across the headlands, and sea otters and whales play just offshore. Guests at *Harbor House* have a perfect vantage point from which to view the spectacle.

Built in 1916 by the Goodyear Redwood Lumber Company, the inn was constructed entirely of virgin redwoods cut from the nearby Albion Forest.

It was used as a retreat and entertainment facility for company executives and guests and as a showcase for redwood construction. Fashioned after the "Home of Redwood" exhibit at the 1915 *Panama-Pacific International Exposition* in San Francisco, the inn has numerous fireplaces, a living room with a hand-carved redwood ceiling, and walls that originally were coated with hot beeswax to preserve their rich red color.

Located in both the main lodge and four cottages on the grounds, the 10 guestrooms offer either ocean or garden views; many have private decks. Fireplaces warm nine of the rooms, and each is furnished with antique oak tables and dressers. The *Redwood Room,* which is paneled in virgin redwood, contains a massive French armoire. There's a sleigh bed in the *Greenwood Room; Shorepine* and *Seaview Cottages* have iron-and-brass beds; *Oceansong Cottage* has a queen-size four-poster, while *Lookout Room* has a iron-and-brass bed and an unobstructed view of the ocean from the wraparound windows.

A stay at *Harbor House* includes both breakfast and dinner (the latter is open to non-guests by reservation only). Extensive vegetable and herb gardens provide many of the staples, and eggs from the inn's chickens are served for breakfast. Outstanding meals are planned around seasonal offerings and are accompanied by fresh-baked breads and desserts. Dinner might be grilled salmon with mustard-dill sauce, followed by a fresh peach crisp.

The inn's gardens create a storybook setting. There are Adirondack chairs on velvety lawns, benches under arbors draped with wild roses, and a sheltered path to a private beach. Tennis, golf, hiking trails, wineries, antiques shops, art galleries, and a botanical garden are all nearby.

HARBOR HOUSE—INN BY THE SEA 5600 S. Hwy. 1, Elk, CA 95432 (phone: 707-877-3203). This redwood lodge on the Pacific Ocean has 10 guestrooms

with private baths and queen- or king-size beds; nine with fireplaces. Open year-round. Rate for a double room (including full breakfast and dinner): $170 to $265. Two-night minimum stay on weekends. No credit cards accepted. Not appropriate for children under 12. No pets. Two outdoor cats. No smoking. Helen and Dean Turner, innkeepers.

DIRECTIONS: From San Francisco either travel north on Highway 1 all the way, or take Highway 101 to Cloverdale, then Highway 128 west, then Highway 1 south for 6 miles to the inn.

CARTER HOUSE VICTORIANS

EUREKA, CALIFORNIA

Innkeeper Mark Carter came by his love of Victorian architecture naturally. He was born in Eureka, a logging and fishing town overlooking Humboldt Bay in the heart of the "redwood empire," where lumber barons built magnificent Victorian mansions to showcase their wealth. To this day, Eureka has some of the most spectacular examples of Victorian architecture in America. Mark became a builder, and by the time he was 30, he had renovated more than 20 of Eureka's Victorian jewels, developing a lasting appreciation for the craftsmanship that went into their creation.

The finest examples of the period were the work of San Francisco architects Samuel and Joseph C. Newsom. When Mark found a book of original Newsom plans, he was intrigued by an 1884 mansion they had designed for a San Francisco banker; it had been destroyed in the 1906 earthquake and fire, but, in 1981, Mark decided to rebuild it as his family's dream home. Sixteen months and $700,000 later, they had a vintage extravaganza, authentic down to the marble fireplaces.

Although the exterior looks as if it had been built in 1884, there are amenities inside (such as Jacuzzis) unimaginable in those days. Using the house as a bed and breakfast inn hadn't been the Carters' original intent, but it had such a welcoming air that they began taking in guests. Today, the *Carter House* offers five guestrooms.

But the Carters didn't stop there. In 1986, they built the 23-room *Hotel Carter* across the street, a re-creation of the *Old Town Cairo Hotel,* one of Eureka's boom-era hostelries. The lobby, with a marble fireplace, massive ceramic urns, Oriental rugs, and antique pine furniture, is a sophisticated blend of the Old World and the New. In 1990, the Carters restored a neighboring house they call the *Bell House,* creating three more rooms.

The rooms in all three Carter properties feature a blend of antiques and modern amenities. TV sets are tucked away in antique armoires, and original local art decorates the walls. Ten of the rooms have fireplaces, and there are views of the bay and the *Carson Mansion.* Most of the thoroughly modern marble baths have dual shower heads.

Fine food is another good reason to visit *Carter House Victorians*. More than 50 types of lettuce and more than a hundred herbs flourish in the kitchen gardens. In fact, the homegrown produce is so important to the hotel's menus that the Carters employ a master gardener, who also gives interpretive garden tours, classes, and seminars. There's an extensive wine room, with a broad selection of California vintages for sale.

A full breakfast (open to outside guests) consists of a fruit course, fresh-baked muffins or sweet rolls, an egg dish or pancakes, and dessert —perhaps a spectacular tart made with buttered phyllo layers, sautéed apples, and almond paste. In the evening, wine, hors d'oeuvres, tea, and cookies are served. With the presentation as carefully planned as the menu, dinner in *Restaurant 301* (also open to non-guests) is in a class by itself. Entrées might include grilled Pacific salmon with mustard-rosemary sauce, or grilled loin of pork with homemade chutney and fresh applesauce.

The inn is near a fitness center, theaters, art and antiques shops, the *Redwood National Park,* and the *Salmon-Trinity Alps Wilderness Area.* Carriage rides and architectural tours of Eureka also are available.

CARTER HOUSE VICTORIANS 301 L St., Eureka, CA 95501 (phone: 707-444-8062; 800-404-1390; fax: 707-444-8067). This inn, comprising three Victorian buildings, has 31 guestrooms with private baths, double, queen-, or king-size beds, and telephones; 27 with TV sets, 11 with whirlpool tubs, 10 with fireplaces. Wheelchair accessible. Open year-round. Rate for a double room (including full breakfast and evening refreshments): $95 to $275; room only $65. Major credit cards accepted. Children welcome. No pets. No smoking. Mark and Christi Carter, innkeepers; Brent Critch and Bob Graves, managers.

DIRECTIONS: The hotel is approximately 280 miles north of San Francisco. Take Highway 101 to Eureka, where it becomes Broadway. At L Street turn left. The inn is on the corner.

GINGERBREAD MANSION INN

FERNDALE, CALIFORNIA

Ferndale is a small village off the beaten tourist trail amid the redwoods of northern California. Settled originally by Scandinavians, the town's primary occupation was, and remains, dairy farming. As the farmers prospered, they built resplendent homes in the Eastlake, Carpenter Gothic, and Queen Anne styles of architecture with the fortunes they amassed. Probably due to Ferndale's hideaway location, many of these "butterfat palaces" remain, making this one of the finest Victorian villages in America. The entire town is a state historic landmark, and Main Street is on the National Register of Historic Places.

The *Gingerbread Mansion Inn* is itself a showplace of Victorian architecture, and it's frequently touted as the most photographed house in California. Built in 1899 as a doctor's residence, it was expanded in the 1920s to become *Ferndale General Hospital.* In 1983, innkeeper Ken Torbert enlarged the rooms, added bathrooms, and opened a bed and breakfast inn. A fantasy of Victoriana, it has turrets, bay windows, and fanciful trim, all highlighted by a peach-and-yellow color scheme.

The inside is as elaborate as the façade. All 10 guestrooms are furnished with Victorian antiques and have fantastic bathrooms. The *Fountain Suite,* for example, has a bonnet-canopy bed and side-by-side claw-foot tubs for romantic bubble baths. A mirrored wall reflects the flames from the bathroom's tiled corner fireplace. The *Rose Suite* has a fireplace in the bedroom, as well as in the bathroom, which also features a claw-foot tub. The *Empire Suite* occupies the entire top floor of the inn and boasts Victorian stained-glass entry doors, Ionic columns surrounding a king-size bed, a massive marble-clad bathroom with a shower and an oversize porcelain tub placed before a fireplace.

A full breakfast, perhaps featuring eggs Benedict or French toast stuffed with cream cheese and blueberries, is served in the dining room. Afternoon tea—small sandwiches, cake, cookies, fruit with Devonshire cream, and petits fours—is offered daily.

The surrounding English gardens include neatly trimmed boxwoods, three-story fuchsias, gigantic camellia trees, and a fountain. The inn is 5 miles from the beach (a nice bicycle ride). Also nearby are the *Redwood National Park,* village tours, theater, museums, and art galleries.

GINGERBREAD MANSION INN 400 Berding St. (mailing address: PO Box 40), Ferndale, CA 95536 (phone: 707-786-4000; 800-952-4136; fax: 707-786-4381). This Victorian mansion has 10 guestrooms with private baths and queen- or king-size beds; five with fireplaces, two with TV sets. Open year-round. Rate for a double room (including full breakfast and afternoon tea): $150 to $350. Two-night minimum stay on some weekends and holidays. Major credit cards accepted. Not appropriate for children under 10. No pets. No smoking. Ken Torbert, innkeeper.

DIRECTIONS: From Highway 101 take the Ferndale exit and proceed west 5 miles to Ferndale. From Main Street turn left at the Bank of America building and continue 1 block to the inn.

CAMELLIA INN

HEALDSBURG, CALIFORNIA

This lovely inn on a quiet side street in Healdsburg, in the Russian River Valley, has an interesting history. Built in 1869, the house was purchased in 1892 by the Seawells, whose son obtained a medical degree and returned to establish his practice in his family's home. The story is that Dr. Seawell's good friend Luther Burbank, the renowned plant breeder, gave him some of the camellia plants that now highlight the gardens. Although Dr. Seawell died in 1938, his widow continued to live in the home until 1969.

When Ray and Del Lewand and their daughter Lucy purchased the house in 1981, it was in nearly perfect condition. Guests at the *Camellia Inn* therefore have the rare opportunity to stay in a 128-year-old house that has never undergone major renovations.

The interior is painted peach with white trim to reflect the many camellia bushes outside. The common rooms have numerous fireplaces, decorative friezes, and sparkling Victorian chandeliers. In the double parlors

at the front of the house are elaborate twin marble fireplace mantels. With its period antiques and Oriental rugs, the house has a gracious ambience similar to that enjoyed by the Seawells more than 100 years ago.

Most of the guestrooms are named for a variety of camellia and all are decorated with antiques. The *Memento Room,* for example, is furnished with a brass bed, Victorian lamps, and wicker chairs; there's a claw-foot tub with brass fixtures in the bath. On display are treasures that belonged to Del's grandmother, including photo albums and old dance cards. The centerpiece of the *Moonglow Room* is a four-poster canopy bed. The two *Tower Rooms* have canopy beds and enormous whirlpool tubs.

In the elaborate dining room, a full breakfast buffet is served from a mahogany sideboard. The menu consists of fresh fruit, cereal, granola, yogurt, fresh-baked sourdough bread, a sweet pastry such as berry coffee cake ring or almond croissants, and perhaps sausage-and-potato pie or Mexican fiesta biscuit bake. An afternoon social hour in the parlors includes cheeses, crackers, iced tea, and lemonade.

The inn sponsors numerous activities, including special teas. One of the most popular events is the annual supper in honor of Scottish poet Robert Burns (Lucy's husband is from Scotland). Naturally, there's a reading or two, as well as the playing of Scottish folk tunes.

Beyond the formal gardens behind the house are a fishpond and a heated swimming pool. Here, guests relax after visiting some of the many wineries in the area, or spending the day bicycling or playing golf or tennis nearby.

CAMELLIA INN 211 North St., Healdsburg, CA 95448 (phone: 707-433-8182; 800-727-8182; fax: 707-433-8130). This Italianate Victorian inn has nine guestrooms with private baths and double or queen-size beds. Wheelchair accessible. Open year-round. Rate for a double room (including full breakfast and afternoon refreshments): $70 to $145. Two-night minimum if stay includes Saturday. Major credit cards accepted. Children welcome. No pets. Smoking permitted outside only. Ray, Del, and Lucy Lewand, innkeepers.

MADRONA MANOR

HEALDSBURG, CALIFORNIA

Madrona Manor is a three-story, High Victorian mansion set on eight acres with spectacular landscaped gardens and views of Healdsburg, the Sonoma Valley, and the mountains beyond. The house was built in 1881 by San Francisco financier John Paxton, who lived here with his wife and 10 servants. In 1983, it was purchased by John and Carol Muir, who have made of it one of the finest inns and restaurants in California.

Listed on the National Register of Historic Places, the inn is furnished in a style that matches the exuberance of the architecture. In the parlor is an array of massive carved walnut and mahogany furniture and an Oriental rug. A hundred-year-old square grand piano dominates the music room.

Five of the nine guestrooms in the *Main House* are decorated with furniture that once belonged to the original owner. *Room No. 301* boasts a High Victorian carved walnut bed with matching nightstands and dresser, as well as a fireplace. Another of the rooms has a 10-foot-high canopy bed (ceilings in the *Main House* reach 14 feet) and a matching armoire. Dripping with Gothic gingerbread trim, the *Carriage House,* which John converted to nine guestrooms, sits just beyond the pool and is furnished with hand-carved rosewood pieces. *Room No. 503* has a fireplace and a large private deck. *Suite No. 400* is the pièce de résistance, with a king-size bed, a fireplace, and a bath that has Greek marble tiles and a Jacuzzi. The *Garden Cottage* offers private gardens and sheltered deck.

The restaurant meanders through three formal parlors, all with fireplaces, overlooking the flower gardens. The inn is renowned for its food, thanks to son Todd Muir, who trained at the *California Culinary Academy* and has been the executive chef since opening day. The menu reflects his interpretation of California cooking and his love of fresh Sonoma County produce. Dinner (also open to non-guests) may include an appetizer of Dungeness crab mousse, an entrée of rack of lamb oven-roasted with Dijon mustard–pistachio–bread crumb crust, served with herbed potato terrine and, for dessert, a white-chocolate mousse napoleon. Breakfast may include Carol's homemade marmalade or jams.

Guests can visit the many wineries of the Sonoma Valley, browse through nearby antiques shops, or explore the area on bicycles.

MADRONA MANOR 1001 Westside Rd., Healdsburg, CA 95448 (phone: 707-433-4231 or 707-433-4433; 800-258-4003; fax: 707-433-0703). This country inn has 21 guestrooms with private baths, twin, double, queen-, or king-size beds, telephones, and air conditioning; 18 with fireplaces, one with whirlpool tub. Wheelchair accessible. Open year-round. Rate for a double room (including full breakfast): $140 to $240. Two-night minimum stay from April through October in the *Main House* rooms and suites. Major credit cards accepted. Children welcome in designated rooms. Pets allowed in some rooms with prior permission only (a deposit is required). Three cats—Tiger, Tux, and Little Bit—in residence. Smoking permitted outside only. John and Carol Muir, innkeepers.

DIRECTIONS: Driving north on Highway 101, go 12 miles past Santa Rosa and take the Central Healdsburg exit. Follow Healdsburg Avenue north to Mill Street and turn left. Mill Street becomes Westside Road. The inn is three-quarters of a mile down on the right.

GLENDEVEN INN AND GALLERY

LITTLE RIVER, CALIFORNIA

The lure of the Mendocino section of California's coastline—a craggy strip of high bluffs and rocky promontories punctuated by tiny coves—is its rugged scenery. On the ocean, 1½ miles south of the historic town of Mendocino, *Glendeven* sits on a headland meadow overlooking Little River Bay. Built in 1867, the inn complex includes the *Farmhouse,* the *Barn,* and the *Stevenscroft Building.*

Innkeeper Jan deVries, an architect and furniture designer, and his wife, Janet, an interior designer, have been part of the local arts and crafts scene since they renovated the inn in 1977. In a gallery in the *Barn*, they show the work of local artists and craftspeople, as well as Jan's furniture.

The parlor in the *Farmhouse* is the inn's social center, especially when a guest decides to pick out a tune on the baby grand piano. The parlor is furnished with antiques and overstuffed chairs gathered around the fire-

place. An Amish quilt hangs on the wall and picture windows admit views of the garden and the distant bay. A pathway leads down to the beach.

The 10 guestrooms are furnished with country French and early American antiques plus Jan's modern upholstered furniture, with its curves and clean lines. Most rooms have fireplaces and views of Van Damme Bay; many have private decks. The *Barn* has been converted into a two-story suite with two bedrooms, a sitting room, a full kitchen, and a sun deck. There are five rooms in the *Farmhouse* and four in the *Stevenscroft Building.*

A continental breakfast—juice, fresh fruit, muffins, and quiche—is delivered to guestrooms on a tray or in a basket. Coffee, tea, wine, and cookies are available in the kitchen all day.

The town of Mendocino is a terrific shopping destination, with numerous art galleries, crafts shops, and restaurants. Also nearby are *Van Damme State Park,* hiking, tennis, and golf.

GLENDEVEN INN AND GALLERY 8221 N. Hwy. 1, Little River, CA 95456; mailing address: Box 252, Mendocino, CA 95460 (phone: 707-937-0083; 800-822-4536; fax: 707-937-6108). This inn has 10 guestrooms with private baths and queen-size beds; eight with fireplaces, seven with private decks and balconies. Open year-round. Rate for a double room (including continental breakfast and snacks): $90 to $220. Two-night minimum stay on weekends; three nights some holidays. Major credit cards accepted. Children welcome in designated rooms. No pets. Smoking permitted outside only. Jan and Janet deVries, innkeepers.

DIRECTIONS: The inn is located on the inland side of Highway 1 between Little River and Mendocino. To travel part of the way by freeway, take Highway 101 from San Francisco north to Cloverdale. Then take Highway 128 north for 65 miles to Highway 1. Continue north on Highway 1 for 10 miles to Little River. The inn is three-quarters of a mile north of Little River, just past the entrance to *Van Damme State Park.*

SAN YSIDRO RANCH

MONTECITO, CALIFORNIA

In the late 1700s, the area where *San Ysidro Ranch* now stands was a stopping place for Franciscan monks on their trek along the Spanish Mission Route. Tomas Olivera, a Mexican rancher, built the oldest building on the property, the *Adobe,* for his bride in 1825. By 1893, the cottage-style bungalows had been built and the ranch was accepting guests. In 1935, matinee idol Ronald Colman purchased the inn, and it soon became an exclusive hideaway for celebrities. Bing Crosby, Jack Benny, and Katharine Hepburn were frequent guests. Vivien Leigh and Laurence Olivier were married in the rose garden. John and Jacqueline Kennedy visited in 1953. Somerset Maugham wrote on the terrace of the *Geranium Cottage,* and John Huston completed his script for *The African Queen* here.

After years of acclaim, the ranch slipped into disrepair. It was purchased by new owners in 1976, and with extensive renovation, *San Ysidro* was again reaping national renown and awards. Today, the 540-acre ranch is owned by Claude Rouas and Bob Harmon (Auberge Associates), who have infused it with their own sophisticated style.

High in the hills above Santa Barbara, *San Ysidro* enjoys spectacular views of the ocean on one side and of the Santa Ynez Mountains on the other. Surrounded by herb, flower, and vegetable gardens, wisteria-covered arches, and ancient, gnarled oak, acacia, and sycamore trees, the ranch's 21 cottages possess a rustic simplicity. With names such as *Jasmine, Magnolia, Lilac,* and *Rose,* the rooms are evocative of their surroundings.

In the cottages are 42 guestrooms and suites, each with a private terrace, a wood-burning fireplace, and a wet bar. Many have private Jacuzzis. All rooms are furnished with antiques that include armoires, buffets, and chests. When guests arrive at their cottages, they find wooden signs bearing their names hanging outside.

The *Stonehouse* restaurant (also open to non-guests) serves award-winning meals, including spa cuisine. There's also a pub, the *Plow and Angel,* carved out of the space that was used as a wine cellar in 1893. Every Thursday and Friday night jazz concerts are held here. Other nights there's dancing to the tunes on the 1952 Wurlitzer jukebox.

Recreational opportunities at the ranch are numerous. Tennis, swimming, a fitness center, *bocci,* horseshoes, mountain biking, and hiking are available. Numerous body and beauty treatments are offered in the privacy of guests' rooms. These include Swedish and sports massage and aromatherapy. Guests also can go to the beach, play golf, or frequent boutiques, all of which are nearby. In addition, extensive facilities are available for children, including a petting zoo and a play area. *Camp SYR* (offered to children ages five to 12 during the summer) keeps the younger set busy panning for gold and learning about Indian lore. There's even a program for visiting pets.

SAN YSIDRO RANCH 900 San Ysidro La., Montecito, CA 93108 (phone: 805-969-5046; 800-368-6788; fax: 805-565-1995). This sophisticated ranch resort has 42 guestrooms with private baths, queen- or king-size beds, telephones, TV sets, fireplaces, private terraces, and air conditioning; 15 with outdoor Jacuzzis or bathroom whirlpool tubs. Wheelchair accessible. Open year-round. Rate for a double room (including use of pool, tennis courts, and other ranch facilities): $245 to $1,400. Two-night minimum stay on weekends; three nights on holidays. Major credit cards accepted. Children welcome. Pets allowed ($45 extra per stay). Smoking permitted outside only. Auberge Associates, owners; Janis Clapoff, managing partner.

DIRECTIONS: The ranch is approximately 5 miles south of Santa Barbara. Traveling south on Highway 101, take the San Ysidro exit and head east, toward the hills. Follow San Ysidro Road to San Ysidro Lane, which ends at the ranch.

OLD MONTEREY INN

MONTEREY, CALIFORNIA

A gracious half-timbered, English Tudor–style home sits on a quiet residential street in the heart of historic Monterey. Ivy covers the front, and wisteria climbs up two stories and wraps around the arched windows. The grounds are studded with majestic oak, pine, and redwood trees; rhododendrons bloom brightly; and the rose garden is a riot of color all summer. This is the *Old Monterey Inn.*

Built in 1929, the house is the longtime residence of Ann and Gene Swett, who raised their six children here. In 1978, they opened their home as an inn and have been offering warm hospitality ever since. The eight guestrooms, a delightful suite, and a garden cottage are all furnished with choice antiques; feather beds are dressed with fine antique linen and down

comforters. Special features include skylights and stained-glass windows, and all but two rooms have fireplaces.

One of the rooms, the *Rookery,* a whimsical retreat with a garden theme and a delightful assortment of white wicker and hand-painted furniture, a skylight over the queen-size bed, and a fireplace. The *Garden Cottage* has skylights, a fireplace, a canopy bed, and a window seat for gazing at the private garden. The *Library,* on the other hand, is a masculine retreat, with book-lined walls, a large stone fireplace, and a private deck.

The high-ceilinged living room offers a variety of comfortable seating, a fireplace, and a garden view. Afternoon tea is served here, as are wine and hors d'oeuvres in the evening. A full breakfast is offered to guests in their rooms, the dining room, or, if the weather is nice, the rose garden. It usually includes juice, fruit, homemade muffins, and perhaps strata soufflé with artichokes and mushrooms or orange-blossom French toast.

The inn is located near Carmel, *Cannery Row,* the *Monterey Bay Aquarium,* 17-Mile Drive, and Pebble Beach; shopping, theater, and symphony concerts are in the area as well.

OLD MONTEREY INN 500 Martin St., Monterey, CA 93940 (phone: 408-375-8284; 800-350-2344; fax: 408-375-6730). This in-village country-house inn has 10 guestrooms with private baths and queen- or king-size beds; eight with fireplaces, three with TV sets, one with whirlpool tub. Closed *Christmas.* Rate for a double room (including full breakfast, afternoon tea, and evening wine and hors d'oeuvres): $170 to $240. Two-night minimum stay on weekends; three nights on holidays and special events. MasterCard and Visa accepted. Not appropriate for children under 13. No pets. A German shepherd, Liza, in residence. No smoking except in rose garden. Ann and Gene Swett, innkeepers; Patti Kreider, manager.

DIRECTIONS: Traveling south on Highway 1, take the Soledad/Munras exit. Follow Soledad Drive, cross Munras Avenue, and turn right onto Pacific Street. Continue a half mile to Martin Street on the left. Traveling north on Highway 1, take the Munras Avenue exit. Make an immediate left onto Soledad Drive and then turn right onto Pacific Street. Proceed as above.

MARTINE INN

PACIFIC GROVE, CALIFORNIA

Located in the charming village of Pacific Grove, the *Martine Inn* is a grand old mansion perched high on the cliffs overlooking Monterey Bay's spectacular coastline. The epitome of elegance, the huge (29-room) house was built in the 1890s, for James and Laura Parke, of Parke-Davis Pharmaceuticals.

Originally, the building was a full-blown Victorian with a cupola and dormers, but these features were removed in the 1920s, when it was transformed into a Mediterranean villa with a stucco exterior. Purchased in 1972 by Marion and Don Martine, the structure underwent additional renovations, though its 1920s façade was retained. The house is now painted rose, and careful attention has been paid to restoring the interior Victorian details. Marion and Don opened the inn to guests in 1984.

Although larger than most bed and breakfast establishments, the *Martine Inn* offers an intimate atmosphere, and each of its 19 guestrooms is distinctive. A unique 1850s American walnut bedroom suite—with busts of Jenny Lind carved in the mirror frame, armoire, and headboard—dominates one room, while another is furnished with a suite that once belonged to costume designer Edith Head. Thirteen rooms, many of which have fireplaces and views of the bay, are located in the *Main House;* there are six more in the *Carriage House,* overlooking the courtyard pond and fountain.

An 1890s billiards table, an antique piano, a slot machine, and a six-person Jacuzzi are found in the conservatory, which previously served as the estate's greenhouse. The library, with its beautiful inlaid oak bookcases, offers a comfortable place to read by the fire. Be sure to ask Don about his collection of MGs, which he drives in vintage-car races. Three are on display in a small auto museum on the grounds.

Breakfast is served in the dining room on a French walnut table set with Victorian china, crystal, and silver. The menu always includes fresh-baked muffins and a hot entrée such as Monterey eggs (eggs and cottage cheese baked with green chilies and cheddar cheese). Afternoon wine and hors d'oeuvres also are served.

The views of Monterey Bay from the dining and sitting rooms can yield some delightful surprises. Binoculars are placed along the window ledges so guests may scan the water for whales, dolphins, sea lions, sea otters, and pelicans.

The inn is four blocks from the *Monterey Bay Aquarium* and within walking distance of *Cannery Row;* also nearby are the Monterey Peninsula Recreational Trail, 17-Mile Drive, and excellent shopping.

MARTINE INN 255 Ocean View Blvd., Pacific Grove, CA 93950 (phone: 408-373-3388; 800-852-5588; fax: 408-373-3896). This mansion inn has 19 guestrooms with private baths, double, queen-, or king-size beds, and telephones; nine with fireplaces. Wheelchair accessible. Open year-round. Rate for a double room (including full breakfast and afternoon wine and hors d'oeuvres): $135 to $240. Two-night minimum if stay includes Saturday night; three nights on holidays. Major credit cards accepted. Well-supervised children welcome. No pets. Smoking permitted in guestrooms with fireplaces only. Don and Marion Martine, innkeepers; Tracy Harris, manager.

DIRECTIONS: From Highway 1 exit onto Highway 68, staying in the right lane and traveling west to Pacific Grove. Once in town continue on Forest Avenue to the beach. Turn right onto Ocean View Boulevard and continue to the inn, which is on the right between Fifth and Third Streets.

RANCHO VALENCIA RESORT

RANCHO SANTA FE, CALIFORNIA

This sun-splashed resort sits high on a 40-acre plateau overlooking the San Dieguito Valley. Nearby, the seaside villages of La Jolla and Del Mar offer sophisticated shops and restaurants, but *Rancho Valencia* is such a peaceful retreat that guests find few reasons to leave.

Climbing the hill to the canyon plateau, a series of sloping lawns is bordered by beds of bright impatiens, agapanthus, hibiscus, and geraniums. The resort's 2,000 citrus trees provide shade as well as a steady supply of Valencia oranges, lemons, and limes.

Although *Rancho Valencia Resort* was built in 1989, it is reminiscent of the grand old haciendas built in Rancho Santa Fe in the 1920s and 1930s, with typical Spanish colonial architecture: stucco walls, red tile roofs, and terra cotta patios. The 43 suites are in *casitas,* each with a cathedral ceiling, a tiled fireplace, a ceiling fan, a private patio, a wet bar, a refrigerator, a CD player, and a VCR. The luxuriously appointed baths offer dressing rooms and oversize walk-in showers. The *Hacienda,* with its own pool and secluded gardens, is an ultra private three-suite retreat.

Meals (also open to non-guests) are a highlight of any stay at the resort, where the fare is a sophisticated blend of California and Mediterranean styles. A salad, for example, might feature warm, crispy sweetbreads with scallions and arugula; entrées include mahi mahi with olive oregano crumbs and sautéed scallopini of venison with celery root fritters. The *Rancho Valencia* orange cake is a medley of orange custard and chocolate mousse. For the health-conscious, a spa menu provides a delicious alternative. No meals are included in the room rate, but a tray with a carafe of juice—freshly squeezed from oranges grown on the property—a rose bud in a vase, and a newspaper is delivered to guestrooms each morning.

Tennis is a draw here, with 18 courts that are in regular use. In addition, there are two outdoor swimming pools, bicycles, a regulation croquet lawn, a putting green, a full-scale fitness center, and a spa featuring a wide array of services, from manicures and Swedish massages to aromatherapy and reflexology. Spirited sunrise walks and scenic hikes prepare guests for the day. Activities especially for children include the *Junior Tennis Academy,* a special amenity package, and a children's menu in the restaurant.

Located in the hills above the Pacific, the resort is 10 miles north of La Jolla and 24 miles north of San Diego. Also nearby are *Del Mar Racetrack, Balboa Park, Sea World, San Diego Zoo,* golf (the inn has privileges at three championship courses), hot-air ballooning, and boutique shopping.

RANCHO VALENCIA RESORT 5921 Valencia Circle (mailing address: PO Box 9126), Rancho Santa Fe, CA 92067 (phone: 619-756-1123; 800-548-3664; fax: 619-756-0165). This luxury resort has 43 suites with private baths, queen- or king-size beds, telephones, TV/VCR sets, fireplaces, private terraces, and air conditioning. Wheelchair accessible. Open year-round. Rate for a double room (including tennis and fitness facilities): $335 to $850 ($2,500 for the *Hacienda*). Two-night minimum stay on weekends; three nights on holidays. Major credit cards accepted. Children welcome. Pets permitted ($75 charge per night, per pet). No smoking. Michael Ullman, general manager.

DIRECTIONS: From Los Angeles take I-5 south to Del Mar. Turn left onto Via de la Valle and then right onto El Camino Real. Turn left at San Dieguito Road. Proceed for 3 miles to the first traffic light and turn right at Rancho Diegueno Road. Turn left immediately onto Rancho Valencia Road. Rancho Valencia Drive is on the left; drive two blocks to Rancho Valencia Circle and the inn. From San Diego take I-5 north to Del Mar Heights Road east. Follow this road to El Camino Real and turn left. Turn right onto San Dieguito Road and follow directions above.

AUBERGE DU SOLEIL

RUTHERFORD, CALIFORNIA

In 1981, Claude Rouas opened the *Auberge du Soleil* (Inn of the Sun), a fine French restaurant on a 33-acre hillside, surrounded by an aged olive grove and overlooking the Napa Valley. As the restaurant and its food began winning praise, patrons requested a similarly luxurious place to stay. In response, Rouas opened the first of the inn's romantic guestrooms in 1985; the number has since grown to 50.

The guestrooms, each of which has a private terrace, a fireplace, and a fabulous view of the valley, are located in a series of one- and two-story Mediterranean-style villas. With their wood-shingled roofs, they look for all the world as if they've just arrived from France. The rooms have exposed-beam ceilings and terra cotta floors; tiles decorate both the headboards and the fireplace hearths. Illuminated by skylights, many of the large baths have Jacuzzis as well as separate stall showers. The in-room refrigerators are stocked with Napa Valley wines and gourmet snacks.

The restaurant at the *Auberge* (open to non-guests) serves exceptional wine country cuisine, using local meat, seafood, produce, and herbs. Dinner might feature grilled hamachi (a white fish) and cashew rice with Zinfandel-sangria sauce, or garlic-rosemary crusted lamb rack with truffled scalloped potatoes and red wine sauce. The setting and ambience reflect California's distinctive informal style. Decorated in stucco and tile, the dining rooms have fireplaces and a terrace with breathtaking views. A bar with a fireplace leads to an open deck with a wisteria-covered trellis.

Facilities include a full-size pool, a fitness center, a beauty salon, three tennis courts, and private dining rooms. A sculpture garden featuring work by local artists can be viewed from the nature trail that has been cut into the hillside. Guests can pursue bicycling, ballooning, gliding, golfing, and horseback riding nearby. With more than 200 of California's finest wineries in the area, wine touring is one of the most popular activities.

AUBERGE DU SOLEIL 180 Rutherford Hill Rd., PO Drawer B, Rutherford, CA 94573 (phone: 707-963-1211; 800-348-5406; fax: 707-963-8764). This inn has 50 guestrooms with private baths, twin or king-size beds, telephones, TV/VCR sets, CD players, private terraces, and air conditioning; 48 with fireplaces, 12 with whirlpool tubs. Wheelchair accessible. Open year-round. Rate for a double room: $275 to $1,200. Two-night minimum stay on weekends. Major credit cards accepted. Not appropriate for children under 16. No pets. Two cats, Cortney and Emma, on premises. Smoking permitted in guestrooms and bar but not in the restaurant. George A. Goeggel, general manager.

DIRECTIONS: From San Francisco, take Highway 101 north through Marin County to the Highway 37 cutoff south of Novato. Follow Highway 37 to Highway 121 and turn toward Sonoma. South of Sonoma bear right (east) onto Highway 12 toward Napa. Turn left onto Highway 29 and continue north through Napa, Yountville, and Oakville. At Rutherford turn right onto Highway 128. Drive 3 miles to the stop sign at the Silverado Trail and turn left. Go 200 yards and turn right at Rutherford Hill Road. The inn will be on the right up the hill.

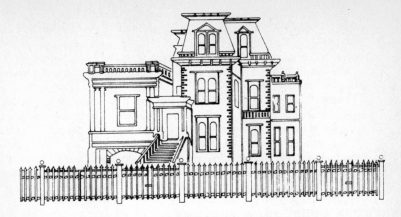

SHERMAN HOUSE

San Francisco, California

Don't be surprised if you hear ghostly sounds of music echoing through the hallways of the *Sherman House*. Built in 1876, this magnificent mansion in fashionable Pacific Heights originally was the home of Leander Sherman, founder of the Sherman Clay Music Company. For 50 years, he lavishly entertained artistic, literary, and musical stars, including such greats as Enrico Caruso, Lillian Russell, Ernestine Schumann-Heink, and Ignacy Jan Paderewski. In 1901, he added a music room the size of a ballroom so that his guests might better enjoy the impromptu concerts he hosted.

After Sherman died, the building served variously as a restaurant, a ballet school, and a sculptor's studio, but even after a stint as a decorator show house, it seemed destined for demolition until a group of public-spirited citizens were successful in having it designated a San Francisco landmark. In 1982, Manou and Vesta Mobedshahi (he a San Francisco hotelier, she an art historian) bought the building and began its restoration.

Today, the Italianate mansion reflects the grace of a bygone era. The spectacular double stairway has been extended to the top floor, ornate plaster friezes have been repaired and painted, and crystal chandeliers hang from ornate ceiling medallions. Priceless antiques are found throughout. A Coromandel screen and a Flemish tapestry are focal points in the lobby. Afternoon tea is served in the sitting room, with its Louis XVI–style commode and a Regency-style table.

All but one of the 14 guestrooms have fireplaces, and most feature canopied feather beds. They also offer views, often from private decks or plush window seats, either of San Francisco Bay and the Golden Gate Bridge or of the English gardens in back. Guestrooms in the mansion are richly furnished with brocade and English or French antiques. The *Carriage House,* in the garden, has a country French decor.

The *Leander Sherman Suite,* on the mansion's top floor, has a black marble fireplace mantel, an antique desk, and a polished antique chest concealing the TV set, CD player, and VCR. French doors open to a tiny side balcony. The pièce de résistance, however, is the 800-square-foot terrace off the suite's living room, with a view that extends past the Golden Gate Bridge to the bay beyond.

Dinner in one of the two dining rooms (open to house guests only) is a treat. Entrées might include pan-seared monkfish on creamy polenta or grilled and braised pheasant in a black currant sauce. Breakfast is also served, although it's not included in the room rate. A house specialty is brioche French toast with apple wood–smoked bacon.

The inn is near the shops and restaurants on Union Street, *Fisherman's Wharf, Ghirardelli Square,* the *Cannery,* museums, and historic walks.

SHERMAN HOUSE 2160 Green St., San Francisco, CA 94123 (phone: 415-563-3600; 800-424-5777; fax: 415-563-1882). This luxury mansion has 14 guestrooms with private baths, twin or queen-size beds, telephones, and TV sets; 13 with fireplaces, three with terraces, one with a whirlpool tub. Wheelchair accessible. Open year-round. Rate for a double room: $295 to $825. Two-night minimum stay on major holiday weekends. Major credit cards accepted. Children welcome. No pets. Boots, a calico cat, in residence. Smoking permitted in one public room only. Manou and Vesta Mobedshahi, proprietors; Christine Berlin, manager.

DIRECTIONS: Traveling north on Highway 101, follow signs to the Golden Gate Bridge but exit onto Fell Street. Travel a half mile and turn right onto Webster Street. Continue for approximately 2 miles and turn left onto Green Street. *Sherman House* is on the right.

SPENCER HOUSE

SAN FRANCISCO, CALIFORNIA

Located in the Haight-Ashbury section of San Francisco, the *Spencer House* is an 1887 Victorian beauty, built by a milliner named Spencer. It has a round tower, Palladian windows, marble stairs, a triple-arched main entry porch, elaborate stained-glass windows with faceted crystals, and a profusion of exterior ornamentation. Numerous gables crown the graceful roof. They didn't build many like this, and there certainly aren't many left.

Barbara and Jack Chambers purchased the *Spencer House* in 1984, embarked on a major restoration project, and opened it as a bed and breakfast establishment in 1985. The results of their work are spectacular.

The Chamberses surrounded the property with an ornate wrought-iron Victorian fence, accented with gilt and designed to complement the arched windows. Inside, they retained the original plaster walls but covered those in the double parlor in silk. The main floor also features vaulted 12-foot ceilings and fanciful hand-painted Bradbury and Bradbury wallpapers. The

front parlor is cozily elegant with down-filled couches, a Kirman rug, and spectacular antiques—the player piano is especially popular.

A grand staircase of hand-carved oak leads to the six guestrooms. Here, the hallway retains the original gilded Lincrusta Walton wallpapers, and oversize, solid wood doors open into enormous rooms with bay windows. The feather beds have down comforters; Barbara traveled to England to select the special bed linen. Three rooms have glorious views of *Buena Vista Park* or the Golden Gate Bridge; all are furnished with antiques. The *French Room*, for example, contains a delightful antique French Eastlake bed and a matching armoire, an Oriental rug, hand-stenciled walls, and a "notorious" Victorian chandelier–it once belonged to a madam. As exquisite as the furnishings are, the decor is elegant, not fussy. A full breakfast is served in the formal dining room. The entrée might be cheese blintzes with brandied cherry sauce and *crème fraîche*.

The inn is near *Golden Gate Park, Buena Vista Park,* museums, and the many interesting shops on Haight and Union Streets.

SPENCER HOUSE 1080 Haight St., San Francisco, CA 94117 (phone: 415-626-9205; fax: 415-616-9230). This Victorian mansion has six guestrooms with private baths, queen- or king-size beds, and telephones. Open year-round. Rate for a double room (including full breakfast): $105 to $165. Major credit cards accepted. Not appropriate for children under 13. No pets. Two cocker spaniels, Percy and Perry, and a macaw, Carmen, in residence. No smoking. Barbara and Jack Chambers, innkeepers; Chrysanthe Soukas, manager.

DIRECTIONS: Traveling north on Highway 101, follow signs to the Golden Gate Bridge but exit onto Fell Street. Follow Fell Street to Baker Street and turn left. The inn is on the left, at the corner of Baker and Haight Streets.

SIMPSON HOUSE INN

SANTA BARBARA, CALIFORNIA

As if plucked from an English village and set down in the midst of the adobe and red tile of Santa Barbara is the *Simpson House Inn.* Situated on an acre of land behind a tall hedge, English gardens laced with pathways lead to this British-style country house, which provides a quiet respite from the workaday world. The English tone is no accident: Glyn Davies, who owns the inn with his wife Linda, hails from England.

The grand Eastlake-style Victorian mansion was built in 1874 by Robert Simpson, who had emigrated from Scotland. He built the house of red-wood and he installed oak floors, high ceilings, and stained-glass windows. Glyn and Linda purchased the house in 1976 and raised their family here. When the children were off to lives of their own, they turned the gracious house into a spectacular bed and breakfast establishment. It's now listed on the National Register of Historic Places.

Glyn is a contractor and Linda an artist, and it shows in every detail of their inn. Inviting and gracious, the common rooms and guestrooms are furnished with elegant Victorian-era antiques, fabrics, and rugs. The beam-ceilinged sitting room has wedgwood-blue walls, a lovely fireplace, and 1920s-style furniture. The dining room features a Victorian brass chande-lier with hand-painted globes hanging over an antique English mahogany table. The guestrooms are exquisite. The walls and ceiling of the *Margaret Simpson Room,* for example, are covered in a spectacular green-and-gold Victorian wallpaper; furnishings include an antique European bed, and a bath with pedestal sink, claw-foot tub, and an antique brass shower.

In 1993, the Davieses completed a renovation of an 1876 barn on the property and Glyn built three private cottages, increasing the number of rooms and suites from six to 14. The *Old Barn Suites* have antique pine floors, wood-burning fireplaces, antique furniture, and private decks overlooking the gardens. The cottages, called *Abbeywood, Greenwich,* and *Plumstead,* are tucked away in the gardens. They have private fountain courtyards, antique canopied feather beds, wood-burning fireplaces, and in-room Jacuzzis.

Breakfast is served each morning in the dining room. A typical menu will include baked pear with whipped cream, savory eggs, hot scones, home-made granola, organic orange juice, and coffee. In the afternoon, Santa Barbara wines or iced tea are served with an extensive selection of hors d'oeuvres. The food is so delicious and the conversation often becomes so animated that guests sometimes make this their evening meal.

The inn will provide bicycles, beach chairs, and umbrellas for a trip to the beach, which is a mile away. The inn is only two blocks from downtown Santa Barbara, home to excellent shops and restaurants, plus the *Santa Barbara Mission,* the *Santa Barbara Historical Museum,* and the *Santa Barbara Museum of Art.*

SIMPSON HOUSE INN 121 East Arrellaga St., Santa Barbara, CA 93101 (phone: 805-963-7067; 800-676-1280; fax: 805-564-4811). This elegant historic in-city bed and breakfast establishment has 14 rooms, suites, and cottages with private baths, queen- or king-size beds, and telephones; 13 with air conditioning, 10 with fountain patios or balconies, seven with TV sets, four with whirlpool tubs. Wheelchair accessible. Open year-round. Rate for a double room (including full breakfast and afternoon refreshments): $140 to $300. Two-night minimum if stay includes Saturday; three nights on some holidays. Major credit cards accepted. Children welcome. No pets. Two black Labradors, Bella and Mia, on premises. Smoking permitted on one porch only. Glyn and Linda Davies, innkeepers; Dixie Adair Budke, general manager.

DIRECTIONS: From Highway 101, take the Garden Street exit and follow Garden Street north for 1 mile. Turn left onto Arrellaga. The house will be on the right in the first block.

INN ON MOUNT ADA

AVALON, SANTA CATALINA ISLAND, CALIFORNIA

Catalina is just an hour from Los Angeles, yet it's light-years away in ambience and attitude. Reached by ferry from the mainland, this serene island enchants with spectacular sunrises and sunsets, the sea, and ocean breezes. Automobile permits are rationed; most people get around by walking, bicycling, or driving golf carts.

On five and a half acres high atop a hill overlooking Avalon Harbor, the *Inn on Mount Ada* was formerly the summer home of chewing-gum magnate William Wrigley Jr. The large, stately Georgian home, listed on the National Register of Historic Places, is ornamented with elaborate columns in the foyer and hand-carved moldings throughout. About 25 years after

Wrigley last used the house (he died in 1932), it was donated to the *University of Southern California* for use as a marine institute. Eventually, the property came to the attention of the Mount Ada Inn Corporation, a group of local residents intent on saving it from further deterioration. In 1985, the corporation signed a lease with the university, and the inn was born.

The inn's numerous common rooms, including a den, a sunroom, a living room, and dining room, are decorated with Chippendale and Hepplewhite antiques and local crafts, including several examples of rare Catalina pottery made in the 1920s. All the rooms afford ocean or harbor views. The four guestrooms and two suites also are decorated with Old World antiques, including canopy and four-poster beds.

The hearty breakfast may consist of juice, bran muffins, poached pears with strawberry sauce, and banana-pecan pancakes with sausage. Fresh-baked cookies are served in the afternoon and hot and cold appetizers, along with wine, sherry, port, beer, and champagne, are set out before dinner. Both a deli-style lunch and a complete dinner—which might feature filet of beef or pork tenderloin—are included in the rate as well. All meals are available to non-guests.

Santa Catalina Island offers many activities, such as swimming, tennis, golf, snorkeling, parasailing, hiking, and shopping. Golf carts are available for guests' use.

INN ON MOUNT ADA 398 Wrigley Rd. (mailing address: PO Box 2560), Avalon, CA 90704 (phone: 310-510-2030; fax: 310-510-2237). This inn has six guestrooms with private baths, queen-size beds, and TV sets. Closed *Christmas Eve* and *Christmas*. Rate for a double room (including breakfast, lunch, afternoon refreshments, and dinner): $350 to $650. Two-night minimum stay on weekends.

MasterCard and Visa accepted. Not appropriate for children under 14. No pets. No smoking permitted. Marlene McAdam and Susie Griffin, innkeepers.

DIRECTIONS: Ferries leave from San Pedro, Long Beach, and Newport Beach; the crossing takes an hour. The inn is also accessible by helicopter from Long Beach and Newport Beach; the ride takes 15 minutes. Guests are met at the dock and the heliport.

MANSION AT LAKEWOOD

WALNUT CREEK, CALIFORNIA

Through the white wrought-iron gates of the *Mansion at Lakewood* lies a world of sweeping verandahs and lush lawns skirted by colorful flowers. The three-acre estate, shaded by hundred-year-old oaks, magnolias, and redwoods, and featuring a cactus garden and a pond where *koi* slide beneath the water lilies, is a tranquil oasis only a quarter-mile from downtown Walnut Creek and 25 miles from San Francisco.

The rambling, two-story Victorian mansion was constructed in 1861 with tongue-and-groove siding and raised verandahs. The 8,000-square-foot structure still has an etched-glass transom over the door showing a flag with 34 stars, the full complement in those days. Mike and Sharyn McCoy purchased the property in 1986, launched a major renovation, and opened their bed and breakfast establishment in 1988.

The main floor boasts a majestic library with arched 14-foot ceilings, redwood bookshelves, and a black marble fireplace. The parlor also has a fireplace and a small boutique. A cherry table and two matching buffets grace the dining room. Toy bunnies, part of Sharyn's collection, peek around corners throughout the inn.

Country-fresh charm pervades the five guestrooms and two suites, which are decorated with fine antiques. The unusual *Summerhouse* has hand-painted floors and a claw-foot tub on an enclosed porch. All rooms have private baths (one suite has a black marble bath with a double Jacuzzi), and the suites include fireplaces.

After a breakfast of fresh-baked croissants, baked eggs, and "Dutch babies" (a puffed pancake) served with fresh fruit, guests might enjoy a game of croquet or stroll on one of the nature paths. A formal high tea (open to non-guests) is served from Friday through Sunday in the *Secret Garden Tea Room,* a charming room with painted mural walls of a garden complete with a faux archway, stonework ledges, and a faux fountain.

The *Regional Center for the Arts,* a playhouse and performing arts center, and a summer Shakespeare festival are both nearby. Also in the area is *Mount Diablo State Park* for hiking.

MANSION AT LAKEWOOD 1056 Hacienda Dr., Walnut Creek, CA 94598 (phone: 510-945-3600; 800-477-7898; fax: 510-945-3608). This secluded Victorian inn has seven guestrooms with private baths, queen- or king-size beds, and telephones. Wheelchair accessible. Open year-round. Rate for a double room (including full breakfast): $135 to $300; corporate rates available. Major credit cards accepted. Children welcome. No pets. Smoking permitted on outdoor balconies or terrace only. Sharyn and Mike McCoy, innkeepers; Angie and John Senser, managers.

DIRECTIONS: From San Francisco cross the Oakland Bay Bridge and then take I-580 east to Route 24. Follow Route 24 through the Caldecott Tunnel to Walnut Creek. Bear left when the highway forks and get onto I-680 north to Ygnacio Valley Road. Continue to the seventh traffic light and turn right onto Homestead Avenue. Proceed 3 blocks, then turn left onto Hacienda Drive. The house is just down the street behind white wrought-iron gates.

Pacific Northwest, Alaska, and British Columbia

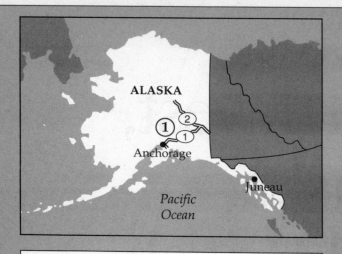

ALASKA
1. Denali National Park: NORTH FACE LODGE/
   CAMP DENALI

OREGON
2. Cannon Beach: STEPHANIE INN
3. Gold Beach: TU TU' TUN LODGE
4. Portland: HERON HAUS

WASHINGTON
5. Bremerton: WILLCOX HOUSE
6. Orcas Island—Eastsound: TURTLEBACK
   FARM INN
7. Port Townsend: OLD CONSULATE INN/
   F. W. HASTINGS HOUSE
8. Poulsbo: MANOR FARM INN
9. Seaview: SHELBURNE INN
10. Whidbey Island—Langley: INN AT LANGLEY

BRITISH COLUMBIA, CANADA
11. Mayne Island: OCEANWOOD COUNTRY INN
12. Sooke: SOOKE HARBOUR HOUSE
13. Victoria: BEACONSFIELD INN

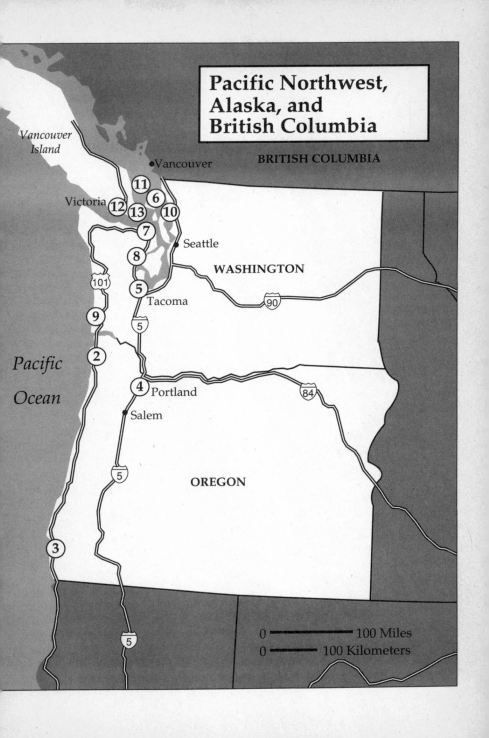

Pacific Northwest, Alaska, and British Columbia

Vancouver Island

Victoria

Pacific Ocean

BRITISH COLUMBIA

Vancouver

WASHINGTON

Seattle

Tacoma

Portland

Salem

OREGON

101

90

5

84

5

5

5

0 ——— 100 Miles

0 ——— 100 Kilometers

Pacific Northwest, Alaska, and British Columbia

Alaska

NORTH FACE LODGE/CAMP DENALI

DENALI NATIONAL PARK, ALASKA

The rising sun casts a golden glow across the jagged white peaks of Mount McKinley (the highest mountain in North America). Beneath it, a moose and her calf amble across a field strewn with wildflowers to drink at the lake. The air is crystal clear; the scent of spruce is on the breeze; and the only sound is the buzz of a bee seeking nectar from a flower.

　　This awesome spectacle begins the day for the privileged guests at *North Face Lodge/Camp Denali,* two separate properties in the heart of *Denali National Park.* Owned and operated by Wallace and Jerryne Cole for more than 20 years, the properties offer distinctly different experiences.

Camp Denali, on a mountain ridge with breathtakingly beautiful views, seems almost of another world. It offers a true taste of Alaska's rugged, wild nature. The camp's 17 log cabins were built on land acquired in 1951 through the Alaska homesteading grant. The accommodations are rustic, although certainly not primitive. Each of the cabins can accommodate from two to six people and has a woodstove (with a wood box that's refilled daily), propane lights, a hot plate for making coffee and tea, and a porch. The country decor includes handmade quilts (made by staff members) on comfortable beds and pretty blue calico curtains at the windows.

Nearby, three common buildings house showers and restrooms, a living room, a natural history resource center, and a dining room, where all meals are served at communal tables. (For those who want to get away from civilization altogether, there is also a separate homestead cabin nearby. It has neither electricity nor running water; an outhouse is down the hill, and guests use the showers at *Camp Denali,* 1½ miles away.)

North Face Lodge is a modern motel-like building. It has 15 small guestrooms, all with electricity and private baths. The rooms fill one wing of the building, and a living room with a massive stone fireplace and a dining room are in another wing.

At both facilities, the day begins early with a full breakfast, perhaps pineapple muffins and green-chili soufflé or asparagus quiche. Lunch is buffet style, so that sandwiches, fruit, drinks, and dessert can be packed for a day's journey into the wilderness. In the evening, when guests return from their treks, hors d'oeuvres await. A typical dinner might feature barbecued salmon with black-bean sauce, homemade bread, and "mud cake" for dessert. Guests sit at communal tables and share their day's experiences.

The variety of activities in this naturalist's paradise is staggering. There are organized nature programs and expeditions, self-guided hiking trails, flightseeing, canoeing, biking, rafting, and fishing. Visitors are likely to see moose, caribou, grizzly bear, mountain sheep, beaver, fox, and wolf.

NORTH FACE LODGE/CAMP DENALI Denali National Park (mailing address: PO Box 67), AK 99755 (phone: 907-683-2290; fax: 907-683-1568). These rustic properties offer 17 cabins (sleeping two to six people) with shared baths, twin, double, or queen-size beds, porches, and woodstoves, and 15 guestrooms with private baths, twin, double, or queen-size beds and balconies. Closed late September through May. Rate for a double room (including breakfast, lunch, dinner, transportation to and from railroad station at park entrance, and activities): $570. Two-night minimum stay at *North Face Lodge;* three nights at *Camp Denali.* No credit cards accepted. Not appropriate for children under 10. No pets. No smoking indoors. Wallace and Jerryne Cole, innkeepers.

DIRECTIONS: Guests arrive by railroad, bus, or car; the railroad station is at the entrance to *Denali National Park,* 90 miles (a 4- to 6-hour drive) from the properties. A bus transports guests to and from the station.

Oregon

STEPHANIE INN

CANNON BEACH, OREGON

Highway 101 twists and turns up the Oregon coast between California and Washington, offering breathtaking views of the crashing Pacific Ocean from craggy promontories. It's one of nature's great spectacles, with blowholes spouting water into the air like geysers, calm sandy inlets, and massive rocks rising from the sea.

The *Stephanie Inn,* built in 1993 by Steve and Jan Martin, is well positioned to take in all this grandeur. Set on a broad stretch of sandy beach, its windows look out on one of Oregon's favorite monuments, Haystack Rock, a monstrous boulder that juts some 800 feet heavenward. It's a bird sanctuary and off-limits for climbing, but at low tide, pools at its base reveal a wealth of sea life, including starfish and purple and green anemones.

The inn's exterior design combines the sharp angles of contemporary Pacific Northwest architecture and the shingled façades associated with New England. Inside, the lobby features beamed old-growth fir ceilings and pillars, a polished oak floor, and a river-rock fireplace. The chart room and library has another fireplace, a leather sofa, and bay windows that reach out to the ocean. Binoculars are provided to watch the changing scene, which is particularly fascinating when the gray whales are migrating. There's a nightly nibble hour here, with Pacific Northwest wines, cheeses, and crackers, that gives guests an opportunity to become acquainted.

The spacious guestrooms are named for women who have contributed to Oregon history and for family friends (the inn itself is named for the owners' daughter). All have ebony four-poster beds strategically placed before a fireplace, an abundance of upholstered seating, and private decks. Each room has a wet bar, a refrigerator stocked with soft drinks, and a VCR for watching movies from the inn's extensive library. Every bath in this romantic retreat features a two-person whirlpool tub.

The full breakfast includes such entrées as pancakes with bacon or homemade biscuits with a sausage-mushroom gravy. The prix fixe dinner (which is open to non-guests) is served in elegant surroundings, with a view toward the coastal mountains. Dinner is served at a specific time (7 PM Mondays through Thursdays; 6 and 8 PM Fridays through Sundays). The evening begins when the chef, who specializes in local produce, fish, and meat, enters the dining room and describes the components and preparation of each course. Entrées might be Pacific rockfish wrapped in parchment paper or roasted rack of Ellensberg lamb with parsnip purée. Desserts include an almond Florentine basket filled with fresh berries and served with vanilla-bean sauce or raspberry-chocolate cake.

Amenities include the services of an in-house masseuse and complimentary use of the *Cannon Beach Athletic Club*. In addition to walking along the misty beach, attractions include the *Coaster Theater* for performing arts, bicycling, and horseback riding nearby.

STEPHANIE INN 2740 S. Pacific St. (mailing address: PO Box 219), Cannon Beach, OR 97110 (phone: 503-436-2221; 800-633-3466; fax: 503-436-9711). This inn on the Oregon coast has 46 guestrooms with private baths, queen- or king-size beds, telephones, TV/VCRs, fireplaces, balconies or patios, whirlpool tubs, and air conditioning. Wheelchair accessible. Open year-round. Rate for a double room (including full breakfast): $139 to $379. Two-night minimum stay throughout August and weekends in July; three and four nights for some holiday and special-event weekends. Major credit cards accepted. Not appropriate for children under 13. No pets. No smoking. Steve and Jan Martin, owners; Sharon Major, manager.

DIRECTIONS: From Portland take Highway 26 west for 75 miles to Highway 101 in Seaside. Follow Highway 101 south for 3 miles to Cannon Beach. Take the third exit for Tolava Park. At the end of the ramp turn right, go 100 feet, and turn right again onto Hemlock Street. Continue on Hemlock about 7 blocks and turn left onto Mantanuska. The inn is straight ahead, one block down the hill.

TU TU' TUN LODGE

GOLD BEACH, OREGON

A breeze whispers through the trees, and fresh pine, cedar, and salt scent the air. A river flows gently by, while deer graze in the apple orchard and a bald eagle soars overhead. *Tu Tu' Tun* (the accent is on the second syllable) is not so much a guest lodge as it is an attitude—a serene and tranquil retreat from the workaday world.

Dirk Van Zante's stepfather, an architect, built this spacious cedar-plank lodge in 1970; in 1977, Dirk and his wife, Laurie, were married in front of the floor-to-ceiling, river-rock fireplace in the inn's living room; today, they are the innkeepers. They have created a unique hideaway beside the Rogue River, 6 miles east of Oregon's spectacular coast.

The lodge is a linear building, its architecture reminiscent of Frank Lloyd Wright. It would be a mistake to call the guestrooms rustic, although they have log beds; with their clean lines and comfortable furniture, the interiors recall Wright's Prairie style. Each of the rooms has a private deck or balcony with a six-foot-wide door that brings the outdoors in. Seven rooms are equipped with outdoor hot tubs, and ten have fireplaces. Floral and geometric cottons and woolens adorn the beds and upholstered furniture. The walls are decorated with old fishing gear and mining equipment (nearby Gold Beach got its name from a flurry of mining activity in the mid-1800s) and scenic watercolors by local artists.

Breakfast and dinner are offered to guests (for an additional fee) as well as to non-guests. The full buffet-style breakfast is served in the dining room and includes juice, fruit, fresh-baked breads, and two entrées. (A breakfast basket with coffee appears at the door of those who plan an early-morning guided fishing trip.) At dinnertime, everyone assembles in the living room for hors d'oeuvres and Oregon wine; then guests are seated in the dining room at tables with views of the setting sun across the river. Fires in two stone pits on the terrace add to the drama. Dinner features the bounty of the nearby river, ocean, and forests: fresh salmon, mesquite-grilled meat, baked cod, and desserts made with local berries. Following the meal, guests may linger on the terrace, sipping a sweet wine and conversing with new friends. On returning to their rooms, they'll find the beds turned down and a plate of homemade cookies.

The inn's wooded grounds include a heated lap pool, a four-hole pitch-and-putt golf course, horseshoes, and croquet. Inside are an antique player piano, a pool table, and a variety of games and books. The Rogue is a designated National Wild and Scenic River: A jet boat makes the trip to its whitewater section from the inn's dock. Fishing for salmon and steelhead trout is a popular pastime, and ocean beaches, hiking, and bird watching are nearby.

TU TU' TUN LODGE 96550 N. Bank Rogue Rd., Gold Beach, OR 97444 (phone: 541-247-6664; fax: 541-247-0672). **This lodge has 20 guestrooms with private baths, queen- or king-size beds, patios or decks, and telephones; ten with fireplaces, seven with hot tubs. Wheelchair accessible. Open year-round; dining room closed November through April. Rate for a double room (including evening hors d'oeuvres): $130 to $310; breakfast and dinner: $37.50 per person per day. Two-night minimum stay from July through September. Discover, MasterCard, and Visa accepted. Children welcome. No pets. One black Labrador, Duke, and a Jack Russell terrier, Leaper, in residence. No smoking. Dirk and Laurie Van Zante, innkeepers.**

DIRECTIONS: **From Highway 101 take North Bank Rogue Road, which starts at the north end of the bridge over the Rogue River in Gold Beach. Travel 7 miles to the inn.**

HERON HAUS

PORTLAND, OREGON

Julie Keppeler's years in Hawaii are reflected not only in the overall airiness of her spacious three-story home, but also in the names of the guestrooms: *Kanui, Kulia, Ko, Manu,* and *Makua.* Despite her love of the islands, she was drawn back to the Northwest, where her grandfather was an early settler.

Heron Haus, a magnificent 7,500-square-foot English Tudor mansion, was built in 1904 by a fish cannery owner, but when Julie discovered it, in 1986, it was in sorry shape. Nevertheless, she couldn't resist its beautiful hilltop site with expansive views of Portland and the Cascade Mountains. Today, with her renovations completed, guests enjoy the ultimate in luxurious quarters and scenery: Mount St. Helens is visible from the living room and the mahogany-paneled library. From the enclosed sunroom, which overlooks the pool, guests enjoy a garden that displays a profusion of blooms from spring through fall.

The house has leaded-glass windows, intricate ceiling moldings, and parquet floors. Ballast stones from an old sailing ship were used to build walls at the entrance and around the pool. There's also a small orchard of pear, apple, and cherry trees.

The spacious guestrooms, decorated in soft shades of blue, lavender, and rose, also have spectacular views. For example, *Kulia* boasts a raised spa on a porch with a view of the city, Mount St. Helens, and Mount Rainier. *Kanui* looks eastward and has a view of Mount Hood. *Ko*'s bath contains the original seven-nozzle shower stall. The three guestrooms on the top floor, in the former servants' quarters, all have brass beds. The room rate

includes a continental breakfast, which is served in the dining room and consists of fresh fruit and pastries.

The inn is located in Portland's Northwest Hills, a residential district studded with fine homes and only blocks from a bustling shopping area. Because of the inn's popularity with business travelers, Julie offers a computer, fax, and work area for guests. Boutiques, fine restaurants, the *Oregon Museum of Science and Industry,* and *Washington Park,* with its rose gardens, are nearby.

HERON HAUS 2545 NW Westover Rd., Portland, OR 97210 (phone: 503-274-1846; fax: 503-248-4055). This bed and breakfast establishment has six guestrooms with private baths, queen- or king-size beds, telephones, TV sets, whirlpool tubs, and air conditioning. Open year-round. Rate for a double room (including continental breakfast): $85 to $250. MasterCard and Visa accepted. Not appropriate for children under 10. No pets. No smoking. Julie Keppeler, innkeeper.

DIRECTIONS: Traveling on I-405, take the Everett Street exit onto Glisan (a one-way street). Turn right on 24th Street and travel 3 blocks to Johnson Street. Turn left onto Johnson, then right onto Westover. Proceed half a block up the incline and look for the address on the rock wall.

Washington

WILLCOX HOUSE

Bremerton, Washington

Despite its Bremerton address, *Willcox House* is actually located about 17 miles from town on Hood Canal. A long private road dips past glades of lush ferns and around massive cedar trees for more than a mile before reaching the gatehouse. The arched log-and-stone structure that spans the roadway used to be the servants' quarters.

The massive house was built in 1936 by noted Northwest architect Lionel Pries for a retired Marine Corps colonel, Julian Willcox, and his wife, Constance. Pries's clean, linear design evidences a Frank Lloyd Wright influence. No expense was spared, and the 10,000-square-foot mansion reportedly cost a quarter of a million dollars, an astronomical figure in a Depression-era economy.

After retirement, Willcox became a war consultant to the movie industry, and his celebrity visitors lent a glamorous cachet to the new home. Locally the house was called the "grand entertainment capital of Hood Canal," and records indicate that Clark Gable, Errol Flynn, Spencer Tracy, and Ernest Hemingway all stayed here. Mrs. Willcox continued to live in the house until 1971, but by the time Phillip and Cecilia Hughes purchased it in 1988, it had also been a boys' boarding school and a conference center.

The large entry hall is clad in faux marble panels. There are oak parquet floors throughout. The massive *Great Room,* with its burnished walnut walls, copper fireplace, and overstuffed sofas, overlooks the restored gardens and the unheated saltwater swimming pool. The adjacent dining room and terrace beyond afford spectacular views across Hood Canal to the Olympic Mountains. A favorite with guests, however, is the clubby library, where walnut shelves are stocked with books on everything from cooking to local history. In winter, the leather chairs in front of the fireplace encourage immersion in a Hemingway novel. Downstairs, a clock that runs backward hangs over the mahogany bar, and a gameroom provides pool, boardgames, puzzles, and darts. Be sure to ask to see the "secret" room—a closet camouflaged within a closet—and the hidden passages between bedrooms.

The spacious guestrooms are decorated in country English style. Many retain features original to the house. In *Constance's Room,* for example, the marble Art Deco fireplace and the built-in vanity are reminders of the many years Mrs. Willcox spent here. *Julian's Room,* however, contains luxuries of which the owner never would have dreamed: a king-size bed and a Jacuzzi. *Clark Gable's Room* has a balcony overlooking the rose garden.

In addition to the garden, the grounds offer wisteria-covered terraces, goldfish ponds with water lilies, an Oriental pond surrounded by Japanese sculptures, and a path to the beach, where visitors tie up their boats at the 300-foot pier.

Cecilia prepares breakfast (as well as lunch and dinner upon request)— perhaps cream cheese–stuffed French toast or apple pancakes. In the afternoon, wine, cheese, and fruit are served. The set dinner includes seasonal produce and fish or shellfish. A salmon steak with chive-and-lime butter might be followed by a peach-and-ginger cobbler.

Hiking trails lead from the inn across the surrounding hills; golf, fishing, and biking are nearby.

WILLCOX HOUSE 2390 Tekiu Rd. NW, Bremerton, WA 98312 (phone: 360-830-4492; 800-725-9477; fax: 360-830-0506). This mansion on Hood Canal has five guestrooms with private baths and queen- or king-size beds. Open year-round. Rate for a double room (including full breakfast and afternoon wine and cheese): $115 to $185. Two-night minimum stay from June through August and on weekends the rest of the year. Discover, MasterCard, and Visa accepted. Not appropriate for children under 16. No pets. A cat, Felix, outdoors. Smoking permitted outside only. Cecilia and Phillip Hughes, innkeepers.

DIRECTIONS: From Seattle take the ferry from Colman Dock to Bremerton (1 hour). In Bremerton drive west on Sixth Street, which becomes Kitsap Way; continue for about 1½ miles to Northlake Way and bear left at the fork. Drive 1 mile and bear left again onto Seabeck Highway. Drive almost 3 miles and turn left onto Holly Road. After another 5 miles (past *Camp Union*), turn left at the stop sign onto Seabeck-Holly Road. Drive 5 miles to Old Holly Hill Road and bear right at the fork. Go 200 yards and turn right at the mailboxes onto Tekiu Road.

Follow the paved road for just over 1 mile, turning left at the cabin and driving through the gatehouse.

TURTLEBACK FARM INN

EASTSOUND, ORCAS ISLAND, WASHINGTON

Orcas Island, a jewel in the string of enchanting islands in the San Juan archipelago, is snuggled into the elbow of Puget Sound, protected, on the west, by Vancouver Island and, on the east, by the mainland. Access to the islands is via ferry from Anacortes, 75 miles north of Seattle. Bring a camera, as the trip through narrow, glistening channels with lush, forested islands on either side is a shutterbug's delight. The views are one of the things that make the journey worthwhile. *Turtleback Farm Inn* is another.

When Susan and Bill Fletcher purchased their 80-acre farm in 1985, it was run-down and overgrown. Built in the 1870s, it had been a dairy farm and later a cattle ranch. Bill was a real-estate broker from San Francisco when they began looking for a summer cottage. Thoughts of operating an inn hadn't crossed their minds, but when they saw the farm, they changed their career paths.

Today *Turtleback Farm* is still a farm—the Fletchers raise Suffolk sheep, chickens, geese, bees, and pigeons—but after years of painstaking work and the addition of a new wing, they have also created a cozy human retreat in a handsome setting overlooking acres of pastureland.

The distinctive evergreen clapboard exterior with white trim seems to blend into the surrounding trees. Inside, the original shallow Rumford fireplace still stands in the living room, where there's also a corner game table and Oriental carpets on polished wood floors. Furnished with antiques and contemporary pieces, the seven guestrooms are simple and uncluttered, with hardwood floors and floral duvets. Several rooms have private decks;

nearly all have claw-foot tubs in the bathrooms. In the evening, candies are left on bedside tables.

A full breakfast is served either in the dining room or on the broad deck in warm weather. It features homemade granola, home-baked breads, and a main course using fresh eggs. The sideboard in the dining room is always supplied with fruit, coffee, tea, and sherry.

The San Juan islands are breathtakingly beautiful and enjoy a relatively mild climate. Guests will find golf, theater and musical productions, swimming, tennis, fishing, boating, sailing, kayaking, hiking in *Moran State Park,* and bicycling nearby.

TURTLEBACK FARM INN Crow Valley Rd. (mailing address: Rte. 1, Box 650), Eastsound, WA 98245 (phone: 360-376-4914; 800-376-4914; fax: 360-376-2151). This country inn has seven guestrooms with private baths and double, queen-, or king-size beds. Wheelchair accessible. Open year-round. Rate for a double room (including full breakfast): $80 to $160. Two-night minimum stay from May through October, as well as on weekends and holidays the rest of the year. Discover, MasterCard, and Visa accepted. Not appropriate for children under 8. No pets. Two dogs, Vicar, a briard, and Spud, a Jack Russell terrier, and farm animals on property. Smoking permitted outside only. William and Susan Fletcher, innkeepers.

DIRECTIONS: From Seattle take I-5 north for 65 miles to Route 20, just beyond Mount Vernon. Follow Route 20 for 10 miles to Anacortes and the ferry. From the ferry dock on Orcas Island go north on Horseshoe Highway for almost 3 miles. Take the first left turn toward Deer Harbor and travel almost 1 mile. Turn right onto Crow Valley Road and continue about 3 more miles to the inn.

OLD CONSULATE INN/F. W. HASTINGS HOUSE

Port Townsend, Washington

Port Townsend occupies an enviable site on Admiralty Inlet at the entrance to Puget Sound beside the Strait of Juan de Fuca. Settled by Loren Hastings in 1850, its history predates Seattle's. It soon became the main port of entry to the sound, and a fine customshouse was built. Increased trade also attracted consulates from such far-flung countries as Chile and Sweden, and grand houses were built for their representatives.

In the 1880s, speculators thought Port Townsend was going to be the terminus for the *Union Pacific Railroad* and believed their town would become the New York City of the West. In anticipation, a clutch of impressive brick buildings was erected along the waterfront and elaborate gingerbread Victorian homes were built on the bluff above. The railroad didn't come, however, and the prosperous little boom evaporated. Fortunately, there was no reason to modernize so the buildings remained; they now form

a National Historic District of some 70 structures, thought to be the best remaining example of a Victorian seacoast town north of San Francisco.

The *Old Consulate Inn* is a prime remnant of that era. Built in 1889 by Frank Hastings, son of the town's founder, it served for a time as the German Consulate. Nicknamed the "Red Victorian on the Hill" and the most photographed house in town, it is a soufflé of turrets, gables, chimneys, and gingerbread trim, its wraparound porch complete with a swing.

When innkeepers Joanna and Rob Jackson purchased the house in 1987, it was sorely in need of an overhaul, but the Jacksons were undaunted (Rob is a building contractor). They rebuilt the ornate carved oak staircase and the front porch, installed a private bathroom for each guestroom, and painted the exterior burgundy with deep green, pale green, charcoal, and black trim. In back, they fashioned an octagonal gazebo to match the style of the house and installed an eight-person hot tub that affords soakers a spectacular view of the bay.

The common rooms on the main floor have 10½-foot ceilings and include an entrance foyer where guests have morning coffee; there's also a formal parlor with a wood-burning fireplace, a grand piano, and an antique organ. In the library, another fireplace and numerous books and jigsaw puzzles provide diversions and, in the gameroom, a pool table and a VCR with an extensive video library round out the indoor entertainment options. The most popular tape is *An Officer and a Gentleman,* which was filmed in Port Townsend. Joanna's collection of glamorous dolls decorates tables in the common rooms (an elegantly clad "madam" presides over the gameroom) and fills a glass-enclosed cabinet in the foyer.

Guestroom furnishings include antique Victorian pieces such as marble-topped dressers, a four-poster rice bed, as well as brass, iron, and wicker beds. Every room has a view of the Olympic Mountains, the marina, or the inlet. One suite has a sitting room in the rounded turret, a claw-foot tub in the bath, and a sweeping view from Admiralty Inlet to the mountains.

The seven-course breakfasts served in the ornate dining room are legendary, with juice and fruit, an egg dish with meat, potatoes and vegetables, a cheese platter, freshly baked sweet breads and biscuits, and a dessert such as apricot-amaretto-almond cheesecake. In the evening wine, sherry, and brandy are available.

There are interesting shops and restaurants downtown; theater, concerts, festivals, and seminars are available in nearby Ft. Warden. Tennis facilities are in the area as well.

OLD CONSULATE INN/F. W. HASTINGS HOUSE 313 Walker St., Port Townsend, WA 98368 (phone: 360-385-6753; 800-300-6753; fax: 360-385-2097). This Victorian inn, in the historic town of Port Townsend, has eight guestrooms with private baths and queen- or king-size beds; three with fireplaces. Open year-round. Rate for a double room (including full breakfast, afternoon tea, and evening refreshments): $89 to $220. Major credit cards accepted. Not appropriate for children under 12. No pets. Fred, a German shorthaired pointer, in residence. No smoking permitted indoors. Joanna and Rob Jackson, innkeepers.

DIRECTIONS: From Seattle take the Winslow ferry from Colman Dock to Bainbridge Island (35 minutes) and follow the signs to the Hood Canal Bridge. After crossing the bridge, follow Route 104 for 5 miles to Highway 19. Turn right (north) and continue for 20 miles to Port Townsend. Watch for the *Port Townsend Motel* on the left and drive up the hill beside it (Washington Street). The inn is on the left at the top of the hill, on the corner of Washington and Walker Streets.

MANOR FARM INN

POULSBO, WASHINGTON

The *Manor Farm Inn* is full of surprises. In a pastoral landscape of hay fields and dairy farms, far removed from urban life, you wouldn't expect to find such a high level of sophistication. But, then, you probably don't know innkeeper Jill Hughes.

After completing her education at *Stanford,* majoring in psychology, she moved to the Pacific Northwest and, in 1975, purchased what was then a working dairy farm. Its collection of old buildings still remains. The farmhouse, built in 1886, now houses an enormous kitchen, a warm and light-filled dining room and a sitting room with a fireplace and a built-in sound system. The barn and chicken house in back continue to serve their origi-

nal purpose. The adjacent fields, dotted with Coopworth sheep, are neatly bordered by white rail fences.

In 1982, Jill added two wings of seven spacious guestrooms and a drawing room, which has a fireplace surrounded by comfortable wing chairs and sofas. The TV/VCR and a library of old films, as well as a collection of boardgames and puzzles, are located here. In the center of the U-shaped inn, a courtyard contains a profusion of flowers, and roses climb the posts to the roof of the verandah.

Guestrooms are furnished with natural pine pieces. Fresh flowers add bright touches to the neutral carpets and upholstery. Several rooms have wood-burning fireplaces or private porches or gardens.

Morning begins with a gentle knock on the door announcing the arrival of fresh-squeezed orange juice and hot-from-the-oven scones with fresh raspberry jam. This tasty wake-up call is followed by a three-course breakfast, which might include French toast or an apple crêpe, in the dining room. In the afternoon an array of homemade cookies, including some fabulous brownies, are set out. In the evening, sherry, fresh-baked cake, and fresh fruit await guests returning from dinner in nearby restaurants.

Fishing in the inn's trout pond is popular, as are hiking the 25 acres of fields and woods, playing croquet, badminton, or horseshoes, or taking a ride on the inn's bicycles—but simply reading a book under the vine-covered trellis beside the courtyard is just as tempting. The tiny Scandinavian community of Poulsbo is interesting to visit, and the inn is near boating and golf.

MANOR FARM INN 26069 Big Valley Rd. NE, Poulsbo, WA 98370 (phone: 360-779-4628; fax: 360-779-4876). This country inn on the Kitsap Peninsula has seven guestrooms with private baths and queen- or king-size beds; four with private decks, two with fireplaces. Open year-round. Rate for a double room May through October and weekends November through April (including full breakfast or Sunday brunch and afternoon tea): $110 to $160; rate for double room weekdays November through April (including continental breakfast): $100. MasterCard and Visa accepted. Not appropriate for children under 16. No pets. Farm animals on property. Smoking permitted outdoors only. Jill Hughes, innkeeper.

DIRECTIONS: From Colman Dock in Seattle, take the Winslow ferry to Bainbridge Island (35 minutes). Follow Route 305 across the Agate Pass Bridge to Poulsbo. Turn right onto Bond Road and go a quarter mile; turn left onto Big Valley Road. The inn is 3½ miles down on the left.

SHELBURNE INN

SEAVIEW, WASHINGTON

David Campiche grew up on the 29-mile expanse of beach called the Long Beach Peninsula; he met Laurie Anderson, a native Seattleite, when she was visiting her parents nearby. When the old *Shelburne Inn* was put up for sale in 1977, they bought it, and now operate it as a very special retreat.

The *Shelburne Inn* was built in 1896 and soon became a popular summer resort for Portland folks, who reached it by traveling the Columbia River by stern-wheeler, then continuing the journey by narrow-gauge railway. They made the trek to walk the gray sand beaches, go clamming at low tide, fish, and climb over the rocks by *North Head Lighthouse,* where the Columbia River empties into the Pacific Ocean (near the spot where Lewis and Clark completed their cross-country expedition).

The inn was moved across the street in 1911, and attached to another structure, but many of its original features remain: the tongue-and-groove wood paneling, the brick fireplace in the living room, the ceilings with exposed beams, and the brass chandeliers. Some of the spectacular Art Nouveau stained glass windows were added by David and Laurie after they rescued them from a church in England that was being demolished.

Listed on the National Register of Historic Places, the inn is now filled with antiques the couple picked up on their travels. There are oak dressers, spectacular walnut bedroom suites, and brass beds with quilts. Fresh flowers from the inn's extensive gardens scent the rooms. *Room No. 15* has a massive English armoire, an octagonal table inlaid with an intricate pattern, an elegant bed dressed with a crocheted spread, and a balcony overlooking the herb and flower garden. The tile baths are handsomely appointed with brass and porcelain fixtures.

Breakfasts, cooked by both David and Laurie, are so delicious and so popular that the recipes have been assembled into a cookbook. Fresh herbs, berries, and edible flowers from the gardens enhance the local seafood. Perhaps a seafood frittata or asparagus crêpes with sweet curry sauce will be the day's offering.

The inn's outstanding *Shoalwater Restaurant* is operated as a separate business by friends Tony and Ann Kischner. Its Victorian decor includes oak chairs, interior pillars, and stained-glass windows. It has won numerous awards for its imaginative cuisine that relies heavily on local produce, fish, and shellfish. The meal might include an appetizer of Dungeness crab and spinach ravioli with a cream sauce of saffron, garlic, thyme, and white wine, followed by an entrée of fresh grilled Copper River king salmon on a bed of wild local morels and oyster mushrooms with a lemon-ginger vin blanc sauce. An extensive cellar of Northwest wines figures prominently. Dessert may feature Ann's old-fashioned bread pudding with rum *crème anglaise* or an Italian lemon-almond torta with raspberry-mint sauce.

Beachcombing, art galleries, craft shops, the *Lewis and Clark Interpretive Center,* museums, and a bird sanctuary are all nearby.

SHELBURNE INN 4415 Pacific Hwy. 103 (mailing address: PO Box 250), Seaview, WA 98644 (phone: 360-642-2442; restaurant: 360-642-4142; fax: 360-642-8904). This country inn on the Long Beach Peninsula has 15 guestrooms with private baths and double or queen-size beds; 11 with private decks or patios. Wheelchair accessible. Open year-round; restaurant closed for one week following *Thanksgiving.* Rate for a double room (including full breakfast): $99 to $170. Two-night minimum stay on most weekends and holidays. Major credit cards accepted. Children welcome. No pets. No smoking. Laurie Anderson and David Campiche, innkeepers.

DIRECTIONS: From Portland take Highway 26 north for 75 miles to Highway 101 in Seaside. Follow Highway 101 north for 22 miles across the Columbia River into Washington. Continue on Highway 101 north for 10 miles to Seaview. Continue to the flashing yellow light and turn right onto Highway 103. The inn

is five blocks ahead on the left. From Seattle take I-5 south through Ol
to the Aberdeen/Port Angeles exit to Highway 12. Follow signs for Aberg
Follow Highway 12 for 37 miles to Montesano and turn south onto Route
which leads in 8 miles to Highway 101 south. Follow Route 101 for 62 mil
Seaview, then follow the directions above.

INN AT LANGLEY

LANGLEY, WHIDBEY ISLAND, WASHINGTON

The *Inn at Langley* is a serene retreat, woven of earth and sky and trees.
There are spectacular waterfront views of Saratoga Passage, where freighters
with goods bound for the Orient slip by, while the Cascade Mountains provide a stuning backdrop. Every room has a window wall with doors leading to a tiled deck. A broad, greenery-filled planter with a bench substi-
tutes for a railing. Guests watch in fascination as herons stand in tide pools
and sea otters play just offshore.

The building has a cedar-shake exterior; inside, rough-plank cedar walls
impart that heady aroma that makes you feel as if you're deep in the woods.
Made of logs, glass, and slate, the furniture is of solid, Craftsman-style construction in soothing shades of brown and gray. The bathrooms, done in
quarry tile, have open showers (without walls) and two-person whirlpool
tubs strategically placed to capture views of both the water and the flicker
of the fire in the bedroom hearth.

Continental breakfast—juice, fruit, granola, and muffins—is set out on
the counter in the stunning open kitchen/dining room, with its double-sided
river-rock fireplace. The plank tables and wrought-iron chandelier were

e by local artists. Dinner is served here on Friday and Saturday nights
in additional charge. Chef Steve Nogal (who is co-manager with his
Sandy) first gathers guests for sherry beside the fireplace, where he
ribes the evening's set menu and the wines that will be served. The
p then moves to the dining room. The preparations are creative yet
le, perhaps using oysters from nearby Penn Cove, freshly caught salmon,
mushrooms or loganberries gathered in the woods. The relaxed, con-
evening ends with a glass of port.

he inn's location on Whidbey Island in Puget Sound is convenient for
ncombing, fishing, and shopping.

ANGLEY 400 First St. (mailing address: PO Box 835), Langley, WA
0 (phone and fax: 360-221-3033). This inn has 24 guestrooms with private
, queen-size beds, telephones, fireplaces, decks, whirlpool tubs, and TV
Wheelchair accessible. Open year-round; dinner served Fridays and
rdays year-round, plus Sundays in summer. Rate for a double room (including
tinental breakfast): $179 to $269. Two-night minimum stay on weekends.
jor credit cards accepted. Not appropriate for children under 12. No pets.
o smoking. Paul and Pam Schell, innkeepers; Steve and Sandy Nogal, managers.

DIRECTIONS: The inn is 32 miles north of Seattle, accessible by ferry from the
south and by the Deception Pass Bridge from the north. From Seattle the trip
takes approximately 90 minutes: Take I-5 north to Exit 189 (Whidbey
Island/Mukilteo Ferry), following signs to the ferry landing, where boats depart
every half hour. Arriving in Clinton, follow Highway 525 north to Maxwelton
Road. Turn right and proceed to the end of the road; bear left onto Langley
Road and continue on to Cascade Street, which becomes First Street. The inn
is on the right. From the north take I-5 south to Anacortes and Deception Pass;
cross the bridge to Whidbey Island. Driving south on Highway 20/525, turn left
onto Maxwelton Road and follow directions above.

British Columbia

OCEANWOOD COUNTRY INN

MAYNE ISLAND, BRITISH COLUMBIA

The Gulf Islands are a string of lush green emeralds stretching some 150 miles north from Sidney, through the Strait of Georgia, to Campbell River. With charter boats available for salmon fishing and sailboats skittering through the channels, the area is a veritable paradise for recreational boaters and anglers.

Mayne Island, part of the Gulf Island chain, is a pastoral 8-square-mile spot dotted with orchards and sheep farms. It's rugged, remote, and wildly beautiful, yet it can be reached by ferry in one hour from either Vancouver Island or the mainland.

Marilyn and Jonathan Chilvers pursued careers in advertising and public relations in Vancouver until 1990, when they decided to trade city for country life. They purchased a Tudor-style house located on 10 acres with spectacular views of Navy Channel, which they renovated and expanded. It now boasts 12 luxurious guestrooms, as well as several elegant common rooms.

Reminiscent of a fine English country home, the living room has polished oak floors, Oriental rugs, and floral sofas before the fireplace. The library has a cozy nook with an abundance of books, a window seat, and another fireplace. An outstanding video collection is available for viewing in the small conference room. The inviting, sunny garden room is filled with plants and a multitude of books about gardens and gardening. The gameroom contains tables for bridge, chess, backgammon, and boardgames, as well as puzzles. A hot tub is perched on a secluded deck that affords outstanding views of the channel; there's a sauna as well. Plus, eight of the guestrooms have fireplaces and nine have either whirlpool or soaking tubs in the room or on a private deck; all except one have water views.

Each of the guestrooms is named for a flower or a local bird and some have fancifully stenciled ceiling borders. The *Rose Room,* for example, has a white wicker bed with an arched headboard and a stenciled garland of roses above it. This room also contains a marble-faced fireplace, French doors opening onto a private balcony, stairs leading down to the gardens, and a whirlpool tub with a view of the water. The *Lavender Room* has a marine blue carpet and a spectacular four-poster canopy bed, lavishly draped with blue-and-white striped fabric and accented with blue-and-rose floral chintz. The bed's raised platform provides unobstructed views of the water. Down three steps is a sofa placed before a fireplace and a two-person soaking tub with its own unobstructed view. A private deck completes the picture.

Guests are served a full breakfast—always with a hot entrée and delicious home-baked goods. Afternoon tea, served on fine china with silver spoons, features homemade pastries. Dinner (also open to non-guests) is a major attraction here. The waterfront restaurant has wraparound windows that capture the ever-changing scene on Navy Channel, yet the presentations and the food are as spectacular as the setting. The prix fixe menu offers a choice of two entrées each night and features the bounty of the Pacific Northwest, from fish and shellfish to produce and herbs from the garden. It might include roast free-range quail served on basil polenta or trout with spinach and blackberries. A marvelous selection of California and Northwest vintages is available, by the glass or bottle.

Mayne Island is laced with lanes for bicycling, cliff-edge footpaths for walking, and vest-pocket beaches for sunning. The Chilverses provide bicycles and will arrange kayak excursions to explore the coves and watch the harbor seals at play. Golf is available on nearby Pender Island, and hiking and tennis also are in the vicinity. Mayne Island is noted for its crafts shops, especially those selling goods woven from locally spun wool.

OCEANWOOD COUNTRY INN 630 Dinner Bay Rd., Mayne Island, BC V0N 2J0, Canada (phone: 250-539-5074; fax: 250-539-3002). This country inn in the Gulf Islands has 12 guestrooms with private baths and twin or queen-size beds; nine with decks and whirlpool or soaking tubs, eight with fireplaces. Closed December through February. Rate for a double room (including full breakfast and afternoon tea): CN $120 to $295 (US $88 to $215 at press time). MasterCard and Visa accepted. Not appropriate for children under 17. No pets. A yellow Labrador, Kelly, and a cat, Rupert, on premises. Smoking permitted in the library and outside only. Marilyn and Jonathan Chilvers, innkeepers.

DIRECTIONS: From the Village Bay ferry terminal, turn right onto Dalton Drive. At the junction with Mariner's Way, turn right and then immediately left onto

Dinner Bay Road. Continue on Dinner Bay Road for half a mile until you see *Oceanwood*'s sign on the left. For those who arrive by boat, a mooring buoy is located just off the inn's beach.

SOOKE HARBOUR HOUSE

SOOKE, BRITISH COLUMBIA

Sinclair and Frederique Philip have created an idyllic retreat with luxurious guestrooms and outstanding food on a remote rocky promontory called Whiffen Spit, 23 miles west of Victoria on Vancouver Island. Seldom will you find innkeepers more enthusiastic about their chosen calling or more knowledgeable about how to make it successful. Indeed, Sinclair has been credited with substantially increasing tourism on Vancouver Island.

As you walk toward the entrance of the inn, the raised beds containing more than 200 varieties of vegetables, herbs, and edible flowers give the first hint of the serious attention paid to food here. Sinclair also considers the sea to be an important part of his "garden"—he not only reaps fish and shellfish from the inn's tidal tank, but harvests more than 60 kinds of seaweed. Much of what is on your plate may have been picked from the inn's garden only moments before. The inn's chefs have won the admiration of food writers from around the world for their imaginative use of local fresh and organic ingredients.

Dinner (open to non-guests) is a truly memorable experience. The menu changes daily, but a meal might begin with an appetizer of local beach runner oysters on the half shell with daylily sauce. The entrées—frequently featuring locally raised organic meat or locally caught salmon, halibut, skate, or black cod—are equally impressive. The evening's bill of fare might include roasted veal with a crust of coriander, tarragon, caraway, and pine nuts, served with chive-flower-and-cremini-mushroom sauce, or roasted yellowtail rockfish filet with a cream sauce of island ale, horseradish, and rosemary, accompanied by a pinto-bean-and-cilantro pancake. Be sure to order the house salad of organic garden greens tossed with bright nasturtium and pansy blossoms and splashed with a hazelnut oil dressing. As flavorful as it is colorful, the salad is served on a piece of slate. Among the dessert choices might be the unique and delicious wild rose crêpes filled with warm rhubarb and fir-infused honey compote and served with tarragon ice cream. The excellent wine list includes California, Washington, and Oregon brands, as well as Canadian vintages.

The dining room offers spectacular views as well. A wall of windows overlooks the Strait of Juan de Fuca and the snow-capped peaks of the Olympic Mountains beyond. Guests can watch the seals frolicking on the rocks beyond the garden and may even see a bald eagle soaring above the water. Vines of passion fruit cascade past the windows, and a clump of lavender adds a touch of color to the patio. The light and airy room is decorated with Frederique's imaginative flower-and-herb arrangements, which incorporate such unusual components as cardoon (a thistle-like plant) and crab shells, and unusual Native American artwork.

In fact, the entire inn is a showcase of British Columbian art. Each of the guestrooms has a fireplace and a name that reflects its decor. In the *Victor Newman Longhouse Room,* for example, are masks, paintings, and drawings by local Kwakiutl artist Victor Newman (who even painted a grouping of sacred symbols on the red cedar surrounding the tub); there's also a vaulted ceiling with a skylight, a Jacuzzi with an ocean view, and a four-poster bed. The *Underwater Orchard Room* has stained-glass windows that depict deep-sea life, plus a hot tub for two on a private deck. Every room has a fireplace and a water view. Thirteen additional rooms were under construction at press time.

A full breakfast, which changes daily, is served to inn guests. It might include juice, fruit, muffins, and pancakes or French toast; lunch also is served to inn guests. Sports fishing, beachcombing, and bird watching are all nearby, as is hiking on the West Coast Trail, which extends more than 62 miles. The inn has a gift shop featuring local crafts.

SOOKE HARBOUR HOUSE 1528 Whiffen Spit Rd., RR4, Sooke, BC V0S 1N0, Canada (phone: 250-642-3421; 800-889-9688; fax: 250-642-6988). This inn has 13 guestrooms with private baths, queen- or king-size beds, fireplaces, decks or patios, and telephones; TV sets available on request, seven with whirlpool tubs. Wheelchair accessible. Closed January. Rate for a double room (including full breakfast and lunch): CN $195 to $295 (US $142 to $215 at press time). Major credit cards accepted. Children welcome. Pets allowed with advance permission only (and a $20 charge per day). Smoking permitted outside only. Frederique and Sinclair Philip, innkeepers.

DIRECTIONS: Sooke is on Vancouver Island, approximately 23 miles (37 km) from Victoria. From Victoria take Highway 1 west to Highway 14. Continue west on Highway 14 to the village of Sooke. Approximately 1 mile (1.6 km) past the traffic light, turn left onto Whiffen Spit Road and continue to the end. The inn is on the right, next to the water.

BEACONSFIELD INN

VICTORIA, BRITISH COLUMBIA

This little Edwardian-era jewel even takes its name from a favorite haunt of King Edward VII—*Beaconsfield* was a pre–World War I English hotel. With its abundant flower gardens, turn-of-the-century charm, and air of serenity and ease, this inn would also please a king—or anyone in search of a gracious retreat.

The house was built in 1905 by R. P. Rithet, a former mayor of Victoria, as a wedding gift for his daughter. He hired the popular Victoria architect Samuel McClure, who fashioned the house with 11-foot beamed ceilings, wainscoted walls, mahogany floors, and exquisite stained glass.

From the moment you enter the front door, you know you're in for a treat. The inviting plant-filled sunroom boasts stained-glass windows with a subtle peacock-feather motif, wicker furniture with floral cushions, Oriental rugs on a black-and-white tile floor, and a softly splashing fountain. The entrance hall has oak paneling and an extravagant carved mantel over the fireplace. In the library, where afternoon sherry, tea, and snacks are served, there's another fireplace and the walls are lined with dark oak bookcases.

Con and Judi Sollid, formerly an orthodontist and an attorney, respectively, have owned the *Beaconsfield Inn* since 1993. Possessing a warm sense of hospitality and a refined sense of style, they've decorated the nine guestrooms with interesting antiques, including canopy and brass beds. Most of the rooms have Jacuzzis and fireplaces (they also have hair dryers and alarm clocks, but no telephones or televisions to disturb the peace). All the rooms convey a sense of comfort and understated elegance, without being fussy or ostentatious. There's an air of romance about them as well, underscored by the fireplaces, the Jacuzzis (complete with bathside candles), and complimentary champagne and chocolates.

Each of the rooms has its own personality and decor. The *Attic Room* takes up the entire top floor and offers a feeling of privacy and seclusion. It features an antique four-poster canopy bed, a cozy window seat, a love seat in front of the fireplace, a skylight, and a Jacuzzi. *Duchess* has a fox hunt theme and a regal air, with a teal and apricot color scheme, a wood-burning fireplace, and an antique "fainting chair."

Two new suites (fashioned from four existing rooms) were created in 1995. One, the charming *Gate Keeper's Suite,* has a door leading out to a private garden patio. The adjoining sitting room has a gas fireplace with a stone mantelpiece and a Jacuzzi for two. In 1996, the Sollids created the ultimate romantic getaway: The *Beach Cottage,* located in a quiet water-side location about 10 minutes from Victoria, has a main room with a river-rock fireplace, a bedroom with king-size bed and Jacuzzi, an entertainment room with a TV/VCR and another fireplace, and a hot tub under the stars. Guests prepare their own breakfasts here.

Back at the inn, breakfast is served either in the dining room or the sun-room. (Arrive early to secure a sun-splashed table in the latter.) In the dining room, a built-in oak buffet, a cast-iron inglenook fireplace, and antique English oak tables provide a country-house setting. Breakfast entrées might include French toast with apple topping and vanilla yogurt sauce, eggs Florentine, or baked egg with salsa. The meal also features juice, fresh fruit, freshly baked breads and muffins, and granola and other cereals.

The inn is three blocks from Victoria's downtown, with its museums and other attractions, and only one block from *Beacon Hill Park.*

BEACONSFIELD INN 998 Humboldt St., Victoria, BC V8V 2Z8, Canada (phone: 250-384-4044; fax: 250-384-4044). This Edwardian inn has nine guestrooms and suites, and one cottage, with private baths and queen-size beds; eight with fireplaces, seven with whirlpool tubs, two with private porches. Closed *Christmas.* Rate for a double room (including full breakfast and afternoon tea and sherry): CN $225 to $350 (US $164 to $255 at press time). MasterCard and Visa accepted. Not appropriate for children under 18. No pets. No smoking. Con and Judi Sollid, innkeepers.

DIRECTIONS: Traveling from the Inner Harbour on Government Street, turn right onto Humboldt Street and drive 3 blocks. The inn is on the left, on the corner of Vancouver and Humboldt.

Index

Inns

Maps